WITHDRAWN

D1234562

The Modern History of Israel

956.94
L962m

The Modern History of Israel

Noah Lucas

Praeger Publishers
New York · Washington

Published in the United States of America in
1975 by Praeger Publishers, Inc.
111 Fourth Avenue, New York, N.Y. 10003

© 1975 by Noah Lucas, London

All rights reserved

**Library of Congress Cataloging in
Publication Data**

Lucas, Noah

The modern history of Israel

(Praeger Asia-Africa series)

1. Israel – History
2. Palestine – History – 1917–1948. I. Title
DS126.5.L82 1975 956.94 74-16411

ISBN 0-275-33450-3

Printed in Great Britain

for my wife, Beatrice

GAT Jur.20'75

214954

CONTENTS

ACKNOWLEDGEMENTS

The author and publishers would like to thank the following for granting permission to reproduce the maps on pages 445–450: the Controller of Her Majesty's Stationery Office for the Peel Partition Proposal, from *Cmd. 5479* of 1937; the Longman Group Limited for the UNO Partition Proposal, from Henry Cattan, *Palestine, the Arabs and Israel*; Martin Gilbert for Jewish Land Ownership, 1942 and Israel (Armistice Boundaries, 1949), from the *Jewish History Atlas* (Weidenfeld and Nicolson Ltd).

PREFACE

Israel's population today is a mere three million, but tens of millions are numbered among its victims, enemies, friends and supporters. From the moment of its specific origins in Europe nearly a century ago Israel's history has been intermingled with that of other peoples to a degree extraordinary even in the modern world. Perhaps for this reason, Israel is the subject of an embarrassingly abundant literature. It is therefore remarkable that hitherto no general history of the whole century of Israel's evolution has been available. In offering what I believe to be the first work of this kind, I hope that it will be of interest to the general reader without prior knowledge of the Jews or of Israel. Such a reader should find the narrative intelligible, with many points of reference to patterns of life familiar elsewhere in the contemporary world. To the habitual reader of history such connections will seem like common sense, and will only be challenging if they come up against any prior assumption that Israel's history is mysterious or inaccessible.

I completed the manuscript of this work in June 1973, three months before the outbreak of the fourth Israeli-Arab war of the quarter-century. The six-year war of 1967–73 is still too recent to permit a historical analysis symmetrical with the treatment of the earlier periods. I have therefore added an epilogue in order to bring the discussion of the Israel-Arab conflict up to the end of December 1973.

This work has been several years in gestation, so that it incurred many debts even before being conceived in its present form. Personal friends in Israel who have influenced or helped me over a period of twenty years are too numerous to mention. I hope that my friendships may survive the probability that they will disapprove of many of my views and interpretations. Numerous officials who would prefer to be anonymous have also given generously of their time to help me to clarify various issues.

I began my formal research in the department of political science at Washington University (St Louis), and I am happy to record my gratitude to that superb department of that distinguished university, for which I retain a deep and abiding affection. I should also acknowledge a grant awarded by its Ford Foundation Public Affairs Committee, which enabled me to undertake necessary travel in 1960. Southern Illinois University (Edwardsville) generously assisted me in 1962 to explore the library resources of New York. I am grateful also for awards from the Academic Research Committee of the Histadrut Executive, in 1964 and 1965. Although these debts belong to its pre-history I hope that this work may in some measure redeem them.

To Professor Bernard Crick, now of Birkbeck College, London, I am indebted for prompting the book and guiding me through the shoals that guard the initial approaches to publication. To my colleague Professor Colin Leys I am grateful not only for needed encouragement, but also for generously offering incisive editorial criticism of several chapters.

In addition to private and public libraries in New York, Jerusalem and Tel Aviv, I had ready access to the library resources of London. I am particularly grateful to the staff of the Wiener Library and that of the Institute of Jewish Affairs in London. The Research Fund of the University of Sheffield helped with assistance towards travel. Also, in typing the manuscript with patience, skill and enthusiasm Mrs Elizabeth Dawson made an essential contribution to the completion of the work.

While I know that this work cannot justify the sacrifices its preparation imposed on my wife and children, I hope that its publication may in some measure compensate for these. In dedicating the work to my wife Beatrice, I can only hint at the fortitude and devotion by which she inspired my efforts and coaxed the work to fruition. Any merit that the work possesses is truly a product of her unstinting help and collaboration.

Noah Lucas
Sheffield, February 1974

PART I

THE ORIGINS OF MODERN ISRAEL

It is true we are thrust into a world we did not make.
But who makes the world into which our children are thrust?
Rabbi Mordecai M. Kaplan

PART I.

THE ORIGINS OF MODERN ISRAEL

CHAPTER 1

THE JEWS OF EUROPE IN
THE NINETEENTH CENTURY

*The traditional society of the Pale – emancipation and
Jewish identity – radical doctrines and movements*

The traditional society of the Pale

The state of Israel itself and many of its most characteristic
institutions were a product of the collapse of Jewish life in
eastern Europe during the nineteenth century. In order to
understand modern Israel it is therefore necessary to examine
briefly the traditional Jewish society of eastern Europe.

As a result of centuries of dispersion three broad divisions
evolved within world Jewry: the oriental Jews of the middle
east; the *Sephardi* Jews descended from the mediaeval Spanish
community, distributed mainly around the Mediterranean
basin; and the *Ashkenazi* branch, the 'western' Jews of
European Christendom. At the beginning of the nineteenth
century there were some two and a half million Jews, of
whom the 'western' branch comprised about two-thirds. The
Jews of eastern Europe made up over nine-tenths of the latter,
some three-quarters of these being under Russian rule and the
remainder within the orbit of the Austro-Hungarian and
Ottoman empires.

The Jews of eastern Europe were extraordinarily fertile in
the nineteenth century, increasing to about nine and a half
million, while oriental Jewry remained more or less static at
about one million. Half of the world's Jews at the end of the
century lived within the Russian empire in the territorial
reservation known as the Pale of Settlement, and a further

3

two and a half million or more lived in eastern Europe within the Hapsburg domain.

Although they were not equal in status to their Muslim neighbours, the Jews of Islam fared very much better than those of Europe. The Jews of Europe, on account of their persistent denial of Christianity, were marked as an inferior caste, and excluded from all but despised occupations. They had no part in agriculture. By the time of the middle ages they were segregated in ghettos set aside for them in the towns and cities, and were subject to discriminatory taxation and often to crippling persecution.

Each Jewish community tended to assume the cultural characteristics of the majority society within which it was domiciled, so that there were noticeable divergencies between the various branches of Jewry. The oriental Jews, apart from religious customs and beliefs, were more or less assimilated to the dominant Arab culture and used the Arabic language. This also applied to the *Sephardim*, but they retained their specific identity with the help of Ladino, a *lingua franca* derived from mediaeval Castilian Spanish. The *Ashkenazim* in western Europe adopted the languages of the majority societies, but rapid migrations eastwards and again from east to west, due to frequent expulsion, promoted the use of Yiddish. This language evolved from mediaeval Rhineland German with an admixture of Hebrew, and it enabled the Jews of eastern Europe to maintain continuity of communication despite their frequent transplantation.

Not only on account of size, but in their acknowledged vitality and leadership in religious learning, the Jewish communities of eastern Europe in the nineteenth century were the predominant carriers of the historical inheritance of the Jews. It was they who comprised the main source of Israel's modern history, its human material, its ideas and its social institutions.

At the time of the crusades the Jews persecuted in western Europe had found refuge in Poland, where they were granted royal protection, religious freedom and communal autonomy. When the Polish kingdom declined into anarchy at the end of the eighteenth century most of its territory and its Jews were inherited by Russia. From the beginning of the nineteenth century until about 1915 the Jews were excluded from Russia proper and were restricted almost without exception to the Pale of Settlement extending from the Baltic to the Black Sea. The Jews of the Pale were highly urbanized, sometimes in their ghetto comprising a majority of the population of a large town. But many lived side by side with the peasantry in small towns and villages.

In addition to their residential segregation the Jews throughout the nineteenth century were subject to a series of inconsistent and fluid regulations circumscribing their social and economic pursuits. In the 1860s there was a wind of liberalization allowing many Jews to leave the Pale and establish themselves in industry or the wider world of commerce, or to obtain a secular higher education. Although this emancipation was shortlived it exposed the Jewish intelligentsia to Russian literature and nationalism, and briefly introduced some greater diversification into the economic life of the Pale.

Hedged about by disabling economic laws while at the same time subject to discriminatory taxation, the Jews of the Pale gradually underwent pauperization through the nineteenth century. Under the Polish regime the Jews had been confined to certain occupations in the manner of a feudal corporate estate. They were concentrated in international trade, usury, tax-farming for the government, the liquor traffic and various crafts in addition to petty trade. Forbidden to hold real property or land the entrepreneurial elite realized its wealth in the form of liquid capital and their economic roles were determined accordingly. Although there was a significant stratum of poverty, and although the occupational structure of the Jews was distorted by their finely regulated roles, the Jewish economy was relatively productive during much of the Polish period. The masses were poor but they were for the most part above the level of subsistence, and an extensive middle class including some magnates had emerged. With the breakdown of corporatism, especially after the emancipation of the serfs in 1861, the Jews found themselves pressed not only by arbitrary legislation but by direct competition in fields which had been their acknowledged preserve. At the same time incipient industrialization rendered redundant thousands of petty traders, artisans and manual workers who were sometimes forbidden by law to tend machines. The development of rail transport destroyed the living of thousands of innkeepers, coachmen and horse traders, occupations with a traditionally large Jewish membership.

A Russian government committee investigating the condition of the Jews in the 1880s reported that ninety per cent were a 'proletariat living from hand to mouth'. By the end of the century nearly half the Jews were subsisting on charity provided by those of their brethren who had work. At the same time, in the last thirty-five years of Tsarist rule before the revolution of 1917, direct official persecution of the Jews reached an intensity surpassing that of any previous period. This was the legal environment and socio-economic context in which the Jews were obliged to sustain their communal life.

Jewish communal traditions and practices had survived for centuries with little change until the traditional society began to disintegrate about the middle of the eighteenth century. Although traditional authority continued to decline throughout the nineteenth century, and despite sporadic attempts by the Tsars to break down their autonomy, the practice of self-government and its memory left a residue of political custom within the Jewish culture, and the Jews continued to operate a vestigial network of social institutions which had evolved during the period of benign Polish rule. These institutions originated in religious practice and were reproduced with variations throughout history in all the lands of Jewish settlement since ancient times.

From the middle of the sixteenth century Jewish self-governmental organs in Poland had been endowed with the authority of the state. In addition to conventional religious institutions these organs included revenue-raising and judicial agencies as well as control of education, welfare and economic life. Community self-government in conditions of social isolation was of necessity based on mutual aid. Administrative activities were centred in the synagogue and sanctioned by rabbinical law and traditional religious authority. This was no less efficacious than state coercion and imparted a voluntaristic if somewhat authoritarian cast to political life. The main sanction at the disposal of the authorities was the ban, an edict of excommunication stipulating the specific degree of ostracism imposed.

The governing body in each settlement of Jews was the community council (in Hebrew *kehillah*, referred to by some writers as *kahal*) headed symbolically by the salaried Rabbi and composed of lay notables chosen indirectly by the householders. The notables acted in an honorary capacity and the chairmanship of the council was usually rotated among them monthly. Until 1765 the councils were loosely federated by representative devices into wider regional bodies meeting periodically to rule on matters of high policy affecting the community as a whole. The activity of the community council extended into every detail of the lives of the individuals within its jurisdiction. It was conducted by a sometimes considerable though often impoverished paid bureaucracy, subject to a sophisticated administrative ethic. The overriding concern of the local and regional councils, fully sanctioned by the religious tradition, was to protect the interests and welfare and if need be the survival of the community as a whole, even at the expense of sacrificing the individual when necessary.

More important than the provision of municipal services or the maintenance of charities, the education of the young males was the most cherished preserve of Jewish autonomy. The resistance of the traditional hierarchy to modernizing influences, whether internal or external in origin, was most effectively asserted in the elementary schools and Talmudical colleges. Indeed the essence of the traditional society might be said to lie in its reverence for religious learning, and the social deference and economic support accorded to its most promising young masters.

In addition to implementing the internal government of the community the council conducted relations with the external authorities and neighbouring non-Jewish interests, through the agency of a salaried emissary. (In Hebrew, the *shtadlan*.) This official was usually the most sophisticated man available, versed in the law and diplomacy of the non-Jewish world. The community council was responsible to the external authorities for transmission of the taxes levied collectively upon the Jewish community. It was perhaps the convenience to the Russian government of leaving the Jews to raise their own taxes that accounted for the perpetuation of Jewish autonomy even in times when the Tsar was officially committed to its destruction. Taxes were collected by the council in the main by sworn assessors who determined the proportion of the levy to be paid by each member of the community on the basis of custom and traditions sanctioned by religious authority. Sometimes the community council would also be found directly engaged in economic activity, as when it obtained from the external authorities profit-producing concessions such as distilling, which it then farmed out within the community.

The family was the most vital prop of the traditional society and of the authority of its governmental institutions. The father ruled firmly and was responsible for the religious upbringing of his children. The highest ambition for a boy was to become a religious scholar, for a girl, to marry one. Success in business enjoined the provision of support for institutions of study or for the upkeep of individual scholars. If a man was not so endowed as to excel in study then he must provide for those who were. In this way the successful merchant could vicariously fulfil his duty to put the study of the law before all other concerns and at the same time attain comparable status to the scholar himself. The alliance between learning and money was reflected in the code of marriage practices.

This basic value of the community was equally well reflected in the structure of its government. The rabbinical leadership displayed a dynastic tendency. The notables for the most part comprised a plutocratic oligarchy, often owing their power (sometimes at the expense of their prestige) to alliance with the local Russian bureaucracy. This pattern, corresponding with a decline of religious authority as the source of legitimacy, aggravated the elements of class struggle within the Jewish community. These had become manifest during the implementation of punitive recruiting laws in operation between 1827–56. Under these laws the councils were obliged to supply the authorities with a quota of teenage boys for twenty-five years' military service supplemented by some years of preparatory training, a euphemism for forcible conversion to Christianity. The councils were obliged to employ professional kidnappers in their thankless compliance with the law and it usually transpired that children of the impoverished were the victims. This injected into the community an element of bitterness and class conflict which itself contributed to the breakdown of tradition and the emergence of movements for secular and democratic communal rule.

Emancipation and Jewish identity

A strong common bond amongst the Jews in their dispersion was the folk-memory of the land of Israel and the idea of a messiah who would lead them back to Zion. The religion was and is intimately bound up with the land in which it achieved its original classical expressions. The liturgy and the traditional rituals and festivals of Judaism maintained the consciousness of the land both as history and as messianic promise. Also sustained by reference to the ancestral land was the potent myth of biological or tribal unity, the myth of common descent.

This myth has special significance as a key to the puzzle of Jewish survival. The survival of Judaism is really no more remarkable than that of other ancient religious traditions such as Christianity or Buddhism. Nor is the survival of the Jews any more remarkable than that of other populations with an ancient recorded history. The remarkable fact which distinguishes the Jews is the maintenance of a collective consciousness of cultural continuity with, and common descent from, the biblical patriarchs, *despite* contrary evidence.[1] The unique sociological content of Jewish survival, in fact that which most crucially survived, is the myth of Jewish survival. It is only the absence of such a myth from the consciousness of Greeks, Egyptians or Iraqis in reference to the ancient civilizations that flourished on their soil and to subsequent events that distinguishes the significance of their survival from that of the Jews. The myth is religious in its origin and in its force, couched not in terms of blood and soil but of spirit. Hence the doctrine that converts to Judaism, amongst whom (or their spouses or their descendants) are numbered many of the greatest leaders of the faith from Moses himself down to Rabbi Akiba, are deemed descended from Abraham. The vital core of Jewish survival has been the myth which inextricably linked the spiritual and social dimensions of Jewish identity. The religion buttressed the sense of social unity, and the tribal consciousness maintained the force of traditional religion. The social elements of unity were embodied in religious belief and practice while at the same time unity was a religious injunction implicit in the social content of the faith. The religious content of social unity and the social content of the faith were both primarily expressed in terms of history, geography and law. Israel as the original environment of the law, the land of Israel itself as history and geography and messianic promise, is the link between the two facets of Jewish identity.

So long as the Jews of Europe were confined to the ghetto with its rigid social and cultural boundaries Jewish identity did not itself present any problems. The religious and tribal impulses, the spiritual and social unity, were two sides of the same coin. The Jewish identity was exhaustive, coextensive with the boundaries of individual personality. The life experience of the Jews was Judaism, its study, its implementation, its transmission. Enforced segregation merely reinforced the tendency to separateness originating in religious practice and previously sustained by political institutions during the ancient period of sovereignty in Palestine. The ghetto structure, collectively linked by law to the surrounding society, enhanced the vigour of religious and communal institutions. These were buttressed by the social requirements of the mediaeval ghetto and the special status of the Pale of Settlement. Their outcast status assisted the Jews in the transmission of their inheritance. Persecuted and segregated, the Jews were protected from the lure of alternative values or opportunities which might challenge the hold of their religion and its associated institutions. The ghetto insulated their way of life and contributed to its survival by reducing drift and sustaining the numbers of the people.

Towards the end of the eighteenth century when the ghetto walls began to crumble in central Europe under the impact of the Enlightenment and in the wake of Napoleon's armies, the emancipated Jews were for the first time exposed in large numbers to modern scientific and philosophical currents of thought and to the process of secularization which had already begun to transform European society. The consequent weakening of orthodoxy bifurcated the Jewish identity and rendered it problematical. For the first time, a possibility of choice was introduced at the heart of the duality of Jewish identity between religious commitment and membership in a people. To be a Jew henceforth ceased to imply a life experience necessarily defined by ethnic membership spontaneously conjoined with religious faith. Emancipation and the decline of orthodoxy snapped the institutional bonds which had woven together the social and spiritual strands of identity within the ghetto. At the same time Jewish identity at the moment of its rupture became only one among many formative agents in the shaping of individual personality. The Jews, in common with other traditional groups exposed to modernization, were now launched upon a poignant quest for a viable identity.

Jewish existence in the wider society also required redefinition in the context of the new social structures being stabilized throughout Europe in the throes of its political and industrial revolution. Owing to their wide dispersion, frequent migration and minority status the transition for the Jews was especially complex. The growing number of unorthodox Jews now sought to define themselves in terms which corresponded to the new social categories of the modernizing societies which they inhabited. The Jews were now faced with the problem of adaptation to dynamic secular societies rather than with the sort of conscientious choice between churches which had sometimes exercised their mediaeval ancestors.

The endeavour of the individual to achieve an adult identity in modern societies released from traditional authoritarian sources of definition is a universal human problem. Cultural, social and national boundaries determined by the accident of birth mitigated the problem for most people by providing anchorage if not fulfilment for the individual personality. Paradoxically enough, this element of support was less accessible for Jews than for most peoples because a major element of choice came into play in the delineation of their Jewish identity. Often as migrants with geographically remote family ties and always as members of a minority wherever they have lived since ancient times (with the sole exception of modern Israel), the Jews have had to make choices in the realms of cultural, social and political allegiance, because the specific boundaries of Jewish identity in these domains have so often been incompatible with the demands of the majorities around them. The limits of choice and the degree to which its exercise involved compromising the Jewish identity have varied from society to society and from time to time. Each society has supplied its Jews with a different range of manoeuvre, producing a complex variety in their responses since the beginnings of their emancipation. The responses of the Jews reflected not only the differential influences of the societies which they inhabited, but also the precise time when their emancipation occurred (or when they were first exposed to its idea as conveyed by its occurrence elsewhere). Hence there were broad differences between the Jewish responses in western and central Europe and those in eastern Europe, both on account of the cultural disparities and the lapse of time between the inception of emancipation in the west and its arrival in the east.

The circumstance of choice was frequently clearly seen, so that the collective process of Jewish adjustment often took on an ideological aspect. After the initial emancipation in western and central Europe (and down to the present day among the multitude for whom the quest persists unresolved, recurring anew in each generation), Jewish community life was characterized by intense doctrinal discourse, formulating and seeking to fix the meaning of Jewish existence in the absence of orthodox authority.

The emancipation of the Jews from the burdensome restrictions imposed upon them throughout Europe began in France and Prussia towards the end of the eighteenth century, and at least the influence of the idea if not its consummation had spread to eastern Europe by about the middle of the nineteenth. Rights were nowhere gained without a fierce struggle and there were intermittent reverses, such as the revocation of liberal measures in Russia after the brief liberal period from about 1855–65. However, even in Russia where emancipation was at best a fleeting incident, it opened up new vistas and hastened the breakdown of tradition within the Jewish masses. The removal of legal disabilities did not terminate social persecution but merely altered its constitution. Emancipation substituted for the official regulation of the collective ghetto the more arbitrary forms of hostility now experienced by the individual Jew. Hence the ideological quest of the liberated

Jews for self-definition in their new social context was governed not only by the general constraints inherent in the structures of the majority societies but also by the measure of persecution the individual could withstand. The Jewish identity had to be supportable from the standpoint of the society's way of life, but it must also be realized as a positive value by its bearers in view of the price attached to it by persecution.

Only those who remained strictly orthodox and impervious to modernizing influences were able completely to ignore this price and eschew any compromise of their identity. For them persecution, however harsh, could impose no defeat unless martyrdom be regarded as such. Only those Jews who remained orthodox were able to sustain intact the traditional unity and spontaneity of Jewish experience, supported by strong institutions even without the benefit of enforced insulation, and in daily triumph over the equivocal hospitality of the modern world to their way of life

For the non-practising Jews (who soon became the great majority after the spread of emancipation or of its influence as an idea) assimilation was a favoured route of adjustment. While persecution undoubtedly impelled many Jews to assimilate or to attempt to do so it more often operated as a barrier to assimilation and reinforced the sense of Jewish identity. In the more liberal societies assimilation was a product of opportunity rather than persecution. Abundant alternative opportunities for fulfilment tended to render the Jewish identity redundant. Assimilation occurred by the shedding of Jewish ties as these became irrelevant, rather than by any positive act of renunciation. It was in the western societies, where persecution in its new ideological cloak of 'anti-semitism' seemed to be an aberration not radically distinct from other manifestations of inter-group tension, that assimilation in the nineteenth century proceeded farthest. Since that avenue of adjustment was paved with incentive it is not surprising that it was crowded by the intelligentsia and members of the upper social strata. For the majority, however, opportunity was lacking and persecution was a real barrier. Together with the tenacity of the emotional attachment of the Jews to their heritage, however sparingly they were now touched by it, persecution still perpetuated the existence of the Jews and the vigour of their dilemma.

Leaving aside the orthodox and the successfully assimilated, who in opposite ways solved for themselves the problem of Jewish identity, the adjustment of the Jews may be understood in terms of responses to emancipation as qualified by persecution. The responses, including Zionism, were born of the tension between emancipation, or the idea of emancipation, and persecution. The transformation of the Zionist emotion from a mystical messianic bond into a political ideology sustaining a dynamic movement was one event that emerged from the flux of adaptation. It can properly be understood only by seeing it as one amongst a much larger number of Jewish responses.

Generalizing broadly, in the western societies with well-established linguistic and national identities and evolving liberal traditions about diversity of religious allegiance within their borders, the Jews tended to select the religious principle from their ghetto heritage while discarding the ethnic rationale of their collective life. Within the west itself Britain and France, each with a firmly integrated national identity embracing a multi-national substructure, exerted less pressure upon their Jews to discard the vestiges of tribal personality than did Germany and the United States, both of which were in an earlier less secure phase of national development. However, even in Britain and France the Jews regarded themselves as a religious group and wished to be regarded as such. This was most clearly exemplified in the denationalized religious doctrine issued by the Jewish notables of France in response to Napoleon's demand in 1806 that the Jews account for themselves in terms of their relation to the new political order. In eastern Europe, which by contrast was politically organized in multi-national empires with a single established religion, the Jews commonly abandoned their religious inheritance and asserted a national or cultural sense of identity. This pattern was well exemplified in the census held in 1921 in Czechoslovakia, which revealed that hundreds of Jews registered themselves as of Jewish 'nationality' and Roman Catholic religion.[2]

Radical doctrines and movements

The first robust western expression of the breakdown of orthodoxy occurred as early as 1750 in Berlin with the inauguration of the Jewish counterpart of the Enlightenment by Moses Mendelssohn (1729–86). This philosopher was not merely the first articulate product of incipient emancipation but its foremost Jewish pioneer and agent. Mendelssohn was dazzled by the treasures of German science and philosophy and was determined that these should become accessible to the Jews of Prussia. His efforts as an intellectual mediator between the two cultures, which involved sharp criticism of traditional Jewish society and its institutions, eventually promoted assimilation in the German lands and ultimately led indirectly to the evolution of Reform Judaism. This movement initiated a radical departure from Jewish tradition. While the Reform doctrine reaffirmed religious faith, in the name of adaptation to the modern world it eliminated Hebrew and all Israel-centred allusions from the liturgy and ceremonies, so that no vestige would remain of any implication that Judaism involved a collective allegiance beyond the confessional.

In eastern Europe the Jewish enlightenment flourished about the middle of the nineteenth century, reflecting no less than the Berlin movement the critical attitude to traditional institutions but now rediscovering within the Hebrew tradition a fund of universal secular values matching in their humanistic content the spirit of liberalism and rationalism. Rather than a reaffirmation and reform of religious faith, the cultural product of the Russian Jewish enlightenment was a flourishing Hebrew and Yiddish literature embodying liberal national values and eventually spawning a variety of nationalistic doctrines.

It is as though the Reform movement moved a step away from Judaism in the direction of the modern world, while the eastern enlightenment discovered the values of that world already inherent within Judaism itself. From the orthodox standpoint both of these movements were a step in the direction of apostasy or assimilation, the one retaining a spurious version of the religion, the other a travesty of the national spirit. However, in the context of the actual assimilation that was rife at the time these movements emerged, they could be regarded as important bastions of defence for Jewish survival. When Zionism, the most radical defensive doctrine, emerged to assert a national interpretation of the Jewish dilemma its most vehement critics were the denationalized Jews of the west, its most fertile constituency the middle class intelligentsia influenced by the Hebrew enlightenment in the east.

The initial political sympathies of the enlightened generation in Russia were with the clandestine Russian revolutionary movement, from its liberal right wing to its populist and social-democratic branches. They hoped to achieve a general political emancipation in which Jews would share together with the other peoples of Russia. But with the outbreak of a new wave of pogroms and the intensification of official persecution in 1882, middle class Jews reluctantly abandoned their belief that their future lay with their Russian neighbours. Disillusioned by the antipathy to the Jews which was now finding its cruellest expressions they fell back on a national solution to the Jewish problem, in the form of Zionism.

The enlightened Jews comprised a small minority, the intelligentsia of the middle class, so that the Zionist vision of a regenerated Hebrew nation in Palestine caught the imagination of a relatively small number. The most widespread reaction of the Jews to their desperate plight after 1881 was the desire to emigrate to the west. In the three decades prior to the first world war over two million Jews from the Pale made their way to the United States, and over 150,000 settled in Britain. In these countries they met for the first time the challenges of emancipation, and their adjustment was part of the distinctive pattern associated with the western societies.

The masses of Jews who remained in the Pale untouched by the Hebrew revival and released from the hold of religious authority (not least by their desperate economic plight and its obvious class connotations) were caught up in the general socialist enthusiasms. However, even the Jewish socialist leaders and masses were forced to adopt a pseudo-national programme, given the language barrier dividing them from the mainstream of the socialist movement. In this case Yiddish rather than Hebrew was the medium, the language of the masses as distinct from the intellectual elite. By the end of the century the strongest movement within east-European Jewry was the socialist Bund dedicated to socialist revolution while at the same time pursuing cultural separatism for the Yiddish-speaking Jews. The national principle also found a wide following in a movement for Jewish cultural autonomy and communal political representation led by the historian Dubnow (1860–1941), which did not share the socialist aspirations of the Bund. This doctrine of 'autonomism' opposed mass emigration and sought to strengthen Jewish cultural life in the territories where Jews lived, mainly in Poland but also in principle in other countries including those of the west. These movements were the eastern counterparts of assimilation. Bearing in mind the political legacy of district councils it is not surprising that the radical modernizing movements, including Zionism, sought to redefine Jewish autonomy while retaining something of its territorial dimension.

But it was only Zionism, derived indirectly from the Hebrew revival and enlightenment, which sought the construction of a Jewish nation in Palestine, abandoning the world of Europe altogether. In effect the Zionist doctrine offered an alternative to those inclined to emigrate to the fleshpots of the west. It was to prospective emigrants that the idea of settlement in Palestine first presented its challenge.

The earlier period of the European Enlightenment corresponded with the emergence of the individual whose identity as a free man was held to be founded in his nature as a rational being. Later in the nineteenth century, especially in central and eastern Europe, the individual's place in the forefront of popular imagination and of history was taken by the nation, which was now seen as the source of the individual's being. This change in emphasis as between two important elements of the liberal tradition is reflected in the evolution of Zionism. Emancipation, the product of the early Enlightenment, liberated the individual Jew, offering the possibility of full assimilation or integration within the larger society of individuals. The growth of anti-semitism, however, in its new political version which represented Jews as an inassimilable national group called in question the validity of the rationalist utopia. To be normal, free and equal, was increasingly seen as an attribute of nations, and therefore, it was thought, the Jews could enjoy the fruits of emancipation only by asserting a

17

national identity. Zionism was the antagonist above all of the individual assimilation associated with emancipation. In asserting at the end of the nineteenth century the centrality of the national principle contained within liberal thought, it was conceding the defeat of the individualist principle earlier placed at the centre of that thought. While asserting the Jewish determination to obtain freedom as understood in the modern world, Zionism simultaneously in a sense repudiated that hope by sharing many key assumptions with the doctrine of anti-semitism. Thus in Zionism the intrinsic contradictions of humanistic liberalism were sharply revealed.

Several precursors of Zionism, most notably Rabbi Zvi Hirsch Kalischer (1795–1874) and Moses Hess (1812–75) enunciated Zionist doctrines in analyses as clear as any which followed in later generations. But they came before their time. The orthodox Rabbi Kalischer wrote in 1862 at a time when the Jews of the west were still savouring their new freedom and learning the glamorous technology of the modern world from which they had been debarred by centuries of segregation and enclosure in the mould of tradition, while the masses of Jews in the east were sinking to the margin of subsistence, oblivious to the incipient currents of liberalism and nationalism in Russian society. The orthodox community, on the other hand, was still shielded from the spirit of political and social change which had come to the ken of Rabbi Kalischer, and were not moved to reformulate the messianic theory of redemption or associate it with a mundane perspective in relation to Palestine. Moses Hess, who combined Zionism with socialism in a bold vision, also wrote in 1862 and was even more in advance of his time since liberalism rather than socialism was then the most dynamic western creed, and the revolutionary movement in Russia had not yet ripened.

The idea of Zionism, the nationalist solution to the Jewish problem, found its time in the last two decades of the nineteenth century at the moment of disillusionment with emancipation in the west and the demonstration that it was unlikely to be achieved at all in the east. The disillusionment in the west was limited to the few who had so nearly achieved complete assimilation that they were the more sensitive to anti-semitic outbursts, while in the east the appeal of Palestine as a focus for national sentiment was limited to the few for whom the transition from the world of orthodoxy and tradition had been made under the influence of the Hebrew literary revival. Until the destruction of European Jewry by the Nazis, Zionism was thus supported only by a small minority. After that holocaust the Zionist movement was able to mobilize mass support among the Jews throughout the world for the nationalist cause, but this support was a product of philanthropic impulse rather than ideological conviction.

CHAPTER 2

ZIONIST DOCTRINES AND NINETEENTH-CENTURY PALESTINE

Pinsker and the Lovers of Zion – the first immigration to Palestine – Ahad Ha'Am and Herzl – the Zionist Organization – Labour-Zionism: Syrkin and Borochov

Pinsker and the Lovers of Zion

The founder of the Zionist movement in its preliminary pre-political phase was Leo Pinsker (1821–91). Pinsker was a relatively assimilated Russian Jew who had been raised in the spirit of the Hebrew enlightenment and exposed to the liberalism and nationalism of the wider world. Although he was preceded by several lone precursors of Zionism, Pinsker was the first thinker whose work evoked an immediate response, producing an organized effort to promote immigration to Palestine as a step towards solving the Jewish problem. His pamphlet *Auto-emancipation* was published in 1882, coinciding with the spread of terror and massacre of Jews throughout Russia.

It was this new wave of pogroms which forced enlightened middle-class Jews in Russia to the conclusion that liberalization and equality of citizenship for the Jews within Russia was a vain hope. For in these pogroms it was clear for the first time that mob violence was not solely a propensity of the wretched peasantry. The terror was actively abetted by students, the press and populist revolutionaries, and by their silence even the greatly admired Russian writers of the age were implicated.

Pinsker himself did not at first realize the importance of Palestine for the creation of a Jewish national movement. His analysis pointed to the peculiar 'ghost' status of the Jews as the source of their persecution and concluded that their position in the modern world could only be satisfactorily resolved if they became a normal nation with independence in its own territory. Unless they found a country of their own they would always be aliens in economic competition with and feared by the majorities among whom they lived. The crux of the solution was independent national existence, and it was of little consequence which territory was settled for this purpose.

Pinsker soon realized from the response to his pamphlet that only if Palestine was placed at the centre of the doctrine could the emotional drive of the enlightened Jews be turned to the advantage of the movement. Otherwise, those who contemplated emigration would undoubtedly head for the abundant west, and would find little magnetism in the idea of colonizing virgin territory for the sake of national independence. Only Zionism, the yearning evoked by Palestine, might supply sufficient emotional drive to justify such a leap in the dark.

Zionist ideology in its maturity asserts that the dream of the return to Zion is the mainspring of the movement, and that Zionism is the modern heir to the messianic impulse of Judaism. Zionism has certainly tapped that emotion but (far from being its heir) it represents a radical break with the spirit of Jewish messianism, transmuting it from an essentially religious insight to a doctrine of secular politics. Zionism can be understood as 'political religion' but as with other modern ideologies this has come about by supplanting religious belief, not by carrying forward its logic. Orthodox Jews continued to cultivate the messianic dream; Zionism attracted those who had been touched by it but had rejected it.

Moreover, among the Jewish masses the emotional yearning for return to Palestine was conspicuous by its absence. It was a residue of the broken tradition playing in the consciousness of the tiny minority of middle-class Jewish intellectuals, especially the young, who had been schooled in orthodoxy or Hebrew literature and found both wanting when abstracted from the territory of Palestine which had given them birth. Thus it was through appealing to the fragile sensibility of a marginal group within the Jewish people that Zionism was able to formulate a strategy by which the Jews could become an intelligible part of the modern world, as a nation in the land of its ancestors.

Pinsker readily accepted the primacy of Palestine, the necessity of Zion, for Jewish nationalism, and he became the leader of the movement of Lovers of Zion which his pamphlet inspired. The distinguishing feature of the Lovers of Zion movement, as contrasted with the religious creed or the other and later forms by which Zionism came to be defined, was the personal undertaking of its members to settle in Palestine. The Lovers of Zion, with branches spreading across Russia, had no concept of a political approach to establishing a Jewish homeland, though some did try to obtain the approval of the hostile Ottoman authorities before making their way to Palestine. Their contribution to the evolution of Zionism was the principle that settlement in Palestine was a method of personal emancipation, that each individual could solve the Jewish problem for himself by emigrating to Palestine and striking roots there. Associated with this doctrine was the call for a return to the soil. Pinsker and his followers attributed much of the abnormality of the Jewish fate to the laws prohibiting their ownership of land, and felt that the return to Palestine must also be a return to agriculture as a necessary foundation for a normal national life.

Masses of young enthusiasts joined the ranks of the Lovers of Zion intending to make their way to Palestine to become farmers there. The wave of immigration which took place was the first instance of purposeful effort based on modern ideas linking the Jews of eastern Europe with the territory of Palestine, and by their example bringing Palestine into the consciousness of the dispersed Jews as an existing reality.

The first immigration to Palestine

The history of Palestine from the time of the Roman conquest to the settlement of Jews at the end of the nineteenth century does not properly belong to the history of Israel, except in so far as Zionist doctrine attached weight to the uninterrupted presence of a number of Jews in the land throughout that entire period. The Jews of Palestine were not the progenitors of modern Israel. The Zion of the Zionists was borrowed from a religious tradition that had already ripened at the Roman expulsion eighteen centuries previously. The creators of modern Israel undertook to terminate the exile of religious doctrine by restoring the Jews to their ancient homeland on the political plane. Palestine as a historical society was irrelevant to their scheme. Its history was not incorporated into their ideology except for their awareness of the tenacity displayed by its remaining Jews through centuries of persecution, massacre and foreign invasion.

Since the Romans, the land had come under the successive rule of Byzantines, Persians, Arabs, Seljuk Turks, Crusaders, Saracens, Mamelukes, Mongols and finally the Ottoman Turks who incorporated it within their empire in the year 1517 and maintained their control until 1917.

In the nineteenth century Palestine was a neglected administrative district of Ottoman Syria. It was sparsely populated by an Arab peasantry and various foreign and religious foundations, including the communities of pious Jews engaged in religious study and subsisting on meagre charity. The Arab population is estimated to have numbered about 300,000 in 1882, while the Jews at that time totalled about 24,000. These were located for the most part in the four cities of Jerusalem, Safed, Tiberias and Hebron, where they pursued their devotions oblivious to events in the wider world.

The soil of the country had eroded and the landscape was characterized by stony hills, desert and swamp, relieved only by marginal agriculture. The dominant climate was inhospitably hot and dry. Despite its spiritual significance for multitudes the world over, the land was an impoverished relic of the past supporting but a minimum of human economy and culture.

There was a brief period of Jewish activity in Palestine before the formation of the Lovers of Zion. In 1870 the Mikve Israel agricultural school was established under the auspices of the Alliance Israelite Universelle upon the initiative of Rabbi Kalischer. Then in 1878 a group of Jews in Jerusalem bought land near Jaffa and founded the first modern agricultural settlement, Petah Tikvah. Although both of these ventures initially foundered they inspired the Lovers of Zion movement in Russia with the aim of undertaking agriculture in Palestine, and gave encouragement to the first wave of Jewish immigration from eastern Europe.

The arrival of the first modern immigration from eastern Europe in 1882 was in fact preceded by an influx of some two hundred from Yemen who arrived in the summer of 1881. Their departure from Yemen had been prompted by the spread of rumours there that the French financier Baron Rothschild had bought land in Jerusalem for free distribution to Yemenite settlers. When they arrived they learned that these rumours were without foundation and they experienced a period of bitter penury and unemployment. By 1885 their number had grown to about four hundred and fifty who had become objects of charity swamped in the European tide.[1] In the last two decades of the century nearly twenty-five thousand immigrants came from Russia and Rumania, doubling the Jewish population of Palestine. This migration resembled subsequent Zionist immigration in that it was a minuscule trickle alongside the mass emigration to the west prompted by the outbreak of pogroms and intensified persecution of the Jews in Russia after 1882. But in terms of the history of modern Israel it was nonetheless important.

Of the enthusiasts enrolled with the Lovers of Zion who were ready to undertake the hazardous trip to Palestine only a minority succeeded in doing so. Most of these were of the middle class with substantial property which enabled many of them to acquire land and develop citrus plantations and vineyards. In the event the majority settled in the cities, especially Jerusalem, where their livelihood was at best precarious. By the end of the period of the first immigration in 1903 it is estimated that the total Jewish rural population numbered only 5,210, operating some 700 farming units distributed among twenty-five new villages.[2]

The settlers faced formidable hardships, not least of these being the hostility of the Turkish administration and the indigenous population, the pious Jew as well as the Arab. Many succumbed to malaria, the oppressive climate and the

24

challenges presented by the difficult terrain. Attracting the interest of Baron Edmond de Rothschild of France (1845–1934), who was concerned with the principle of introducing Jews to farming rather than with Zionist ideals, the immigrants were rescued from insolvency by his steady financial support. By the end of the century the new settlements were underpinned by a tremendous philanthropic investment and for the most part were under the direct control of the Baron's administration.[3] Officials appointed by the Baron administered their trust autocratically as a charity without any reference to nationalist aspirations. The settlers themselves had a capitalistic and colonialistic approach to the land and the Arab population which was seen as a reservoir of extraordinarily cheap labour. Under the influence of the Baron the Jewish enterprise assumed the flavour of the French colonisation then evolving in North Africa.

The Zionism of these settlers was construed in terms of personal emancipation rather than a clear vision of national redemption, and their efforts contributed little to the regeneration of Jewish national life in Palestine. By the end of the century their settlements had degenerated into effete charitable foundations, distinguished economically from the pious communities of the towns only by their exploitation of the native peasantry. The Lovers of Zion movement and the immigration it engendered failed roundly in the objective of settling Jewish farmers firmly in Palestine. The younger generation raised on the land for the most part drifted to the towns or emigrated. At one point during the period of the first immigration the flow of emigration from Palestine exceeded the influx. By the end of the century most of the settlements appeared headed for economic ruin and were in any case demoralized by hardship and reliance on charity.

The failure of the first immigration was exemplified by the fate of the subsidiary movement within it known as the *Bilu* association. (A Hebrew acrostic of the slogan, 'House of Jacob, come, let us go!' *Isaiah* 2:5. Members of the group were known as the *Biluim*.) The first immigrants to arrive in 1882 were fifteen youthful members of the *Bilu* group, a radical offshoot of the Lovers of Zion, composed mainly of students who had been influenced by the revolutionary Russian populist movement, *Narodnaia Volia*. It is estimated that about five hundred and twenty youngsters in Russia were identified with the *Bilu* movement but no more than fifty reached Palestine, of whom in turn only some twenty remained at the end of the century.

The *Biluim* alone among the settlers of the first immigration wave were imbued with a strong sense of altruism and idealism. These students saw themselves as social pioneers. Their immediate goal was the establishment of a model agricultural village based on equality, co-operation, mutual aid, group discipline, self-defence and similar principles which were intended to preclude the transplantation of what they regarded as the evils of European feudalism. However they did not have a clearly thought out national programme and there is evidence that they hoped eventually to become members of the landowning class.

The *Biluim* were subjected to fierce attack by the other settlers who suspected them of subversive designs and moral delinquency. The pressure of public opinion secured their disqualification by the Baron for financial aid. Only the Lovers of Zion in Russia gave the *Biluim* any help, and this with some reluctance. As a result of their inexperience and lack of resources they failed to establish their projected model village and were forced to join the several hundred landless labourers dependent upon employment in the plantations. Forced to compete for jobs with Arab peasants who were satisfied with low wages as a supplement to their other sources of income such as sharecropping the impoverished Jewish labourers made several abortive attempts at trade union organization. These attempts succumbed in every case to hostile measures taken by the Baron's officials or to the pressure of unemployment.

The colonialistic approach associated with the lack of a coherent nationalist ideology, the subservience to charity and – at the other end of the social scale – the utopianism and inexperience of the first immigration all combined to relegate their endeavours in 'practical' Zionism to secondary historical significance. Those of their settlements that survived left no substantial imprint on the country. The historical importance of the Lovers of Zion and the first wave of immigration lies in the widespread interest in Zionism and in Palestine that

their efforts generated amongst Jewish communities throughout the world.

Ahad Ha'Am and Herzl

The settlement attempt in Palestine, although it was small in
scale, did accustom the Jews of eastern Europe to consider
immigration to Palestine as a possible concrete solution for
their immediate plight. On the other hand the failures of the
immigrants evoked scepticism about the efficacy of 'practical'
Zionism (as the settlement effort was dubbed) and led to
vigorous debate among Zionist writers and followers as to the
proper strategy for the national movement. The first influential
criticism of the Lovers of Zion and the early settlers came from
the pen of Ahad Ha'Am (1856–1927), himself a Russian leader
of the movement and possibly the most acute thinker of
Zionism.

In his essay *This Is Not the Way*, published in 1889, Ahad
Ha'Am presented the kernel of what became with subsequent
elaboration a sophisticated doctrine of Zionism, advocated by
a critical school of thought within the mainstream of the
movement. Ahad Ha'Am suggested in his essay that the
approach of the Lovers of Zion with the haphazard settlement
activities it sponsored was bound to fail so long as it appealed
to self interest and the desire for personal emancipation rather
than to the inspiring vision of national regeneration with its
cultural potentiality. The development of the national movement required the reinvigoration of Jewish education in the
diaspora for the revival of Jewish spiritual unity and creativity.
Settlement in Palestine was of crucial importance because it
would eventually establish a centre of leadership for such
creativity but not if cultural quality was subordinated to
quantity.

This was the basic line of argument of 'spiritual' or 'cultural'
Zionism: it selected the crisis of Judaism rather than that of
the Jews as the core issue. Unlike Pinsker Ahad Ha'Am did not
negate the diaspora. The rebuilding of the community in
Palestine he saw as only a part, albeit a vitally important part,
of a wider movement for the development of the national
spirit of the Jews wherever they lived. In place of the purely

religious tradition he envisaged a metaphysical national soul capable of giving spiritual leadership to the nations of the modern secular world. His understanding of Jewish history and destiny resembled most closely that of Dubnow, the exponent of cultural 'autonomism', except for the Zionist conviction which Ahad Ha'Am shared and which placed Palestine and the Hebrew language at the centre of his scheme rather than Yiddish and Russian Jewry.

The views of Ahad Ha'Am and the troubles of the Palestine settlers preoccupied the Lovers of Zion movement but brought them no nearer to a political strategy for Zionism. Although it was in eastern Europe alone that conditions were fertile for Zionist sentiment and it was the Pale of Settlement that long continued to supply the membership of the movement, it was only in the west that circumstances favoured a strategic political concept of Jewish nationalism. The concept of political Zionism evolved in Vienna, the metropolis of nineteenth-century nationalist ferment. It is quite intelligible that in the political circumstances of tsarist Russia Pinsker's analysis of the Jewish fate did not lead him to envisage the Zionist movement as part of the secular world of power politics. The Jewish problem for Ahad Ha'Am and the Lovers of Zion was a crisis of Jewish history. Only within the range of western political experience – refracted, as it so happened, through Vienna in its national turmoil – could it clearly be seen as part of modern European history, accessible to the conventional symbols of political interpretation. Only an assimilated western Jew, lightly touched by orthodox tradition, could place the Jewish problem in such a frame of reference, free of the metaphysical and emotional bias of those steeped in the Jewish heritage. It was thus as a European that Herzl came to lead Zionism, and as a Hebrew scholar that Ahad Ha'Am emerged as his leading Zionist antagonist.

The founder of political Zionism, Theodor Herzl (1860–1904), was born in Budapest and educated in Vienna from where he was sent to Paris as correspondent of an important liberal newspaper. An assimilated Jew with but scanty traditional education he showed little interest in Jewish communal life or problems until the Dreyfus Affair of 1894 in Paris forced him to consider the implications of anti-semitism. In his pamphlet *The Jewish State*, published in 1896, he set forth a political solution to the Jewish problem. His analysis added nothing new to that of Pinsker (whose work was unknown to Herzl) except the all-important belief born of his optimistic liberal faith that the powers of Europe could be persuaded to support the establishment of a Jewish state and guarantee its sovereignty. This was the political dimension which had been lacking in the Russian movement and it was immediately amplified by the Zionist Organization which was created in 1897 by Herzl for the planned pursuit of the nationalist policy.

Herzl's essay had a lightning impact in eastern Europe. Because rather than in spite of his being somewhat a stranger to his people his leadership had a magnetic quality. If the sophisticated voice of western emancipation advocated the same policies as the provincial intellectuals of the Odessa ghetto, their clandestine movement must indeed have historical authenticity on a universal scale! Zionism led by Herzl could not be a mere reflection of ingrown Jewish complexity removed from reality, a fantasy. For this was the voice of Vienna and Paris, a doctor of laws, Austrian laws, a man of letters whose imposing and popular presence graced the most fashionable salons of gentile society.

Like Pinsker Herzl took anti-semitism as his starting point and reached the same conclusion: that only Jewish sovereignty in a selected territory could release the Jews for all time from their suffering. Like Ahad Ha'Am he was critical of the tumbledown colonies in Palestine which were all that practical Zionism had to show for its fifteen years of effort. In Herzl's view the overriding primary goal of the movement must be to secure a legal charter for the colonization of a territory, endorsed by the powers of Europe and underwritten by international law. This could be accomplished only by bold diplomacy backed by the resources of Jews the world over. Only when autonomy was legally guaranteed could colonization proceed rapidly on a mass scale, unhampered by uncertainty and by conflict with the indigenous population and authority. Not by infiltration nor by a back door but only by right could a territory be occupied and built into a state. Herzl's view was dubbed 'political' Zionism in contradistinction to 'practical' Zionism.

Herzl's doctrine of political Zionism was derived from the analysis of anti-semitism, many assumptions of which it shared: that the Jews were unique in a metaphysical sense and could not be assimilated, that they constituted a nation in spite of their dispersion and the variety of their circumstances, and that anti-semitism was a natural expression of folk-feeling and hence ineradicable. In his vision the establishment of a Jewish state would for the first time make possible and would hasten the assimilation of those Jews who, by their failure to leave their countries of domicile to join the new state, would be freed of the suspicion that they had national links beyond the boundaries of the countries in which they dwelt. Their situation would thus be normalized no less than that of these Jews living in their own state.

The endorsement of anti-semitic assumptions and assertion of the national character of their community was directly contrary to the beliefs and aspirations of the Jews of the west, and it is not surprising that they vehemently rejected Zionism and regarded it as a threat to their progress and their very security. In the east however the Zionist doctrine accorded closely with the experience of the Jewish middle class. They did indeed display the features of nationhood, a common language, culture and history and even, relative to the Jewish dispersion, a high degree of territorial concentration. But for them Herzl's analysis confirmed and supported only one element of their own vision. While gladly accepting his leadership and the political direction it gave them they pursued a more complex revolutionary design. They were at war not only with anti-semitism and the oppression to which they were subjected by the external population and authorities, but, immersed in Jewish communal life, they were equally radical in their opposition to traditional Jewish institutions and values and to the other movements such as socialism, Bundism and autonomism, that offered themselves as alternatives. Herzl's appearance on the scene gave them a welcome sense of fitting European categories but did not on that account divest them of their specifically Jewish concerns and sensibilities, and certainly not of their emotional attachment to Palestine and the messianic fervour with which they now approached it on the political plane. Like Pinsker before him Herzl appreciated

Palestine as one possible territory for settlement, but it did not have any necessary primacy so far as he was concerned. In the Zionist vocabulary he was essentially a 'territorialist' rather than a Zionist, at least until he became fully aware of the intensity of the emotional appeal of Palestine for his east-European constituents and realized its political importance for the movement.

The Zionist Organization

Acting immediately while discussion of his proposals proceeded at a high pitch, Herzl convened the first Zionist Congress at Basle in 1897. The conference, at which were assembled delegates from communities the world over, declared that 'the aim of Zionism is to create for the Jewish people a home in Palestine secured by public law.'

The ambiguity of the adopted term 'home' was the inevitable reflection of the fact that the Jews did not in fact inhabit the territory they had selected to be the base of their autonomy. However, the phrase 'secured by public law' did imply that a form of sovereignty was the ultimate goal and indicated the endorsement by the Congress of the political rather than the practical strategy. Then as later in the formulation of its diplomacy, Zionism avoided reference to statehood as such. It may be seen that this ambiguity was not so much a devious device as a natural consequence of the absence of the people from Palestine and the hypothetical nature of the assumption that they would eventually settle there. It would at this stage have invited not opposition but ridicule to have talked about a Jewish state in Palestine. Only after about forty years, when such settlement had reached significant proportions, did the Zionist movement officially endorse statehood as its avowed goal.

The conference at Basle established the Zionist Organization to pursue the aim of the movement systematically. Herzl was elected president of the new organization and Vienna was made its initial headquarters to suit his convenience. The Congress was convened annually up to 1901 and thereafter biennially except in time of war to discuss broad policy directions and appoint its intermediate executive organ, the

31

General Council. This body in turn appointed the members of the Central Executive, a small committee empowered to direct day-to-day activities of the organization. Local units of the organization were federally linked within each country and membership, conferring the right to participate in the selection of delegates to the Congress, was contingent upon payment of a small subscription (the *shekel*, equivalent to a shilling) to provide working funds for the administration of the organization.

The Congress had a great inspirational impact on crisis-torn Jewry. The new organization quickly absorbed the old Lovers of Zion branches and stimulated the formation of new Zionist groups throughout eastern Europe and even in the west. By the end of the century the movement registered a membership of over a hundred thousand and had established Zionism as the leading issue of the day among Jews, for its antagonists no less than for its most passionate followers.

The organization gradually evolved appropriate machinery for implementing its programme. The second Congress in 1898 established the Jewish Colonial Trust, a bank registered in London, as the financial organ of the movement. With 140,000 shareholders and a paid-up subscription of £250,000 the bank was able to begin operating in 1902, and in 1903 its first branch in Palestine began to provide credit for all types of enterprise. The fifth Congress in 1901 resolved to establish the Jewish National Fund for the acquisition of land in Palestine to be held in trust as national property. By 1914 the Fund had collected donations totalling £170,000. In 1907 a Palestine Department was created within the Executive and a Palestine Office was opened in Jaffa in 1908 to assist activities on the spot. On the initiative of its first director, Arthur Ruppin (1876–1943), the Palestine Office was instrumental in founding Tel Aviv and also established the Palestine Land Development Company for land amelioration preparatory to settlement.

In the early years of the movement the organization was chronically short of funds. Most of the Jewish magnates sponsored vast philanthropic undertakings of their own, and were not interested in the political approach to relieving Jewish suffering. Consequently the revenues of the movement were mainly subscribed by small donors.

In the first years of the movement the foremost issues dividing the leadership were the merits of territorialism as against exclusive focus on Palestine, and the merits of the political strategy which gave priority to the quest for a legal charter as against the practical strategy based on settling and developing the land pending the bestowal of such a charter. It was not until 1905 that the territorialists were decisively defeated and the movement irrevocably committed exclusively to Palestine. As to the second issue, the failure of Herzl's diplomacy, coinciding with some success in new settlement activities in Palestine after about a decade, led to the practicals taking control of the organization.

Many alternatives to Palestine had been considered as possible candidates for settlement and eventual Jewish autonomy. However, it soon became clear that only Palestine evoked the ardent support needed to fuel the movement, and that the persecuted were unlikely to undertake the hazards of colonization in preference to emigration to the west unless the inspirational power of Palestine was attached to the enterprise. When in 1903 the government of Great Britain offered Herzl the opportunity of autonomous Jewish settlement in the British East Africa Protectorate,[4] Herzl tried to persuade the sixth Zionist Congress to accept it. His efforts in diplomacy carried to all the major capitals of Europe had failed to procure powerful support for the Zionist aim, and he was discouraged about the prospects of the Ottoman Sultan relenting in his opposition to the Palestine adventure. The Congress voted to explore the 'Uganda' matter further, but the next Congress in 1905 after Herzl's death rejected the 'Uganda' proposal outright, and the territorialists seceded from the organization. The outcome was a victory for the Russian Zionists over the western leaders, and it was followed up by another some years later on the score of priority for the promotion of practical work in Palestine.

The dispute between the politicals and the practicals was about emphasis and method rather than ultimate aims. This was most evident in the approach of Chaim Weizmann (1874–1952), later President of the Zionist Organization and first President of Israel. As a leader of the practicals he pointed out that practical activities had great political value. He coined the term 'synthetic Zionism' (sometimes referred to as 'organic Zionism') to stress the close connection between the two approaches, suggesting that they were equally vital. It was a result of pressure by the practicals that the Zionist Organization set up the Palestine Office in 1908 to sponsor and promote development on the spot. From then on the influence of the practicals grew until by 1911 they were able to dominate the executive.

The movement of cultural Zionism led by Ahad Ha'Am did not form a separate faction but succeeded in enlarging its influence within the organization from year to year, obtaining among other results the adoption of Hebrew as the official language of the organization. The cultural movement found itself somewhat closer to the practicals than the politicals on the immediate tactical issues. Weizmann was associated with Ahad Ha'Am from the time of his entry into the movement so that his doctrine of synthetic Zionism also embraced the cultural programme. In the event the synthesis which most effectively combined all three goals, the political, practical and cultural, was the contribution of an embryonic party known as the labour-Zionists. However, their interpretation of the three doctrines in combination differed from those of the foremost exponents of each in isolation.

Labour-Zionism: Syrkin and Borochov

Labour-Zionism, the most common name for a group of doctrines attempting to synthesize socialism and Zionism, eventually became the predominant ideological treasury governing Jewish constructive efforts in Palestine, and it comprised the foremost immediate source of modern Israel's social and economic institutions, values and myths. The original theorists and creators of the labour-Zionist movement in its European phase were Nachman Syrkin (1867–1924) and Ber Borochov (1881–1917).

The Zionists had the greatest difficulty in making any impression upon the Jewish masses who tended to look on them as romantics or at best as representatives of bourgeois sentiment. By the end of the century, with the failure of practical Zionism in Palestine and the consequent politicization of the movement under Herzl's leadership, Zionism appeared to offer less and less for the alleviation of current suffering. As it was transformed into a futuristic vision embracing the entire sweep of Jewish history, and incorporated a doctrine that vitiated all expectation of improvement for Jews within the European environment, Zionism came into direct conflict with the Jewish proletariat's perceived interest. It was in this context that the ideas of socialist-Zionism were formulated, seeking to increase the relevance of Zionism for the masses and to broaden the appeal of the movement beyond its primary middle-class constituency.

Although he was influenced by Marx, Syrkin's theory was more humanitarian than Marxian and was addressed specifically to the solution of the Jewish problem. Attributing antisemitism to the class structure of society Syrkin concluded that only a classless society could solve the Jewish problem. Jews should therefore join the socialist movement. However, since socialist activity in Europe offered only the remotest prospect of the classless society triumphant, the Jewish masses must also seek national sovereignty as a framework for their own social cause. The Jewish masses must therefore participate in the struggle for national independence as well as revolutionary socialism. That the national struggle was currently led by bourgeois elements need not detract from its relevance to the proletariat, since the proletariat had the most to gain from the success of Zionism. The national goal was above the internal Jewish class conflict and should be pursued by all classes in co-operation. Syrkin was convinced in any case that Zionism would never succeed as a political movement unless it incorporated a profound measure of social idealism which alone could render the movement attractive to all Jews regardless of their class location.

Syrkin at first was ignored. His influence spread slowly, perhaps because of the lack of articulation between the two branches of activity endorsed by his theory: socialist agitation in Europe and Zionist effort in Palestine. His ideas did however generate the formation of working-class Zionist groups, and it was these groups that provided the nucleus for a unified labour-Zionist movement inspired by the thought of Ber Borochov.

Borochov's analysis of the Jewish problem requires close attention because of its great influence on those who became the founding fathers of modern Israel. His theory (drastically condensed) may appear rather cryptic to the reader uninitiated in the Marxian vocabulary, for Borochov sought to extend Marxian concepts to the fuller understanding of the national problem which he felt had been neglected by Marx and Engels and misunderstood by their followers. He considered his work to be a fulfilment of Marxian theory rather than a revisionist exercise.

His contribution to the evolution of labour-Zionist ideology falls into two parts, a general theory of nationalism and an application of that theory to the case of the Jews. To deal with nationalism Borochov introduced a new concept, 'conditions of production', supplementing the more familiar 'relations of production'. By conditions of production he meant the total historical, geographical and anthropological setting in which relations of production arose. While the relations of production, as in Marx, determined the class struggle, the conditions of production in Borochov's view determined national struggles. Just as social conflicts arose from the contradictions between the developing forces of production and the existing *relations* of production, so national conflicts arose from an analogous clash between the developing forces of production and the existing *conditions* of production. Under the then normal conditions of bourgeois development, national conflicts tended to obscure class antagonisms, and so from the point of view of the proletariat they were reactionary. Under abnormal conditions, however, as when a nation was subjugated (as in the case of colonial peoples), the proletariat of that nation was bereft of a territory or strategic base from which to wage the class struggle. In these circumstances the national consciousness of the proletariat would arise before class consciousness and the national struggle would become complementary to, if not identical with, the class struggle. The different classes within the subjugated nation would place a different value on the national interest, and the proletariat need not and therefore must not collaborate with the other classes. Hence, class conflict within the nation would proceed unhampered by the fact that the classes shared the goal of normalizing the conditions of production for the entire nation.

Applied to the case of the Jews Borochov's argument held that the Jewish proletariat, as part of a subjugated nation on the margin of the economy, had no base from which to wage the class struggle to correct its plight, and was therefore nationally conscious. The Jewish proletariat would therefore be driven to emigrate and ultimately to emigrate to the only land where it might freely enter all branches of production, the only land wanted by no other nation, Palestine. While other countries might display considerable absorptive capacity and the flow to Palestine would represent only a minority of the people, Palestine alone offered the proper 'conditions' for Jewish settlement. Such settlement was therefore inevitable from a materialist standpoint. Jewish settlement in Palestine in which workers would play a key role was objectively determined by the conditions of production, and so far as the Jews were concerned Zionism had a scientific status analogous to socialism as heir to the future.

Borochov's analysis reflected the fact that the Arabs of Palestine were Turkish subjects with no national consciousness as Palestinians. In this respect his doctrine resembled the other evolving versions of Zionism. But his understanding differed from these in that his socialist theory obliged him to fit the Arab population into his scheme of development. In his analysis the Arabs would not be subjugated or colonized by the Jews but would be assimilated to them economically and culturally, since it would be the Jewish initiative which would launch the new conditions of production. Lacking a national consciousness of their own, they would become part of the Jewish nation. In the struggle with the Turkish power which would inevitably arise concurrently with the newly emerging conditions of production, the Arab population would be united as one nation with the Jews.

Building on the dispersed groups that had formed under the influence of Syrkin, Borochov vigorously organized a coherent labour-Zionist movement known as Poale Zion ('Workers of Zion'), with branches linking several centres in eastern Europe. Although Poale Zion did make some inroads into the ranks of the working class most of the working people attached to the movement stayed in Europe and made no contribution to the evolution of Israel's history in Palestine. The immediate

37

importance of the movement was its provision of an ideology for the socialist intelligentsia and middle-class Zionist youth, who had not yet succeeded in relating their socialist or liberal aspirations to their national idealism. Borochov's analysis with its scientistic overtones gave its devotees a conviction of historical relevance and the confidence in eventual triumph that was needed to sustain a radical movement.

Poale Zion proceeded to the immediate goal of organizing immigration to Palestine with a clear sense of national and social purpose. By the year 1907 shortly after its inception, Poale Zion is estimated to have numbered some 19,000 followers. The majority of these were caught up in the European socialist movement and in the event only a small portion found their way to Palestine. At first these were primarily middle-class youths with a liberal-Syrkinian socialist bias. Among the labour-Zionist immigrants to Palestine the Marxian Borochovists outnumbered the Syrkinians only in the second decade of the century.

Neither Syrkin nor Borochov went to live in Palestine so they did not have the opportunity to develop their ideas in the light of the realities of the Palestinian environment. But Zionist immigrants who came to Palestine during the period of the second wave of immigration (between 1904–1914) found it necessary to adapt their European doctrinal luggage to the new conditions they encountered. It was in Palestine in the first two decades of the century that labour-Zionism evolved to maturity, and became the driving force of the state in the making. The leading thinker of the movement in its initial Palestine phase was Aaron David Gordon (1856–1922) whose ideas and whose impact reflected the transition of Zionism from its character as an aspect of European life to that of a thrusting force in the middle east.

PART II

THE STATE IN THE MAKING (1904-48)

Men make their own history, but they do not make it just as they please: they do not make it under circumstances chosen by themselves, but under circumstances directly found, given and transmitted from the past.

Karl Marx

CHAPTER 3

FOUNDING FATHERS: THE
SECOND IMMIGRATION (1904-14)

*The pioneers of the second immigration – the religion of
labour: A. D. Gordon – emergence of party politics –
the 'conquest of labour' – origins of the kibbutz – trade
unions in embryo – rebirth of the Hebrew language*

The pioneers of the second immigration

Within the second immigration wave that flowed into Palestine
between 1904–14 there was a relatively small group with distinctive characteristics setting them apart from the rest. These
were the teenage founding fathers of Israel.

A minority within the second immigration created the
labour-Zionist pioneer movement, and on the basis of its
ideology built and shaped the institutions that ultimately lent
credence to the claim of Zionism to Jewish national statehood.
The will of this revolutionary minority prevailed upon the
reluctant majority of the population and the recalcitrant terrain. In the first decade of the century as youngsters they
developed the outlines of social and economic organization,
the pattern of party politics, the revival of Hebrew culture
and the framework for defence, which together effectively
moulded the country. After the Bolshevik revolution and in
the early 'twenties their numbers were augmented by a new
influx of pioneers who came with the third immigration wave.
Then their early experiments crystallized into a vigorous
united labour movement which achieved political dominance
in the 'thirties, enabling them to drive successfully to statehood
in the 'forties. The ability of these fanatical youngsters to

modify and adapt their European nationalist and socialist ideals to the new environment of Palestine marked them from the moment of their arrival as makers of history.

Among the labour-Zionists of the second immigration were many whose political careers spanned more than five decades. These included the foremost architect of the state David Ben-Gurion (1886–1973), Israel's first prime minister; Yitzhak Ben-Zvi (1885–1962), the second President of the state; and Joseph Sprinzak (1884–1958), first Speaker of the Knesset (Israel's legislature).

The first immigration to Palestine during the last two decades of the nineteenth century was geared to the alleviation of immediate suffering. With the foundation of the Zionist Organization and the evolution of the movement as a vehicle for national rebirth by political means the character of the settlement in Palestine changed. The newcomers who flowed into Palestine in the period 1904–14 were the first of the practical Zionists to link their efforts and their vision of the future to the requirements of the nationalist cause conceived as a political movement. While the Zionist Organization continued its propaganda, fund-raising and diplomacy, now for the first time settlers in Palestine gave the movement a clear direction in social and economic development in the territory selected by Zionism for Jewish national redemption.

In Russia the situation of the Jews reached a new point of crisis in 1903 with the outbreak of a wave of pogroms which continued intermittently till 1907. Mass emigration gained momentum and was assisted by philanthropic rescue organizations established in the Jewish communities of the west. The vast majority of the emigrants headed for the United States. Between 1882–1914 nearly two million Jews emigrated from Russia alone, some three-quarters of them to America. Two United States officials appointed by the secretary of the Treasury to investigate the causes of European emigration spent several months touring the Pale of Settlement and reported that America was the Jews' great hope, 'towards which their gaze is directed as earnestly as that of their ancestors towards the promised land'.[1] The Zionists among the emigrants were clearly exceptional. The second immigration wave is estimated to have brought between 35,000–40,000 newcomers to Palestine, a figure which included many from the Austrian empire and Rumania as well as Russia, and also a further two thousand or so from Yemen.

It is clear from the direction of migration that the masses of the people were above all concerned to free themselves from crippling persecution and to reconstruct their individual lives wherever economic opportunities were to be found. The Zionists differed from the rest in that they were preoccupied in the main with the fate of the Jewish people and its national future. They were idealists committed to a solution of the Jewish problem, seeking not personal emancipation like the Palestine immigrants of the first wave or the emigrants to the west, but national rebirth. Their cause promised them no comfort, only hardship upon hardship in the hostile environment of Palestine. They were dedicated to a public cause, oblivious to the call of the private career.

The second immigration was variegated in composition, drawn from every class and walk of life and not notably differentiated from those who chose a westerly migration. However the pioneers among them were distinguished from the majority by their youth, their origin in the 'middle and small Jewish bourgeoisie', and by their extraordinary rebelliousness, their fanatical revolutionary temper.

It is estimated that the pioneer movement within the second immigration numbered at its peak some ten thousand or a quarter of the total influx. However not all the pioneers maintained their resolve in the face of severe trials. By 1914 no more than twelve hundred had established themselves in farm labour, and some additional few hundred working in the towns continued to identify themselves with the pioneers.[2]

The pioneers' exposure to secular values was more drastic than that of the previous generation. The transition from Jewish orthodoxy during the heyday of the enlightenment had been bridged by the restatement of liberal Jewish values and by the economic opportunities briefly available to the emancipated of the middle class. But by the 1890s the movement of the enlightenment had already passed from the scene in Russia. For the younger generation the transition was shaped more by the direct confrontation of orthodoxy with Zionism and socialism which had now ripened into magnetic movements. These youngsters, as they graduated from the Talmudical colleges, could find no attraction in the pursuit of a chemist's or doctor's diploma, in the context of sealed economic opportunity. There was no point in exchanging old books for new. Any programme of action exerted a stronger appeal than any new books, the mastery of which in any case would not expand career opportunities.

A curious characteristic of the pioneers of the second immigration was the fact that they were not organized in groups specifically for the purpose of carrying out their migration. In this they differed from the first and from subsequent immigration waves. They came, 'two from each town, one from each village',[3] individuals, in ones and twos. They were rebels against every accepted norm of their society, against every institution of authority. They renounced their very obligation to parents and family. The youths who went to the United States moved together with their families or at least with the blessing of their families. No rebels they, following the most respectable course open to them in the light of prevailing values.

At the time of their departure for Palestine the petit–bourgeois economy from which these stragglers the pioneers sprang had crumbled into bankruptcy, and the various movements to which they had been exposed were demoralized. Most of the membership of Poale Zion remained in Europe. The Zionist movement, divided on the 'Uganda' question, did not urge settlement in Palestine. Even the dispirited remnants of the first immigration included among their number many fanatical exponents of settlement in British East Africa. Hebrew literary activity and cultural dynamism in Russia had succumbed to oppression. The inspirational impact of the first Russian revolution of 1905 was dissipated in the intense political and social reaction which followed it.

Thus the pioneers were a tiny minority moving against the stream of Jewish life and even of Zionist life. They were rebels even within the perspective of a revolutionary culture. They rebelled not only against their plight, but against current radical prescriptions for correcting it. The message of Palestine as it filtered down to Europe at this time portended economic disaster for all but the propertied. And yet these young men and women were determined to become workers and pioneers, determined to restore the occupational structure of the Jews to a normal pattern after centuries of legally determined distortion. Their revolutionary fervour can be better understood in the context of the despair prevalent amongst them in Europe, as vividly expressed in the following passage from the reminiscences of one of the pioneer leaders:

'I do not know whether our elders, as they rose at midnight to pray and spill tears for their slavery and the bitterness of exile, experienced the depths of agony that we youths, tossed in the winds of revolution, felt at the calamity, the ignominy of our people. The tempests of the world swirled us about, the wine of revolution intoxicated us ... but we were few among the majority, those few whose roots in the soil of Israel's being no storm whatsoever could dislodge ... In the dim alleys of Jewish Vilna, in their famine and their filth ... we were breathing the air of annihilation ... clinging together in penury, in cellars and emigré encampments, in disease and affliction ... in despair and beyond hope.'[4]

Paradoxically Zionism was a revolutionary idea, but the average Zionists were not revolutionary in temperament, neither then nor since. With but few exceptions, this distinction belonged to the labour-Zionist pioneers who were anything but average Zionists. The Zionist and socialist movements in Europe were too diffuse to accommodate them. Palestine answered to their needs because there alone could they direct and shape events in the image of their own movement, in the school of action. And yet it is in the specific context of the Jewish problem alone that the pioneer youth emerge as revolutionaries of the most radical cast. In relation to the political culture of the wider Russian world the labour-Zionists were closer in spirit to the humanist social-democratic tradition of intellectual revolt than to the embryonic communist tradition. In their later works the pioneers revealed significant affinities with the Russian mensheviks in their approach to the social order. Their radicalism was more pronounced in relation to the national problem than in their approach to social and economic issues.

The pioneers were eloquent in the vocabulary of European

revolution but found as they grappled with their new environment that their doctrines needed to be adapted to the concrete challenges they now faced. For over a decade following their arrival in Palestine, and with some intensity for decades thereafter, they engaged in heated ideological discourse, refining and rearranging their European symbols to bring them into correspondence with the new reality. The clearest formal expression of the adaptation of their European nationalist and socialist ideas to the circumstances of Palestine was conveyed in the work of Gordon, the foremost philosophical protagonist and mentor of the pioneers.

The religion of labour: A. D. Gordon

Gordon came from Russia to Palestine at the relatively advanced age of forty-eight. He went to work immediately on the land and lived his last twenty years as a labourer and essayist. Gordon, who has been dubbed a 'secular mystic and saint' and the Tolstoy of the Zionist movement,[5] exerted a great influence on the young pioneers of labour-Zionism.

Gordon rejected outright the Marxian doctrine of class struggle and formulated an idealistic theory of nationalism in which social goals were subordinated to national. He considered that the regeneration of the individual human spirit was the starting point of human progress. For him socialism represented a mere mechanistic reflex of capitalism, like a dull recording rather than the vibrant melody of the living soul. Only nationalism in his view addressed the human spirit in a way which released creative human energies. His metaphysic argued to the conclusion that nationalism was the essence of the creative human struggle for individuation. For the Jews in Europe it was the national spirit that had secured their survival, but it was unable to impart to them a creative life for only in the symbiotic attachment of a people to its soil could creativity occur. Only through personal labour on the soil could the individual become free and a nation realize its personality.

From the standpoint of a nationalist rejecting socialism, Gordon came to the same conclusion as the orthodox socialists that socialism and nationalism were incompatible. The nation could only achieve progress and regeneration through unity, the fusion of all its elements regardless of class or party. Not that Gordon rejected the socialist aspiration for justice; but justice was only attainable when the working people, *tillers of the soil* in their forefront, increased their influence until they spoke for the nation. The ideal of justice could not be embodied within a class which was merely a collective group, but only within a national community; and it could not be attained by the method of class struggle but only by the education of the young. Justice would be installed only when the young would *become* workers and, by the force of their moral example, the workers would then come to the leadership of the nation. The labour movement would convert the masses to the religion of productive labour, and then the elimination of parasitic exploitation would ensue.

Gordon asserted that by waging class war the socialists merely carried dynamism into the capitalist sphere, and suggested that by becoming devoted workers rather than spending their energy as agitators for socialism they could bring the centre of gravity of collective life into the sphere of the working people. The victory of social justice would come with the victory of national labour through its growth.

Thus did Gordon see the labour movement as the vanguard of the nation, as the force whose ideology, if it were but based on justice and labour, would come to absorb within its orbit all elements of the society. By identifying itself with the nation as a whole, labour would come to lead the nation.

Quite apart from the possible merits or demerits of his metaphysical theory Gordon's view proved correct as a prediction of labour's role in the future development of the national movement. Although there have been greater thinkers than Gordon associated with the evolution of Zionism, none has had a greater influence on the spirit and course of the national development of Israel. His influence was seminal because his disciples were revolutionary makers of history. Young as they were, the pioneers were deeply moved by Gordon's preaching. His was the only elderly voice to speak in a language that accorded with their feelings and aspirations, while at the same time answering to the realities of their situation.

Those who had been influenced by Syrkin in Europe came quickly under the spell of Gordon in Palestine, while the followers of Borochov found his language less congenial. A dialogue developed between the Gordonians and Borochovists as the pioneers sought to adjust their European symbols to the Palestinian reality. Their socialist ideas rooted in the evils of early European capitalism and Russian feudalism, and their nationalist sentiments formed in the turmoil of central and eastern Europe as traditional nations sought political independence in the territories they inhabited, were both rather remote from the facts of Palestine. Within the Jewish range there were no classes to speak of, let alone class war. As for the alleged nation, it was conspicuous by its absence from the territory. Necessarily the socialist and Zionist doctrines of the pioneers moved somewhat from the descriptive plane to the visionary. It was here that Gordon came into his own.

The notion that by identifying itself with the nation as a whole the labour movement would come to lead the nation afforded a link between the Gordonians and the Borochovists. Although their reasoning was divergent they were equally able to contemplate the assimilation of the entire nation into the orbit of the pioneer labour movement. This is what Ben-Gurion, a Borochovist, meant when he coined the slogan 'from class to nation'. The Gordonians assumed an open society in which could be established a humanistic socialism unhindered by institutional obstacles. The Borochovists assumed the inevitable emergence of classes, and a class struggle which from the standpoint of labour would be identical with the national struggle. The Gordonians said, in effect, 'let us labour, and build a nation'; the Borochovists, 'we are a class, which will struggle to become the nation.' Both perspectives saw the role of labour as a nationalist role. Both were concerned to replace the occupational structure of east-European Jewry by a new national pattern based on Jewish primary production. The Gordonians were less clear than the Borochovists about the inherent difficulty of achieving labour predominance in the context of wage-labour, with its dependency on the Jewish employer. The Borochovists, on the other hand, had difficulty grasping the vision, which to them was at best vague and at worst utopian, of a labour movement based on a class of independent socialist farmers.

The two themes of nationalism and socialism were hence-

48

forth closely intertwined in the labour culture so that it is not possible always to distinguish the one from the other in the mental play of the leadership. Since the constituency for immigration was still centred in eastern Europe the nationalist programme was comfortably couched in European symbols. These gradually atrophied as the centre of gravity of their movement shifted from Vilna and Minsk to Jaffa and Sejera.

Emergence of party politics

From the moment of their arrival in Palestine the pioneers were divided into two competing camps which quickly assumed the character of political parties. The Gordonians, initially in the majority, most of whom in Europe had originally come under the influence of Syrkin, were organized in Hapoel Hatzair (literally, 'The Young Worker'). Those who had followed Borochov in Europe formed the Palestinian branch of Poale Zion ('Workers of Zion'). The ranks of Poale Zion gradually swelled with the later arrival of immigrants indoctrinated in the European movement and it eventually became the larger of the two. The two parties, both founded in 1905, played a crucial role in the lives of the pioneers, assisting them to adapt to their new environment. For long they were the only organizational instruments available to the pioneer movement.

Hapoel Hatzair at its inception resolved to cut its ties with the European Poale Zion. Committed first and foremost to nationalism, its members determined to concentrate on the immediate challenges of agricultural pioneering and to avoid socialist apologetics. They would follow a pragmatic indigenous programme of nationalism and social justice and forget the theoretical pangs of European socialism. The party did not consider itself part of the socialist movement but only as part of the Zionist movement, within which it sought to represent the highest degree of practical Zionism. Gordon was their influential spiritual or moral guide, while Sprinzak, from his arrival in 1908, became the leading practical tactician and spokesman of the party. The group produced many other distinguished leaders who made their mark on the country, and also a remarkable cluster of Hebrew literary luminaries.

Poale Zion, by contrast, maintained its European links for many years, regarding itself as part of the international socialist movement. The Palestine branch, led intellectually by Berl Katznelson (1887–1944) and in practical politics by Ben-Gurion and Ben-Zvi among others, persistently sought acceptance within the revolutionary socialist fold whose orthodox leadership repudiated Jewish national claims. The first paragraph of the Poale Zion platform adopted in Jaffa in 1906 defined the ultimate aim of the party as the establishment of socialism throughout the world by means of the class struggle. However, the programme also called for a Jewish state in Palestine, displaying a tough political orientation which was absent from the rival party circle.

Generally Poale Zion was more militant in outlook than Hapoel Hatzair, more urban in orientation and disposition, less imbued than the Gordonians with faith in the efficacy of brotherhood and pacifism. However, with the passage of time and their adaptation to the conditions of Palestine the members of Poale Zion came increasingly to act like good Gordonians, while using the Marxian vocabulary of Borochov. The two parties were divided on theoretical rather than practical grounds, and their theoretical differences derived from European issues encountered in their formative years, rather than from Palestinian circumstances. Thus they usually came into agreement on concrete policy choices, on the basis of their different theoretical rationales. The debates between the two groups, the intense ideological discourse which comprised their main leisure pursuit, had thus an ethereal quality resembling a European socialist ritual removed from the realities of their surroundings. In practice they were free of dogmatic strictures and in their works they demonstrated a pragmatic rather than doctrinaire approach. Thus it may be seen that their European vocabulary provided a convenient set of fictions easing their adjustment to their new environment, rather than an accurate key to the understanding of their practical activities.

In the process of adjustment the members of Poale Zion had to undergo the greater compromise. In this they were forcefully led by Ben-Gurion who pressed the party to loosen its European ties and concerns ultimately to the point of rupture which took place in 1920. Poale Zion gradually came to give priority to the nationalist range of goals over the socialist, and formulated a viable synthesis of the two perspectives which eventually enabled them to lead and dominate the labour movement as a whole.

Their isolation as a small minority movement and the physical harshness of conditions generated a primitive solidarity and equalitarianism among the pioneers, and evoked a profound commitment to mutual aid. The ideological differences dividing the two parties were relatively minor and obviously less significant than the factors which set them apart from the majority of Jewish settlers. Their ideological veneer tended to obscure the underlying social structure of the parties. In fact they resembled close-knit communities, reminiscent of the *kehillah* (the community organ of the Jewish society in eastern Europe). Upon their arrival in the country in ones and twos the would-be pioneers found their immediate social location within the party circle whose ideology they favoured. The party alone effectively eased the great loneliness of these transplanted teenagers, helped them to find work, provided communal kitchen facilities, shelter, newspapers, discussion clubs, and generally looked after their daily needs. In the range of services they provided and their style of ideological discourse they became prototypes of the pattern of party politics which later became characteristic of Israel.

Observers of Israeli politics have perhaps somewhat glibly attributed the system of proportional representation and the vigour and style of party politics to the organizational necessities and issues that evolved within the international Zionist Organization; but the emergence of Israeli party politics can better be understood by assuming the decisive importance of conditions in Palestine and the extraordinary influence of the pioneer labour parties upon all subsequent politics. In this light the parties may be seen to reproduce in no small degree the structure of the *kehillah*, and in large part its political values, as tempered by pioneering conditions.[6]

The 'conquest of labour'

In the peak years of immigration, 1905–07, there arrived over six thousand new immigrants, including many would-be pioneers. They were horrified to discover the demoralized state of the old settlers and to witness the stream of emigration from Palestine of native-born Jewish youth. Immediately they set about groping for an economic foothold and a voice in the building of the country. Having renounced Europe and their alien status in European society, the pioneers now found themselves aliens within the Jewish community of Palestine! The fact that they were unwilling to assimilate to the community established by their predecessors accounts for their dynamism and their impact upon the country: it is this fact that marks the moment of their arrival as the inception of modern Israel. Had they gravitated socially and culturally towards their predecessors as subsequent immigrants did towards themselves, it is unlikely that the labour movement or the state later founded upon it would have come into being. Much of their creative energy was generated by reaction to the failure of the first immigrants, and by the determination to avoid the errors, from the point of view of the national cause, of the decadent host community. In rejecting the traditional society of Europe the pioneers were in competition with a multitude of alternative prescriptions, all vigorously sponsored. But in the narrower context of Jewish Palestine, although they were still a minority, they were able to exert a much greater influence.

As their immediate antagonist the pioneers selected the Jewish farmer with his colonialist social norms. They were appalled by what they saw as the curse of idleness, the lack of esteem in which labour was held by the plantation owners who saw themselves as the organizing minds of agriculture in the style of the French colonists of Algeria. The pioneers attributed the lack of spirit among the native Jewish youth to the influence of the French Levantine culture imported by the Baron's administration. To this they opposed the ideals of the socialist economy and the regeneration of Hebrew national culture. The old colonists saw their right to land, conventionally, as based on a charter or title deed. The newcomers under the influence of Gordon, favoured the theory that the right to land could only be based on labour upon it. Daily contact with the soil through toil was in their view the moral and legal basis of land ownership. The idea of colonizing the native Arab peasant was repugnant to all the pioneers whether they drew their socialist predilections from Borochov or Gordon. Their aim was to colonize the bare land not its people, to become themselves peasants and workers not masters. They wanted a Jewish national community based on its own labour with a normal occupational structure, not a Jewish colonial enterprise based on exploitation of the native population. This was where, in their view, the first immigrants had gone wrong, and it was in grappling with the issue of Arab labour, and in their resolve not to build the new nation on a colonial foundation, that the pioneers took the first decisive step in the creation of modern Israel.

Against this background, in 1905, Hapoel Hatzair coined its first slogan 'conquest of labour'. By this they meant two things: their own personal transformation into workers and secondly, the establishment of Jewish wage-labour in the agricultural economy. The slogan served both the Gordonians and the Borochovists equally well, if for different reasons.

The priority given by the pioneers to agriculture, especially as this was formulated in the almost Tolstoyan mystique of Gordon, may tend to obscure the broader historical significance of their enterprise. Given the economic vacuum confronting the pioneers, national development clearly required the preparation of a Jewish agricultural foundation. The drive for a Jewish job-structure in agriculture was a necessary preliminary to the industrialization of the country, not an essentially agrarian movement. So it was seen by the Borochovists if not by the Gordonians, and so, in the event, would history prove it to be. Although the modernization of an underdeveloped economy normally requires breaking away from a solely agrarian base, it so happened that so far as the Jews were concerned in the conditions of Palestine at that time it required first the creation of an agrarian base. The essential modernizing spirit informing the movement thus placed it historically in a common category with industrialization movements led by intellectuals in other countries in the twentieth century, rather than in the utopian limbo of agrarian romanticism.

For the Gordonians the 'conquest of labour', in the sense of securing job positions for Jewish farmworkers, was the

c

necessary foundation for a humane national society based on individual effort and proximity to the soil. They did not regard their opposition to the Jewish employers of native Arab labour as class opposition but as a conflict about the proper means of attaining national goals. The Borochovists on the other hand saw Jewish employment in primary production as the necessary base from which to wage the class struggle, and looked upon the Jewish plantation owners as capitalists exploiting cheap labour.

Both Hapoel Hatzair and Poale Zion made the slogan 'conquest of labour' into the central principle of the national movement at that stage in its development. Although they envisaged ultimately making common cause with the Arab peasants, they neglected to think through the immediate problem of their relation to that group. The immediate antagonist, in their minds, was not the Arab worker they sought to replace, but the Jewish employer. A key element in the doctrine of conquest of labour was the assumption that Jewish capital had no national value without Jewish labour. The ideology of nationalism gave them a claim on the Jewish employer, a very real claim and not merely a philosophical one to the extent that Jewish public capital was invested in colonization. The pioneers were determined to eradicate at its source the colonialist mentality with which the earlier Jewish settlers had led the national movement into a cul de sac.

The pioneers were resolved to secure work and to live at a higher standard than the Arab peons on the margin of subsistence. The quasi-feudal Arab system, with its extraordinarily wealthy upper class, would surely at some point emerge into focus as an antagonist of the Jewish labour movement, but in the meantime the Jewish employer must first be nationalized. The pioneers, however, proved too weak directly to break the resistance of these employers, whose attitude is summed up: 'My Jewish heart won't let me pay you four piastres a day which is all that I pay to these little Arab girls. And my pocket won't let me pay you more. So you had better give up this folly.'[7] The defeat of the pioneers in their battle with the employers to put national considerations before personal gain forced them to modify their tactics of pressure and persuasion, and brought them to a new creative threshold.

Origins of the kibbutz

The pioneers failed to break the resistance of the plantation owners and operators in the coastal plain. The availability of 'cheap' Arab labour vitiated their bargaining power. But they did not give up their quest in despair. Their defeat drove them forward to a new concept of 'conquest of labour', and into a new part of the country as yet untouched by Jewish farming. They moved on foot to Galilee where the Zionist Organization had begun to purchase land, and were resolved upon direct labour settlement; not as owners but as custodians for the nation, not as employers but as workers, not for profit but for long-term development.

As a means of protecting the altruistic purposes of Zionist donors the Zionist Organization had set up the Jewish National Fund to purchase land and hold it perpetually in trust for the nation. The land would be leased for development but not sold for profit. This fortuitous circumstance did more for the labour-pioneer cause than perhaps any other factor, since it institutionalized the idea of nationally owned natural resources and cancelled their economic weakness as a group without capital. If capital were supplied by the Zionist Organization the labourers need only become its trustees to put them effectively on an economic par with private owners. Land would be virtually free to any who could work it. Since only the pioneers were willing to tackle malarial swamps they were able at the inception of agricultural development to introduce their own social principles at the grassroots of economic organization.

At first the Galilee lands purchased by the National Fund were administered autocratically in a style reminiscent of the Baron's regime in the coastal plantations. Workers were paid the same wages and subject to the same conditions as prevailed in the private sector. But the head of the Palestine Office of the Zionist Organization, Dr Arthur Ruppin, quickly came to understand the vision of the pioneers and grasped the important role they might play in economic development. He was therefore more hospitable to their revolutionary notions than most, and although he was no socialist he sought to co-ordinate the objects and procedures of the agencies he headed with the desires and spirit of the labourers on the job. From this conjunction of minds developed the *kvutza*, progenitor of the kibbutz movement which was to become the best-known institution in Israel. At the heart of this movement which changed the face of the country within a generation was the alliance between the embryonic labour movement and the Zionist financial institutions. The pragmatism of the more radical socialists among the pioneers was revealed in their readiness to enter such an alliance with the Jewish bourgeoisie abroad.

Using the strike weapon a group of the pioneers in the Galilee lands demanded that the land be leased to them as a group, asserting that they needed no 'administrator'. With Ruppin's help they gained their point and the co-operative principle was thus introduced in agriculture. By working the land collectively on their own responsibility, and marketing their produce co-operatively, the pioneers were able to gain a foothold in the market notwithstanding Arab competition. The first kvutza, Degania, was formally established in 1911 and within a few years was followed by more than a dozen similar groups.

A colleague of Ruppin's, Professor Franz Oppenheimer (1864–1943), propagated co-operative theories in Palestine and his ideas undoubtedly had an influence on the pioneers, but the development of the kvutza and the social and economic principles governing its structure grew more directly out of the daily experience and imagination of the pioneers and their leaders. The kvutza did not originate as a deliberate social experiment. Its forms were elaborated by accretion in the school of circumstance. The kvutza was vigorously defended by Ruppin against much criticism in Zionist circles unsympathetic to collectivism. Ruppin constantly stressed the importance of grasping the psychology of the pioneers whose enthusiasm he regarded as the greatest asset of the Zionist movement. Instead of the relationship of tutelage in which farmers had stood *vis-à-vis* colonization agencies in the period of the first immigration, Ruppin saw the advantages of equal partnership between the pioneers and national organs, and correctly predicted that these latter would eventually become in effect a subsidiary instrument of the settlers, whatever form of social and economic organization the settlers adopted.

The initial period of the kvutza movement was marked by its Gordonian philosophy. Gordon himself settled in Degania and his spirit was the strongest influence upon the young pioneer founding fathers. Although they did not originate on the basis of a clearly thought out social philosophy, a number of principles common to all the kvutza groups soon became institutionalized. These principles came not only to influence greatly the pattern of agricultural settlement for years to come, but also permeated other institutions of the labour movement as they came to fruition.

In its initial social and economic structure the kvutza embodied a number of revolutionary ideas of general significance. Cherished above all was the principle of mutual aid, by which was meant nothing less than the absolute organic interdependence of all members. Also, they were committed to 'self-labour', by which they meant that they would farm as much land as they could manage by their own labour, without resorting to the 'exploitation' of hired workers. (As times changed this principle was the one most honoured in the breach, but its vigour as an ideal was never lost.) Economically, they established co-operative relations. All assets were held in common by the group, and all the needs of individuals including medical care and the raising of children were met by the group. It followed that there was no need for money in the internal transactions of the kvutza.

The principle of co-operative trading extended as far as possible to the external relations of the group. The kvutza settlements together developed joint co-operative institutions which helped them to gain a foothold in the produce market and to secure their supplies as cheaply as might be. Their own needs were first supplied before surpluses were marketed so that the kvutza came close to self-sufficiency, and with this aim a pattern of 'mixed' farming was established, early supplanting monoculture.

Up to 1914 a dozen kvutza settlements were established and proved economically viable. Besides developing considerable tracts of wasteland, the settlements performed an important function as training centres for farm labourers, a fact which undoubtedly augmented their influence within the pioneer movement as a whole. As the groups were stabilized in some cases with no more than a dozen members, it gradually began to be realized that a permanent new form of settlement had been created. At first the creators of kvutza had been itinerant pioneers learning a variety of trades and moving from one part of the country to another under the aegis of their political party, wherever job opportunities arose or where a nucleus of workers appeared to stand in need of organization. It transpired, however, that the social norms of the group generated an inherently strong community not unlike the family. Rather than move on to open up new territory the pioneers increasingly stayed within their new community and absorbed new members into their way of life.

At the core of the developing philosophy of the pioneer movement was the concept of self-defence, a principle which met its prime test in the early kvutza settlements. It should be understood that this was a radical notion in Jewish life. The Jews of eastern Europe had for centuries assumed a pacifistic posture in face of attack and massacre. A horror of violence was inculcated in early childhood and was an integral element of the traditional Jewish culture. But already in Russia many of these youths had become concerned with self-defence and were among those who had organized the first defence actions against the pogroms which broke out before their departure for Palestine. When they came they found that defence against Bedouin marauders was entrusted by the Jewish settlers to other Bedouin hired for this purpose. In effect, they paid protection money. In 1907 a small group of Poale Zion members founded *Bar-Giora*, a corps of Jewish guards which hired out its services to various villages, usually demanding at the same time that Jewish labour be employed on the lands it protected. In this way they dramatized their concept of a national militia. Taking the name Hashomer ('The Watchman') in 1909, they soon gained the respect of the Arabs and Bedouin violence declined. Inspired by the feats of Hashomer the kvutza groups undertook their own defence from the first, though not without argument. Gordon and many of his followers were opposed to the idea, one of whose most assiduous exponents was Ben-Gurion. The militia movement soon became an integral part of the labour ideology and profoundly influenced the character of Zionism. For once the principle of self-defence against economic marauding became 'structured' within the evolving nationalist doctrine, its application could easily be switched to another focus. The Bedouin of course were not nationalists but later on Arab nationalism would arise. With their initiative on an issue not yet contemplated by the Zionist movement at large, the labour-Zionists instituted a decisive mode of response to the Arab national problem, before that problem arose. The consequences of their initiative for the impending national struggle were not understood except perhaps by Ben-Gurion who began to reveal a sense of the direction of events in which he greatly outdistanced his young comrades.

Trade unions in embryo

Although the political party was the more congenial forum and the organ more appropriate to the requirements of a rudimentary nationalist movement, members of Poale Zion were committed by their ideological predilections to explore the avenue of trade unionism. While the towns did not attract public capital to the same extent as agriculture, they absorbed more immigrants than the land during the period of the pioneer movement, as they did throughout the later history of the country. Most of the town population made a living in commerce arising out of the building industry and the agricultural economy. The towns nevertheless did harbour a small population of Jewish workers and artisans, centred in the printing establishments of Jerusalem and many small manufacturing plants there and elsewhere, in addition to construction and transport. Many Poale Zionists, urban in disposition, sought work in the towns although their relatively less inspiring mission there ensured that they would occupy a lesser place than the agricultural pioneers in the pantheon of the movement. They tried to propagate socialism and trade unionism among the town workers, the majority of whom were either attached to the pietistic traditional community or were unorganized drifters. The agitators launched sporadic strikes which inevitably failed. Even the initial building of Tel-Aviv, the first all-Jewish city founded in 1909 with a loan financed by the National Fund, was carried out mainly by Arab labourers.

The farm workers were more responsive to trade unionism, but they tended to look on their party as the prior focus of allegiance and as caterer to their needs, even in securing work and pressing for improved conditions. However the first stable trade union in the country was founded in 1911 by the hired agricultural workers, in two regional units. Giving a different form to the same original doctrine to which the kvutza owed its origin, the union sponsored the idea of groups working together as contractors to strengthen their competitive position. They also developed rudimentary machinery for mutual aid and the pooling of resources. However they found themselves in chronic flux between employment and unemployment, fitness and sickness, hunger and hardship, and continually lost members through emigration and decimation. They numbered an estimated six hundred in 1914,[8] the peak of their activity until after the great war.

The union movement was significant in providing a bridge between the two ideological groups organized in their respective parties. This role fell to Berl Katznelson, the founder of the trade union and an influential leader from the moment of his arrival in 1909. The farm labourers' union gave Katznelson a political base which eminently qualified him to bridge the rift between the Gordonian co-operators and Marxian militants, since its members were drawn from both parties and also included the kvutza pioneers. Although Katznelson was then temperamentally closer to Hapoel Hatzair his credentials as a trade union leader enabled him to communicate effectively with Poale Zion. Thus he made a major contribution to the convergence of the parties towards unity, a process which advanced by stages until its consummation in 1930 with the formation of Mapai.

The institutional vacuum of the time enhanced the play of ideological controversy among the pioneers, at the same time lending it a creative thrust with practical institutional consequences. An uninitiated contemporary observer might have thought comic the solemnity and intensity of discourse about tactics and strategy among these bedraggled destitute youths in their tents, in their paltry numbers on the edge of the swamps of Galilee. Certainly they were not seen universally by their compatriots or foreign supporters as the harbingers of history.

But they took themselves very seriously and had full faith that their deeds would give birth to and form the character of a new Jewish state.

Between 1911 and 1914 one convention after another of the two regional union groups debated the merits of alternative protest tactics and organizational forms, the optimal degree of discipline to be imposed, the various forms of settlement and their potential, the proper approach to the unorganized Jewish workers and above all, the relation of the political parties to the trade union movement. This latter problem occasioned the most serious disputes within the movement, as indeed it typically did in those labour movements of Europe where labour parties had a prior existence to trade unions.

Both parties opposed the assumption by the union of any other than orthodox trade union functions. Under Katznelson's leadership a 'non-party' party was formed, demanding that the role of the union be expanded into every area of activity so that it would be a roof organization of labour-Zionism, relegating the parties to the cultivation of abstractions. Katznelson found in Ben-Gurion a most persistent and effective advocate of labour unity, although his concept never seemed entirely free of the assumption of Poale Zion hegemony. During this period a variety of Zionist assignments took Ben-Gurion abroad, but he continued from a distance to maintain close contact with his comrades and to supply them with a torrent of written advice.

It is noteworthy that Ben-Gurion was consistently more concerned with the propagation of labour-unity, self-defence, organization and trade unionism, than in pursuing the inaugural socialist experiment of the kvutza. It is a significant sidelight on his personality that almost alone among those who grew to national leadership, he was never on the inside of that initially Gordonian movement. His own initiation as a pioneer was limited to a short experience as a gang-labourer. Towards the kvutza (and later the kibbutz movement) his personal attitude was somewhat ambivalent. In any case he was wholeheartedly committed to the strategy of co-operative land settlement, and on this issue broke with the more doctrinaire Marxists of the movement in Europe, who denounced the financial alliance with the bourgeoisie and considered the

C*

kvutza Utopian. Ben-Gurion successfully pressed the Palestinian Poale Zion to shed the ideological constraints which limited its appeal, and to modify its urban outlook to enable it to attract rural workers to its ranks. For Poale Zion, though it assimilated much of the essential Gordonian philosophy, this compromise led to a doctrine of trade unionism on the land rather than to a concept of communal farming, and to a vital theory of the mutual interests of farmworkers and town-dwelling workers, rather than to direct social experimentation. Thus both parties became equally devoted to the new interpretation of conquest of labour as implying settlement on the land. This principle afforded a core of common ground between them, and between both of them and the adherents of the 'non-party' party. Land settlement, whether in the form of the kvutza or groups of contract workers or any other form, came to be seen as the primary purpose of trade unionism.

The first years of the second immigration witnessed the growth of a tough solidarity among the pioneers, translating them from a state of individual isolation to membership in a close-knit fraternity. This reinforced the reverence for manual labour and the fanaticism of their devotion to their cause, while at the same time enhancing their derision for private property and scorn for detached intellectual pursuits and values.

Rebirth of the Hebrew language

No decision of the labour-Zionists was more enduring in its national significance than their sponsorship of Hebrew revival. If as they concluded upon observing the state of the first settlers, demoralization and idleness went hand in hand with the culture of French Levantinism, then national dynamism and labour would go hand in hand with Hebrew culture. Many of the pioneers undertook this challenge with great reluctance, especially those of Poale Zion, since they were linked by Yiddish to their members in Europe. However the Gordonian nationalists, much less anchored to their past, energetically pursued this aim and their advocacy of Hebrew literature and culture and their use of the language in daily transactions became a fundamental commitment of the movement.

62

The labour-Zionists were by no means the originators or even the foremost active exponents of the Hebrew revival in the wider national arena. They were preoccupied with the development of their own movement and with the concerns of their own membership. Others, especially those involved in educational institutions, translated the Hebrew revival into a national movement. But the acceptance of the goal by the socialists was crucial to its ultimate triumph, as increasingly they proved to comprise the most dynamic lever of national revolution. Just as Gordon the minor philosopher might have entered history as a mere footnote had not his hearers been the young pioneers, so too was a lone Hebrew pioneer of the first immigration rescued from possible oblivion by the dedication of the labourers to the propagation of Hebrew within their own fold. This was Eliezer Ben-Yehuda (Perlmann) (1858–1922) who came to Palestine in 1881, and who at first conducted a lonely and unpromising struggle within the settled religious communities and among the immigrants of the first wave on behalf of Hebrew revival.

The orthodox traditionalists considered Hebrew a holy tongue, reserving it for prayer and study and forbidding its use in profane pursuits which they conducted for the most part in Arabic, Ladino or Yiddish. This had been customary for centuries. Even two millenia ago during the declining years of the second Jewish commonwealth in Palestine Hebrew had followed the Bible into canonicity, being reserved for religious devotions while Aramaic became the vernacular. Since that time, in their dispersion, a multitude of languages had come into the experience of the Jews, foremost among them the Yiddish argot of eastern Europe. Until the enlightenment introduced by Moses Mendelssohn had spread to Russia in the middle of the nineteenth century the literature of Hebrew had been limited to religious works. The first Zionist leaders, notably Herzl among them, failed to appreciate the importance of adopting a single mother tongue for the national adventure. The settlers of the first immigration, among whom were many who had been touched by the enlightenment, were sympathetic to Hebrew, but saw no need to use it exclusively. They spoke a variety of tongues. Only with the arrival of the pioneer immigration in the first decade of the new century did an appreciable number see the importance of linguistic unity to national development.

The selection of Hebrew had more than nominal value. It was not merely a language which happened to be suitable for promoting social unity. Hebrew amplified in daily speech the Zionist vision, with its geographic and historical dimensions recalling ancient glories and borrowing from the religious impulse some of its force. Many pointed to the obvious disadvantages of adopting an archaic language without a vocabulary to comprehend the modern world and with many technical deficiencies for the precise conceptualization of new knowledge. But this seemed a small price to pay for the nourishment of the national movement from its own cultural sources.

Ben-Yehuda, perhaps the fiercest fanatic in the annals of Zionism, refused to the end of his days to speak anything but Hebrew, even within his intimate family circle. He devoted his life to preparing a monumental Hebrew dictionary incorporating into modern usage many biblical word-roots, a major contribution to Hebrew lexicography. He proved that the language of the Bible could be adapted to modern needs without violence to its integrity and his passion was in time transmitted to other educators.

Not for some decades could the battle for Hebrew be deemed irrevocably won. But its exponents displayed as much tenacity as any of the martyrs of national reconstruction. In most of the schools available to the Jewish community of the towns the language of instruction was French or German, reflecting the cultural interests of the endowments that established them, while the mother-tongue of the pupils was Yiddish, Arabic or Ladino. In the rural areas there was less vociferous orthodox opposition and Hebrew was taught by followers of Ben-Yehuda, spreading quickly among children. By the end of the nineteenth century Hebrew-language kindergartens had begun to proliferate, and the necessity was increasingly acknowledged of using a common tongue for the instruction of children drawn from diverse cultural backgrounds. Herzlia Gymnasia, the first Hebrew secondary school – a radical venture given the doubts about the capacity of Hebrew to envelop modern studies – was founded in Jaffa in 1905 and was enabled to grow rapidly through the assistance of Zionists abroad and the enthusiasm of many parents in eastern Europe who sent their children there for schooling. Teachers were drawn from foreign universities and engaged in the translation of textbooks. Henceforth teachers played a decisive role in the implementation of the Hebrew revival.

The schools of the time were under an extraordinary variety of sponsorships without any central control, so that the teachers tended to enjoy an unusual measure of initiative. At a conference in 1903, at the instance of Menahem Ussishkin (1863–1941), a leader of the original Odessa branch of Lovers of Zion, the Union of Hebrew Teachers was founded. It formulated a model school syllabus and established qualifying procedures for teachers much as might a craft union of workers, and in effect assumed some of the functions of an education ministry. The Union had no legal status and no way of establishing its authority in the schools except through the commitment of its members.

The teachers showed their mettle at a turning point in the language battle just before the outbreak of the European war. The *Hilfsverein*, a society of German Jews interested (like its French counterpart the *Alliance Israelite Universelle*) in propagating German culture and aiding Jews in distress abroad, set up several schools in Palestine, employing about a third of the members of the Union of Hebrew Teachers. In 1912 with the support of the German government which was then in competition with other European powers for influence within the Ottoman domain, and in conjunction with other Jewish and Zionist groups elsewhere, the society promoted the establishment of a technical college in Haifa. Although not opposed to the use of Hebrew in their elementary schools, the German sponsors of the projected institute assumed Hebrew to be inadequate for advanced technical studies and insisted on German which they regarded as 'the most cultured language'.[9] The teachers throughout the *Hilfsverein* network of schools went on strike in protest, and enlisted the support of the Zionist Organization for the opening of new schools based on Hebrew instruction. Thus the Zionist Organization secured control of the Hebrew school system, and accorded authority to administer it to a board of education appended to the Union of Teachers. In these circumstances Zionist pressure on the board of governors of the new Technion succeeded in 1914 in effecting a compromise whereby Hebrew would become the general language of instruction after four years. This, as it happened, coincided with the conclusion of the European war and the lapse of German influence in the region.

Although the battle for Hebrew was by no means fully won, the dissemination of Hebrew among ever-increasing numbers of children had a cumulative effect and the Zionist movement was now set in an irreversible cultural direction.

CHAPTER 4

FOUNDING FATHERS: THE THIRD IMMIGRATION (1914-24)

Palestine in the world war – Weizmann and the Balfour Declaration – Jabotinsky and Ben-Gurion – towards labour unity – founding of the Histadrut – constitution of the Histadrut – evolution of moshav and kibbutz

Palestine in the world war

As a result of Turkey's entry into the first world war on the side of Germany, and its defeat in 1917, Britain gained control of Palestine. The country came under interim British military rule as occupied enemy territory until the inauguration of civil administration in 1920. This was followed in 1923 by the formal award to Britain of a League of Nations Mandate to administer the country.

Herzl and the early Zionist leaders had laboured for a Turkish concession to permit large-scale Jewish colonization in Palestine in return for the offer of financial assistance to the bankrupt Ottoman regime. Until the outbreak of the war Ben-Gurion and most other leaders in Palestine had also assumed that the future of Zionist aspirations lay with the Turkish government. But Turkey maintained a consistently negative attitude to Zionist overtures, not least because it feared that a growth in the number of its people under foreign protection would only increase the already considerable influence of the European powers over the internal affairs of the empire. The loose imperial administration in Palestine bordered on anarchy and Jewish immigrants had been able to settle relatively unhampered in spite of the contrary policy of

Constantinople. Often a well-placed bribe at the local level was all that was needed to be assured of freedom to pursue Zionist aims.

The requirements of the war brought about a sharp change which bore heavily on the Palestinian population, and especially on the Jews. The Turkish commander in the Syrian theatre, Jamal Pasha, correctly suspecting the Jews of active sympathy with the allies, imposed a variety of repressive measures including mass deportations and imprisonment or exile of Jewish officials. Thousands escaped to the British side in Egypt. As a result of these upheavals and also of disease and famine the Jewish population of the country was reduced from some 85,000 in 1914 to little over 50,000 in 1917.

Among those exiled to Egypt was Joseph Trumpeldor (1880–1920), a visionary leader of the pioneer youth who, alone among them, had acquired professional military experience.[1] At the outbreak of war he left Degania, of which he was one of the founders, and made for Egypt certain that victory would be with the allies and that the prospects of the Palestine enterprise would be greatly enhanced if the Jews could play a role in the liberation of the country from Turkish rule. In Alexandria he joined Vladimir Jabotinsky (1881–1941), then a leading Zionist publicist, who later emerged as a formidable critic of the leadership of both the Zionist Organization and the Palestine pioneers. Jabotinsky shared Trumpeldor's view of the war and the opportunity it presented to Zionism.

Rounding up a following among the Palestinian refugees in Alexandria, Jabotinsky and Trumpeldor sought to persuade the British commander in Egypt to form a Jewish army under a Jewish flag to take part in the expulsion of the Turks from Palestine. No plan for the invasion of Palestine existed within the purview of the British general and in any case he did not have the authority to follow such an unorthodox procedure. Interested nevertheless in recruiting volunteers he proposed to form a transport battalion for service under a British officer wherever it might be required in the middle east. Its Jewish credit would be recognized in its title, the Zion Mule Corps. Jabotinsky withdrew in scorn and made for London to press for a full-fledged Jewish military unit while Trumpeldor accepted a commission as second-in-command of the Corps, and succeeded in raising some nine hundred volunteers. The Zion Mule Corps served in Gallipoli and earned some publicity if not distinction in that campaign. It was unfortunate for Trumpeldor's hopes that the Corps was deployed in that disastrous engagement whose outcome portended its disbandment in 1916 just one year after its formation. Among the survivors over a hundred now followed Trumpeldor to London where he joined forces again with Jabotinsky in his battle for Jewish military honours.

In the meantime Ben-Gurion and Ben-Zvi were among the exiled Jewish leaders although, ironically, their sympathies in the war were with the Turks and they were still convinced that the future of the Jewish enterprise lay in its integration within the Turkish political structure. It was in this belief that they had gone to Constantinople in 1911 to study Turkish law and enter into the politics of the capital on behalf of the Zionist interest. Ben-Gurion was disturbed about the tendency in Zionist circles to support the allied cause, believing that the outcome of hostilities was by no means certain. He felt that the most important issue was the maintenance and defence of the Jewish foothold in Palestine regardless of the direction of events in the global arena. Accordingly when forced to leave Palestine in 1915 he and Ben-Zvi made their way to America to undertake an arduous tour of Jewish communities in the hope of arousing interest in Palestine and obtaining recruits for the pioneer movement. Concerned primarily with the replacement of the population losses in Palestine Ben-Gurion was opposed at first to the efforts of Jabotinsky and Trumpeldor, which he feared might bring Turkish reprisals upon the Jews in Palestine. However, with the entry of America into the war Ben-Gurion came to appreciate the political importance of Jewish participation on the Palestine front and he joined a group of volunteers from the United States and Canada posted to the Jewish Legion which Jabotinsky had by then succeeded in creating within the British command. The strength of the Legion was about five thousand men, some of whom participated under General Allenby in the pursuit of the Turks after the surrender of Jerusalem in December 1917.

Weizmann and the Balfour Declaration

The divergent activities of Ben-Gurion, Jabotinsky and Trumpeldor (who hastened to Russia after the 1917 revolution) reflected the lack of central direction on the part of the Zionist Organization and the Palestinian settlers. Each individual leader made his own assessment of the war situation and acted accordingly, with the result that Zionist leaders were ranged on both sides of the war without any co-ordination of policy. The same arbitrariness occurred in the diplomatic arena where Chaim Weizmann acted on his hunches based on his belief in an allied victory, although the Zionist Organization which he headed was officially neutral and had members in the fighting forces of both sides. Upon the outbreak of the war the Zionist Organization, finding itself with important leaders and membership branches on both sides of the conflict and its headquarters in Berlin, sought to assert its neutrality by setting up a liaison bureau for the duration of the war in non-combatant Denmark. But the organization could not function effectively across national boundaries with the loyalties of its members engaged on opposite sides. It was in these circumstances that Chaim Weizmann, although not then a member of the official Zionist Executive, by means of personal diplomacy hitched the fortunes of the movement to the British interest.

In the decade preceding the war Weizmann, from his base at Manchester University, had established his leadership of the Zionist movement in Britain. Gifted with extraordinary diplomatic skill and personal magnetism Weizmann made contact with several important politicians and engaged their interest in Zionism. In spite of the vigorous opposition to the Zionist cause expressed by the foremost acknowledged leaders of Anglo-Jewry and in spite of the relatively small following of the movement among the wider Jewish public, Weizmann managed to convey the conviction that he spoke for the masses of Jewry including the large communities of Russia and the United States, and that he represented a political force of great potential.

Weizmann ignored the preponderance in the Zionist Organization of continental leaders dedicated to the victory of the Central Powers and their Turkish ally, and with some contempt ignored also the façade of Zionist neutrality. He was convinced of an eventual allied victory, and on the basis of this conviction turned to advantage the rumour of a possible Zionist initiative by the Kaiser in a bid for Jewish support in eastern Europe. Grasping the evolving British imperial interest in the postwar control of Palestine Weizmann saw in British sponsorship and protection the greatest opportunity for Zionist fulfilment. His diplomacy was crowned on 2 November 1917 by the Balfour Declaration in the form of a letter from the Secretary of State for Foreign Affairs to Lord Rothschild (the most prominent of the Jewish leaders sympathetic to Zionism), announcing the support of the British government for Zionist aspirations in Palestine.[2]

Foreign Office
November 2nd, 1917

Dear Lord Rothschild,

I have much pleasure in conveying to you, on behalf of His Majesty's Government, the following declaration of sympathy with Jewish Zionist aspirations which has been submitted to, and approved by, the Cabinet.

'His Majesty's Government view with favour the establishment in Palestine of a National home for the Jewish people, and will use their best endeavours to facilitate the achievement of this object, it being clearly understood that nothing shall be done which may prejudice the civil and religious rights of existing non-Jewish communities in Palestine, or the rights and political status enjoyed by Jews in any other country.'

I should be grateful if you would bring this declaration to the knowledge of the Zionist Federation.

Yours sincerely,
Arthur James Balfour

There has been much sophisticated analysis of the complex considerations governing the evolution of British wartime policy in the middle east as a whole and the formulation of the Balfour Declaration in particular. It may not be possible to establish with any certainty the precise grounds of the British government's initiative but it is in any case clear that the declaration bore a different value for Britain than for the Zionist movement. It is doubtful whether for Britain it was any more than a superficial gesture designed to mobilize Jewish public opinion in Russia and the United States (and indeed in Germany itself) in favour of the allied war effort. It was in all probability a tactic of war rather than a solemn definition of a war-aim and it might have passed into the historical limbo of political rhetoric had it not been for the zeal and seriousness of purpose of the Zionists to whom it was addressed. From the British standpoint it was but a minor diplomatic incident but for the Zionist leader Weizmann, who had participated so effectively in its crystallization over a period of months, the Balfour Declaration was the long-cherished charter which had eluded every initiative of Herzl. The declaration was acclaimed throughout the Zionist world as a decisive coup and was indeed seen by many as the consummation of the Zionist enterprise rather than its threshold. It gave a tremendous boost to Zionist morale and lent the movement a new prestige. It brought Weizmann to the pinnacle of Zionist leadership, his personal authority now being widely recognized as the most valuable asset of the movement.

Although their diplomacy played on the myth of Zionist enthusiasm amongst the world-wide Jewish masses the Zionist leaders knew from experience that they could not depend on effective mass effort towards promotion of the Palestine venture. The vagueness of the doctrine – 'establishment in Palestine of a national home for the Jewish people' – reflected the uncertainty of the Zionist leaders who helped to formulate it as to the scale and vigour of the response which might be expected from the Jews throughout the world, much as the same uncertainty had governed the wording of the Basle programme twenty years previously. Weizmann and the majority of his colleagues favoured a cautious approach leaving quite open and unspoken the issue of sovereignty or statehood until results or events might render such a question relevant as a practical matter.

In this the practical Zionists concurred. But differences arose on the proper policy to follow in the light of the British intervention on behalf of Zionism. Weizmann now found himself flanked on one side by Jabotinsky and his followers claiming the authority of Herzl for the pursuit of a more radical British commitment, while on the other side he faced the pioneer movement with Ben-Gurion becoming known as its spokesman, demanding urgent mass immigration and settlement in Palestine. In the early years of the Zionist Organization Weizmann had emerged from the 'cultural' school as the advocate of a synthesis of political and practical Zionism, thereby helping to rescue the latter from subordination in the councils of the movement. In the intervening years a change had occurred in the ambition of the practical pioneers in Palestine. They now raised their sights in the conviction that they had laid the social and economic foundations of a viable political community. For the new politicals led by Jabotinsky Weizmann's accomplishment was merely a halting step in the right direction. From the standpoint of the practicals the celebration of the diplomatic coup was excessive and premature, revealing the limitations of political Zionism.

Jabotinsky and Ben-Gurion

Jabotinsky pursued to its most logical conclusion the doctrine of Zionism derived solely from the prevalence of anti-semitism and consequent plight of the Jews. The mainstream of east-European Zionism, whether it flowed from Ahad Ha'Am's concern for the future of Judaism (as in the case of Weizmann) or by way of the commitment to a socialist society (as in the case of Ben-Gurion), was significantly shaped by the pattern of traditional Jewish life and the desire to modernize it while yet retaining many of its values. Jabotinsky was more radical in his repudiation of the entire experience of diaspora Jewry which he considered to be a slave culture. His view of national reconstruction required the mass transfer of Jews to Palestine on the basis of absolute political sovereignty there, which he considered to be a necessary condition for effecting the transfer. The Balfour Declaration must be amplified to compel Britain to establish the Jews as of right and on a large scale in the ancient boundaries of biblical Israel. If Britain could not or would not undertake such a responsibility then this would be a challenge for the Jews who must use every means necessary for its fruition. In Jabotinsky's view the practical Zionists

73

were dreamers lacking in the revolutionary thrust which alone could create large new political arrangements. Inspired by the national movement of Italy where he lived and studied for several years, Jabotinsky envisaged a Jewish risorgimento. He refused to recognize any distinction whatsoever between the practical efforts of the labour pioneers and those of the planters of the first immigration. To him, the pioneers' settlement attempts were puny and futile, cowardly and costly, and quite unrelated to the challenge of political revolution. The socialist dream of the pioneers merely clouded the authentic vision of Zionism as national regeneration above class and beyond issues of social and economic organization.[3]

Jabotinsky's magnetism and profound rhetorical and polemical skill, his originality and his fanaticism, ensured that he would remain a constant irritant to the leadership of Weizmann in the international arena and that of Ben-Gurion and his comrades in Palestine. But he was never able to command a large enough following to determine the course of the movement during his lifetime.

The Balfour Declaration also highlighted the divergence in historical view which already existed between Weizmann and Ben-Gurion, although Ben-Gurion had not yet come to the fore as a recognized major leader of the world movement. In his American wartime tour Ben-Gurion found himself constantly obliged to argue against the notion that a Jewish state could be handed to the Zionist Organization by the allied powers. To him Weizmann's diplomacy in the anterooms of gentile power savoured of Jewish advocacy in the style and tradition of the professional communal emissary of Polish Jewry, and as such was of minor interest and in any case retrograde in spirit. As early as 1915 he wrote:[4]

'There are several ways of conquering a country; it can be obtained through political moves and diplomatic treaties, it can even be bought with money. All these methods have but one aim ... to seize power and enslave and exploit the native population. We, however, are seeking something very different in Palestine ... a homeland. And a homeland cannot be taken just like that, like a gift, it cannot be acquired by concessions or political agreements, it cannot be bought, neither can it be seized by force. A homeland has to be built by the sweat of your brow. . . .'

For Ben-Gurion it was the pioneers in Galilee who held the key to statehood, not Weizmann nor Jabotinsky much less Balfour. In an article after the publication of the Balfour Declaration (but before Allenby had received the surrender of Jerusalem by the Turks), Ben-Gurion wrote:[5]

'England has not given Palestine back to us. It is not in England's power to give Palestine back to us. . . . Even after England conquers the whole country it will not become ours again just because England has agreed to this, nor even if all other states agreed. A country is not given to a people except by its own toil and creativity, its own efforts in construction and settlement. . . . The Hebrew people itself, body and soul, with its own strength and its capital must build its national home and make good its national redemption.'

The contrast with Weizmann's approach is most sharply illustrated by the remark attributed to Weizmann that the years 1904-14, that is the years between Herzl's death and his own first diplomatic successes, were uninteresting and uneventful years of Zionism: the very years in which Ben-Gurion and his teenage comrades were laying the social and economic foundations of the Jewish state. Nevertheless Ben-Gurion appreciated the intervention of Britain and he realized that the British presence could be of use to the movement. To the extent that there might be a coincidence of interest between Britain and Zionism he would seek to exploit it. For the immediate future, at any rate, it provided an adequate political and legal framework for the furtherance of settlement.

The new situation created by the Balfour Declaration now obliged the Zionist Organization to consider its approach to building the national home as a practical rather than hypothetical project. At meetings held in London in 1920 Ben-Gurion and other spokesmen for Palestine labour pressed for immediate mass immigration and settlement. Well aware that prospective pioneer immigrants from eastern Europe would come without capital, and fearing that extensive private land purchase would generate speculation and raise prices, they pressed for exclusive national ownership of land. The labour spokesmen were in the minority but although encouragement of private as well as public land purchase was endorsed, it went by default in the absence of investors, while the principle of public ownership was publicized and established. Immigration policy was a tense issue in dispute. Ben-Gurion chafed at the caution of the official leadership of the organization in their anxiety to foster rapport with the British authorities in Palestine. Referring to officials of the Zionist Organization then appearing in increasing numbers in Jerusalem he complained, 'In the old days we settlers had direct access to Jamal Pasha. Now we have to do everything through intermediaries.'[6] He felt that the overriding urgent need was to strengthen the Jewish foothold on the ground in Palestine. The official Zionist leadership looked on the pioneers as a useful but relatively minor force amongst the many agencies of national construction. They favoured caution, envisaging the planning and promotion of gradual development by a multiplicity of national organs in essential conjunction with British aims. The pioneering labour movement had come to see itself as a pacesetter, looking on the Zionist Organization as a welcome source of funds but conceding to it neither the initiative nor the responsibility for the arrangement of priorities and selection of policies. The labour pioneers were fanatically sure of the crucial importance of their own historical role. They tended to scorn the subtlety of the official leadership and its preoccupation with British sensibilities, considering this activity and its arena as secondary. They were resolved by all means to seize upon external Zionist efforts and the protection provided by Britain in so far as these were necessary props for their own pursuits, but they would not accord to these any historical primacy. The inchoate labour movement now turned in upon itself and determined to deploy its potentialities more effectively to exploit its new political environment.

Towards labour unity

The Israeli labour movement in its early pioneering phases and also later as the bearer of political hegemony within Israeli society, has been characterized by disunity and often bitter ideological conflict on every issue of policy and level of organization. But efforts to extend the range of united endeavour never ceased and the great historical impact of the movement upon the country can be attributed to such successes in this direction as were achieved from time to time. None was to prove more enduring than the complex general pioneer organization known as the Histadrut, none more ephemeral than the periodic linkage of the political parties under united leadership.

By the year 1919 the 'non-party' party led by Katznelson had outstripped both Hapoel Hatzair and Poale Zion in size, thereby enhancing the vigour of Katznelson's pressure for the creation of a framework for unity. Katznelson demanded that the role of the agricultural workers' union be expanded into every arena of activity to supplant the political parties in all but ideological agitation and discourse, and thus to provide a general roof organization for all practical undertakings catering to the needs of all the workers. It appears that Katznelson's initial concept was the first explicit statement of the organizational theory eventually to be enshrined in the constitution of the Histadrut.

During this time, though much of his leadership was exerted from abroad, Ben-Gurion emerged as the most persistent supporter of unity along the lines advocated by Katznelson. Ben-Gurion's concept of unity never seemed entirely free of the assumption of dominion by Poale Zion. While he brought Poale Zion ever closer in its ideology to Hapoel Hatzair, making compromises and assimilating the nationalist philosophy of Hapoel Hatzair in its essentials, his call to unity was nevertheless an invitation to others, in effect, to join the domain of Poale Zion. Hapoel Hatzair also viewed the unity movement in this light and was reluctant to submerge itself in an organization that might be governed by the ideology of class conflict. Such indeed was the nature of the new party, Ahdut Ha'Avodah, which emerged in 1919 as an abortive first consummation of the unity drive. Ahdut Ha'Avodah failed to substantiate its desired image as a general workers' union and came on the stage rather as an expanded Poale Zion party now making room for the followers of Syrkin as well as of Borochov. At its foundation the new party succeeded in absorbing the members of the old Poale Zion except for a small group of left-wing dissidents, many of the non-party adherents including Katznelson himself, and but a few members of Hapoel Hatzair. It may be that the resistance of Hapoel Hatzair to the blandishments of Ahdut Ha'Avodah was bolstered by reports from Europe that Zeire Zion ('The Youth of Zion'), the youth movement which provided a natural reservoir for recruits of its own persuasion, had grown greatly by comparison with Poale Zion, giving the expectation of new immigration in Hapoel Hatzair's favour. In the event Ahdut Ha'Avodah confirmed the suspicions of Hapoel Hatzair by adopting a platform linking the new party with the international socialist movement and including much other language repugnant to the political spirit of the Gordonians.

At the time of the foundation of Ahdut Ha'Avodah a considerable infusion of new blood was pumped into the pioneer movement with the influx of the third immigration wave. This major immigration wave took place during the period 1919-23, bringing an estimated 35,000-40,000 newcomers from eastern Europe. A conjunction of events prompted this new migration, particularly the issue of the Balfour Declaration which inspired optimism about the national future in Palestine; the revolution and civil war in Russia, accompanied as these were by renewed attacks upon the Jews, even to the extent of massacre under the auspices of the counter-revolution; and the further disintegration, in the aftermath of war and revolution, of the lopsided Jewish economy of the Pale.

The third immigration was unique among the waves of Jewish settlement in Palestine in that it included a high proportion of committed labour pioneers. A majority of the ten thousand newcomers who arrived in the years 1919 and 1920 had been trained in the pioneer youth movements in eastern Europe. There they had carefully planned their migration and prepared for it in every possible way, even undergoing intensive agricultural training. These youngsters were well-informed about conditions in Palestine and well-versed in the achievements and the chronic disputes and problems of the first generation of pioneers. Most of them had been organized and trained for their adventure by Hechalutz ('The Pioneer'), a non-political youth movement founded by Trumpeldor, in Zeire Zion, an offshoot of Hapoel Hatzair, or in Hashomer Hatzair ('The Young Guard') originally an idealistic scout movement but at that time politically sympathetic to Hapoel Hatzair. Poale Zion failed to bring significant numbers of new pioneers since most of its followers veered into the communist camp following the Bolshevik revolution.

These pioneers merit the designation 'founding fathers' of Israel together with those of the second immigration. They threw themselves into the embryonic labour movement with great energy and enthusiasm, sparking many historic innovations and cutting some of the ideological and organizational knots in which their predecessors were becoming tied. The strength of motivation imbuing the new pioneers was reflected in the enormous difficulties they overcame in order to reach Palestine, not least being the need to outwit many bureaucracies including that of the Zionist Organization which at the time was officially opposed to unpropertied immigration.

The new pioneers barged into a depressed economy against the better judgement of the Zionist Organization which had then no financial resources for additional settlement. The two labour parties Hapoel Hatzair and Ahdut Ha'Avodah ignored the obstacles in a manner which became characteristically their own, and organized the immigration. They were vindicated in the long run by the fact that the new flood of immigration itself inspired inert Zionist sympathizers to raise new funds for land settlement. In the meantime however unemployment was the immediate fate of the would-be workers.

Upon the initiative of the two labour parties the British administration came to the rescue by granting them a share, together with the Arabs, in large-scale public works. Each political party became a direct contractor in the building of needed roads, a project which sufficed for a time to employ thousands of new immigrants. The principle of small groups of workers contracting their labour collectively had already been applied successfully in agriculture but it had not yet been attempted on such a large scale as now envisaged. And if the earlier agricultural gangs had acted under the direction of the party to which they belonged, the parties themselves, in their capacity as political parties, had certainly not yet been tested as entrepreneurial agencies. Now Hapoel Hatzair and Ahdut Ha'Avodah each undertook contractual responsibility for completion of the work. This unusual procedure, devised under the pressure of circumstances, had no historical precedent, unless it be the occasional operation of economic concessions by community councils in the Pale of Settlement.

The parties were able to acquire essential equipment with the help of loans from Zionist sources. For handling the difficult organizational problems involved they called upon veteran (though still in their twenties) members of the kvutza movement. By the end of 1920 some two thousand workers were engaged in road-laying and had learned a new trade. The success of the operation was made possible by the kibbutz form of organization implicit in the 'work legions' set up by each party for mutual aid and the pooling of resources. This movement, which was shortlived in its original form, developed the concept of linking agricultural and urban workers within the same labour camp or work legion to ameliorate the effects of seasonal fluctuations in employment.

The road-building project engendered extraordinary duplication of institutions by the two parties. They worked on separate contracts on separate roads, and each formed separate contracting offices, labour exchanges, immigration offices and sickness funds. Since the foundation of Ahdut Ha'Avodah, taking the union of farmworkers with it, Hapoel Hatzair had also developed an agricultural workers' union of its own. The proliferation of parallel institutions with similar functions revealed the extent to which the two parties were divided by their European symbols giving them opposed views of the future, rather than by practical aims. The gulf between them had clearly become one of temperament rather than of policy.

The two parties contended bitterly for the allegiance of the newcomers and in so doing provoked the emergence once again of a 'non-party' party. The fresh arrivals soon made up a majority of the pioneers, and by standing aloof from the jaded ideological disputations of their predecessors they hoped to procure unity for the whole labour-pioneer movement. Led by Trumpeldor, now returned from Russia, the 'non-party' group proposed the establishment of a general labour council to operate institutions on behalf of all workers regardless of party. A fierce debate raged in the labour periodicals throughout 1919–20.[7] Ahdut Ha'Avodah called for complete unity of all the workers within one comprehensive organizational framework, while Hapoel Hatzair offered to co-operate on all matters suited to joint action without impinging on its survival as a separate political party. If Poale Zion by merely changing its name had succeeded in swallowing the old 'non-party' party it was not now to be allowed to absorb Hapoel Hatzair by changing its name yet again!

Hapoel Hatzair doubted the nationalist élan of Ahdut Ha'Avodah, not merely on account of its socialist ties abroad but also on the score of the prevalence of Yiddish in its ranks despite its formal commitment to Hebrew. Also, the biggest stumbling block to the entry of Hapoel Hatzair into the merger of 1919 had been the close organizational link established in Ahdut Ha'Avodah between town and farm workers, depriving the latter of sole control over their own affairs. Hapoel Hatzair was unwilling to discuss any arrangement of unity which allowed political party control over trade union activities. Its concern on this point centered upon the agricultural workers who constituted its primary constituency and whose national spirit it wished to foster and protect from the temptations or the rhetoric of class war. This issue proved to be the most difficult to resolve, but Ben-Gurion for Ahdut Ha'Avodah agreed to enter into negotiations with Hapoel Hatzair eschewing prior assumptions about the status of unions or the future role of the parties.

After many months of negotiations between leaders of the two groups, and possibly galvanized by the death of Trumpeldor in battle defending a settlement against Arab attack, they agreed to call a convention to thrash out differences and create a united organization. The convention delegates were elected on the basis of proportional party representation and participation was open to all who identified themselves with the labour-pioneer movement. In December 1920 the eighty-seven delegates met and established the new labour organization known as the Histadrut,[8] which now became the foremost instrument of the pioneer movement, the powerful lever which in the hands of the young founding fathers contributed more than any other force to the making of the state and the shaping of its culture.

Founding of the Histadrut

Of an estimated 7,000 Jewish workers in the country at the end of 1920, 4,433 cast their votes for delegates to the Histadrut founding convention. On the basis of electoral participation the Histadrut claimed only 5,000 members, indicating the extent of hostility or apathy among the workers themselves towards the aims of the pioneer movement. The total Histadrut membership at the time of its founding embraced about 11 per cent of the adult Jewish population of the country. Ahdut Ha'Avodah obtained approximately 42 per cent of the votes as compared with some 31 per cent to Hapoel Hatzair, 19 per cent to 'non-party' new immigrants and the rest going to a small left-wing dissident group. Thus the new immigrant group held the balance of power at the convention and it was they who in the event exerted the greatest influence in achieving unity and defining its terms in the structure of the new organization.[9] Hence while the foundations of the movement had been laid by the second immigration, its crystallization in an enduring form was attributable to the impact of the third immigration.

The three main groups at the convention each submitted a detailed unity prospectus and the ensuing debate once again traversed the issues that had been articulated in the periodicals for more than a year past. The new immigrant proposals were designed to afford an arena for compromise rather than to represent fixed demands. Behind the scenes the new immigrants worked to hammer out areas of agreement while polemics on the floor expressed and aggravated ideological and personal antagonisms. The convention adopted a pilot constitution as a basis for operation until a permanent constitution could be prepared in the light of experience. Each point at issue was voted on separately, starting from the very name of the organization, and on every score the resolution passed was the one supported by the new immigrant delegates. Sometimes they swung their weight with Ahdut Ha'Avodah, sometimes with Hapoel Hatzair, according to their estimate of the extent to which the integrity of either group appeared to be involved in the issue. On the whole the programme of Ahdut Ha'Avodah, aiming for the maximum degree of unity, predominated, not merely on account of the weight of numbers but also owing to the superior tactical skill of its spokesmen.

It was resolved that the Histadrut would be composed of trade union associations organized by occupation. Membership in the Histadrut would be open to all workers who did not 'exploit' the labour of others. In addition to promoting trade union organization on a non-political basis the new body resolved to undertake activities in land settlement, work contracts, the improvement of working conditions and productivity, vocational training, co-operative trading and mutual aid, defence, the reception of immigrants and promotion of pioneer immigration from abroad, and the promotion of Hebrew language and culture. All institutions of the political parties hitherto operating in these spheres were to be transferred immediately to the jurisdiction of the Histadrut. It was resolved to establish a workers' bank to finance the movement's operations. At that time the penurious pioneers were unable to provide revenue for the functioning of the organization. The Workers' Bank was successfully established with the aid of a loan from the Zionist Organization and the sale of shares to sympathizers abroad. In its first years the organization was unable to support a full-fledged bureaucracy and was conducted by an informal part-time leadership. Ben-Gurion was appointed joint general secretary[10] and he immediately impressed his imprint upon the movement by his contribution, together with Katznelson and others, to the drafting of a definitive constitution. This was completed and ratified in 1923.

Two threads of unity were woven through the resolutions of the Histadrut founding convention: the uncompromising national vision of large-scale organized immigration and pioneering land settlement, and the social vision of a self-sufficient workers' commonwealth. These were the essential ideological principles differentiating the five thousand members of the Histadrut from the majority of the Jews in Palestine and in the Zionist movement abroad, and indeed from the British administration and the Arab population of the country. The unity achieved within the Histadrut on the basis of its eclectic ideology brought together not only the established political parties but also the political generations. The pioneers of the second immigration had experienced all too sharply the lack of rapport with the previous generation of settlers. Now within the framework of the Histadrut the pioneers within the third immigration found a common language with their immediate predecessors, and such continued to be the case with the pioneering element in subsequent immigration waves. The framework of the Histadrut made possible the immediate absorption of newcomers of like mind, forming a bulwark against a re-occurrence of the pronounced dislocation which had characterized the confrontation of the second and first immigration waves. Not that the original pioneers completely submerged their chronological identity within the new organization. Differences and tensions between them and the later arrivals continued to occur.

The general ideology of immigration, land settlement, and the workers' economic and social commonwealth was predominantly Gordonian in content, while the chosen approach to its implementation through the disciplined medium of the Histadrut was more indebted to the school of Borochov. The dialogue between the two schools of thought during a decade and a half thus eventuated in the adoption of the goals of the one group and the means of the other. Gradually the cultivation of political thought had given way to the solving of problems. Broadly, the two parties were differentiated primarily in terms of the relative precedence they accorded to nationalistic (Hapoel Hatzair) and socialistic (Ahdut Ha'Avodah) values. Similarly, the two generations of the second and the third immigration waves were differentiated by the precedence they accorded to the norms of individualism and collectivism respectively. The immigrants from post-war post-Bolshevik Russia inspired by the splendid success of the 1917 revolution were more pronouncedly collectivist in outlook than their predecessors schooled in the abortive 1905 revolution and the challenge of late-Ottoman Palestine. After Poale Zion and its successor Ahdut Ha'Avodah had assimilated the robust nationalism of Hapoel Hatzair the members of the second immigration wave were all nationalists who tended to approach the issues facing the new organization in terms of choice between individualist or collectivist values. The pioneers of the third wave were all collectivists to whom the issues presented themselves in terms of choice between a nationalist or a socialist strategy. The second immigration instituted the hegemony of Gordonian ideals while the third immigration produced the victory of Borochovist methods. Their joint creation, the Histadrut, was dedicated to the pursuit of nationalist aims by socialist means.

Constitution of the Histadrut

Ben-Gurion and Katznelson, most prominent among the architects of the Histadrut, grappled with two complex problems in particular as they took part in drafting the constitution for ratification. First they had to determine the working relationship between the political parties and the new organization especially as to its trade union functions and secondly, they had to find a means of reconciling what appeared to be the potentially divergent interests of the trade unions and co-operative associations being brought together within the Histadrut.

The pilot resolutions adopted by the founding convention had repudiated the proposal sponsored by Hapoel Hatzair according to which the political parties would function as partners in the conduct of joint non-political trade union activities. However the alternative version of federalism advocated by Ahdut Ha'Avodah, although it won the day in 1920, proved inadequate in practice. The concept of the Histadrut as a congress or federation of trade unions was merely rhetorical in the circumstances of an undeveloped economy in which occupational differentiation had hardly yet arisen. Only the union of agricultural workers represented significant numbers with a relatively stable job commitment. In the light of immediate realities therefore, the 1923 constitution established a structure whereby the Histadrut became a 'general' union based on direct individual membership rather than a federation of craft or industrial unions with block memberships. Each individual member upon joining the Histadrut was automatically allocated to an occupational union, thus maintaining the fiction so dear to Ahdut Ha'Avodah that militant trade unionism would be the driving force of the socialist commonwealth on the way. It was not for another thirty years or so that the scale of economic development

85

allowed for sizeable occupational unions to grow and become the characteristic if not the dominant components of the Histadrut.

While the Histadrut as an autonomous primary association of individuals formally shed its original federal image it nevertheless retained an ambiguous federal aspect through the functioning of the political parties in their transformed role. The creation of the Histadrut divested the parties of many of their service functions but did not reduce them to mere ideological clubs, for they now found within the arena of the Histadrut itself their major challenge: competition for the glamorous prize of control of the whole organization. Through the play of the majority principle it now became possible for a political party to seek control of the ramified services newly enlarged by unification under one roof, and hence to wield the power of the labour movement as a whole and enhance itself as a political force in the community at large. Since there was no political criterion of eligibility for membership in the Histadrut, workers might belong to any party they chose or to none at all. The majority indeed were unaffiliated in the early 'twenties. Since Ahdut Ha'Avodah and Hapoel Hatzair had been the active vehicles of labour unification, each offering alternative programmes, it was natural that members would continue to look to them for leadership. Although there was not a word about political parties in the constitution, they emerged from the first as organized elites within the movement contending for control on the basis of their respective policies. The circumstances of its origin thus determined the future pattern of decision-making within the Histadrut. The non-political rank and file looked to the established parties and indeed to any new parties as those were formed to articulate the issues and lead the movement in its periodic selection of policies and executive officials. Thus was the Histadrut fortuitously patterned as a parliamentary community on an unacknowledged federal basis. For although the Histadrut by constitution drew its authority from and was responsible to the mass of members rather than to the parties, there was no possibility of its functioning as a general framework of labour activity beyond the extent to which the separate parties sustained the consensus imparting unity to the framework.

A separate parallel constitution was drawn up to define and govern co-operative activities. It was in their approach to the integration of co-operative and trade union activities within one structure that the founders of the Histadrut made their most original contribution to labour organization, and perhaps their most effective contribution to social and national strategy. In a fine stroke of vision Ben-Gurion proposed in outline the framework which he thought would, and which in the event did, inextricably bind the co-operative and trade union interests within a unitary movement.[11]

Contradictions inevitably abounded in the attempt to develop a coalition of defensive-protest and entrepreneurial-colonizing interests. Ben-Gurion reduced the manifold structural problems inherent in this endeavour to one essential issue: maintaining the class character of the movement. Apart from the technical issues involved in devising an organizational structure simultaneously serving trade union and co-operative units, the overriding substantive issue exercising Ben-Gurion was to forestall the emergence of a privileged class of co-operators with a higher standard of living than the hired workers who consumed their products and whose aid would have been needed by the co-operators to become established in the first place. At that time, so far as agriculture was concerned, the problem was theoretical rather than actual since to the rural co-operators undergoing the rigours of pioneering, autarchy harvested from lush green fields was still a remote dream. It was in the circumstances of subsistence economy that the agricultural co-operators had introduced the doctrine of identity of interest between producer and wage-labourer. But in building and other branches of the economy the problem was an immediate one. Already at the time of its founding the Histadrut embraced no less than seventeen producers' co-operatives in the towns, which had been sponsored by the old Poale Zion and owed nothing to the Histadrut itself. How to subject these potentially independent groups to a discipline aligning them with the hired workers, how to reconcile the divergent interests of producers and consumers? It was indeed its own vision of national construction that elicited the Histadrut's concern with co-operative enterprise, but the fruition of co-operation depended on a high degree of class rather than national consciousness. The co-operative constitution devised by Ben-Gurion was perhaps the best example of the collusion between nationalist goals and socialist means institutionalized by the Histadrut.

The founders of the Histadrut abhorred particularism within the labour movement. In the trade union sphere this meant the elimination or preclusion of any vestige of syndicalism. In the co-operative sphere the repugnant prototype was the 'irresponsible' narrow interest. The most vehement antipathy was reserved for the occasional co-operative group which had seceded from the movement upon achieving a secure standard of living. Following the precedent of the kvutza, co-operators were called upon *as* trade unionists to subordinate their energies to the requirements of national development as directed by the labour movement as a whole. This meant in practice that individual co-operative groups must be willing to subject their economic goals to the scrutiny of the general labour organs, and if need be to subordinate their policies to the aims of the wider movement. Not only in their selection of initiatives and in their investment decisions but above all in their pricing policies they must remember that their first obligation was to supply the needs of wage-earners. To achieve this Ben-Gurion's proposal stipulated constituting the Histadrut as a primary co-operative society (to be known as *Hevrat Ovdim* ('Workers' Commonwealth') in which the membership would be precisely coextensive with the membership of the Histadrut in its capacity as a trade union organization. Thus the economic activities of the movement whether conducted by small independent groups of co-operators or by the contracting agencies of the Histadrut, came under the control of the generality of workers. With the adoption of Ben-Gurion's draft constitution hired workers no less than co-operative entrepreneurs became full members of the co-operative movement, with an equal voice in its development. The executive organs of the co-operative society were identical with those of the trade union movement. Thus co-operative groups would be entitled to assistance from the central organization and at the same time would be subject to its discipline.

Although formally a primary association, in effect Hevrat Ovdim exercised the functions customarily undertaken in classical co-operative practice by central wholesale societies. In addition to carrying out the leadership and economic functions of a central society on behalf of its affiliates, Hevrat Ovdim was constituted simultaneously as a holding company for enterprises purchased, created or otherwise developed by the Histadrut as entrepreneur. In this guise the Histadrut operated more conventionally along the lines of a central society, but with an important difference. By constitution all the profits of economic enterprise conducted by Hevrat Ovdim were committed automatically for re-investment. Although technically every worker in the Histadrut was a shareholder in Hevrat Ovdim with a voice in its management, he could not consume its dividends. In this doctrine lay the secret of the Histadrut's phenomenal growth to the status of the largest employer and largest creator of employment in the country. In the principle of the automatic reinvestment of all the surplus of labour enterprise lay the key to the power of the Israeli labour movement and the unusual form of socialist economy which it promoted. In the light of this principle the ownership of labour enterprise by the rank and file membership may be seen as a fiction. Ownership, if not control, was in effect public and national.

Although he was opposed to any legal determination of the Histadrut's trade union activities Ben-Gurion used the provisions of the co-operative law to underwrite the standards of labour solidarity and cohesion to which he was dedicated. Under legal codes introduced in the first years of the British administration economic agents such as co-operatives were required to register and acquire juridical status and liability. Ben-Gurion grasped this as an opportunity to place the weight of the law behind the Histadrut's norms of internal co-operative discipline, including the prohibition on distribution of profits. Thus the constitution was written in such a manner as to induce the administration, in all probability unwittingly, to lend its authority to norms of control of co-operative values far in excess of the minimum objectives of the law, and to the exercise of such control by the Histadrut over its co-operative subsidiaries. In addition to organizational unification of co-operative groups and hired workers, initiation of economic enterprises by the same central organ and obligatory reinvestment of the profits of labour enterprise, another novel feature of the co-operative constitution of the Histadrut was the appointment of men drawn from the ranks of the labour movement as managers of labour enterprises at the same wages as were paid to skilled workers. This led to the emergence of a group of labour leaders whose main role was entrepreneurial, and whose calibre was in later years to become the envy of the private capitalistic sector of the economy. The great saving in executive costs due to the idealism of these leaders (and their desire for power rather than personal economic gain) balanced the extra costs of operating plant in working conditions better than those which obtained under private capital, and so enabled labour enterprise to compete.

The first article of the 1923 constitution which remained in force until 1959 when the constitution as a whole was amended and brought up to date, listed the functions of the Histadrut under four main categories of activity: trade unionism on the basis of disciplined organization; economic enterprise on the basis of co-operation; education to be geared to the national integration of new immigrants; and the promotion of social welfare on the basis of mutual aid.

As to the fields of education and social welfare, the Histadrut promoted an intricate network of institutions embracing all members and their families, thereby implementing to some degree the social vision of a commonwealth of labour responsible for its own fate. Members' children were educated in schools run by the movement and dedicated to transmitting the labour ideology to the rising generation in the medium of modern Hebrew. In the field of social welfare the Histadrut absorbed the sickness fund of the agricultural workers' union founded in 1911 to promote the health of workers, provide them with medical service and insure them against the losses exacted by malaria and the other hazards of pioneering. The constitution now obliged all members to belong to the sickness fund and endowed the Histadrut with general responsibility for the health of the pioneering community.

Although the Borochovist rhetoric gave the Histadrut constitution the flavour of trade union militancy, in the early decades of the organization its educational and social welfare institutions and its economic enterprise were more vital than conventional trade union activities, especially in the absorption of newcomers. The social services and especially the health services provided by the Histadrut were by far its most important attraction for new members amongst the masses of immigrants.

The intensity of ideological discourse amongst the founders of the Histadrut might mislead the untutored observer seeking to evaluate their political style. That they were thoroughgoing pragmatists rather than dogmatists is well illustrated by the ease with which the experience of less than two years was assimilated into the constitution, crystallizing the structure of the Histadrut along many lines which were neither apprehended nor intended at the founding convention. The pragmatic test of effectiveness in the actual circumstances facing the movement was from the first the cornerstone of its architecture, and the initial confusion arising from attempts to reconcile abstract political doctrines was readily resolved in the realm of experience.

Evolution of Moshav and Kibbutz

In their first groping efforts to realize a form of socialist community the founders of the kvutza fixed on the idea that the individual could best fulfil his human potentialities as the member of a small organic group numbering about a score, tied together by the practice of mutual aid in every sphere. The regeneration of the individual human soul through close communion with nature within a co-operative framework was the Gordonian approach to building a new order of social justice. The kvutza members believed that only by remaining small and autonomous could the group achieve a high level of socialist practice, and they sought to expand the movement in the interest of national development by multiplying the number of groups rather than by assimilating new immigrants into the established settlements. To maintain the social purity of the group each kvutza would attain some insulation from the monetary economy by means of subsistence farming.

During a decade in which two dozen such settlements were established, revealing a common pattern of organization, their members started to explore and debate the theoretical and ideological implications of their undertaking. The discovery

91

of the itinerant pioneers that they had stumbled upon a permanent form of settlement prompted analysis and generated new concepts of their historical role in relation to the national and socialist movements.

The first critical appraisal of the kvutza from within the movement came from several of its founders who had received their preparatory training in the United States where they were influenced by the individualist ethos. Affiliated with Hapoel Hatzair, they devised a blueprint for a form of settlement aiming to restore the family unit to the centre of social and economic organization while retaining a high level of co-operation and mutual aid. They felt that the kvutza choked individual initiative and upset the balance of family life. The form of settlement they advocated, the moshav, was essentially a smallholders' co-operative based on the family farm. They believed that in settlements of fifty to a hundred families they would achieve better economic results than the kvutza and would attract larger numbers, thereby making a greater contribution to national development.

Simultaneously an alternative and at the time more influential critique emerged, suggesting that the kvutza was prone to become a self-serving institution for the beatification of its members and that it would therefore fail to realize its potential for transforming the country. As it became clear that the kvutza had established a permanent form of social organization many of its leaders focused on its potentiality for economic development on a large scale. They advocated a form of organization, the kibbutz, a collective settlement that would incorporate the essential values of the kvutza but extend its principles to the *masses* of workers and pioneers. Proponents of the kibbutz envisaged the communal organization of large numbers, embracing both agriculture and manufacture and combining rural and urban workers under collective discipline through machinery linking the separate groups. The advocates of the kibbutz considered that the social benefits of communal living could be achieved in a large collective without loss, while the economic advantages of collective organization on a large scale would enable the movement to play a major role in national development and colonization through the absorption of masses of immigrants into the pioneer movement.

The intensity of discussion was heightened in 1921 by the purchase of some fifteen thousand acres of land in the Jezreel Valley by the JNF, opening up a major new opportunity for colonization. This in conjunction with the momentum of the third immigration brought about the establishment of the first moshav in 1921, Nahallal, with the initial participation of some thirty-five kvutza families. A few days later Shlomo Lavi (1882–1963) was the foremost leader in founding the first kibbutz, Ein Harod, with over two hundred members in its initial period. The kibbutz concept of social innovation as a key to economic development appealed strongly to the socialists of the third immigration. Lavi was persuaded that the work legion which had been formed to carry out the roadworks would be the best starting point for organizing collectivism, and it was the elite of this movement which provided the manpower for the first kibbutz.

Within a few years of their establishment the first moshav and the first kibbutz were followed by several others on the same lines and the pioneer labour movement at least in agriculture began to be widely seen as the vanguard of national construction. The first kibbutz incorporated many diverse occupational groups and hoped to become the centre of a nationwide collective of workers and pioneers. However the ideological ferment acted to produce greater diversity rather than uniformity and the movement was much fragmented from its first years. The members of the kvutza with their Hapoel Hatzair orientation were unwilling to submerge group autonomy in a discipline directed by the Ahdut Ha'Avodah leadership of the kibbutz. And the members of Hashomer Hatzair who had established a number of small communes of their own began in the early 'twenties to crystallize an independent orientation which proved an obstacle to their assimilation within Ein Harod.

Once again the attitudes of the second immigration as reflected in their creation, the kvutza, could be seen in relief against those of the third immigration, and their formula the kibbutz. However, as with the Histadrut itself and other agencies of the labour movement, the changes brought about by the third immigration carried with them many of the original veterans.

93

D*

THE ARABS, THE JEWS AND THE BRITISH (1917-39)

The League of Nations mandate – the Palestine Arabs – the Zionist Organization and Jewish Agency – Jewish immigration and land purchase – the British administration

The League of Nations mandate

By the end of 1917 the Egyptian Expeditionary Force of the British army led by General Allenby had secured the Ottoman *sanjak* of Jerusalem and in the following year extended its control over the whole Ottoman-Syrian province. The northern and eastern portions of the territory were provisionally parcelled out to French and Arab jurisdictions in accordance with understandings (or misunderstandings) arrived at during the war. The British force remained in direct control of the Palestinian area which was placed under military administration as enemy-occupied territory. The boundaries of Palestine, a political creation of the war settlement, remained indeterminate for some years pending diplomatic resolution of Franco-British rivalry, Zionist aspirations and diverse Arab claims to sovereignty in the region. The middle east diplomacy of London was in flux at the time and conflict between Britain and France especially contributed to delay in procuring a definitive settlement. Difficulties in concluding a peace with Turkey and problems connected with American rights as a non-member of the new League of Nations also caused delay. It was not until 29 September 1923 that the League of Nations mandate for Palestine came formally into effect and not until May 1924 that the definitive boundaries of the mandated territory were incorporated under British rule. However, the expectation that Britain itself would retain control of Palestine was supported from the moment of Allenby's arrival in Jerusalem by the terms of the Balfour Declaration and the physical British military presence.

Although its definitive terms were not yet drafted the Palestine mandate was assigned to Britain by the allied powers meeting in conference at San Remo in April 1920. It was determined at that meeting that the territory to become Palestine would extend from the Ladder of Tyre in the north to the Gulf of Akaba in the south, and from the Mediterranean in the west to the Jordan Valley and the Dead Sea in the east. Arab sovereignty, swiftly abrogated by French military action, was just then being imposed in Damascus by the British protégé Faisal. Two northern Jewish settlements within the Syrian jurisdiction, Metullah and Tel Hai, came under Arab seige. This circumstance gave political substance to a Zionist claim that all Jewish settlements be included within the British mandated territory. This and adjacent disputed territory surrounding Lake Huleh to the north was disposed by an Anglo-French boundary commission. In 1922 the Commission reached an agreement which was implemented in May 1924 by the transfer of a number of northern villages to the British administration.

The Zionist aspiration included within the boundaries of Palestine the land to the east of the river Jordan as far as the Hejaz railway, but before San Remo this territory was already incorporated within the jurisdiction of the abortive Faisal regime centred in Damascus. When the French crushed the Faisal regime in July 1920 Britain annexed its southern portion to Palestine, much along the lines of the Zionist concept. The first draft of the mandatory instrument completed at the end of 1920 envisaged Palestine on both sides of the Jordan but a 1921 revision incorporated as Article 25 of the final version, with Zionist assent, entitled the mandatory power 'to postpone or withhold application' of provisions relating to the Jewish national home from the Transjordanian territory. Thus although Palestine as a political creation formally transcended the Jordan valley, two separate administrations grew up under British auspices on each side of the river and Zionist activities were henceforth to all intents and purposes confined to the western region.

Immediately upon its establishment in Palestine the military administration set about restoring order and providing necessary services. Its jurisdiction as an occupying force under the Hague Code was subject to the doctrine of political *status quo*, implying neutrality, which proved incompatible with the evolving policy of the government in London. Seeking to give some effect to the Balfour Declaration while the war was still in progress the government sponsored the despatch in April 1918 of a Zionist commission led by Weizmann to act as a link between the Jewish population of Palestine and the military authorities. The military administration was sceptical of the national home policy and accordingly less than enthusiastic in its welcome to the vaguely structured commission, not least on account of an increasing concern to mollify Arab resentment and contain a growing volume of Arab protest against both the British occupation and the Zionist programme. The assignment of the mandate in the spring of 1920, coinciding with Arab attacks on the outlying northern Jewish settlements and an outbreak of communal rioting in Jerusalem, hastened a decision by London to remove the military personnel who were lukewarm towards the government's policies and to establish a civil administration. On 30 June 1920 the first civilian High Commissioner, Sir Herbert (later Viscount) Samuel (1873-1962) arrived and inaugurated the new administration. At the end of 1920 the framework of British rule was further modified by the transfer of responsibility from the Foreign Office to the Colonial Office in London. Although the mandate was not yet formally effective pending agreement with Turkey, the mandatory instrument in its various drafts (until its final version was completed in 1922) was widely known to the interested parties and was taken as the basis for the British civil administration.

Whatever the motives of the British government in issuing the Balfour Declaration in 1917 and however vague and rhetorical the commitment as then conceived may have been, in the years immediately following the policy ripened to a full-fledged undertaking to promote Zionist aspirations. It is perhaps easier to determine the reasons for the growing firmness of London Zionism at this time than for the Balfour Declaration itself. It is at least probable that strategic imperial considerations and especially French rivalry had come to supplant the tactical considerations of wartime. However that may be, the Zionists made the most of the opportunity. Vigorous Zionist diplomacy conducted by Weizmann and his international circle of colleagues ensured close Zionist participation in the drafting of the mandatory instrument, which accordingly emerged from the diplomatic melting pot with a pronounced Zionist cast.

The mandate empowered Britain to administer the country with wide discretion, subject to explicit directives to foster the Jewish national home, develop self-governing institutions and to safeguard the civil and religious rights of the whole population. Article 4 of the mandate recognized the Zionist Organization as 'an appropriate Jewish agency' to assist the administration in the establishment of the national home and development of the country, while Article 6 enjoined the administration in co-operation with the Jewish agency to facilitate Jewish immigration and 'close settlement by Jews on the land'. Article 11 provided that within certain limits the administration might arrange with the Jewish agency to operate services and utilities and develop natural resources. These provisions gave substance to the Zionists' opportunity to make what they could of the national home and allowed for the growth of semi-autonomous social and economic institutions. At the same time the principles of the mandate were so general and on matters such as rights so vague as to permit much flexibility in interpretation according to the dictates of expediency. This was particularly evident in the matter of self-government. It is therefore not surprising that each item of the mandate and its theory as a whole were the subject of close conflict between the Jews and the Arabs and between each of these and the British throughout the period of mandatory rule.

The Palestine Arabs

Estimated at about 300,000 in 1882 the Arab population had doubled by 1920.[1] Continuing to grow by a high rate of natural

97

increase supplemented by a small flow of immigration from the surrounding countries with which the people had links, it reached approximately 850,000 in 1931 and over a million by the end of 1939. The sedentary population was concentrated in the hilly northern district and also in the hill-range overlooking the coastal plain while some 70,000–100,000 Bedouin, or nomadic desert livestock breeders, were dispersed in the south. The great majority lived in small towns and villages, with about a seventh distributed amongst the half dozen large cities. The population was overwhelmingly Muslim with a Christian minority comprising about an eighth of the whole. With about three-quarters of their number living by agriculture the Muslims were predominantly rural, while the great majority of the Christians lived in the larger towns and cities. The *fellahin* or sedentary cultivators for the most part held in peonage, comprised the great majority of the Muslim Arabs. The urban community included those of the large landowners who did not reside abroad, the Muslim religious bureaucracy, employees of government and the professions, merchants, manufacturers, artisans and labourers. The peasantry and urban labourers were impoverished while the urban intelligentsia, merchants and manufacturers were linked by family and other social ties to the landowners and clergy, with whom together they constituted a ruling oligarchy. This official class disposed of great wealth.

Apart from its political implications for the Arabs the Zionist incursion exerted a direct impact on their economic life. All groups with the exception of the Bedouin and certain city-dwellers in the long run benefited economically from the Zionist initiative. The Bedouin were economically injured by the modernization of settled agricultre and its improved defence, as also by the modification of their age-old grazing and gleaning rights consequent on the Zionist enterprise. The fellahin from the 1880s until the first world war were more often than not hurt by the competition of the pioneer Jewish farmers using modern methods. Also, they were often displaced by land sales to the Zionists conducted over their heads. With the establishment of British rule and the improved regulation of land transfers this became much less common and when it occurred was ameliorated by provisions for compensation.[2] By the late 'twenties and thereafter increased Jewish investment and immigration and the associated expansion of the produce market with rising prices afforded the fellahin considerable economic gains. These were supplemented by the proliferation of employment opportunities and by the upward Jewish pressure on wage levels. Rising standards amongst the fellahin were fully shared by the urban labourers and artisans who benefited from the increased demand for services and building materials. A probable quarter of the entire Jewish investment in the inter-war period found its way into the Arab sector of the economy.[3] The fellahin additionally gained by easement of the tax burden upon them as Jewish immigration enlarged the administration's revenue base. At the same time social services were developed and the health and life expectancy of the Arabs was greatly improved.

The landowners and clergy were further enriched by lucrative land transactions concluded with the Jews and they often obtained grossly inflated prices for the tracts of swampland to which they held title. Although their long-term political interests were undermined by the sale of land to the Jews they continued to sell land while opposing Zionism. The Zionist enterprise was advanced by the circumstance that the cupidity of the landowners exceeded their patriotism. As for the merchants and manufacturers, although increased competition probably affected adversely their standing relative to other groups, they benefited in absolute terms from economic growth. The intelligentsia on the other hand, including professionals and government employees, was undoubtedly hurt by Jewish competition. This affected the Christian more than the Muslim Arabs who were less prominent in these fields. However, some of their losses in the private market for their services were offset by British patronage which was often dispensed in favour of Christians.

Arab society was not integrated politically but attained a measure of cohesion through general acceptance of a common traditional authority. The social structure at all levels was based upon the gerontocratic extended family derived from the Bedouin culture. The basic social units were patriarchal village clans linked in a pyramidic network to the clans of

99

their creditors or landowners at the social pinnacle in the cities. Administration was rudimentary and more or less limited to the clerical sphere and the regulation of indebtedness. Education was negligible and illiteracy almost universal among the Muslims at the beginning of the mandatory period. By the mid-'thirties the administration had promoted a network of schools providing education for nearly a third of the Muslim children. Christian education was conducted mainly by foreign missions.

Political life consisted in the rivalries and intrigues of the heads of the landowning and clerical families. The lower classes were malleable and subservient to the ruling elites. Divisions among the notables were reflected in corresponding feuds within the peasantry. Two families in particular, with their respective allies, dominated the political life of the Palestine Arabs, the Husaini and the Nashashibi. In 1922 the Hussaini faction attained political dominance over its rival with the appointment of the Mufti of Jerusalem, Hajj Amin Al'Husaini (b. 1895?) to the Presidency of the Supreme Muslim Council.

The Arab notables firmly rejected British overtures inviting them to participate in the machinery of colonial administration. They recognized neither the legality nor the authority of the British mandate nor the validity of Zionist rights incorporated within it. They did however accept the framework of religious administration devised by the British along the lines of the Ottoman model, providing the various confessions with machinery for extensive autonomy. The presidency of the supreme Muslim council, established and financed by the administration, commanded full control over religious, cultural, educational and judicial institutions throughout the Muslim community. Its tenure enabled Hajj Amin to wield enormous patronage, develop a powerful political machine and dispose of relatively vast revenues.

The Arab notables constituted themselves as the Palestine Congress whose executive committee, the Arab Executive, became the recognized agent of Arab opinion *vis-à-vis* the British administration. The Arab Executive supplied a forum for the development of policy and propaganda in relation to the Zionists and the mandatory regime. The Husaini gave voice to extreme anti-Zionist and anti-British sentiment while the Nashashibi adopted a more moderate public posture. The latter were no less opposed to Zionist or British interests but they showed a willingness to negotiate on issues, thereby enhancing their influence through the credit this earned them with the British officialdom. Although the Nashashibi had strong support within the Executive and possibly enjoyed greater popularity in the country the Husaini Mufti succeeded in dominating the Executive until the mid-'thirties, when he was forced into exile by the British for incitement. Thereafter he continued to exert his influence from abroad. The rudimentary political articulation of the Palestine Arab population in conjunction with the British desire to maintain the semblance of representative government made possible the total concentration of power and leadership in the hands of Hajj Amin. To this in large part must be attributed the disasters which befell the Arabs of Palestine.

Although the Arab population was not welded together as a political community it *was* united in national sentiment formed in the conviction that its patrimony was put at risk by the powerful British and Zionist intrusion. They recognized neither the authority nor the legality of the British mandate or its Zionist protégé, but feared the power of the former and the potential of the latter. They had not been consulted at any level in the preparation of European plans for the disposal of their homeland and felt in no way bound peaceably to accept their implementation. It is possible that Zionist enterprise might have been acceptable if not ecstatically welcome to the Arabs had it continued along the lines of the pre-war immigration. But coming as it did under British auspices under cover of western legality made it clear that Zionism was part of an imperial plan for the country rather than a movement of 'return' to the orient by a people intent upon becoming integrated within the wider imperial Islamic order. The issue of Jewish immigration was the very crux of Arab opposition. British rule itself might have been more or less acceptable to the Arab oligarchy, as it appeared to be in other parts of the middle east. But a British regime sponsoring alien settlement in the name of law made by European powers was another matter. Other countries (including Britain in 1905 under the premiership of Lord Balfour!) regulated the proportionally minute immigration of Jews who desired only to assimilate. On what ground were the Arabs expected to accept a proportionally large immigration seeking to transform Palestine?

The incipient nationalism of the Palestine Arabs was not a coherent social movement, and therein lay its political weakness: it was an expression of fury. The educated professionals within the official class desired national regeneration of the Arab people, modernization and independence. They alone among the Arab population were economically injured by Zionism, and they alone initially displayed an authentic nationalist response to the Zionist encroachment and its British sponsors. Although they had links with the wider Arab nationalist movement which was beginning to spread throughout the middle east, the Palestinian intellectuals were more immediately concerned about the foreign presence in Palestine itself. An intelligentsia had not crystallized as a class apart, but the Zionist incursion had the effect of stimulating its emergence. Although the professionals were not well represented within the Arab Executive, their vocal rejection of Zionism was felt as an influence amongst the inarticulate masses.

The ruling oligarchy itself was drawn by the Zionist presence into an uncharacteristic, though ambivalent, nationalist posture. The modern ideas and social practices of the Jews no less than their economic dynamism with its impact on the living standards of the masses threatened the legitimacy of the oligarchy and the bases of its wealth. The Zionists threatened the hegemony of the official class and presented the main obstacle to its capture of the succession to British rule. Hence the traditional oligarchy was obliged to oppose the foreign nationalism of the Jews. Since Zionism was sponsored by Britain, this meant that the Muslim oligarchy could not, like its counterparts in the neighbouring countries, enter into an alliance with the colonial power to stem the tide of indigenous nationalism. Zionism thus brought the Arab Executive into alliance with elements prone to nationalism and potentially subversive of its own power. The official class evolved a nationalist rhetoric which was directed against the Zionists and in support of the traditional order, rather than one which expressed social identification with its co-lingual peasantry.

Although displacement due to land transactions with the Zionists was reduced to a minor scale by the early 'twenties the fellahin had already acquired deeply ingrained attitudes of hatred towards the Jews on this score. It is highly probable that the peasants were little stirred by the activities of the Jewish colonists of the first immigration since their effect was to improve their conditions without otherwise changing it. But the pioneer socialists were another matter. What appeared to be their outrageously lax social and sexual morality outraged the religious sensibilities of the peasants (as also those of the pious Jewish community). As for the socialists who evinced concern for their fate, what were the peasants to make of the idea of fraternal equality for Arabs and Jews? While it was in the Jewish employ that the fellahin first apprehended the possibility of rising above the margin of subsistence, it was also there that they observed that they received less pay than Jewish workers. Injury upon insult, it was there too that they encountered the socialist claim to exclusive Jewish employment in Jewish-owned plantations, and it was there that they learned the risks of living above the margin of subsistence, such as unemployment and competition. Thus the economic benefits of Zionism far from reconciling them to the project merely quickened their sense of national humiliation. Together with the urban artisans and labourers the fellahin thus approached the threshold of national consciousness even if more often than not through the medium of their religious consciousness. Although the lower class was politically inarticulate, entirely dependent upon and easily manipulated by its economic masters and spiritual mentors, it comprised a reservoir of more than willing recruits for campaigns of violence.

The Zionist Organization and Jewish Agency

From the first, even before the terms of the prospective mandate crystallized, the British government envisaged its own role in relation to the national home as essentially protective, leaving to the Jews the initiative and responsibility for its construction. It was in this spirit that the government in London authorized the Zionist Organization to send the

Zionist commission to Palestine in April 1918 to provide an official link between the Jewish population and the military authorities and to pick up the threads of Jewish community organization disrupted by the war. The commission was a temporary wartime expedient prompted by Weizmann's determination to lose no time in giving concrete political expression to Zionist claims. The commission absorbed the functions of the Palestine Office established in 1908 and exercised public initiative in a variety of directions.

A series of Zionist conferences in London in 1919 and 1920 effected the transfer to London of the headquarters of the movement, formally elected Weizmann President, and prepared the reconstitution of the Zionist Organization to take account of the new political conditions and also of its now greatly increased membership. At these meetings also the *Keren Hayesod* ('Foundation Fund') was established as the central financial organ of the movement. The new constitution was ratified and implemented by the first post-war Zionist Congress, the twelfth, meeting in Carlsbad in 1921. The Congress substituted for the old 'smaller actions committee' an enlarged executive and replaced the Zionist commission by the Palestine Zionist Executive, consisting of those members of the executive who resided in Palestine. These headed the various operational departments corresponding to the range of initiative allowed to them by the administration.

A basic assumption of the Balfour Declaration and the terms of the mandate, attributable in large part to Weizmann's diplomacy, was the expectation that Jews throughout the world would respond with enthusiasm to the challenge of the national home. The Balfour Declaration and the award of the mandate certainly boosted Zionist morale and the membership of the movement grew to a nominal three-quarters of a million, but its active supporters still embraced only a small minority of the world-wide Jewish people. Yet even amongst the most vigorous and influential Jewish opponents of Zionist ideology there were those who believed that a strong community in Palestine would be valuable to Jewry. The majority were for the most part apathetic to Zionism rather than hostile, willing to help the venture in Palestine if pressed but not willing to become involved in the political excitements of the movement.

It was to tap these Jewish masses for support without imposing on them the political commitment of membership in the Zionist Organization that Weizmann and others sought to create an enlarged Jewish agency incorporating all shades of non-Zionist opinion to direct the development of the national home. American Jewry had now become the most important Jewish population since the virtual loss to Zionism of the Russian masses caught up in the revolution. Hence American Jewry, which had engaged considerable resources in international relief activity but tended to stand aloof from Zionism (and continued to do so until after Hitler), was Weizmann's particular target.

Discussion at the 1921 Congress of a formal proposal to mobilize non-Zionist effort on behalf of the national home revealed that it would not be easy to reconcile divergent views within the Zionist camp as to the proper grounds of cooperation and the appropriate organizational machinery. To ideological differences dividing affiliated parties was added a persistent cleavage between American and European Zionist leaders over the relation between national Jewish communities and the Zionist movement at large. It was not until the next Congress in 1923 that Weizmann was authorized to negotiate with representative Jewish organizations for the formation of a partnership in an enlarged Jewish agency. Although differences amongst the Zionists persisted Weizmann was now able to concentrate on bridging the wider differences separating the non-Zionists and Zionists and moderating the claims of each group upon the other in the quest for a basis of cooperation. Six years elapsed until the task was complete and the new Jewish Agency was established in 1929. In 1930 it was recognized by the mandatory power as the successor to the Zionist Organization as the official agency of Jewish participation in the national home. The Palestine Zionist Executive and its administrative departments were thereupon merged within the new Jewish Agency Executive which now nominally included representatives of non-Zionist interests.

The constitution of the Jewish Agency provided for equal representation of Zionists and non-Zionists on all executive organs. The highest organ was the Council called upon to meet every two years like its Zionist counterpart the Congress.

An Administrative Committee would meet every six months like the Zionist General Council. The President of the Zionist Organization was automatically to be President of the Jewish Agency and would work with an Executive made up of four Zionists and four non-Zionists. Headquarters were to be located in Jerusalem with a supporting office in London under the President to conduct affairs with the British government and the League of Nations Mandates Commission. The Keren Hayesod was formally detached from the Zionist Organization to become the main financial instrument of the Jewish Agency. The Jewish National Fund on the other hand remained subsidiary to the Zionist Organization but was nominated sole purchaser of land on behalf of the Jewish Agency. The structure of the Jewish Agency ensured Zionist hegemony within it not least because interest in Palestine was but a secondary commitment for the non-Zionists. Also, the 'non-Zionist' representatives on Agency organs were often in fact more or less active Zionists, on account of the formal definition of non-Zionist as a person associated with the Agency otherwise than as a representative of the Zionist Organization. Thus, for example, the Palestine Jewish community like any other obtained a portion of the non-Zionist places. Furthermore, and naturally enough, all questions coming before the Agency for decision were first discussed by the Zionist General Council or Congress.

The emergence of the Jewish Agency added complexity to the political constitution of the Jewish community. On the theory that the national home was a province of the Jewish people as such rather than merely a minority Zionist venture the formal responsibility for its promotion was now lodged in the Jewish Agency, regarded as representative of Jewry at large. From the first however it was dominated by the Zionist leadership and was to all intents and purposes controlled by the Zionist Executive. The non-Zionist elements were active at the outset but gradually abdicated their potential over the years. They made financial and political contributions to the furtherance of the national home but never exerted any major influence on broad policy nor on the practical conduct of affairs in Palestine.

Jewish immigration and land purchase

One of the first acts of the civil administration in 1920 was to issue an ordinance permitting the resumption of immigration and leaving to the Zionist Organization the responsibility for the absorption of newcomers. In June 1921 following an outburst of violent Arab protest the regulation was modified to limit entry to those with definite prospects of specific employment. A series of further refinements followed leading to the implementation of a definitive Immigration Ordinance in 1925. This instrument remained substantially in force subject only to minor amendments until the mid-'thirties, after which time political considerations came to supplant economic criteria in the limitation of entry.

The Ordinance based the regulation of entry on the estimated economic absorptive capacity of the country, classifying eligible immigrants in economic categories: those of independent means (including such people as orphans and students with assured maintenance), those qualified in a profession, those with definite employment available upon arrival and dependants of permanent residents or immigrants. The category of workers with employment prospects, which became known as the 'labour schedule', accounted together with dependants for the great majority of immigrants during most of the inter-war period. The operation of this regulation brought about the closest participation of the Zionist Organization and later the Jewish Agency as a quasi-governmental authority and at the same time occasioned the greatest friction between the Zionists and the authorities.

Twice yearly the Palestine Zionist Executive and later the Immigration Department of the Jewish Agency Executive submitted to the chief immigration officer its estimate of the number of workers who could be absorbed into employment during the next six-month period, giving details of the precise trades and occupations in which jobs would be provided. The High Commissioner, acting upon the recommendation of his immigration officer, then fixed the number of certificates to be issued under the labour schedule. These were transmitted directly to the Zionist Organization which was given a free hand in their distribution through its network of Palestine

Offices abroad. This assured that the certificates would be taken up by Jews although the immigration controls made no specific provision as to nationality or religion.

As Arab protest grew in vigour over the years the issue of Jewish immigration became the main battleground of the three-cornered conflict in Palestine. The administration, prone at first to respond to Arab grievance by merely tightening the application of economic controls, drifted by the mid-'thirties to an avowedly political formulation of immigration policy. This shift from economic criteria coincided with the enhancement of Jewish need as the Nazi persecution reached the threshold of mass extermination.

The accumulated amendments of the 1925 Ordinance were incorporated in a new Ordinance in 1933 which applied somewhat stricter controls but maintained the economic basis of assessment. In 1936 although the Ordinance remained in effect it was now interpreted in a more restrictive manner, especially as regards the labour schedule. In 1937 a new Ordinance gave the high commissioner the authority to prescribe a political ceiling on immigration. The restrictive approach culminated in the reduction of immigration to a trickle and its prospective termination on political grounds under a new policy elaborated by the London government in a White Paper issued in 1939.

The administration from the first invariably disputed the estimates of the Jewish authorities as too optimistic and consistently marked down the number of certificates under the labour schedule, disregarding the detailed justifications presented in support of the Jewish estimates. Whether or not the Jewish estimates of capacity were too optimistic, in fact the flow of immigrants was not usually so great as to press unduly on the official ceilings. As pointed out at the time in a Jewish Agency memorandum, the fundamental questions in the industrial development of Palestine were *whether* there were Jews in sufficient number prepared to immigrate into Palestine who could bring with them sufficient capital and business experience if they were encouraged, and *whether* there were other Jews ready to come to Palestine to supply the skilled and unskilled labour required. In some years in the 'twenties re-emigration was substantial and in 1927 exceeded immigration.

Illegal Jewish immigration did not take place on any considerable scale until the implementation of the stringent restrictions following the new policy laid down in the White Paper of 1939. However throughout the inter-war period a steady trickle entered the country unrecorded by evading frontier controls or overstaying visitors' visas or by securing the right of entry on the basis of fictitious marriages. The official population count of 1939 missed some thirty thousand Jews shown in more reliable Jewish estimates which included unrecorded immigrants of the preceding two decades.

Including former residents allowed to return under the auspices of the military administration, the net Jewish immigration between 1918 and 1939 is estimated to have been approximately 310,000. Only about a quarter of the total Jewish growth during the period was due to natural increase. The population grew more than eightfold from about 55,000 at the beginning of 1918 to an estimated 475,000, including unrecorded immigrants, at the end of 1939. Arab net immigration was relatively low but natural increase contributed to the rapid growth of the Arab population to over a million during the same period. Nonetheless the Jews as a proportion of the whole population of the country grew from less than one-tenth at the beginning of British rule to nearly one-third at the end of 1939.

Just as the earlier immigrants had moved to Palestine in clearly differentiated waves, so during the inter-war period there was a rhythmic tide in which each influx displayed specific social and cultural characteristics associated with its geographic origin and the circumstances prompting the migration.

As has been seen, the period of the third immigration from 1919–23 brought a net increase of some 30,000, mainly from eastern Europe, and included a high proportion of young people and labour pioneers. Between 1924 and 1926 the fourth wave resulted in a net influx of some 50,000. The fifth immigration from 1932–9 increased the Jewish population by over 220,000 newcomers three-quarters of whom came during the four years from 1933–6. The year 1935, with nearly 62,000, was the peak year of immigration prior to Israel's accession to statehood in 1948.

The fourth immigration originated primarily in Poland and

was occasioned by anti-semitic measures of the Polish government rather than by any new outburst of Zionist enthusiasm. This wave differed from the third immigration in its social composition, including amongst its number only a minor element of pioneer youth and containing many hundreds of independent small businessmen. These brought capital into the country which extended citriculture and stimulated the urban economy with the establishment of numerous small manufacturing concerns. They also introduced a speculative fever which culminated in a serious recession in 1927. The fourth immigration did not make any notable impact on the social and cultural institutions or political life of the Jewish community. They imported something of the business ethos of the Polish ghetto, a petit-bourgeois culture which was becoming characteristic of the national home in spite of the efforts of the socialist founding fathers.

Following a lull in the late 'twenties and early 'thirties which was due in part to adverse economic conditions in the country, immigration swelled again in 1933 when the Nazis came to power. Some 165,000 immigrants arrived between 1935–6 of whom nearly one-fifth came from Germany. The largest element continued to be drawn from Poland but for the first time now Germany, and towards the late 'thirties also Austria and Czechoslovakia as they in turn came under the Nazi heel, accounted for a significant proportion of the immigration.

The fifth immigration was marked by a relative reduction in the share of the labour certificates as against the categories of independent persons, professionals, orphans (especially in the late 'thirties) and students. At this time it was still possible for Jews to take capital with them out of Germany and a significant number came with larger means at their disposal than the Polish immigrants of the 'twenties had typically possessed. From Germany also came a high proportion of professional people more educated than any previous group of immigrants. These made a lasting contribution to the culture and public life of the country without however displacing the grip of the east Europeans on the political institutions and leadership of the community. In the long run the central Europeans had to adapt themselves to the way of life shaped by those from Russia and Poland.

The immigration of the inter-war years continued to display the urban disposition of the Jewish community. By the end of the 'thirties Tel Aviv had grown to a population of nearly 150,000 and about three-quarters of the total Jewish population was accounted for by those in urban centres. The most intensive rural development took place in the Jezreel Valley, the Jordan Valley, the stretch of coastal plain between Haifa and Tel Aviv and to the south of Tel Aviv where the earliest settlers had struck roots. Jewish agriculture was also extended in the hilly terrain of Galilee, Samaria and Judea.

The Zionist leadership was content in the main to leave to private initiative the promotion of industry and commerce, while reserving its own energies and resources for the acquisition and settlement of land and the furtherance of agriculture. Given the need to reclaim the land from swamp and desert and to underpin virgin agriculture with adequate research and experimentation, it was clear that rural development could not proceed on a commercial foundation but required public investment and sponsorship. Also, the Zionist leadership hoped to conserve funds by concentrating land purchase in order to obviate undue upward pressure on prices from private speculative activity. The administration's Department of Agriculture and Fisheries provided some facilities but its relatively minor efforts in this field were geared primarily to the needs of Arab agriculture, and the Jews were expected in the spirit of the national home to undertake responsibility for themselves. Under the terms of the Land Transfer Ordinance introduced in 1921 all land purchases required the consent of the administration, which was conditional upon satisfactory provision being made for any tenants displaced by the transfer of ownership. No further limitations were placed upon Jewish acquisition from Arab proprietors until the White Paper policy of 1939 came into effect.

The main Zionist organs responsible for the purchase of land in large tracts were PICA (Palestine Jewish Colonization Association), founded in 1924 as the successor to Baron Rothschild's administration; the JNF (Jewish National Fund), founded in 1901 by the Zionist Organization; and the PLDC (Palestine Land Development Co.), founded in 1908 as an adjunct of the Palestine Office headed by Ruppin. PICA, as heir to the agricultural initiatives of the late nineteenth century, was the largest Jewish landowner until the mid-'thirties when it was overtaken by the PLDC and the JNF. PICA's tenants were in the main private farmers obliged to defray their capital debt over time, while the agencies of the Zionist Organization sponsored the settlement of labour-pioneer groups as well as private farmers.

There was some duplication of function between the JNF and other public agencies such as the PLDC and Keren Hayesod. The JNF was responsible both for raising funds on a world-wide basis for land acquisition and for negotiating land purchases 'on behalf of the Jewish people'. This formula was enshrined as a basic doctrine in the constitution of the JNF, according to which the lands it purchased became the inalienable property of the Jewish people. Such lands could not be resold but only offered on hereditary leasehold to those who worked it, in practice at a token rental and indeed only to Jews. Thus the pioneer settlers without any capital of their own were able to pursue their avocation acting virtually as national custodians of the land. Reclamation, amelioration and other necessary initial investments were also financed by the JNF, but this activity was in the main conducted by Keren Hayesod.

Most of the lands acquired were purchased in large tracts from absentee private Arab proprietors. The mandatory administration itself controlled over a quarter of a million acres classed as state domain but it leased only a minute portion of this to Jewish agriculture. By the late 'thirties the Jews held little over a quarter of a million cultivable acres, approximately twice the area they had owned in 1920, although the Jewish population had increased nearly eightfold in the same period. In 1939 about five per cent of the total land area of the country was in Jewish ownership, including, according to the administration's calculation, about one-ninth of the total cultivable land. (The official definition of cultivable land brought only about one-third of the whole country under that category.) The Jews, however, considered well over half of the land to be cultivable and hence regarded their holdings as much less than one-ninth of the cultivable area. In fact much of the land they held had been rendered cultivable by their own reclamation efforts and had not been regarded as such at the time of purchase.

The British administration

While the Balfour Declaration as a political measure originating in wartime diplomacy and Anglo-French imperial rivalry served its purpose more or less effectively, it proved inadequate as a philosophical foundation for the administration of the country. The declaration gave expression to an imaginative nineteenth-century brand of Zionism characteristic of the British upper class. Based on a romantic biblical and orientalist cult of which Balfour and Churchill were among the most distinguished exponents and which was shared by others such as Lloyd George, the ardent idealism of British Zionism was also associated with a sense of Christian guilt in relation to the trials to which Christendom had for centuries subjected the Jews. Ironically, British Zionism of the period was in all probability closely related in its socio-cultural provenance to an equally romantic Arabism. In the Palestinian context exponents of the latter necessarily became antagonists of the former, but they shared a similar concept of the Arabs. The doctrine of promoting Jewish national development while protecting (undefined) Arab rights, revealed an intrinsic dependence of British Zionism on certain prior assumptions about both Jewish and Arab behaviour. British Zionism as a source of policy was therefore enervated and its ideals dissipated in proportion to the deviation of Jewish and Arab behaviour from the norms that it imposed on them. Jewish Zionism, especially as manifested in its Palestinian branch, increasingly diverged from the British concept as it became ever more closely identified with the activities of east-European Jews of socialist persuasion. In Britain a new Zionist concept was increasingly voiced by labour leaders some of whom shared in the old romantic concept but were even more responsive to the social possibilities of the national home. This neo-Zionism did not assimilate the wartime generation of British Zionist statesmen whose conservative or liberal dispositions were offended rather than intrigued by the social innovations of the east-European Jews. Thus the new social dimension of British Zionism, given that it was expressed for the most part in the ranks of the opposition party, was unable to fill a growing philosophical void in the foundations of British policy. Within about fifteen years of the assumption of the mandate the idealistic aspirations of the original policy-makers had been reduced to a distant echo.

Also, and perhaps more significant than the gradual loosening and shifting of its British-Zionist moorings, the Palestine policy was implemented by colonial service personnel who for the most part did not share the original idealistic assumptions of the statesmen to whom they were answerable. At first the upper echelons of the administration were filled by prominent British-Zionists like the first High Commissioner Sir Herbert Samuel, his Attorney-General Norman Bentwich, the Governor of the Jerusalem District Sir Ronald Storrs, the chief immigration officer Albert Hyamson and others.[4] The gradual decline of British Zionism as a philosophy informing the Palestine policy was reflected and accentuated in the numerical reduction of Zionist sympathizers at the top levels in successive administrations.[5] Such sympathizers were seldom in evidence at all at the lower levels and over the years outright hostility to Zionist activities became characteristic of the lower British officialdom in Palestine.

Underlying the initial British concept of the national home was the assumption that Jews and Arabs would become integrated within a broader Palestinian national identity. The British goal was to promote neither Jewish nor Arab sovereignty as such, but a polity of Palestinians. The Hebrew and Arabic languages, it was assumed, would afford the two peoples the means of separate cultural expression while the English language would provide a bridge for their political integration. Arab nationalism at the time of the British arrival was still an inchoate movement and did not yet encompass the Arab masses of Palestine, whose religious ties transcended all other relations. There seemed every reason to expect that a sense of Palestinian nationality might be nurtured and serve the political needs of the Arabs, Muslim and Christian. There was also a sound historical basis for assuming the possibility of developing a Palestinian consciousness among the Jews. Those of the first immigration and their children, born Ottoman subjects, were Palestinian in outlook and their Levantine culture had more in common with that of the Arabs than with the pioneer ethos of the second immigration.

The Ottoman legacy supported and enhanced the British perspective. The Arabs were accustomed to the Ottoman *millet* system allowing significant autonomy to religious minorities within the empire and the *millet* also accorded well with the east-European experience of the Jews and with the requirements of Zionist development. The alacrity with which the Arab notables, in spite of their refusal to acknowledge the authority of the mandate, accepted the machinery of Muslim autonomy devised by the British on the Ottoman model supported the expectation that the Muslim majority might be satisfied with confessional rights as compensation for their loss of dominion within the old imperial framework. The convenience and appropriateness of the constitution of self-government along confessional lines enabled the British administration to sustain the illusion of Palestinism for some time. However, the idea that the essential element of differentiation within the population was religious rather than national was soon turned into a fiction by the accelerating development of the two nationalisms.

In its initial years the mandatory administration erroneously assumed that Arab fears were based on the claims voiced by Zionist extremists and that moderation on the Zionist side would suffice to obviate conflict. Constrained by the British diplomacy of conciliation and making essentially the same appraisal of Arab opposition, the official Zionist leaders in the first years were in close rapport with the British in their broad understanding of the national home and its assumed compatibility with Arab rights and interests. Arab opposition to the Zionist project although not precisely 'nationalist' in its sources in the aftermath of the war, was nevertheless vociferous, violent and unequivocal. The Arab official class displayed a unanimous hostility to the project of the Jewish national home. However, Anglo-French collusion thwarted the only attempt on the part of the Versailles powers to ascertain the wishes of the population of Palestine in regard to their future government. On the insistence of President Wilson the King-Crane Commission was despatched to the middle east for this purpose despite the withdrawal of co-operation by the European powers. Even if it had in principle been possible to determine the state of popular opinion in the absence of representative or participatory institutions the King-Crane Commission would have been futile since it was informed by the Wilsonian doctrine of self-determination. This was incompatible with French and British designs and in particular with the British commitment to the Jewish national home as eventually enshrined in the League of Nations mandate.

Anti-Jewish violence on a significant scale was first manifested in Arab rioting in the spring of 1920 which inaugurated a period of sporadic bloodshed continuing for about a year. Taken aback by the vehemence of Arab opposition to the policy of the Jewish national home, the British government sought to mollify the Palestine Arab leadership by issuing a moderately worded statement of its intentions. This was the purpose of the Churchill White Paper of 1922 drafted for the Colonial secretary by Sir Herbert Samuel, which served for some fifteen years as the controlling interpretation placed by Britain upon its mandatory obligations.

The White Paper unequivocally maintained the British commitment to the Jewish national home but gave a more concrete interpretation than the mandatory instrument of the approach to Arab rights. It mentioned the Arab community explicitly, which the mandatory document failed to do, pledged non-domination by the Jews and intimated that in future immigration would be regulated by economic criteria. Also by promising to review the question of self-government after a few years the White Paper shifted the emphasis of ambiguous previous pronouncements carrying the inference that self-government would be conditional upon Jewish national development, and implied that it would be effected while the Arabs remained the great majority of the population.

The Zionists for the most part envisaged the eventual emergence of a Jewish majority which would lead to accession to some form of sovereignty. Some British policy-makers tended to a similar view and although there is evidence that Churchill himself thought in terms of a Jewish state, the government preferred to leave the question open pending the test of Jewish efforts. Even allowing that the prevalent British view fell short of assuming eventual Jewish sovereignty the British government and the Zionist Organization were at one in viewing caution as a diplomatic tactic rather than an indication of ultimate goals. The Arabs knew this and were concerned with the ultimate implications of British policy rather than with its immediate effects. Accordingly the Zionist leaders, disappointed though they were with the tendency of the White Paper, gave it their consent. The Arab notables rejected it out of hand and made it abundantly clear that their intransigence was addressed to the very principle of Jewish immigration and settlement.

Political developments within the Arab community under the Husaini writ on the one hand, and the direction of national construction by the Jews on the other, diverged much too sharply to permit the creation of an integrated bi-national Palestinian polity. The ideals of mandatory policy proved hopelessly inadequate to subdue the political, social, economic and cultural mainsprings of conflict between Arab and Jew, and between each of these and the British themselves. The characteristic British posture of fairness in administration proved to be an insufficient substitute for incisiveness and feasibility as criteria of policy. By the mid-'thirties external events began to impinge on British policy in a way that reinforced the contra-Zionist pressures within Palestine. As the Nazi threat loomed in Europe and Italy overran Ethiopia the possibility of war heightened Britain's concern for strategic control of the region as a whole and so enhanced the bargaining power of the neighbouring Arab regimes, enabling them to exert leverage on behalf of the Arabs in Palestine. British policy in Palestine, hitherto relatively finite and insulated despite the hypothetical strategic content of its origins, now slipped into explicitly subservient status in relation to concrete regional, European and global calculations.

By the time of the outbreak of the second world war the optimistic and altruistic sentiments underlying the Zionist aspect of the Palestine policies framed in the first world war were fully spent. The doctrine of the national home had become a historical curiosity. The culmination of this transition on the British side coincided with a transition within Zionism no less radical, impelled by the same external events.

117

E

The first decade of the mandatory administration, in which the Jews were relatively weak, was characterized specifically by Arab-Jewish conflict which, after a lull following the riots of 1920 and 1921, erupted in a crescendo of violence in 1929. During this period an early step towards the modification of British policy was discernible in a growing tendency of the administration to interpret its function primarily as arbiter of Arab-Jewish conflict rather than as sponsor of Zionist aspirations. Hajj Amin had succeeded in driving a wedge between the British and the Zionists. The second decade of the regime, in which the Jews were stronger but still dependent on British protection, was marked by Arab-British conflict. A recurrence of violence in 1933 and a full-fledged rebellion in 1936 took a toll in Jewish life but were mainly aimed at British rule. As the Arab-Jewish conflict thus became overlaid by direct Arab-British struggle a disposition to appease Arab demands gradually swung the administration from the posture of arbiter to that of protector and finally sponsor of the Arab interest. However, this occurred only after the vigorous suppression of the Arab revolt and decimation of the Arab political leadership. The third and last decade of British rule, in which the Arabs were now relatively much weaker, was marked by Jewish-Arab and Jewish-British conflict and the collapse of British control. The conflict of the 'forties explicitly assumed the aspect of a struggle for the succession to British rule, all parties including the British having by then irrevocably abandoned the theory of the mandate and the national home. The Arabs had brought about the collapse of the national home policy, whereupon the Zionists proceeded to bring about the collapse of British rule.

CHAPTER 6

FOUNDATIONS OF JEWISH SELF-GOVERNMENT (1917-39)

The Jewish economy and labour movement – political parties – the Jewish quasi-government

The Jewish economy and labour movement

The nationalist ideology underlying Jewish development was refracted through the socialist ideas of the most energetic pioneers, who quickly attained political predominance within the Jewish population. The most forceful expression of Zionism as implemented in Palestine was the 'conquest of labour' strategy of the Histadrut. This policy secured the containment of Arab employment in the Jewish sector to a minimum. It was this which most markedly distinguished Zionism from other European settler enterprises such as those in Kenya and Rhodesia. The Jewish settlers not only did not seek to exploit the Arab economy but did everything possible, including the exercise of violence in the labour market, to prevent the occurrence of any such tendency. Economic nationalism was then extended from the labour market to the produce market. The growing Jewish population provided a market for Arab produce, but only to a very limited extent did the Jewish economy employ Arab labour or sell its products to the Arab sector. In consequence of this policy the Jewish economy was independent of the Arab labour force and the Arab market. This was perhaps the single most important source of its strength. In the context of the differing social structures of the two peoples and the difference between the living standards acceptable to the Arab peasantry and the Jewish settlers, the

Jewish economy was thus insulated and segregated from the Arab economy. The desire to avoid colonial exploitation thus laid the basis for the eventual partition of the country, perhaps even rendering this inevitable.

The growth of the Jewish economy was closely tied to the pattern of immigration and the import of capital by the immigrants themselves. It is estimated that in the period between the two world wars the Jews introduced some £125 million of capital into the country. About one-fifth of this amount was at the disposal of the public Zionist agencies, in particular by Keren Hayesod and the JNF, being the revenue of voluntary donations raised among Jewish communities abroad. The largest share of such philanthropy was contributed by the Jews of the United States and other English-speaking countries. Private capital was, however, the predominant source of investment funds. Some £75 million was introduced in the form of personal capital of the immigrants, most of this in the mid-'twenties and mid-'thirties, and about £26 million came as private foreign capital in pursuit of profit.[1]

Contrary to the expectation of many observers who noted that a steep economic decline had followed the peak immigration of the mid-'twenties, and in spite of the almost universal depression then gripping the industrial world, the fifth immigration inaugurated an unparalleled surge of prosperity in Palestine. This was in large measure due to the substantial capital sums imported by the Jews who came from Germany, Austria and Czechoslovakia. Almost one-fifth of the total capital imported between the wars was brought in the years 1934 and 1935. The largest part of investment capital was absorbed by land purchase and settlement. This was divided between a smaller portion devoted to intensive mixed farming conducted in the main by co-operative groups financed by the Zionist development agencies, and a larger share invested in citriculture mainly on privately owned plantations. Private capital in the rural sector and concentrated in citriculture accounted for the largest single share of investment. Urban construction took almost as large a portion of capital, followed by light manufacture and commerce, transport and other social investments. By the outbreak of the second world war new industry had absorbed a tenth of the total investment. Jewish industrial activity was diversified, with electric power, food, chemicals and building materials comprising the main branches. Less than a tenth of industrial establishments employed more than ten workers, the vast majority of plants being small family-owned firms in light manufacture. Before the second world war industry was geared to the supply of consumer goods for the domestic Jewish market and foreign trade was relatively limited. The foremost export was citrus fruit for which Britain was the leading market, while imports were brought mainly from Europe, the middle east and Britain. Amongst the few major economic initiatives of the British administration was the opening of the deep-water port at Haifa in 1933. When Jaffa port was closed by the Arab general strike in 1936 the Jews developed an auxiliary port at Tel Aviv which was commissioned in February 1938.

Amongst the most important concerns in the country was the Palestine Electric Corporation, a public utility established in the early 'twenties on the basis of mixed private and public capital. A prominent Zionist entrepreneur, Pinhas Rutenberg (1879–1942), secured a concession from the British government in 1921 for the supply of electric power, in circumstances which generated sharp controversy. Much criticism of Zionism at the time pointed to the concession as evidence that the movement was a profit-hunting adventure for the enrichment of private individuals with suitable political connections. This criticism was soon muted as it became evident that Palestine was no goldmine. So far as the electric power undertaking was concerned it took several years to become established on an economic footing. By the mid-'thirties the corporation had raised adequate capital and completed three power stations based initially on fuel oil and later on hydro-electric power. These grew in capacity in pace with industrial investment and laid the basis for future industrial expansion.

Another important Zionist undertaking was the Palestine Potash Company operating a concession for the extraction and processing of the rich chemical deposits of the Dead Sea. This company, like the electric power company, was headed by a dynamic Russian entrepreneur with specialized technical experience, M. Novomeysky (1873–1961). A cement factory, a soap and edible oils plant and a textile concern were also sizeable in scale. All these companies were established by private initiative, but many of them succumbed to the great risks posed by the uncertain conditions of the economy in the 'twenties and the 'thirties and were eventually taken over by public interests amongst which the Histadrut was foremost.

The Jewish labour force, which increased from about 20,000 at the beginning of the mandate to an estimated 188,000 in 1939, was distributed amongst the various branches of the economy in a fairly stable pattern throughout the period. Agriculture and industry each employed between a quarter and a fifth of the labour force, construction between a sixth and a twelfth, while employment in various services grew gradually over the period from approximately two-fifths to about a half of the total Jewish labour force.

Throughout the mandatory period the Histadrut grew relative to the Jewish population as a whole. Its membership increased at a compound annual average rate of over fifteen per cent compared with about ten per cent for the adult Jewish population as a whole. From about eleven per cent of adult Jews at the time of its founding in 1920 the Histadrut had grown by 1939 to some thirty-six per cent. From about half of the Jewish workers in the early 'twenties those organized within the Histadrut reached two-thirds by 1939.[2] Histadrut members comprised a higher proportion of rural than of urban workers, a fact readily intelligible in the light of the importance of agricultural settlement in the Histadrut's programme. The majority of its members were nevertheless settled in the cities. Since membership in the organization was limited to working people, whether co-operators or hired workers, the Histadrut included a significantly higher proportion of adults under fifty years of age than did the Jewish population as a whole. From less than five thousand at the time of its founding the total membership of the organization grew by 1939 to nearly one hundred and ten thousand, including housewives employed only in their own homes, or almost eighty thousand in remunerative employment.[3] Of the one-third of workers who did not belong to the Histadrut many were members of religious organizations which co-operated closely with it in trade union activities, while others were organized in the National

Labour Federation, a rival union of the right-wing opposition. As the Histadrut expanded it increased the range and improved the quality of the various social services it supplied to its members. Its responsibilities in education, health and welfare were consolidated until the social activities of the labour movement became a comprehensive social and cultural force reinforcing the voluntary character of autonomous national life. The Histadrut maintained its own network of schools from kindergarten to high-school level in which general education was combined with indoctrination in the 'religion of labour'. It also established its own daily newspaper and publishing house, adult education institutions and youth movement. All members automatically belonged to the sickness fund which provided comprehensive medical care to their families, while other institutions of the labour movement catered to the needs of orphans, widows and the aged.

With the expansion and consolidation of the Histadrut a considerable bureacracy arose to administer its services and interests. After a decade of haphazard and rather tenuous central co-ordination the Histadrut by the early 'thirties achieved a position of central command over the range of labour institutions. Not until 1937 did the organization succeed in establishing a central dues collecting agency. However the greater part of the revenue of the organization for the finance of its administration continued until the end of the mandate to come from contributions of the American labour movement.[4]

The unusually high degree of organization enabled the trade unions within the Histadrut framework to secure wages and working conditions as advanced as the relatively undeveloped economy could possibly yield. The crux of the Histadrut's bargaining power was its control of the labour exchanges enabling it to maintain a 'closed shop'. This control was heavily contested by employers and by the opposition union, sometimes aided by the British police, but it was sustained by the effective use of the strike weapon. The Histadrut's trade union power was greatly augmented by its manifold network of co-operative enterprises which was often used as a pace-setter in determining wages. Almost half the gainfully occupied members of the Histadrut earned their living within the co-operative institutions lumped together in common parlance as the 'labour economy'. After twenty years this comprised about a hundred directly owned subsidiaries of the Histadrut and about a thousand autonomous co-operative societies in every branch of the economy. By consistently ploughing back profits as required by its constitution the leadership of the Histadrut established a nearly autarchic socialist economy alongside the private sector.

Although the Histadrut was predominantly urban in composition its co-operative activities were greatly influenced by the ideas and practices of the agricultural pioneers who had brought the comprehensive labour movement into being. These at no time exceeded a fifth of the total Histadrut membership. However, by dint of their ideological mobilization and high degree of discipline they created a network of sectarian institutions comprising one of the most powerful elements within the Histadrut during its formative years. They were at once the greatest asset of the movement in so far as they set a standard of self-sacrifice and social discipline that inspired emulation, while at the same time they often exerted a centrifugal influence detracting from the general authority of the Histadrut.

During the 'twenties the kibbutz movement was still weak and embattled. In its first dozen years over four hundred youths had joined Degania but less than fifty remained in 1923. The kibbutz movement as a whole in that year embraced about two thousand seven hundred members dispersed in sixty-six groups of varying organizational form. The urban boom inaugurated by the fourth immigration weakened the agricultural pioneer movement and exacerbated its divisions. In 1926 the work legion disbanded. After years of embroilment in conflict with the Histadrut leadership its members had moved so far in the direction of militant revolutionary socialism that its majority eventually renounced Zionism and made their way to the Soviet Union. At the same time the efforts of the kibbutz founders to form a united national movement failed to overcome the disputatious habits characteristic of the ideological culture. The metapolitics of the agricultural movement brought about its organizational fragmentation, which in turn rigidified differences even while these declined in practical importance. Party politics then supervened to exacerbate the disunity. The result was the creation of three separate kibbutz federations which within a few years converged in all practical particulars while at the same time their political differences became more pronounced.

In its first years, pursuing the original conception of its founders, Ein Harod acted as the central core of a number of groups organized as a unitary kibbutz although they were dispersed far afield in various occupations and branches of the economy. By 1927 the kibbutz comprised four rural settlements and eight groups employed in the cities with a total membership of over nine hundred. Opposition to the spreading of the kibbutz grew amongst those settled at Ein Harod who wished to give first priority to the development of their own settlement. They proposed that Ein Harod should shed its central co-ordinating functions and that these be vested in a federal association in which each group would be responsible for its own affairs. On this basis in the autumn of 1927 was established *Hakibbutz Hameuhad* (The United Kibbutz), embracing those groups within the orbit of Ahdut Ha'Avodah which were dedicated to the theory of the large settlement and the close linking of agricultural workers with those in other branches of the economy. The new federation failed to attract the kvutza pioneers in the Hapoel Hatzair fold, who insisted on the primary value of the small group and the importance of its autonomy.

In the meantime in April 1927 four of the settlements associated with Hashomer Hatzair formed *Hakibbutz Ha'Artzi* (The Countrywide Kibbutz) which sought to secure tight central discipline binding all groups within one kibbutz while at the same time preserving the social doctrine of the kvutza by limiting the size of the individual units. Also Hakibbutz Ha'Artzi adopted the principle of strict political unity designed to give its members an independent role within the wider labour movement and Zionist arena.

The kvutza movement maintained its preference for control by the individual settlement of its own activities, and remained reluctant to transfer significant influence to any central association. However the movement needed federal machinery to strengthen and protect the kvutza economy now exposed to the competition of the dynamic new federations. Accordingly

E*

in 1928 *Hever Ha'Kvutzot* ('Association of Kvutzot') was established as a framework for inter-group co-operation. The kvutza was rescued from decline by the arrival of new manpower trained in 'Gordonia', a movement in Europe inspired by the ideals of A. D. Gordon.

The kibbutz movement grew steadily from less than one per cent of the Jewish population at the beginning of the mandatory period to over five per cent by 1939. Hakibbutz Hameuhad by then embraced thirty-three settlements with a population of over 12,000; Hakibbutz Ha'Artzi with thirty-nine groups had a population of over 6,000; and Hever Hakvutzot with thirty-three groups totalled over 4,000 souls in 1939.[5] An additional two thousand belonged to kibbutzim associated with the orthodox religious parties.

From the moment of their formation the kibbutz federations never ceased to explore the question of organizational unity for the whole movement.[6] As the years passed the social and economic practices and forms of the various movements came ever more closely to resemble each other, but unity eluded them as political differences hardened and competition for public funds was institutionalized. Hashomer Hatzair was unwilling to permit ideological diversity within its ranks, insisting on political and ideological unity in the constitution of its settlements. Hever Hakvutzot on the other hand was unwilling to submerge the autonomy of the individual group in a collective discipline such as that imposed on its members by Hakkibutz Hameuhad.

In the inter-war period the moshav movement grew to forty-seven settlements with a total population of over ten thousand.[7] The importance of the moshav as a factor in Jewish colonization in a sense surpassed that of the kibbutz, in so far as the latter grew by assimilation of immigrant pioneers trained and indoctrinated in the European youth movements, while the moshav depended almost entirely on recruits from the population within Palestine, including kibbutz defectors. After many false starts giving rise to ephemeral local or regional organizations the moshav movement succeeded in establishing a firm central organ in 1930 at a time when it numbered nine settlements with less than a thousand members. In the mid-'thirties a new form was created within the moshav movement, the 'moshav shitufi' ('co-operative *moshav*'), which combined the kibbutz principle of collective ownership of assets with the social pattern of the classic moshav based on the family unit.

Apart from its interest in land settlement financed by public funds the Histadrut also took economic initiative or made acquisitions in industry, construction, banking, retailing and transportation. Passenger transport by road became a co-operative monopoly. However in all other branches of the economy the labour-controlled enterprises in the inter-war period comprised a relatively small part of the whole. Even in co-operative agriculture the numbers employed within the Histadrut framework were lower than the numbers in the employ of private farmers and plantations. Thus the private sector was much the more important foundation of Jewish economic life and development. But the centralized control of the Histadrut augmented the relative importance and potentiality of its economic undertakings. The co-operative economy as a unit employed nearly a third of the Jewish labour force. The ideological and institutional mobilization of the labour movement enabled the Histadrut to 'deliver' the labour economy as a political power. The various groups in the private sector, by contrast, stood in relations of competition and were pronouncedly individualistic in outlook, politically dispersed and weakly motivated.

The Histadrut leaders seemed to apprehend intuitively that in an underdeveloped economy political power was the primary source of wealth, while the entrepreneurs of the private sector appeared to be trapped in their European perspective in which economic power seemed necessarily to yield political power. This view was given clear expression by one of its most prominent leaders in the course of a discussion within the farmers' federation about its role as an organization:[8] 'If the private farmers will but strengthen their economic organization, and on an economic basis alone, and if all other propertied interests in the country will do likewise, these will in the end become the decisive political power in the land.' The leaders of the Histadrut thought otherwise. Using their economic power, such as it was, in the 'thirties to assist their drive to political hegemony, they were then able in the war economy of the 'forties to enlarge their economic role by political means until the Histadrut sector did indeed become the most important developmental factor in the national home. The political ascendancy of the labour movement virtually placed control of the capitalistic economy in the hands of the labour bureaucracy, a unique feature of the national home. However, even given this and also the prestige and influence of the pioneer movement, the socialist leadership never succeeded in fully counteracting the petit-bourgeois ethos of the Jewish economy.

Political parties

It has already been noted that Zionist political parties in Palestine had their origin in the ideological differences of the labour pioneers in the first decade of the century. From the first the labour parties took the form of communal organizations with extensive service functions. Only later did electoral politics arise, when the institutions of the Palestine settlers and the external Zionist movement were ramified. Thereupon new parties arose from time to time. These tended to follow the same communal service pattern as the labour parties rather than merely responding to electoral necessities.

By 1920 when the Histadrut was founded the socialist pioneers tended to follow either Hapoel Hatzair or Ahdut Ha'Avodah or the lesser fringe groups on the left, all of which catered to their social needs. With the establishment of the Histadrut the parties shed many of their functions to the new comprehensive organization, but retained their initiative as ideological elites contending for control of the general movement and its ancillary institutions.

The desire for unity between the two major labour parties never abated following the abortive attempt of 1919 which resulted in the founding of Ahdut Ha'Avodah. At the Histadrut founding convention in 1920 Ahdut Ha'Avodah had gained a plurality but not a majority of the vote. At the succeeding conventions in 1923 and 1927 Ahdut Ha'Avodah secured an absolute but narrow majority.[9] This served Ahdut Ha'Avodah well in heightening the pressure upon Hapoel Hatzair to join with it in a complete merger. The main resistance to unity was based on nationalist grounds in the case of Hapoel Hatzair and on socialist grounds in the case of Ahdut Ha'Avodah. The petit-bourgeois immigration of the fourth wave in the mid-'twenties undermined labour's wider influence and helped to drive the two parties towards presenting a common face in meeting external attacks upon their ideas and methods. The economic crisis of 1926–7 in conjunction with increased urbanization and industrial strife shifted the Histadrut frontline moment-arily from agriculture to trade union activity in the towns, thereby somewhat detracting from the influence of Hapoel Hatzair and weakening its resistance to Ahdut Ha'Avodah's unity overtures. In spring 1929 the leaderships of the two parties drew up a joint platform combining nationalist and socialist rhetoric and put the issue to a referendum of the rank and file. Over eighty per cent of the membership of each group voted for unity. The political crisis occasioned by the Arab riots of 1929 hastened the process and unity was consummated on the eve of 5 January 1930 with the establishment of Mapai (an acrostic of *Mifleget Poalei Eretz-Israel*, the 'Palestine Workers' Party').

At its founding Mapai claimed 5,650 members, of whom nearly three thousand were of the Ahdut Ha'Avodah persua-sion and most of the rest from Hapoel Hatzair. Ben-Gurion was the leader of the former and Sprinzak of the latter, though both they and their immediate colleagues were at that time somewhat overshadowed by Haim Arlosoroff (1899–1933), Weizmann's 'favourite son' in Palestine. Arlosoroff had come from the ranks of Hapoel Hatzair but rose to national leader-ship in a meteoric career in which he displayed extraordinary linguistic and diplomatic gifts and, alone amongst the labour leaders, a brilliant grasp of economics. It was the murder of Arlosoroff by an unknown hand[10] in 1933 that brought Ben-Gurion to the pinnacle as leader of Palestine Jewry. The merger enabled Mapai to speak for the vast majority of Histadrut members[11] and to consolidate the power of the organization to yield labour hegemony in the national home. From the mid-'thirties to the present time, without inter-ruption, Mapai has been the dominant factor in the leadership of the Palestine-Israel community.

Ahdut Ha'Avodah held a majority and the platform of the

new party gave emphasis to the socialist symbolism favoured by Ahdut Ha'Avodah. Accordingly Mapai could be regarded as the lineal heir of Ahdut Ha'Avodah. However, Hapoel Hatzair received more than a proportional share in the leadership. As Mapai became responsible for national decisions its concentration on national problems took a toll of socialist commitment, so that in practice the party was increasingly identified in the line of succession to Hapoel Hatzair. This process stimulated the elevation of left-wing dissident groups within the Histadrut to the status of a coherent core of opposition. Controversy within the labour movement now shifted from Hapoel Hatzair's nationalist critique of Ahdut Ha'Avodah to a new socialist critique of Mapai's nationalist policies.

The left-wing opposition to the Mapai leadership came from within the party as well as from the outside. As the Mapai leadership tended more and more to subordinate socialist to nationalist considerations the original (Ahdut Ha'Avodah) advocates of a strong centrally directed Histadrut came increasingly to favour devolution and sought to retain the sinews of economic and political power within the more limited range of Hakibbutz Hameuhad. At the same time the kvutza association and the moshav movement lost their original (Hapoel Hatzair) view, and now displayed greater loyalty to Mapai in its efforts to centralize and consolidate the Histadrut authority which comprised its most important power-base.

Left-wing opposition within the Histadrut was led by Hashomer Hatzair. This movement considered itself to be the ideological centre of Hakibbutz Ha'Artzi and refrained until the mid-'forties from formally constitutioning itself as a political party appealing to the wider public outside the kibbutz.[12] From the time of Mapai's founding Hashomer Hatzair hoped to influence the labour majority by socialist criticism, envisaging itself as the vanguard of a united labour movement if and when Mapai would endorse class warfare and bi-national socialist revolution. Thus in the name of a higher unity Hashomer Hatzair stood aside from the existing framework of unity; it feared that by forming itself as a competitive political party it might weaken its own kibbutz movement and diminish the prospect of the rise of a broad-based revolutionary party. In 1936 it nevertheless formed the 'socialist league' to reach socialists outside the kibbutz, and functioned to all intents and purposes as a political party. By the end of the 'thirties Hashomer Hatzair succeeded in increasing its support within the Histadrut from about eight per cent at the beginning of the decade to nearly twenty per cent. This was more probably a result of immigration derived from its vigorous youth movement in Europe than of its making inroads into the Mapai following.

The rise of the labour movement to control of the national institutions in Palestine was eased by a process of fragmentation in the sphere of middle-class politics simultaneous with the extension of organizational unity on the left. The most thrusting and well-organized right-wing movement in the Zionist Organization was ideologically oriented to the wider international political arena so that by its very nature it was handicapped in the struggle for influence within Palestine. The ultra-nationalist movement led by Jabotinsky in the external Zionist arena formed the Revisionist Party in 1925 to contest the 'practical' Zionism favoured by Weizmann and implemented in large part by the labour movement.

In the revisionist view the pioneer movement in agriculture and the militant trade unions in the towns squandered national resources and diverted energies in pursuit of a socialist chimera which would ultimately place the interests of the Palestine community in conflict with the general aims and interests of the Zionist movement. The vested interests of the Palestinian settlers in the socialist structures they created would come to supersede the overriding goal of working for a Jewish state. A state was the prior condition for Jewish mass immigration and colonization. In the 'twenties the first priority was to force Britain to take full partnership in building the national home with all the resources of state power at its disposal. If Britain could not be compelled to undertake such a role then the Jews must arm and struggle by every means to capture state power. Social aims and theories within the national home were irrelevant in this perspective. Given the middle-class sources of immigration, the economic initiative of the private sector was the backbone of practical construction and class struggle an insidious subversion of the national struggle. From this standpoint the revisionists in Palestine fought the Histadrut

as a cancer on the national body politic. The revisionist analysis
exerted considerable influence within the Zionist movement at
large but did not sufficiently correspond with the perceived
interest of the middle-class settlers as to become the representative voice of the non-labour majority in Palestine.

The crystallization of left-wing opposition within Mapai
first occurred in connection with the relations between the
Histadrut and the rival revisionist trade union. Ben-Gurion
believed that the best way to contain the disruptive labour-
market tactics of the revisionist union would be to restrict its
initiative by incorporating its members within the Histadrut.
It appears that Ben-Gurion and Jabotinsky had developed a
sneaking admiration for each other. They came to an agreement according to which the Histadrut would take over the
revisionist trade union in return for granting the latter a
minority veto over strike action by the Histadrut. This episode
occurred when anti-revisionist sentiment within the Histadrut
was at its peak following the assassination of Arlosoroff. The
Mapai hierarchy was furious with Ben-Gurion, who had
negotiated with Jabotinsky without consulting them, and by
a hairbreadth majority they voted to dishonour the agreement.
A Histadrut-wide referendum on the issue brought the dissident left within Mapai into line with the Hashomer Hatzair
opposition to defeat the proposal.

The small-property interests, including private landowners
in the rural villages and independent artisans and manufacturers in the cities, embraced a majority of the settlers and
formed the characteristic social and economic ethos of the
national home. However, they were organizationally weak and
ideologically inarticulate and proved to be no match for the
idealistic self-conscious labour movement in the competition
for political hegemony. Outside the labour movement the most
effective association was the Farmers' Federation comprising
private agriculture, citriculture and small plantation interests.
The small landowners were often in direct conflict with the
Histadrut when they came under pressure to hire only Jewish
labour. Not unnaturally the private farmers felt unable to bear
this economic burden which was equivalent to their subsi-
dizing out of their own pockets expensive and often in-
experienced Jewish labour. Especially in citriculture which

was geared to the export market, such altruism could be suicidal. Although their resistance to the Histadrut was often effective in the labour-market the farmers failed to form political bridges to the urban middle classes. Like the latter, the farmers were preoccupied in the main with their craft and economic problems and were individualist in outlook. Unlike its counterpart in independent countries the urban middle class in Palestine was not class conscious. Accordingly it was ideologically inarticulate. These groups made little attempt to influence the wider Zionist movement from a Palestinian standpoint, whereas the national goals of the labour movement were shaped in Palestine and from there carried to the external movement. The middle-class interests, ironically, were politically handicapped in that they were not dependent on public funds. The dependency of labour on allocations from the public Zionist treasury for land acquisition and support at every stage of colonization gave the labour parties an immediate interest in controlling or influencing the administration of Zionist revenues and institutions. Thus the labour movement had a vital political motivation quite apart from its ideological commitments and aspirations.

To the extent that they were involved in party politics the propertied interests in Palestine were identified with 'general' Zionism. The mainstream of the international movement organized on territorial lines was designated general-Zionist to reflect the broad sentiment of Jewish nationalism without specific social commitments or ideological discipline. The pressure of the emerging ideological parties cutting across territorial lines gradually influenced general-Zionism to sharpen its position and tighten its organization until by the late 'twenties it came to resemble a political party representative of moderate middle-class views. However, the party remained a loose framework and never achieved the discipline or unity of the other groups. The General-Zionists in Palestine were weakly led and produced few personalities of the calibre of the Histadrut and kibbutz elites. Their 'ethnic' origins, particularly with respect to the main divisions between the oriental Jews, the Polish and the German, were more divisive than in the case of the homogeneous east-European labour movement. The General-Zionist party was split in 1931 into two factions 'A' and 'B', the former favouring many of the policies of the labour movement and the latter opposing them. In Palestine the former group had the support of about a tenth of the population while the more right-wing group embraced about a quarter of the following enjoyed by its associate.

Approximately similar in size to the General-Zionists in Palestine and similarly divided in their attitude to the labour movement were the parties devoted to religious Zionism: Mizrahi (an abbreviation of *Merkaz Ruhani*, 'Spiritual Centre') and Hapoel Hamizrahi, its labour wing. Mizrahi was the first ideological union to form within the Zionist movement at the beginning of the century, in response to the challenge presented by the Zionist extension of secular influence over education in the Jewish communities of eastern Europe. Predominantly middle class in composition the Mizrahi party adopted a posture on social issues resembling that of the General-Zionists, but social and economic issues were a secondary concern subordinate to the aim of establishing a Jewish national home in accordance with traditional religious Judaism. Within Palestine the followers of Mizrahi were mostly of the working class and in 1921 they formed Hapoel Hamizrahi as a rival labour framework to the Histadrut. However, although opposed to the Histadrut labour market policies and to its role in education, Hapoel Hamizrahi co-operated with the secularist labour institutions in many activities. As in the case of the General-Zionists the labour-oriented religious party was the larger of the two wings in Palestine, so that the religious movement also was a weak centre of opposition to the ascendancy of labour.

Descriptions of Israeli politics uniformly stress the importance of the Zionist organization and its structure as the main determinant of the political system of the country and especially of its party politics. Such emphasis, however, misses the importance of the rootedness of the labour parties in Palestinian conditions in contrast with all the other parties which were indeed a product of international Zionist politics. The rise of the labour parties to control of the movement as a whole was assisted by their gaining control of the Palestinian arena at the time when the national home attained a size and importance

134

sufficient to give it the major influence in the world-wide movement.

The Jewish quasi-government

At no time did the British administration succeed in obtaining the support of both Arabs and Jews for any measure designed to promote self-government of the population as a unitary Palestinian polity. In the first years of the regime when the national home was the dominant focus of policy the Zionists tended to support such proposed measures, which in itself sufficed to preclude Arab co-operation. Later, when the appeasement of Arab demands became a decisive determinant of British policy, the Arabs showed a better disposition towards such proposals, whereupon the Zionists withdrew their support. Apart from minor exceptions in local government in 'mixed' Arab-Jewish centres all attempts to establish advisory, legislative or executive organs with joint Arab-Jewish participation failed. As the Jewish national home grew in momentum the difference between the Jewish and Arab sectors of the society widened. Not only through cultural and economic separatism but also in governmental life the gulf between the two populations became more and more marked.

The legally formed role of the World Zionist Organization, and after 1929 of the Jewish Agency, in the direct development of the national home afforded the Zionists significant opportunities for self-government. These were supplemented by the British policy of permitting the Jewish community in its aspect as a religious minority to exercise autonomy in several jurisdictions. The administrative apparatus of the Jewish Agency Executive, formally controlled by the external Zionist movement and its non-Zionist allies, together with the locally controlled political institutions of the settled population in Palestine comprised in effect a Jewish quasi-government. This stood the Zionists in good stead as a foundation for sovereignty when statehood was achieved.

The members of the Jewish Agency Palestine Executive functioned virtually as cabinet ministers at the head of the various administrative departments which comprised the embryonic Jewish quasi-government. Next to the chairmanship occupied by Ben-Gurion from 1935, headship of the political department was generally acknowledged to be the most important position. This department, headed by Moshe Shertok (later Sharett) (1894-1965), represented Zionist opinion to the British authorities in Jerusalem and to the Arabs, and was in effect a shadow foreign ministry. Departments of trade and industry, health, public welfare and education carried out the practical activities indicated by their titles. The selection of immigrants from amongst the applicants at Jewish centres abroad was conducted by the immigration department, and the organization of their settlement on the land by the settlement department. The labour department was concerned with the employment of the immigrants whose livelihood depended on wage-labour. Overall financial responsibility was vested in a treasurer. Since development was closely bound up with the allocation of public revenues this position was influential in shaping social and economic institutions. All the key posts in the quasi-government were filled by Mapai leaders after 1933.[13]

In the nineteenth century the Jewish community had enjoyed a measure of local autonomy within the Ottoman framework. In the first decades of the twentieth century strenuous attempts were made to convene an elected representative organ to speak for the Jewish population of the country as a whole. These efforts culminated in the first meeting in 1920 of the Elected Assembly (*Asefat Hanivharim*) on which were represented about twenty parties or groups, the largest of which was Ahdut Ha'Avodah. The assembly elected a thirty-six-member executive organ, the National Council (*Va'ad Leumi*), empowered to speak for it between meetings. It had been intended that the assembly should meet annually but this proved unwieldy. In fact the National Council met regularly and became the pivotal 'legislative' organ of community government, with its own executive committee varying from six to seventeen members.[14]

After several years of negotiation with the British authorities these organs were granted juridical personality by the Jewish community regulations issued in 1927 under the Religious Communities (Organization) Ordinance of 1926. The Jewish community was recognized as *Knesset Israel* ('Community of Israel') on the basis of voluntary participation through enrolment in an official register maintained by the National Council. The Elected Assembly and the National Council were empowered to conduct autonomous religious courts, to carry out a variety of local government functions and to impose taxes on a voluntary basis. Taxes were raised in proportion to house rents by local community boards (*Kehillot*) constituted under the regulations. The great majority of the Jewish population enrolled in Knesset Israel (with the notable exception of the extremely orthodox groups), thereby consenting to be taxed for the maintenance of services authorized under the regulations. The inner executive of the National Council conducted a network of services which overlapped with those of the Jewish Agency in their range of concern, but were limited mostly to the local level and assimilated within the framework of local government.

The National Council tended to be overshadowed by the Jewish Agency Executive financed from abroad, but as the national home grew in size and importance the controlling influence within the world-wide Zionist movement passed from Jewish leaders abroad to the Palestinians. The interests of the Palestinian settlers gradually became the dynamic source of Zionist policy. The process registered a transition in Zionism, inevitable in the nature of the enterprise, in which from being the creature of Zionist interests abroad bent on advancing their solution to the Jewish problem, the Palestinian settlement by the mid-'thirties became a self-serving community directing its external allies in its own interest, defining their interests in terms of its own. In the context of the mandatory theory which held the Jewish people responsible for the development of the national home and in view of the British doctrine of Palestinism which limited uni-national autonomy to confessional concerns, the transition was not effected by the transfer of Jewish Agency jurisdictions to the local Palestinian organs, but by the accession of Palestinians to control of the Jewish Agency Executive. A chronic shortage of funds in 1932 occasioned the transfer of welfare and education functions from the Jewish Agency to the National Council, but this was an exceptional rather than typical modification of the relations between the two quasi-governmental frameworks. The Palestinian leaders soon straddled both wings of the quasi-government and achieved ascendancy in this manner rather than by bringing development under the control of the community organs. The Jewish Agency was in effect a halfway house absorbing the shift in power from the external to the Palestinian wing of Zionism. The Jewish Agency Palestine Executive became the nerve centre of the world-wide movement in the mid-'thirties at the same time as it became the instrument of the Palestinian leaders.

The route of the labour movement to overall leadership was thus from dominance within the Palestinian organs to leadership of the international movement as a whole. The labour parties were assisted by their firm Palestinian focus while the middle-class interests were handicapped by the complacency induced by their initial dominance in the external movement and their failure to anticipate the transfer of power to the Palestinian wing.

The labour parties were the most energetic early advocates of countrywide Jewish political organization. They were rewarded in the elections to the first unofficial assembly in 1920 with over a third of the seats on that body, as compared to about a tenth of the delegates to the Zionist Congress of 1921. Thus already at that time the labour movement's prominence in local politics compensated somewhat for its weakness in the international Zionist Organization. An oriental ethnic group tended to combine its forces with the orthodox religious interest in the assembly, while the small propertied interests remained fragmented.

The representative structure of the Zionist Organization favoured the Palestinian settlers by mechanical weighting of their votes. They nevertheless remained at a numerical disadvantage throughout the 'twenties. By the early 'thirties, with the growth of the national home and the emergence of coherent political parties cutting across the general-Zionist societies, it became possible through the party system for a minority movement in Palestine to gain control of the world-wide organization and its revenues. While it had been most difficult for the Palestinian community to attain a dominant influence in the world movement as one of its geographic branches, it now became easier for specific groups in Palestine to obtain the leadership of their respective parties throughout the world and thereby through the party system to strive for control of the world movement. The labour movement made the most of this opportunity. Especially after the foundation of Mapai and of a world union of labour-Zionist societies in its wake the initiative of the party leaders in Palestine was secured by party loyalty and discipline abroad. Grassroots organization of Zionist members in Jewish centres abroad was gradually removed from the initiative of their indigenous leaders and passed to the hands of roving party emissaries from Palestine.

In elections to the second meeting of the assembly which was convened in 1925 the two main labour parties maintained their 1920 strength, while in 1931 after Mapai was established it became the dominant party with thirty-one seats out of seventy-one. Mapai was allocated eleven of the seats, then numbering twenty-three in all, on the National Council. Labour strength in the international Zionist Organization grew from less than ten per cent in 1921 to nearly thirty per cent in 1931, and after Mapai had taken hold in the wider arena rose steeply to forty-four per cent in 1933. From that year Mapai maintained its dominance in Palestine and abroad.

CHAPTER 7

THE TRIANGULAR CONFLICT
(1920-39)

*The Zionist movement and the Arabs – the Histadrut and
Arab labour – the Arab Revolt – the Peel Report and
sequel*

The Zionist movement and the Arabs

The early period of Zionist thought and discussion was marked
by almost total ignorance of the country of its devotions. It is
recorded that when the first immigrants came to Palestine in
the 1880s under the auspices of the Lovers of Zion they were
surprised to find the country inhabited. Many youngsters of
the second immigration including Ben-Gurion recoiled in
horror from the social reality they encountered upon arrival
in the land of their dreams.

Ahad Ha'Am in one of his reports from Palestine published
in 1891 pointed out the gravity for Zionism of the Arab
presence but at the time he drew no conclusions and few
echoes. The prevailing concept of political Zionism as elaborated by Herzl was exclusively concerned with the arena of
power politics and imperial diplomacy. Abortive attempts by
Zionist agents to work together with Arab nationalist interests
in Ottoman politics were part of that diplomacy, not part of a
grassroots approach to their neighbours by the new immigrants
in Palestine. Early voices calling for a political appraisal of
what for Zionism became the 'Arab question' were ignored in
the higher counsels of the movement and virtually silenced
within Palestine by the fury of the reaction they evoked. One
such voice was that of an early settler Yitzhak Epstein (1862–
1943) who in 1905 said:[1]

'Among the grave questions linked with the concept of our people's renaissance on its own soil there is one question *which is more weighty than all the others put together*. This is the question of our relations with the Arabs. Our own national aspirations depend upon the correct solution of this question.'

Epstein was given short shrift by his contemporaries who were for the most part contemptuous of the Arabs and associated any tenderness on their behalf with the sort of 'minority psychology' which was typical of European Jewry and which was repudiated by Zionism. Seeing Epstein as one who worried too much what the gentiles thought and too little about the Jewish need, they failed to consider the possible political validity of his thesis. It was indeed some decades before the Zionists came to view the Arab presence in a political light.

Although the Zionist movement outside Palestine subsumed a variety of views of the Arab question, until the late 'twenties there were few differences of view concerning the essential nature and scope of the problem. Zionist analysis was almost invariably a contingent response to specific expressions of Arab hostility such as violent outbursts or diplomatic representations. Hence with few exceptions the thorough analysis of the Zionist-Arab issue did not occupy a central place in Zionist ideology: its consideration was seldom prompted by any spontaneous appreciation of the fact that the country claimed for Jewish national regeneration was inhabited by another people. The Zionist purblindness can only be understood if it is appreciated that the Zionists were convinced of the *absolute* quality of Jewish rights in Palestine, whether argued from the millenial mystique, or British promises, or League of Nations legality or the socialist logic of national construction. This is what gave rise to the peculiar tendency of the Jewish minority, when challenged by the Arabs, to respond by *sincerely* offering the majority *guarantees*. Like the British, the Zionists could neither face the fact nor concede, even when on occasion they could see, that Arab hostility was directed at the Zionist project in its entirety and in principle. The vital illusion be-clouding Zionist contemplation of the Arabs (*and thereby enhancing the effectiveness of the movement*) was that well-timed compromises or well-worded gestures of moderation would, by overcoming piecemeal the particular instances of Arab opposition, suffice to resolve the problem of the relations between the two peoples.

Some Zionist leaders were indeed more exercised than others by the political implications of Arab hostility, some more than others were sensitive to the broad issues of justice that it entailed. Weizmann was greatly concerned about the issue as it increasingly bore on Zionist pursuits in the short term, but he did not think it through to any useful secular conclusion. Although his correspondence reveals an increasing awareness of the major proportions of the issue, Weizmann tended to lead from behind on this score, and it appears that he was overwhelmed by the pressure of the Zionist following with its cruder understanding. Outside Palestine the Zionist approach to the Arabs combined a somewhat flabby if undoubtedly sincere rhetoric of goodwill with an active diplomacy of conciliation on specific issues, neither of which corresponded with the tendencies of Zionist policies within Palestine.

Like other Europeans of the time the Zionist leadership typically took a static view of the Arab presence, not appreciating the effect that Zionism itself, let alone other influences, would have in generating nationalism amongst the Arabs of Palestine. Under Turkish rule Arab nationalist activity had been necessarily clandestine, and this also made it harder to discern. The Zionists thus consistently underestimated the strength of Arab feeling, the depth of Palestinian Arab hostility. To the extent that they did appreciate that Zionism would inevitably have an impact on Arab society, the Zionists unanimously assumed that its likely economic effect in raising the Arab standard of living would be enough to elicit Arab acquiescence. But although mistaken about the intensity of Arab opposition the Zionists were correct in their estimate of its political weakness relative to Zionist potentialities.

The Zionists encountered the Arabs of Palestine at a time when the Arabs lacked the European badge of political worth – a society politically organized as a nation-state. Accordingly any increasing Zionist awareness of the Arab potential tended to be oriented towards the semi-independent regimes of the surrounding Arab countries. With these a form of agreement was often sought and sometimes momentarily reached on the basis of trading Zionist support for their wider aspirations against the promise of unhampered Zionist development in Palestine. Such was the nature of an understanding between Faisal and Weizmann arrived at in 1919 and aborted when Faisal's bid for Arab dominion was defeated. Many Zionists advocated this approach in its ripest form in which a Jewish state would be integrated within a wide Arab confederacy. Such explorations came to naught but on occasions when they involved spokesmen of the neighbouring countries they revealed that the Arab leaderships no less than the Zionists or the British in the same context overlooked the interests of the Palestinian Arabs who had to wrestle with the effects of Zionist development in their daily lives.

The Zionist settlers within Palestine exhibited a more sophisticated response to the Arab question. Much better informed than their external allies they had a more vivid grasp of the scale of the conflict and its intractability. However, they too tended at first to give the issue little attention until the deterioration of British control.

In its vagueness the national home formula exactly suited the circumstances of Zionism in Palestine. Given the relative weakness of Jewish support for Zionism until the defeat of Hitler, the settlers were able to implement only a gradualist development and were under no immediate pressure to think about ultimate aims. These remained vague and ambiguous for the first three decades of the century before the issue of who would succeed to British rule became concrete. As in the case of the Zionists abroad few within Palestine were willing to formulate their final goals, least of all in relation to the existence of the Arab population.[2]

Only by the end of the 'twenties and the early 'thirties did Zionist discussion of relations with the Arabs and the search for agreement with them reach a high pitch of intensity within Palestine. This was occasioned specifically by British proposals for a measure of popular political participation through a legislative council including Arabs and Jews. Exploring possible formulae of representation brought into question the political status of the two populations and the relations between them. At the very crux of the matter, preventing any collaborative discussion, lay the issue of immigration, its very continuation and its scale. As a result of this blockage the intensive diplomacy of the 'thirties was in reality a round of shadow-boxing between the three parties concerned. The internal discussions within the mainstream of official Palestinian Zionism were prompted and governed mainly by tactical considerations. There was sufficient challenge to be found in the matter of persuading the Jews to become Zionists and settle in the country and build its national base.

One movement alone within Zionism placed the Arabs at the centre of the Zionist challenge and pressed indefatigably within the elites of Palestine Jewry for a more profound appraisal of the Arab issue. This was a movement comprised of many strands which came together under a broad doctrinal commitment to 'bi-nationalism'. The historical importance of the movement consisted in its failure. Bi-nationalism was shorthand for the view that since Palestine was occupied by others besides the Jews Zionism must for its own fruition develop in conjunction with the nationalism of the Arabs, in agreement and co-operation with it. The bi-nationalists concurred in the Zionist perception of the Jews as a nation and did not propose to diminish the absolute quality of Jewish rights in the country. Rather it gave these rights boundaries in contrast to the open-ended national-home formula of mainstream Zionism. The Jewish national home must be autonomous in its internal development, as must the Arab, but the two nations must together share in the responsibility for the common fate and interests of the country as a whole. The view was in some respects similar to the British concept of Palestinism as expressed in the Churchill White Paper, though it differed in so far as that rather vague view lent itself to the interpretation that Palestinism envisaged the complete submergence of the two nationalities in a larger whole.

The movement was distinguished by its intellectual quality and by the personal eminence of many of its spokesmen. With the benefit of hindsight, four wars later, it may also be thought that it was distinguished by the accuracy of its essential analysis. For although they could never prove that a different approach to the Arabs would have succeeded in securing their goodwill and bringing the two peoples together, events confirmed their belief that official Zionism was pulling them apart and heading for violence. Most of the Zionist leaders failed to see this while at the same time they accorded overriding importance to the peaceable realization of Zionist aspirations, so that if they had seen the violence implicit in the course of the movement their will might well have been paralysed. Their peaceable intentions contained an element of illusion sustained only by ignoring the patent need for British protection for their activities. As long as Britain held the ring the Zionists need not fight and could believe that violence was in no way implicit in their goals.

Ahad Ha'Am, the major philosopher of Zionism, was a significant precursor of the bi-nationalist movement but in his own lifetime the Arab issue had not crystallized sufficiently within the Zionist mainstream to enable him to develop his views in a form applicable to practical politics. Martin Buber (1879-1965) was an early disciple of Ahad Ha'Am and became a luminary of the bi-nationalist movement. Amongst its many other prestigeful advocates were Judah Magnes (1877-1948), the first head of the Hebrew University, Arthur Ruppin and Norman Bentwich (1883-1971).[3] These men formed their predilections in an essentially liberal humanist tradition but they found their most important ally in the collective membership of Hashomer Hatzair.

Many of the individual exponents of bi-nationalism were of central-European origin and with Hashomer Hatzair they shared the cultural influence of the German youth movement. These temperamentally opposite types were further linked by an analytical thread in their early appreciation of the dangers inherent in the association of Jewish nationalism with British bayonets. The anglophile Weizmann, Ben-Gurion the practitioner of *realpolitik* and Jabotinsky the 'maximalist' were not worried by this aspect of the Zionist predicament. But Buber, Magnes and the others could not countenance the imperial context in which Zionist development was nurtured and thereby ineluctably drawn away from the 'semitic symbiosis' they cherished as a core value of the Jewish national renaissance. Hashomer Hatzair was impervious to this mystical lure but by the route of socialist analysis was equally opposed to attaching Zionist fortunes to British imperial interests, and committed to Arab-Jewish brotherhood as a necessary and minimum condition for Jewish reconstruction. Hashomer Hatzair of course differed fundamentally from the independent bi-nationalists in its estimate of the emerging Arab nationalist movement. For Hashomer Hatzair this movement was reactionary and could not supply the basis for Zionist-Arab co-operation. That would require the activation of the Arab masses in a joint Jewish-Arab socialist movement. The liberal independent bi-nationalists by contrast regarded Arab nationalism as the representative and progressive Arab movement with which Zionism must find a *rapprochement*. In spite of this basic difference in their world view and their particular understanding of local history, Hashomer Hatzair and the independent bi-nationalists were able to co-operate occasionally in their advocacy of bi-nationalism and later also managed to come together in a common organizational framework.

The first organized expression of the bi-nationalist movement was Brit Shalom ('Peace Alliance'), founded in 1925 on the initiative of Ruppin to propagate the better understanding of Arab aspirations within the Zionist movement at large and within Palestine in particular. The group failed to attract an active following of more than two hundred. The spokesmen of Brit Shalom emphasized that bi-nationalism was not an ideology in the sense of a blueprint for the future but rather a description of the existing Palestine reality that Zionism must grasp. By the end of the 'twenties, long before the Zionist movement was willing to formulate definitive political goals in relation to the Arabs and British rule, Brit Shalom had moved from merely advocating study of the Arab question to endorsing specific political aims in regard to the constitution and government of Palestine. The essential issue between Brit Shalom and the Zionist majority concerned the very terms of Jewish national life. The bi-nationalists were unwilling to contemplate terms unacceptable to the Arabs who lived in the country as of right. They believed that if Zionism would internalize and fully accept the goal of Jewish-Arab co-operation in a bi-national polity approximately along the lines adumbrated in the Churchill White Paper then the two peoples would live in peace and the Jewish national home would be integrated within its oriental environment. In their view a

Jewish majority, or Jewish sovereignty, were misleading and illusory targets. The Zionists should therefore officially renounce the aspiration to majority status, which was in any case unattainable, a phantom of propaganda which would mislead the movement into imperialism and compel it to develop all the vices of a warlike nation.[4]

The Zionist majority regarded these views as bordering on the treasonable. Although in the absence of a sizeable Jewish population in Palestine the Zionist movement could not seriously contemplate statehood or sovereignty as a reasonable target it was nevertheless bemused by the myth of sovereignty, and however unrealistic its reluctance it was quite unwilling to rule out Jewish sovereignty from the bounds of future possibility. If the Zionists were few who would in principle preclude Jewish statehood there were fewer who would in principle accept any ceiling on Jewish immigration even though the prospect of a Jewish majority was as unrealistic as it appeared and as events proved it to be. Even some of the independent supporters of Brit Shalom were unwilling to rule out an eventual Jewish majority. This was also far removed from the concept of bi-nationalism entertained by the Marxian socialist supporters of the movement. Typical Zionist feeling on the matter was expressed by Ben-Gurion as early as 1925 in replying to a delegation of Brit Shalom enthusiasts who discussed bi-nationalism with him as head of the Histadrut:[5]

'The formula you have proposed does not say anything, it only confuses and therefore damages us without giving anything to the Arabs. Is it not sufficient that we have one formula, "national home", the meaning of which no one knows, without you adding a second formula which says nothing? A bi-national state?

What does the formula bi-national state mean? Sprinzak says we do not wish to be a majority, but to be many. What is many? A hundred thousand? A hundred and fifty thousand? Many in relation to whom, to the Arab population in Palestine or the Jewish population abroad? ... I have an Arab problem only on a Zionist basis, when I want to solve in Palestine the problem of the Jewish people, that is to say to concentrate it in Palestine and make it a free people in its land. Apart from this Zionist basis there is no Arab problem in Palestine but a Jewish problem, just as there is a Jewish problem in all the countries of the dispersion including those in which we are "many" . . . this expression "many" is just an evasion of the central and principal problem of Zionism [the promotion of large-scale Jewish immigration] and we cannot educate the public in this way. . . .'

And yet in the late 'twenties in the context of the British proposals for the participation of Jews and Arabs in the legislative process Ben-Gurion was himself exploring the constitutional possibilities of bi-nationalism. Disturbed by the Arab riots of 1929 and by the British response which displayed a propensity to appease the Arabs at the expense of the national home, Ben-Gurion put before his colleagues a detailed draft constitution along federal lines. His proposal was conciliatory in tone but was aimed not so much at soothing the Arabs as at detaching from the British administration a portion of its executive power and placing it in the jurisdiction of the two peoples. He hoped that such an objective might afford sufficient common ground to make possible a joint effort of Jews and Arabs. It was in this context that he undertook with the help of Magnes a round of personal diplomacy in direct discussions with Arab leaders during 1934. If he had any doubt until then these meetings confirmed his conviction that peaceful relations with the Arabs in their existing political arrangements would be unattainable. The issue of immigration was an absolute barrier. In January 1935 Ben-Gurion explained the absolute importance of immigration to the fulfillment of Zionism, taking it beyond the reach of negotiation:[6]

'The disaster which has befallen German Jewry is not limited to Germany alone. Hitler's regime places the entire Jewish people in danger, and not the Jewish people alone. Hitlerite Germany is in conflict not only with the Jewish people. Hitler's regime cannot long survive without a war of revenge against France, Poland, Czechoslovakia and the other neighbouring countries with German communities, and against Soviet Russia. Germany will not go to war today for she is not ready, but she is preparing for the morrow. I do not wish to prophesy the future but so far as it is possible to see what is afoot there is no doubt that we now stand before the danger of war not less than before 1914, and the war which will break out this time, if it does, will be greater in its destruction and its horrors than the last war. The Jewish people is not a world factor with the ability to prevent or delay this danger or to weaken or diminish it. But there is one corner of the world in which we are a principal factor if not yet the decisive one and this corner determines our whole national future as a people. What will be our strength and our weight in this corner on the day of judgement when the great world disaster will begin? Who knows, perhaps only four or five years, if not less, stand between us and that awful day. In this period of time we must double our numbers, for the size of the Jewish population on that day may determine our fate at the post-war settlement.'

In the wake of Ben-Gurion's draft constitution and other proposals the labour movement refined its doctrinal culture to accommodate the Arab question, but most of its members did not put the issue in the forefront of their thinking. The diplomatic and verbal output of Ben-Gurion on this question consumed much time and print but when placed in the context of his monumental prolixity it assumed only minor importance. His attempts to grapple with the question analytically for some thirty years before he was vested with the leadership of Palestine Jewry revealed a fertile political imagination, a deep intuitive grasp of the essential structure of the conflict and a fleeting half-wish that he could be free to lead the Arabs in their need. He never lapsed into the pious rhetorical vein to which the Weizmann circle in the external Zionist arena was susceptible, but always stressed his view that Arab opposition was just and only to be expected. In common with other settlers and in contrast to the external Zionist leaders Ben-Gurion grasped the essential fundamentalism of Arab enmity. Years ahead of the others he realized that this portended the settlement of Zionist claims by violent means. After his election to the leadership in 1935 Ben-Gurion directed the movement in Palestine on its collision course well understanding the risks incurred while most of his colleagues for years continued to believe that a peaceable resolution of the conflict might be possible. There is no reason to doubt the sincerity of Ben-Gurion's conciliatory diplomacy, but so long as it was rebuffed by the Arabs he never allowed it to interfere with the ripening of the strategy by which he was taking Zionist development in a direction that would carry it beyond the range of negotiable issues.

In the meantime his colleagues in the labour movement continued to consider essentially bi-nationalist possibilities as an approach to the immediate challenges of colonial politics. For the official leadership bi-nationalism was mainly of tactical interest and it fell short of adoption as a framework for terminal goals. As, for its different reasons, the official leadership thus took up the cause Brit Shalom suffered many defections and faded from the scene in 1933.

Ruppin himself parted company with the bi-nationalists on grounds of loyalty to Zionism when he came to the conclusion that the position of the Arabs had become so strong that voluntary concessions to Zionism could no longer be expected of them. He therefore considered that the problem had become incapable of peaceable resolution since a Zionism at the mercy of the Arab majority would fail to maintain its Jewish support abroad and would become a 'Zionism without Zionists'. He concluded that Zionism would henceforth be locked in perpetual war with the Arabs.[7]

With the outbreak of the Arab revolt in 1936 the bi-nationalist movement acquired a new lease amongst the liberal intellectuals. Once again prominent individuals of great prestige lent their energies to the movement for an agreement with the Arabs and entered into personal diplomacy to this end. But now in the new circumstances created by the Arab revolt and the impending British inquiry commission, in which Jewish Agency officials were involved in more delicate and intense political manoeuvering than ever before, there was great reluctance on the part of the bi-nationalists to incur the odium that had fallen on Brit Shalom as an 'irresponsible' factor in Zionist diplomacy. Accordingly they subordinated their initiative to the guidance or indirect control of the

Agency which gave lip-service to their aims but was itself acting on different principles. These were summed up by Ben-Gurion:[8] 'We need an agreement with the Arabs, but not in order to create peace in the country. Peace is indeed vital for us – a country cannot be built in a state of permanent war. But for us peace is only a means. Our aim is the complete and absolute fulfillment of Zionism. It is only for this that we need an agreement.' Ben-Gurion consistently pointed out that the Arab response to Zionist claims and particularly immigration – the crux of the conflict – was perfectly understandable, that the conflict was irreconcilable from a Zionist standpoint, and that its ultimate resolution would ensue only from an Arab appraisal of Zionist power which must therefore be maximized in every possible way. It is probable that most of his colleagues understood his words as stirring rhetoric to strengthen their will rather than as an analysis which incorporated the probability of major violence. At no time did the Palestine Zionists as a whole recognize a need to seek the acquiescence of the Palestine Arabs by direct advocacy and persuasion. It is therefore impossible to judge whether had they done so at the outset the Arab attitude might have been different. In the event the obdurate enmity of the Arab official class reinforced, and for many justified, the Zionist neglect. As for the Arab masses as a political factor, most Zionists were quite willing to ignore them considering the intrinsic difficulty of apprehending the wishes or interests of an illiterate peasantry trapped in the struggle for subsistence and at the mercy of its economic and spiritual masters. Only the socialists entertained any interest in the peasantry and saw the resolution of Arab-Zionist conflict as bound up with the fate of the Arab masses. Only the socialist wing of Palestinian Jewry were confident that their vision yielded the appropriate prescriptions corresponding to the interests of the peasantry. But the implementation of these prescriptions involved the labour-Zionists in direct conflict with the peasantry. By the time the labour movement came to power within Palestine-Zionism in the mid-'thirties that conflict had already dissipated whatever potential there might have been for leading the Arab masses along socialist lines.

The Histadrut and Arab labour

The Histadrut's struggle with the Arab problem, like that of other Zionist groups, came to the forefront of its consciousness in pace with the disintegration of the national home policy. As Zionism began to be concerned with the practical issue of succession to the mandate, theories of Jewish-Arab relations became an important political dividing line within the movement as a whole, within the Palestine community and within the Histadrut itself.

Unlike other Zionist groups the Histadrut policy-makers were subject to a double burden since their Arab ideologies had to answer to socialist as well as nationalist, moral and strategic principles. To maintain any semblance of relevance socialist doctrine had to address itself to the national problem and offer some guidance for its resolution. Yet an additional dilemma imposed itself upon the Histadrut theoreticians, for not only did its Zionist analysis of the Arab issue have to be synthesized with the socialist view but it must also cope with the specific question of the Arab worker in the context of the myth of labour solidarity.

The first crucial struggle of organized Jewish labour in Palestine had been for the right to work. It is not likely that the labour pioneers ever considered the Arab employer as a potential source of work or that Arab employers ever considered employing immigrant Jewish labour. The Arab economy was almost entirely agrarian, without the intrinsic developmental momentum that would have been necessary to absorb a new labour force. 'Conquest of labour' therefore meant the right of Jewish workers to be employed by Jewish employers, most of whom in the first two decades of the century had been concentrated in plantations institutionally linked to the Arab economy. Looking forward to the mass immigration of Jews with 'western' cultural needs it seemed clear to the visionaries of the second immigration that the Jewish national future would of necessity be founded on a modern economy geared to development and the creation of new job opportunities on a large scale.

With the failure of the pioneers to influence the habits of the old Jewish employers in agriculture the 'conquest' strategy was reformulated as a movement for settlement on the land, on the basis of co-operation and mutual aid. As public investment capital from external Jewish sources began to accumulate, its trustees agreed with the labour pioneers that Jewish labour alone could realize the national value of the investment and provide a sound economic and social basis for the national home. On the basis of this ideological consensus was formed the partnership between external public capital and the labour movement which made possible extensive colonization. While land settlement proceeded the Jewish workers continued the struggle for job positions in the Jewish private sector in the towns. Although they had made little headway with the old planters they did succeed, by appealing to national sentiment, in making some inroads among the entrepreneurs who began to arrive in the mid-'twenties. The Histadrut saw no reason to modify its nationalist doctrine in application to private as distinct from public Jewish capital since it considered the conditions providing security for private investment to be a product of the national endeavour underpinned by public investment. 'However private his capital, a settler can only possess his land by grace of Zionism and its works,' asserted Ben-Gurion. The labour movement therefore opposed as a parasite any employers who failed to acknowledge their indebtedness to the nation by hiring Jewish workers. Foremost among his national obligations the private entrepreneur must play an economic role assisting the absorption of Jewish immigrants, and for this reason the Jewish economy had to be insulated from the depressed Levantine environment, rather than seek to exploit it.

Extension of the Histadrut's foothold in the labour market was favoured by the demand for skills that were lacking in the Arab economy, but it made its greatest advances as a result of its high degree of organization and militancy. By the early 'thirties the Histadrut unions succeeded in gaining control of a large segment of the labour market through the enforcement of hiring rules administered by a network of union-controlled labour exchanges. Once this wedge was firmly lodged the demand was increasingly heard that *only* Jewish labour be hired, and this soon became the official Histadrut doctrine. In a situation in which Arabs employed Arabs alone it seemed not unreasonable to the labour leaders to claim from Jewish employers that they should hire Jews alone.

It is probable that the entrepreneurs of Jewish nationalism, if they thought about it at all, assumed that the Arab economy would be carried forward by Jewish dynamism. Many Zionist entrepreneurs shared the Histadrut view that a normal occupational structure achieved by Jewish adaptation to the manual labouring trades was a basic requisite of national construction. But together with a probable majority of entrepreneurs who were innocent of such concerns, they did not in principle exclude Arab labour from a role in development. On the contrary, especially in the early years when 'Palestinism' was a live prospect, many private Jewish employers elevated the notion of Arab employment alongside Jewish to an enlightened principle of non-discrimination. A number of British companies and the administration itself whether in the name of 'Palestinism' or on more general grounds, vigorously practised 'mixed' employment.

The Histadrut thus found itself in the paradoxical position of defending what appeared to be a reactionary doctrine from what appeared to be a liberal critique by the political right wing. The embarrassment of the Histadrut leadership in this connection was not eased by the repudiation of its labour-market policies on socialist grounds by the left-wing opposition within the movement. The socialism of the Mapai leadership did not follow the logic of Borochov to its conclusion in bi-nationalism, as on the left. Although the nationalist rationale of its policy had some persuasive influence on external opponents and was in any case well supported by its institutional power, the Histadrut also needed a socialist rationale to requite its own moral sense and to ward off the claim of its own left to sole proprietorship of the socialist conscience of the movement.

The broad outline of the socialist reasoning endorsed by the Histadrut shared with its nationalist doctrine the polemical advantages accruing from plausibility and simplicity. Far from reflecting an enlightened attitude, it was asserted, the penchant for Arab labour merely signified the capitalist exploitative urge. Arab workers were but a convenient tool to hold down the wage level. In the view of the Histadrut leaders employers were using the issue as a screen for opposition to the principle of organized labour as such, as a means of undermining the power of the labour movement. Not all employers were as free of hypocrisy as the person quoted by Ben-Gurion:[9]

'... lots of Jews will come to work here, we can dispense with the peculiar [organized] kind: the plain, ordinary worker will adjust to the rigid law of husbandry and abate his standards: the main thing is to prepare the kind of worker overseas in advance, and fight the Histadrut to a standstill.'

The majority of employers with whom the Histadrut was locked in combat used the liberal clichés to which the Arab issue lent itself, in order to wage the Jewish class struggle. By linking their policy to the internal Jewish class struggle in this way the Histadrut leaders were able to enhance its socialist respectability in their debate with the left.

The discrimination practised by the Histadrut, it was asserted, was not based on race or religion but on the need to combat feudalist exploitation. The struggle for Jewish job positions was the avenue to dignity for Arab and Jewish workers alike. In the long term this was the way to socialist victory over serfdom. Rather than allow cheap Arab labour to depress his standards, the organized Jewish worker from the bastion of secure employment would proceed to raise the Arab worker to his standard. Equal wages for Arab and Jewish workers were mandatory, but they must be equal to the wages of the Jewish worker, achieved through organization. The principles of non-discrimination and equality were stressed only to conceal the fact that the wages offered were in fact too low to support the Jewish worker. The Jewish economy must therefore be insulated from the threat of devaluation posed by the Arab labour supply until such time as Arab standards rose to equal the Jewish. Of course the Jewish labour movement must in the meantime give every assistance to the Arab worker to organize and raise his standards by means of militant trade-unionism within his own economic sector.

As socialists the Histadrut leaders believed that none of the Jewish vantage points were taken at the expense of the Arab masses. The issue was not whether the Jews had a right to take existing jobs from Arab workers but whether they had an obligation to share with Arab workers the new opportunities created by Jewish investment. There could be no obligation to share the revenue of Jewish national effort with unorganized workers who displayed no solidarity with that effort but merely sought to undermine its goals. First the Arab worker must become identified with the labour movement, as eventually he would be. As Ben-Gurion argued:[10]

'The Arab worker, too, whom unthinking employers regard as a robot, will throw off his torpor and enter into the ranks of combatant labour, he too will behold the vision of his freedom ... Tomorrow or the next day Arab labour will echo the demand, for who is so shortsighted as to think that the Arab will meekly consent to be robbed forever ...?'

As for the few Arab workers who were indeed organized and devoted to trade union ideals, the Histadrut recommended that they concentrate on the organization of their own sector, to which they alone had access, until it ceased to be a lever for lowering Jewish wages. When the Arab wage-level rose to that of the Jews then the barriers would be removed and work freely allocated.[11]

'The non-Jewish labour market is surrounded by a high wall against the Jewish worker. The wall has a queer character: it does not allow the Jewish worker to penetrate inward, but does not cease propelling to the Jewish economy masses of Arab workers. In this situation the Jewish worker cannot trifle with the problem of who erected these walls, or whether the Arab worker is responsible for them ... he has no choice but to surround himself with a protective wall.'

As the Histadrut leaders frequently pointed out, although the Arab in Palestine was for the most part indigenous while the Jew was an immigrant, the Jewish worker was nevertheless in a position comparable to that in other countries of the indigenous organized worker protecting his standards against the incursion of unorganized immigrant labour. Thus, starting from the nationalist imperative of creating jobs for Jewish immigrants, the Histadrut shifted to the socialist ground of insistence upon organized labour and then, to deal with the case of organized Arab labour, reverted to the nationalist rationale now couched in socialist language.

Its historical priority in the evolution of labour ideology suggests that the nationalist consideration was the basic determinant of the Histadrut Arab policy. But as socialists the Histadrut leaders preferred to look on the issue as a social rather than a national conflict. In this way they could reassure themselves that recurrent violent expressions of Arab resentment were not due to incompatibility between Zionism and Arab nationalism. Arab aspirations, they could tell themselves, were not hampered by Zionism but by the adverse Arab political and social structure. Socialist reasoning selected the torpor of Arab society and its ruling class as the source of Arab-Jewish conflict. It was a small group of landowners, usurers and clergy that stood in the way of the Arab masses. The moment their overlords were overthrown the Arab masses would realize that Zionism and Arab nationalism could co-operate in peace and progress. This theory was widely diffused throughout the Zionist movement but it had a special value for the labour-Zionists. By beclouding the essentially nationalist élan of their own programme their socialist reasoning enabled them to evade the logical conclusion that the Arab opposition could also be interpreted in national terms, as incipient nationalism. Incidents of co-operation with Arab peasants or workers and occasionally with intellectuals were exaggerated out of all proportion. While the socialist analysis of Arab society was largely valid it led its exponents to the false conclusion that international conflict need not arise. If the energetic anti-Zionism of the Arab intellectuals seemed to challenge the socialist assumption that education would wash the contours of hatred from the visage of the Arab peasant, this could only be because the Arab intelligentsia was non-proletarian, tied by threads of kinship to the ruling class. The empirical vigour of the socialist doctrine blinded the Histadrut leaders to the probability that education would not dispel the illiterate's resentment of Zionism but would enable him to express it more articulately.

The most sensitive element in the socialist justification of the Histadrut's Arab policy was the fact that, while its theoretical long-term target was the Arab overlord, the brunt of its implementation fell upon the Arab worker. This was so in the double sense that the Arab worker was the short-term victim of the labour-market struggle and also in that he was elected by circumstances to the task of conducting a revolution within the Arab economy. Some discomfort was felt within the Histadrut at the vulnerability of the Arab workers. Embarrassment was heightened when left-wing critics within the Histadrut seized this issue and accused the leadership of striking the underdog. The Histadrut could but try to assist the Arab worker in his struggle but it lacked access to the Arab sphere, not least on account of the language barrier. The difficulties of the leadership on this score were augmented by the apathy of the rank and file membership of the Histadrut, who saw the Arab question as a rather boring foreign issue.

The resolutions passed by the founding convention of the Histadrut in 1920 made no reference to the Arabs. The issue was seen by the pioneers as a secondary aspect of their struggle with the Jewish planters. The first policy challenge to the labour-Zionists in this connection came with the 'mixed' employment of Arabs and Jews in the communications services maintained by the British administration. The Jewish union of railway, post and telegraph workers associated with the Histadrut was defeated in 1925 in its attempts to bring the Arabs into line in joint efforts for better wages and conditions. On the basis of this experience the Histadrut convention in 1927 resolved to establish the Palestine Labour League for joint organization of Jews and Arabs in the trade union sphere. The league was conceived as an avenue of co-operation through which the Histadrut could help the Arab workers in the Arab economy while also resisting the downward pressure of Arab labour on wage levels in the 'mixed' economy. The issue of joint organization in the Jewish economy was at that time evaded, eventually to be superseded by the absolute doctrine of exclusive Jewish labour. It was hoped that as long as national autonomy within the league was honoured it might be possible to develop a common language of bread-and-butter unionism. The hope was not vindicated. The original concept of the league as a federation of Jewish and Arab unions on a large scale was soon reduced to a federation of all-Arab unions linked organizationally to the Histadrut Executive Committee. The attraction of the Histadrut health services drew some Arabs into the association and the league registered some minor successes in co-operation but its attainments on the whole fell short of expectation. Membership never rose above one per cent of Arab workers.

There can be little doubt that the nationalist labour-market policies of the Histadrut aggravated Jewish-Arab relations while accentuating the national nature of the conflict. At the same time it is equally certain that these policies procured a firm economic foundation for the national home, precluding its dependency on colonial exploitation. Whatever the political cost of these policies and whatever may have been the possible alternatives at any time, it was the concrete impact of the Histadrut and its vice-like grip on the labour market that eventually determined the political terms upon which the national home would be translated into a sovereign state.

The Arab Revolt

The Palestine Arabs were slow to react to the British intrusion. The nationalist movement made its first appearance at the end of the war as an offshoot of the more advanced pan-Arab movement led from Damascus. The country was under military rule. The military administration, itself out of sympathy with London's Zionist policy, was less than frank with the population about British intentions.

An Arab riot in April 1920 in which six Jews and six Arabs were killed was local in scale and did not represent an organized nationalist response. Following the installation in Palestine of Samuel's civil administration in 1920 and the defeat in Damascus of Faisal's bid for Arab leadership, the nationalist movement became a Palestine-centred force with the founding at Haifa of the Palestine Arab Congress and the Arab Executive. The Congress called for British withdrawal and the establishment of an independent representative Arab government to be elected by Arabic-speaking residents who had been in the country before 1914.

A major riot broke out in May 1921 in which nearly a hundred Jews and Arabs were killed (the latter mostly by

British troops) and over two hundred wounded. This was followed by an official inquiry[12] and an increase in the British garrison, which sufficed to hold the peace for some years. The inquiry established the fact of Arab hostility to Jewish immigration and was followed by the Churchill White Paper and other gestures calculated to subdue Arab fears.

Although it used democratic Wilsonian rhetoric it was soon clear that the Congress was an instrument of the wealthy landowners and particularly the Husaini family headed by Musa Kazim Pasha (1850-1934) and the Mufti of Jerusalem and president of the Supreme Muslim Council, Hajj Amin. For several years the movement was torn by internal dissension as the Nashashibi clan struggled to depose the Husaini faction. The Husaini triumphed towards the end of the 'twenties and consolidated the Congress as virtually a personal retinue of Hajj Amin. The period of Arab dissension coincided with Weizmann's quest to broaden Jewish support for the national home by including non-Zionists in the leadership of the movement, a period marked by a relatively slow pace of Jewish immigration and many setbacks in economic development. Accordingly Arab anti-Zionism appeared quiescent. The subsequent period of Hajj Amin's ascendancy coincided with the formation of the enlarged Jewish Agency to the accompaniment of fierce opposition in the name of greater militancy led by Jabotinsky. This occasioned the revival of Arab opposition.

A major eruption of violence in 1929 set the stage for a trial of strength between Arab and Zionist diplomacy. A riot originating in a tawdry dispute over religious rights at the 'western wall' (a Jewish holy place which formed part of the Muslim *Haram as-Sharif* comprising the Dome of the Rock and the mosque of El-Aksa) spread throughout the country in a pattern of Arab massacre of Jewish settlements which had all the hallmarks of a planned action. Some 250 Jews and Arabs were killed and over 500 wounded. Once again as in 1921 the Arab casualties resulted from British police action and almost matched those of the Jews. The Shaw commission and the Hope Simpson commission were immediately sent from London to investigate the disturbances and made recommendations, particularly in regard to immigration and land transfers, which were decidedly anti-Zionist and favourable to the Arabs. The colonial secretary accepted these and incorporated them in the Passfield White Paper of 1930 only to meet a furore of opposition within parliament and a barrage of effective diplomacy and propaganda mounted by Weizmann and other leading Zionists. As a result Passfield retracted and early in 1931 the government reaffirmed that its national home policy remained unchanged. Although Weizmann's diplomacy won the day for the Zionists, the Arabs now had every reason to assume from the tenor of the Shaw-Hope Simpson-Passfield findings that Britain could be budged.

In the early 'thirties with the rapid increase in Jewish immigration the Arab national movement grew and a number of political 'parties' emerged alongside the Congress contending for leadership of the population. These came together at the end of 1935 in an attempt to establish unified representation in dealings with the British authorities.

By the beginning of 1936 events in Europe had begun to press more directly on Palestine politics than heretofore. The plight of the Jews in Europe galvanized Zionism into a new sense of urgency in which diplomatic considerations and ideological niceties lapsed into secondary status. After the peak of immigration in 1935 the Arabs began to see a ripe opportunity in Britain's concern for regional security as axis propaganda reached a high pitch and the threat of war loomed. Nationalism in the neighbouring countries had only recently shown that Britain could be made to succumb to pressure and the Palestine Arabs became more militant. The political 'parties' now articulated grassroots nationalism on the local level throughout the country and supplanted the Congress as the forum of Arab leadership. In April 1936 the parties succeeded in suspending their rivalries and came together in a new united executive (still dominated by Hajj Amin), the Arab Higher Committee, which immediately issued a call for a general strike. This was to be continued until the administration put a stop to Zionist immigration, forbade land transfers from Arabs to Jews and also met the wider nationalist demand for independence. The administration was disposed to suspend immigration pending further inquiry but under Zionist pressure agreed to a limited entry under the labour schedule in May. The Arabs then instituted an economic boycott of the Jewish sector and sporadic violence increased in volume. This soon mushroomed into widespread rebellion with guerilla groups aided by volunteers from neighbouring countries mounting a persistent campaign of sabotage, pillage and terror aimed at Jewish settlements and British installations and also engaging British troops. The High Commissioner Wauchope acted at first with restraint although he made it very clear that the administration would not negotiate under duress and would suppress the revolt. With British consent the Jews were enabled to organize their self-defence. This was conducted by the Zionist leadership on a strictly defensive basis avoiding provocation or retaliation, so that the issue was confined more or less to the basic Arab-British confrontation rather than becoming a general showdown between Arabs and Jews.

Abdullah of Transjordan and Nuri Said of Iraq, whose diplomacy at that time was bent upon improving relations with Britain in the interest of their own regimes, attempted to mediate with the Arab Higher Committee, but to no avail. The Jewish Agency refused Nuri's plea to agree to a temporary suspension of immigration as a gesture of goodwill. The crisis worsened and the London government announced the delay of its prospective Royal Commission enquiry until the disorders ended. British troops were increased to 20,000 and the emergency powers of the High Commissioner enlarged. The strike and revolt were quickly broken, unable to withstand British military force. Since the Jewish economy did not depend to any great extent on the Arab sector the Arab population bore the brunt of economic losses due to the strike, and unemployment spread. Political unity within the Higher Committee began to falter and the revolt was already virtually broken when on 11 October the Higher Committee was enabled to save face by accepting a joint plea from the rulers of Iraq, Saudi Arabia, Yemen and Transjordan that they call off the revolt and rely on British good intentions and justice. The Royal Commission headed by Earl Peel, a former Secretary of State for India, came to Palestine in November 1936 and conducted its investigation until the end of January 1937. There was a lull in violence until the publication of the Peel Report in summer 1937. The commission recommended partition of Palestine.

The Arab revolt was immediately revived and within a short time reached the same pitch of violence as in the previous year. On 30 September the administration acquired new powers. The Higher Committee was disbanded and most of its leaders imprisoned or deported. Hajj Amin was deposed from the presidency of the Supreme Muslim Council and fled to Lebanon, from where he continued to direct the revolt. Guerilla activity increased and was now directed as much against Arab dissidents as against British installations. Violence and disorder continued until by the summer of 1938 British control of the countryside was virtually lost. The crisis was intensified in the summer of 1938 by the emergence of a Jewish terrorist group following a policy of retaliation in disregard of the official Zionist leadership. By this time the London government had come to the conclusion that partition was unworkable and abandoned the policy. In October 1938 full military force was brought to bear and the revolt was once again crushed. Thereafter it continued intermittently but in the form of blood feuds within the Arab population. As a political movement the revolt was virtually ended early in 1939 before the outbreak of the world war.

The year 1936 was a decisive turning point in the Palestine conflict. The Arab revolt and its failure created the conditions for the ultimate success of Zionism. Under Hajj Amin's rule the Arabs had failed to mobilize a constructive movement directing the energies of the people towards attainable political goals. The mufti could not have chosen a worse time to challenge British rule by violent means. With but a modicum of political insight he might have realized that Britain's concern for regional security did indeed afford an opportunity to wring concessions, as the Zionists feared it would, but that a violent confrontation was bound to be unacceptable to Britain in these very circumstances. The partition proposal as an admission of the unworkability of the mandate followed by the British conclusion that partition too was unworkable were indeed political victories for Arab nationalism, but they were victories whose fruits were reaped by the Zionists. In the revolt the Arabs lost some three to five thousand killed (about a quarter of these victims of Arab intimidation of dissidents), their leadership was decimated (in large part by Husaini efforts to eliminate rivals), their economy was ruined and plunged into the deepest depression, and their spirit was crushed. The Palestine Arabs henceforward were a negligible political factor. The strike and disorder strengthened the Jewish economy, for example by the opening of Tel Aviv harbour to replace strike-bound Jaffa. It also enabled the Jews for the first time, with British acquiescence, to arm themselves and greatly to raise their level of military training and preparedness. In the 'forties it was the Zionists who were able to challenge British rule *after* Britain was exhausted by the world war and engaged in the liquidation of its empire.

The Peel Report and sequel

The terms of reference of the Peel Commission were to investigate the causes of the disturbances in Palestine and the performance of the administration in executing the mandate. The Peel Report was an exhaustive review and analysis of the Palestine conflict from the mandatory perspective. The report found that Arab grievances were not legitimate under the terms of the mandate but that the mandatory obligations to the Jews could only be fulfilled by repression of the Arabs, and that therefore the mandate was unworkable.

As immediate 'palliatives' the report recommended restriction of the area of Jewish settlement and the regulation of immigration by 'political, social and psychological as well as economic considerations'. A ceiling of 12,000 immigrants per year should be imposed immediately and remain in force for at least five years. The report considered these palliatives necessary to contain the conflict but did not believe them capable of solving the root problem. For this it would be necessary to abrogate the mandatory basis of government. The report recommended this and proposed the partition of the country into a sovereign Jewish state, an Arab state to be joined with Transjordan, and British mandatory zones comprising the main holy places and seaports. The Jewish state would occupy about a fifth of the country. Pending the transfer of authority Jews would not be allowed to buy land in the territory of the prospective Arab state.

The London government was less than enthusiastic about

Peel's findings but initially it endorsed the recommendations and despatched the Woodhead Commission to Palestine to explore the practical problems of partition and draft a detailed blueprint. In the meantime the palliative approach was put into operation by the enactment of an amendment to the immigration ordinance authorizing the imposition of a political ceiling on immigration at the discretion of the high commissioner. The Permanent Mandates Commission of the League of Nations was very cool towards partition but was willing to have the question further explored. The Woodhead Partition Commission reported in November 1938 refuting in effect the practicability of partition and London accepted this with alacrity, having already apparently come to a similar conclusion. Instead the Colonial Office announced that it would convene an Arab-Zionist conference in London.

Just as the Arab revolt coincided with the extension of Britain's strategic perspective in the light of European events, so these events for the first time drew the neighbouring Arab regimes actively into the Palestine issue. The German-Italian axis for the first time presented a European challenge to British hegemony in the Arab world and thereby gave the Arab regimes leverage against British dominion. The pace of agitation on behalf of the Palestine Arabs was set by the opposition nationalist groups in the surrounding countries rather than by the established regimes, but these latter were increasingly drawn into the struggle by the pressure. In convening the London conference in February 1939 Britain acknowledged the primacy of its broader middle-east concern by inviting the representatives of the Arab states to participate in the discussions of Palestine. This proved to be a fateful new departure both for the Zionists and the Palestine Arabs, rather to the detriment of the latter. Henceforth the neighbouring Arab regimes became contenders for the Palestine succession rather than effective exponents of Palestine Arab interests.

The conferences between Britain and the Arabs on the one hand and Britain and the Zionists on the other failed to find any basis of agreement, whereupon the London government determined to impose a solution. This was outlined by the Macdonald White Paper issued in May 1939. From the British standpoint the White Paper went as far as possible towards meeting the Arab claims. The White Paper announced that the government would now prepare the ground for the establishment of self-government in which Arabs would remain the overwhelming majority but in which the Jews as a community would share in the exercise of authority. Jewish immigration would be limited to a total of seventy-five thousand over the next five years and thereafter be subject to Arab consent. Land sales by Arabs to the Zionists would be regulated in certain areas and prohibited in others. In effect the White Paper terminated British promotion of the national home. From a legalistic standpoint it could be held that the new policy deemed the building of the national home complete rather than that the mandatory obligation to the national home was being renounced.

Arabs and Zionists alike rejected the policy, the Arabs mainly on the grounds that by continuing to acknowledge Jewish rights in the issue of self-government it rendered such independence merely illusory. The Permanent Mandates Commission in its initial consideration of the new policy in June 1939 expressed the view that it was contrary to the mandate. The presentation of the British government's case before the Council of the League, due in September 1939, was foiled by the outbreak of war, so that it cannot be known whether the League of Nations might have devised an alternative procedure for terminating the mandate.

CHAPTER 8

FOUNDATIONS OF JEWISH
SELF-DEFENCE (1920-39)

*Origins of the Haganah – a unified militia – from local
militia to national defence force*

Origins of the Haganah

During the period of British military rule at the end of the
first world war steps were taken to bring together the various
elements of the self-defence movement that had grown up in
the previous decade. Many leaders had come to share the aim
of creating a united defence network on a countrywide basis
directed by a central command. The growing volume of Arab
protest, and the violence of 1919 and 1920 hastened the
process, bringing the problem of Jewish defence into the urban
arena and thereby into a countrywide perspective for the first
time.[1]

Early discussions within the defence movement of the agricultural settlements at the end of the war revealed basic differences of concept in relation to a number of key issues. The
most crucial division of opinion was on whether defence
organization should be under the command of the political
leadership of the Jewish community, the view taken by those
newest to the defence movement and by the labour leaders,
or whether, as in the view favoured by the veterans of
Hashomer (see above, p. 58). Hashomer, the early defence
organization, is not to be confused with the socialist movement
Hashomer Hatzair and its kibbutz federation), the active defence
leaders should hold ultimate responsibility for their own
decisions. There was also a dispute as to whether the organiza-

167

tion should aim to embrace the whole population or should be a limited organization like Hashomer, co-opting its own members only after careful scrutiny. For many years these differences recurred in the form of sharp personal antagonisms within the movement. The influence of the Jewish Legion, which had spread defence consciousness amongst hundreds in all walks of life, and the growing political character of the opposition to Zionism with the corresponding growth in the political importance of Jewish defence policies all combined to weaken the Hashomer case, and assisted the formation of a mass defence organization controlled by the political leadership.

The founding convention of Ahdut Ha'avodah at the end of 1919 resolved to undertake responsibility for defence. The party became a focal point for the wider defence movement. The new labour party aimed to establish the nucleus of a national defence arm and to attract to it other groups beyond the scope of labour-Zionism. This was not accomplished without a struggle against the Hashomer veterans who wished to continue in their tradition of limited professional membership. (The total membership of Hashomer in 1919 was registered as seventy-eight, not all of whom had yet returned to the country from their dispersal during the war.)[2]

The new party (Ahdut Ha'avodah) set up a 'defence centre', whose representatives, Eliahu Golomb[3] and Dov Hos, joined with Jabotinsky, Rutenberg and others in the spring of 1920 to set up the first urban defence command in Jerusalem. Jabotinsky, although he was committed to the idea of a national militia to be recognized and armed by the British, was at that time persuaded of the need for Jewish defence initiative even if of necessity on an illegal basis. With the setting up of the defence command and the outbreak of Arab disturbances a defence network involving hundreds of volunteers came into being. Jabotinsky was more concerned with the uses of defence organization as a political lever towards securing a recognized militia, than with defence for its own sake. He did not have much faith in the efficacy of defence by small groups in the labour-movement tradition of rural defence. He was more interested in defence activity as a demonstration of mass militancy, and accordingly conducted the training of volunteers in the open, intending that the administration should be fully aware of these activities. However, such arms as were available were clandestinely deployed. The Jewish Legion members were still in uniform under British command and their freedom of action was limited until general demobilization took place at the beginning of 1921. The defence leaders associated with the labour movement opposed Jabotinsky's policy. They pressed for the tight clandestine organization of defence, for the sake of defence, regardless of the political context.

In May 1920 at the height of the disturbances Hashomer convened its general council to consider its future role. Golomb and Tabenkin, representing the view of the political leadership of the labour movement, forcefully advocated a wider defence organization subject to political control by community organs, but were met by fierce resistance on the part of the Hashomer veterans, representing the majority within the association who insisted on the autonomy of the defence movement. The outcome of the meeting was a surprise decision to liquidate Hashomer and to place its members at the disposal of Ahdut Ha'avodah for the widening of the defence movement. It appears that the Hashomer veterans intended to be rid of the perennial debate about political control, which now placed them in dispute not only with the wider public but with the labour movement itself, and to carry on in their own defence tradition at a deeper level underground. Many members of Hashomer did in fact resume their separate activities after the new defence authority was firmly established on the basis of a wide consensus.

In June 1920 the convention of Ahdut Ha'avodah sent a message to Jabotinsky and his colleagues, now imprisoned for their illegal defence activities, expressing the wish of the labour party to work together with them in a national defence organization. Golomb and Hos emerged at the convention as the new defence leaders, supplanting the Hashomer veterans. The convention resolved on 5 June 1920 to undertake all the responsibilities previously reposed in Hashomer, and to develop a national defence movement under the leadership of the party, to be known as the Haganah (the Hebrew term for 'defence').

The convention appointed a committee of five, including three of the Hashomer veterans together with Golomb and Hos, to take the initiative in establishing the new defence organization. The argument about political control did not abate. Hashomer, as a self-elected elite subject to a rigorous code of discipline, saw itself as the vanguard of the nation, and could not readily accept political control from outside its ranks. They continued to work clandestinely according to their habits even after the association was formally abolished. Golomb and Hos persisted in their view that the Haganah was the nucleus of a future independent Jewish army which must be subject to popular control in accordance with democratic processes. They felt that the future security of the people would be endangered if left to the devices of a small number of individuals, however professional and however dedicated they might be.

At the Histadrut founding convention in December 1920, against the opposition of the pacifistic members of Hapoel Hatzair, it was resolved to take responsibility for countrywide self-defence. Ahdut Ha'avodah formally ceded its initiative to the Histadrut. For some months the Histadrut had difficulty in asserting its leadership over defence activities and especially in obtaining access to weapons, which the various settlements preferred to control themselves. There was also complacency to overcome. The lull in violence following the eruption of 1920 and the high hopes for security under the friendly civil administration of Samuel for a while reinforced a tendency in the rural wing of the defence movement to ignore urban defence problems. In the spring of 1921 the Histadrut established a full-time post for the co-ordination and supervision of defence, answerable to a five-man committee known as the Haganah Centre. The committee sought funds from local communities and from the central Zionist coffers, but of course resources were sparse. The lack of public response seemed to confirm the analysis of Hashomer that defence could not be dependent on the wider public. However, general complacency was dispelled by the outbreak of new Arab disturbances on a significant scale in various parts of the country in May 1921.

The riots exposed the unpreparedness of the defence movement and the inadequacy of its existing cadres to provide protection for the population. The work legion (see p. 80 above) engaged in roadworks in the north comprised the only firm organizational framework within the Haganah. Members of the work legion spent their spare time in military training under the guidance of those who had experience in foreign armies during the world war. Otherwise the Haganah had made little headway. The shortage of firearms and ammunition was acute. The main source of supply was by theft from British army stores carried out by Jewish Legion members still in uniform. Lesser quantities were made available with the help of Jewish policemen in the administration, and by the purchase of used small arms from local Arabs. The authorities officially allocated only a small number of rifles to rural settlements.

As a result of the disturbances in 1921 the issues of defence came before the community organs and the Zionist executive. Rutenberg, the nominal head of the Palestine community in his capacity as chairman of the National Council, had taken personal charge of defence in Tel Aviv during the riots and he studied the problem at close quarters. Although he was assisted by members of the Haganah centre and worked in harmony with them, he was opposed to the Haganah approach and identified the movement with its Hashomer faction, which he repudiated. Jabotinsky for his part continued to press for the formation of a legal Jewish militia under British command and as a price for his continuing to serve on the Zionist executive insisted that it commit itself to this goal. Ben-Gurion, representing the Haganah in the wider debate, affirmed the goal of a legal militia, but insisted that while pursuing that goal the community organs should still give full support to the clandestine self-defence movement.

Resistance to the Haganah approach to defence came also from the independent farmers in the plantations and the older villages. They feared that a countrywide defence organ would arouse the hostility of their neighbours and expose them to greater danger of attack by the Arabs. In common with middle-class circles in the cities the independent farmers also feared the implications of military organization under the control of the political left.

The difficulties of the Haganah were multiplied when it

came under fierce attack in the British press as a communist front bent on violent revolution, and when the administration, becoming aware of the theft of arms from its military depots, inaugurated a countrywide search for illegal weapons.

The high commissioner proposed to provide an official allocation of weapons for all Jewish settlements and to establish a legal Jewish defence unit in return for the disbandment of the Haganah and the surrender of its arms. Jabotinsky used the opportunity to call for the immediate recognition of a Jewish militia under the British command, and continued to heap scorn on the Haganah. The Zionist leadership, at best lukewarm towards the Haganah, was inclined to pursue Samuel's offer, and took up discussions with the Haganah command. The Haganah leaders remained obdurate. While recognizing the political importance of a legal defence force they refused to tie this to the liquidation of the Haganah and made it clear that members would not surrender the weapons in their possession. They rebutted Jabotinsky (who suggested that their military training and discipline was so poor as to constitute a threat to security) with the argument that the friendly British disposition of the moment could easily change with political circumstances and that it would therefore be an illusion to see security in an alliance of that kind rather than in self-defence. The Haganah leaders successfully stalled negotiations between the administration and the Zionist officials. The Haganah continued its underground procurement and training, now without even the informal support of the Zionist organs that it had previously enjoyed.

For several years until the major disturbances of 1929 an atmosphere of peace again settled on the population. The Haganah remained, low in prestige and in a losing battle against public complacency, as an underground group of a few hundred fanatics.

A unified militia

In the 'twenties the Histadrut itself had not yet established effective authority over the multitude of institutions which made up the labour movement. The Haganah committee of the Histadrut therefore experienced similar difficulty in bringing defence under its supervision. Settlements were reluctant to reveal the quantities of arms in their possession lest the central authority might see fit to distribute them elsewhere. Close co-operation with the Histadrut defence officials came only from the committed members of Ahdut Ha'avodah, the party which controlled the Histadrut. The Haganah machinery in these years was most effective in the cities where enrollment for defence required active volunteering, rather than in the rural areas where all workers were by dint of their location automatically involved in defence duties.

In 1924 the Haganah adopted its first formal constitution, on the initiative of its urban commanders rather than of the Histadrut authorities. The organization defined itself as an underground military organization which aimed to defend the Jewish population and to prepare itself to become a people's militia. A period of active training was specified for new members, after which they would be enrolled in the reserve. Each branch was placed under the control of a committee nominated by the Haganah command. The national structure of the organization was emphasized in detailed procedures for the transfer of members to a new command when they moved their place of residence. The constitution empowered members to criticize their commanders and to convene meetings for this purpose.

The formal semblance of tight-knit organization did not rescue the Haganah from general neglect during the years of peace, nor even from derision. The few hundred members were dispersed in isolated units with little real co-ordination or central guidance. Ben-Gurion, Golomb and the other major leaders were busy with other tasks and they did not concern themselves with the details of Haganah activity, leaving these to the personal control of their nominee. The climate was radically altered by the outbreak of the 1929 riots.

Once again, as in 1920 and 1921, the Haganah proved to be ill-equipped to conduct defence on a scale commensurate with the Arab eruption. Although its leaders had all along insisted on the need for preparedness for just such a situation, the organization was lacking in machinery and resources for countrywide defence. However, the Haganah did show that it was able to prevent an even greater disaster to the Jewish population. Its public prestige rose enormously when it was seen in 1929 to be the only effective means of defence available. Even Jabotinsky, its long-time enemy, now lavished praise on the Haganah and conceded that it had saved the Jewish population during the four days that elapsed until the British forces brought the outbreak under control. Rutenberg too acknowledged that only the Haganah had prevented a great massacre in Jerusalem such as that which overtook the Jews of Hebron and Safed where the Haganah was absent.

The public organs of the Jewish community now reconsidered the whole question of defence in the aftermath of the 1929 riots. Jabotinsky stuck to his view that only a legal army, quite apart from its political value, could attain the required standard of training and discipline. But the Haganah was now taken seriously. The public was now less confident in the quality of security afforded by the regime and was more inclined to accept the doctrine of self-defence, even if that be of necessity illegal. The National Council formed a defence committee under the chairmanship of Rutenberg, which sought to bring the Haganah and the non-labour groups together as parallel units within a unified command under the direction of the National Council. This corresponded with the Histadrut's own aim of widening the Haganah into a national militia.

Negotiations now took place between the labour representatives and the non-socialist interests for the formation of a united defence movement. Amongst the independent farmers and other middle-class groups there was a tendency to favour separate organization as a means of countering the power of the labour movement. Golomb on behalf of the Histadrut conducted a conciliatory diplomacy while Smilansky, the most able and respected of the farmers, turned the scales against separatism. The Jewish Agency and the National Council both ratified a new defence structure that evolved from the 1931 negotiations.

A broad defence command responsible to the national institutions was formed on the basis of equal representation of the Histadrut and the non-labour groups in the population, with three members from each wing. The Histadrut now gave closer attention to defence, and Golomb and Hos were placed on the command on the labour side. Each branch of the

Haganah continued within its own political forums to prepare its own policy preferences, and there was frequent tension and lack of mutual confidence within the unified command. On the whole, however, the parallel structure worked and prevailed until 1948. The weight of the labour wing was initially much greater owing to its superior organizational discipline, its defence experience and its numbers. The labour leaders continued to carry the main burden of Haganah leadership within the framework of equal representation.

The perennial conflict between the socialist and middle-class interests, dating back to the first decade of the century, was sharpened in the 'thirties with the emergence of the revisionist movement as an alternative centre of militant leadership in Palestine. In the Zionist organization abroad the revisionist impact was largely theoretical. The split which took place in 1935, when Jabotinsky and his followers formed the New Zionist Organization, had arisen from issues of high policy in the formulation of Zionist strategy. Inside Palestine, however, revisionism took a more prosaic form as a movement opposed to the Histadrut and all its works. If Jabotinsky opposed socialism it was as a liberal democrat dedicated to an alternative national strategy. Living abroad, he was cut off from the details of political life in Palestine and exerted little direct influence over the activities of his nominal followers in the country.

In the spring of 1931 the Jerusalem commander of the Haganah with about a hundred followers broke away from Haganah discipline and formed an independent defence unit. The great majority of the dissidents were of the non-labour affiliation and resented labour dominance in the defence movement. The dissident organization, known as Haganah 'B',[4] attracted many young members of the Maccabi athletic movement and also some university students, in addition to many revisionists. The influence of the revisionists spread within the breakaway group through their youth movement *Betar*, from which came many recruits to Haganah 'B'. The dissidents' organizational structure was similar to that of the parent Haganah, but they were more militant and enforced a more strenuous discipline on members. The older leaders of the dissidents hoped to develop their defence network to a point where they could bargain with the Haganah for a greater non-socialist voice in policy-making in return for reuniting. They came close to reunion in 1933, but the move was aborted by the worsening of relations at that time between the labour movement and the revisionists.

The Arlosoroff murder trial greatly exacerbated tension between the labour movement and the right-wing of politics among the public at large and within the defence movement in particular. The Histadrut following was convinced that the murder was the work of the revisionists while many others, not only revisionists, thought otherwise. Hatred between the two persuasions was intensified when the trial itself, on appeal, proved inconclusive. The atmosphere of the drawn-out trial boosted the dissident following. Now for the first time the leaders of Haganah 'B' were able to persuade Jabotinsky to lend his support to the organization. Although he had insistently opposed illegal military organizations in the past, he now saw the dissident defence movement as a useful political outpost for his New Zionist Organization, hoping that it might come under revisionist control. Other leaders opposed to the emerging socialist hegemony in Palestine were now also attracted, and the dissident group was able to form a political command including religious leaders and representatives of the General Zionist party in addition to Jabotinsky himself. This enabled the group for the first time to obtain support for arms procurement in Europe.

The religious and General-Zionist leaders associated with Haganah 'B' hoped to renegotiate the Haganah structure in favour of the non-labour interests, using the dissident organ as a bargaining lever. In the meantime the revisionist influence within Haganah 'B' spread. There was keen competition in recruiting new immigrants and the dissident organization grew to about two thousand in 1936 on the eve of the Arab rebellion. Its growth was assisted by the personal links of many of its members with the Maccabi movement abroad. Amongst its commanders the dissidents numbered many youngsters who had grown up in their ranks. These raised the level of militancy and introduced a militaristic ethos which was contrasted in their propaganda with what they saw as the pacifism of the regular Haganah. After the formal breakaway of the revisionists from the Zionist Organization in 1935 these young revisionists opposed the desire of their older commanders for unity with the Haganah, and sought to make Haganah 'B' the military arm of the New Zionist Organization. With the outbreak of the Arab rebellion the non-revisionist members of the movement became more anxious for unity with the parent movement and close negotiations were begun to this end.

Jabotinsky did not think much of the Haganah 'B' as a military force but he hoped that by using it for leverage he could negotiate an agreement between his movement and the official Zionist Organization which would commit the latter to a more militant strategy. By 1936 only the revisionists within Haganah 'B' remained opposed to reuniting with the Haganah. With the exception of the revisionists the Haganah 'B' commanders in any case agreed with the official Haganah line of 'restraint' rather than retaliation against the Arabs. Jabotinsky himself recommended the policy of restraint but he was unable to influence the younger militants among the dissidents, who pressed for an offensive response to Arab attack.

Negotiations for unity with the Haganah were conducted directly with Ben-Gurion as head of the Jewish Agency. There were many obstacles to be overcome and it was not until 26 April 1937 that agreement was reached between the dissident commanders and the Haganah. The agreement provided for broadening the authority which supervised the Haganah on behalf of the national institutions, and for the implementation of parity of command (as between the labour and non-labour wings) at the local level in addition to the central command level.

The conclusion of the agreement occasioned high tension within the dissident movement as the revisionist members repudiated it. A referendum was carried out within Haganah 'B', with the result that about half of the then three thousand members voted to return to the regular Haganah fold. The remaining half voted to retain their separate organization, which now became known as the Irgun.[5] At the time of the return of the dissidents to the Haganah its ranks numbered over twenty thousand, including some four thousand women, although the available arms sufficed for probably no more than ten thousand.

From local militia to national defence force

The Arab revolt of 1936–9 created the conditions for a Zionist succession to British rule in Palestine. Amongst its most important effects was the speeding of the Haganah's development from a locally oriented militia to the nucleus of a Jewish national army. As a voluntary movement the Haganah had not been able to mobilize fully the energies of the Jewish population in the absence of sustained attack upon it. The violence of the Arab revolt and its threat to the population everywhere in the country galvanized the Jewish youth, bringing it into the orbit of the Haganah and spreading defence consciousness throughout all levels of the society. The first phase of the rebellion released the Haganah's latent organizational capacities, while the peak of violence in the second phase from autumn 1937 to mid-1938[6] provided the test of fire that enabled the Haganah to become a mature fighting force.

No agricultural settlement, however isolated and beleaguered, was abandoned during the period of terror. On the contrary, the Arab challenge generated a new concept of settlement in a military format, which extended the strategic boundaries of Zionist colonization. Erecting prefabricated stockades and watchtowers by night under cover provided by the Haganah thirty-seven new kibbutzim were established during the period of the terror in virgin lands that had been purchased and held in reserve. The Haganah was placed at the very core of the new settlement programme which combined the political and military objectives of national security with the development of the Jewish economy.

It was during the Arab revolt that for the first time the Zionists were permitted legally sanctioned military activity. In the spreading chaos and disorder the administration had no choice but to respond positively to a Jewish proposal to enlist the help of the Jewish population in policing vital roads, railways and pipelines, and eventually even in suppressing the revolt itself. The Jewish community organs imposed on the Haganah an official policy of restraint which limited it to more or less passively resisting attack, ruling out retaliatory terror against the Arab population. The administration rewarded this policy in the early summer of 1936 by enlisting Jews as supernumerary policemen,[7] by ignoring the continued illegal activities of the Haganah and also occasionally by co-operating with these informally. Within a few months nearly three thousand supernumeraries were recruited in a campaign organized by the Haganah itself, with a view to giving its members access to superior training and equipment under the British command. In the interlude following the conclusion of the first phase of the revolt the administration attempted to exploit the supernumerary force to strike a bargain with the Zionist leaders: its continuation as a legal instrument would be contingent on the liquidation of the illegal Haganah and the surrender of its arms. Discussion amongst the Jewish leaders had not advanced far on this issue before the resumption of the Arab revolt on an intensified scale in 1937 gave a new lease of life to the supernumerary force. By 1939 over twenty thousand, comprising nearly the whole membership of the Haganah, were mobilized as supernumeraries. Their organization was converted by that time from the form of an auxiliary to a full-fledged para-military uniformed force known as the Jewish Settlement Police.

In the summer of 1938 another important development in collaboration with the British was that Captain Orde Wingate,[8] a British intelligence officer and passionate Zionist, overcame the resistance of his superiors and was given freedom to assist Jewish defence efforts. Wingate established formations known as Special Night Squads in which the best military talents of the Jewish youth were trained in guerilla warfare by night. This laid the foundation for the Jewish military superiority by night which proved to be of decisive importance in the war of 1948 by which Israel won its independence. Wingate's tactical genius proved an enduring reservoir of doctrine for the embryonic Zionist army and his leadership contributed to the growth of military self-confidence amongst the Zionists, which had been lacking in the previous decades. The youth in particular now came to see themselves as soldiers, overcoming the traditional pacifistic leanings of their parents. Wingate introduced the practice of great mobility and speed which became characteristic of the Haganah, and he also taught the importance of military intelligence and reconnaissance and, above all, of surprise. Although it was in the nature of a temporary honeymoon, the political and military collaboration between the Zionists and the British during the period of the Arab revolt had incalculable, perhaps decisive importance, for the future military capacities of the Jewish population.

Of great importance to the development of Jewish military potential was the internal evolution of reforms within the Haganah, generated by the Arab challenge. The magnitude of the revolt and its terror brought about a transformation of the Haganah's organizational structure and modes of operation. The first phase of the revolt converted the Haganah from its traditional locally oriented pattern of defence to a habit of countrywide planning, and from static to mobile active defence. These changes were gradually formalized during the second phase of the revolt and in effect they ushered in the formation of a national army. The transformation was conducted within the framework of the political doctrine of restraint which ruled out offensive or punitive action.

At first local commanders continued to exercise full initiative in accordance with Haganah custom, but gradually the national command took control and effected the co-ordination of activities on a countrywide basis. Regional and district organization began to supplant the local perspective. Instead of being responsible as hitherto only for the protection of the population from which its members were recruited, local branches of the Haganah were now ordered to take active responsibility for the defence of weaker neighbouring areas. Each of the stronger branches, especially in the cities, became the headquarters for the defence of its wider vicinity, including outlying settlements on the periphery. The most isolated settlements were covered by the national command itself by means of reinforcements drawn from volunteer recruits from the cities. Within a few months volunteers from Tel Aviv alone numbered over three hundred, engaged in remote defence by rotation on tours of duty averaging about a month. Some volunteers were used for agricultural work to relieve settlers for defence duties, while the more experienced volunteers were placed immediately on guard. This did much to raise the morale of the settlements and to generate a sense of national unity.

There was great pressure from the rank and file to burst the bounds of restraint and go on the offensive against the Arab bands. Restraint was discredited among the young as a foible of the older generation synonymous with cowardice. The political foundations of the policy were not well understood. The command managed, however, to maintain discipline, yielding in the direction of active and mobile defence but still avoiding offensive action.

Instead of static defence to prevent Arab bands from entering the residential centre of a settlement the practice grew, on the initiative of Itzhak Sadeh (next to Wingate the most brilliant military mind in the annals of the Haganah), of sending guard units further afield to camp at the perimeter of the settlement's land. From this practice Sadeh evolved the formation of mobile night patrols to anticipate and ambush Arab attackers. Sadeh's way of thinking as a tactician closely resembled that of Wingate and his methods prefigured those of the Special Night Squads. Sadeh's experience was studied by the Haganah command and at the end of 1937 it was resolved to formalize it as official Haganah canon. This resulted in the formation of 'field squads' at the beginning of 1938. These were the first mobile units of the Haganah organized in the manner of army platoons, with the task of pursuing and engaging the enemy in battle. They were shortlived in their original form as a result of political differences within the Haganah command itself and between the squad commanders and the regional commanders to whom they were subordinate.

The field squads were placed under local control except in emergencies, at which time the national command was empowered to deploy them away from their bases. In this case, however, they still came under the control of the regional commander in whose sphere they operated. The squad commanders were torn between their responsibility to the national command concerned with security in a countrywide perspective and the regional commanders with a more limited view. Underlying this arrangement was a political compromise between the labour wing of the Haganah command, which favoured the accelerated development of centrally directed units for countrywide operations, and the non-labour element, which continued to be hesitant about military ramification beyond the local level. The conflict resulted in the liquidation of the field squads at the beginning of 1939, by which time they numbered over two thousand of the best-trained supernumeraries. Sadeh and the socialist elements in the Haganah command did not give up their efforts to develop from the concept of the field squads a national force responsible for countrywide security. This was eventually accomplished by separating the two incompatible functions through the establishment of a field corps for regional operations and a commando force not linked to local frameworks, for national defence.

Throughout the period of the Arab revolt the Haganah command was riven by tension and mistrust between its two parallel factions. Important decisions were arrived at by a process of political trading, for only in this way could parity of command function in practice. Each wing of the command formulated its views in discussions within its own party forums: the labour wing in the Mapai or the Histadrut executive, and the non-labour wing in the Farmers' Federation, the Tel Aviv municipality (one of its main centres of strength) or the religious or General-Zionist party organs. Organizational innovations were weighed in the inter-party political balance as much as on their military merits. To these obstacles to smooth control and speedy decision were added the confusions of operating in two guises, the legal and illegal, each responsible to a different authority. Political balancing was rendered more difficult by the fact that the Jewish Agency executive, which was acknowledged as the supreme political command, was not based on the same parity formula as the Haganah command. Thus the labour wing tended on important issues to use its predominance in the Agency to enhance its influence in the Haganah command. The non-labour elements, on the other hand, gained countervailing strength from the ever increasing dependency of the command on the wealthier non-labour interests for its supply of funds through the community defence treasury which they controlled.[9] Tensions reached a peak at the end of 1938 when the political climate changed and the strength of activist opinion in the Agency executive grew, while the non-labour elements clung to a moderate approach in the fear of a direct clash with the British.

To get round these impediments to effective central control of the Haganah's operations Ben-Gurion pressed for the establishment of a 'technical' or professional military head to be directly responsible to the Jewish Agency executive. In the summer of 1938 Professor Yohanan Rattner[10] was appointed the first 'Head' of the Haganah command, with the task of mediating political pressures and protecting the military functions from having to absorb these. This was the first step towards the evolution of a military general staff which had been sorely lacking through all the years. Rattner had the greatest difficulty in establishing authority since he was vulnerable at any time to the withdrawal of support for his office by any faction disagreeing with his decisions. The function of his office was essentially to secure, by persuasion, political acquiescence in vital military decisions.

Rattner pressed ahead for organizational changes that had been under discussion. The issue crystallized around a view which saw the local units of the Haganah as the source of its organizational being and advocated their direct linkage to the central command, and an alternative view in which the national institutions at the political pinnacle were seen as the source of military powers from which organizational practice must flow. The former view affirmed the traditional structure while the latter sought to shape the Haganah more firmly in the image of a modern army. The argument and struggle between the two concepts continued unabated until after Israel attained its independence. In the meantime Rattner managed to implement at least in part a reorganization in the direction of the army model. At the end of 1938 the local units numbered twenty-one. These were now distributed among seven new regional commands based on political parity but subject to the ultimate discretion of the regional commander. The field squads were replaced in the summer of 1939 by a new field corps made up of units under regional command at a level of about a quarter of the available manpower. The creation of the field corps enhanced the prestige and importance of the regional commanders. The reorganization was only partially implemented in practice. Lacking a central military authority with formal powers, the organization at the grassroots continued to operate in accordance with personal habits and links, while the central command was frequently paralysed in political deadlock.

Rattner now sought to create a command structure which would differentiate the separate tasks appropriate to the political command from those best handled by military staff. His proposal was that the central command should continue to conduct budgetary responsibilities, military industry and procurement, while the military staff would engage in defence planning, instruct the regional commanders, determine the principles of leadership and training and all other military matters. The chief of the general staff would be responsible for appointing commanders. These plans were blocked by the right-wing faction, which continued as ever to fear the creation of central military institutions that would come under socialist control. Early in 1939 the central command reached the point of disintegration due to chronic deadlock. The situation became worse with the withdrawal of Golomb from active participation in the command when he failed to bring his own ideas to fruition. It was at this point that Ben-Gurion, returning in April 1939 from the abortive negotiations in London with the British government, took the situation in hand. After studying the details he resolved that in the new political circumstances the Haganah would have to undertake a vital political role in the Zionist struggle against the hostile British policy, and for this reason as much as for defence considerations it would be necessary to overhaul the organization from top to bottom. His efforts resulted in the establishment of a military general staff in August 1939. Thus twenty years from the time when Ahdut Ha'avodah donned the mantle of Hashomer and founded the Haganah, the organization now assumed the form of a national army. Such at least was the formal framework, though sharp conflict continued for many years to delay its full development.

The new political context of Jewish self-defence now took the form of unrelenting struggle against the administration in its implementation of the Macdonald White Paper policy. The Haganah now became a political instrument in the struggle for the Zionist succession to British rule.

CHAPTER 9

THE STRUGGLE FOR THE SUCCESSION: PALESTINE AND THE EUROPEAN HOLOCAUST (1937-45)

The issue of statehood – Jewish Palestine in the world war

The issue of statehood

The Zionist Congress met in August 1937 to discuss the Peel partition proposals which had generated a furore of controversy throughout the movement, abroad and in Palestine. Was a Jewish state confined to one-fifth of Palestine west of the Jordan indeed to be the terminus towards which half a century of Zionist sacrifice had been invested? Was this better than continuation of the open-ended national home? In the absence of a settlement with the Arabs would not such a state be a mere British dependency?

From his position outside the official Zionist organization Jabotinsky vehemently rejected partition and called for a Jewish state on both sides of the Jordan. The more radical nationalists within the organization similarly rejected partition on maximalist grounds. One wing of the socialist left repudiated partition as being premature given the limited extent of Zionist colonization, while the other wing rejected it as incompatible with the goal of a bi-national socialist Palestine. The spokesmen of the religious parties rejected in principle the amputation of the holy land.

Mapai was unable to establish a 'whip' on the issue which was regarded as a matter of individual conscience. Katznelson and other important leaders of the party in Palestine rejected partition outright. Ben-Gurion, however, shared the view of Weizmann that the proposal presented a major historic opportunity which must be grasped. Weizmann and Ben-Gurion mustered support for partition within the social-democratic mainstream of Mapai and the progressive wing of the General-Zionists. The level of tension within the organization was so high as to rule out an explicit resolution being adopted on the issue, with the risk of fragmentation that this would incur. By a two to one majority the Congress, evading a direct endorsement or repudiation of partition, authorized the executive to negotiate with Britain on the lines of partition without committing the movement pending the next Congress.

In the meantime with the resumption and intensification of the Arab revolt Britain itself dropped the partition plan, and the specific recommendations of the Peel commission fell from the agenda of discussion. The consideration of partition within the Zionist movement had, however, brought the question of Jewish statehood explicitly into the official Zionist vocabulary for the first time.

It is doubtful that Ben-Gurion believed even for a minute (as Weizmann did) that Britain would implement the partition plan, but he drew two important conclusions from it. First, that the partition formula itself demonstrated that for the first time Jewish statehood was in principle an internationally acceptable notion; and secondly, that since the proposal was based on the assumption that the mandate was unworkable, it would no longer work for Zionism or for Jewish immigration. Given the first conclusion he believed that the time had come for Zionism to work for Jewish statehood, and given the second, it must settle for any manner of statehood as soon as might be. Even the small portion of the land designated for the Jewish state by Peel would be sufficient: the issues of size and viability he considered negotiable, that of dependency surmountable over time. Ben-Gurion also reached the conclusion that the United States and its Jews, who he believed represented a tremendous untapped political potential, must now be placed at the centre of the Zionist struggle abroad. He came to the conclusion that Britain might no longer be found serviceable, and he even contemplated the possibility of armed struggle against Britain. Ben-Gurion was unable at first to dislodge his associates from the sway of habit which accorded primacy to the British connection. It was on this issue that for nearly a decade Ben-Gurion and Weizmann came into bitter conflict, until events confirmed Ben-Gurion's view and brought him to full ascendancy in the movement.

As a result of the 1937 Zionist Congress giving favourable consideration to partition the non-Zionist members of the Jewish Agency withdrew from the organization. Their willingness to work with the Zionists in supporting the life of Palestine Jewry stopped short of co-operating in any drive towards creating a Jewish state. The Jewish Agency now to all intents and purposes became identical with the Zionist Organization itself. At the same time the gradual rise of the Palestinian leaders to hegemony within the movement was nearly complete, and with the outbreak of the general war and the consequent dispersion of organizational capacities abroad political initiative rested with the inner circle of leadership in Jerusalem. Along with these the American movement, less fully cut off by the war, became the foremost Zionist political instrument abroad, much as Ben-Gurion had foreseen,

The twenty-first Zionist Congress meeting in the summer of 1939, after the publication of the Macdonald White Paper, still refrained from a reformulation of the goals of the movement in its new political circumstances. But the topic of statehood had attained wide currency and pressure grew for the drafting of a clear programme that would meet the challenge of the inevitable European war and post-war settlement. As the European holocaust erupted Ben-Gurion saw it as a decisive opportunity for Zionism. Just as Weizmann in the first world war had realized the opportunities presented by the fluid political situation, so now Ben-Gurion above all others sensed the tremendous possibilities inherent in the dynamic of the chaos and carnage in Europe. He saw that the opportunities that would occur in the war aftermath would not linger, that there would be but a few years at most to grasp statehood before powerful forces might arise to defeat Zionism.

Fifteen years after the Balfour Declaration the Jews in Palestine had still numbered less than two hundred thousand and after the influx of the 'thirties prompted by the initial

Nazi persecution, the Jews at the beginning of the world war were still less than half a million and less than a third of the total population of the country. In conditions of peace, it was clear, Zionism could not move the masses of world Jewry. The forces unleashed by Hitler in all their horror must therefore be harnessed to the advantage of Zionism.

If the looming European crisis in the mid-'thirties impinged on British interests in a manner that favoured the Arab cause in Palestine, these same events drove the Zionists to a more urgent, militant assertion of their demands. The Nazi menace athwart Europe in the late 'thirties had not yet appeared to portend the total doom of European Jewry, although the certainty of general war was already clear to the more far-sighted leaders in Palestine and elsewhere. The scale of the Nazi 'final solution' of the Jewish problem was undreamt of even by the most habitual pessimists in the Zionist leadership. Who could imagine that in the midst of a savage war on several fronts the Nazi machine would deploy resources methodically to massacre between five and six million individuals on account of their 'racial' origin? The secret war against the Jews of Poland and other territories occupied by the Nazis at the beginning of the war did not come to public notice in the allied countries until late in 1942, and was then met for the most part with incredulity. Even the Zionists, who had expected something of the sort, had difficulty in accepting the truth of reports of millions slaughtered and millions more marked for extermination. By the end of 1942 little doubt remained about the enormity of the Nazi purpose. By this time the Zionist movement itself was transformed. While hopes and efforts for the rescue of Europe's Jews continued, the struggle for a Jewish state became the primary concern of the movement.

Differ though they did in their appraisal of Britain's place in the determination of Palestine's future, Weizmann and Ben-Gurion agreed that the Jews of the United States must be galvanized to take a more active part in support of Zionism. In the early years of the war both men campaigned energetically to persuade the movement of the imperative need for a Jewish state. In Weizmann's case this was a slogan whose precise political meaning would not be formulated until relations with Britain after the war were renegotiated according to the new circumstances. In Ben-Gurion's case, however, the Jewish state was a deadly serious claim that the Zionist movement would assert in the period of the post-war settlement, even if this meant direct struggle against Britain.

The Hitler holocaust succeeded where three decades of Zionist propaganda had failed in moving the masses of American Jews to support Zionism. The change in outlook was timely in terms of the acculturation of American Jews. Hitherto their energies had been absorbed in the challenges of assimilating to American society. Like other immigrant groups in America their assimilation reached a point at which they could re-define themselves in relation to their old-world ties. From a position of security in their American identities they were now better able to associate themselves with the strange romantic movement of the Palestine settlers, although they did not become positive Zionists in the sense of contemplating personal migration to Palestine. Their sense of security as members of American society did not, however, attain a level that would have enabled them to campaign for the liberalization of immigration laws to accommodate masses of Jewish refugees. Their desperate desire to rescue the Jews of Europe was conveniently structured by the Zionist programme in a way that involved only helping Jews to reach Palestine, without impinging on their lives in America. Thus the identification with political Zionism exactly answered to their needs and those of the Zionist movement. They were mobilized and energized on behalf of what they regarded as a foreign philanthropic enterprise, with little knowledge of or interest in the political situation in Palestine.

Returning to Palestine in the spring of 1941 after a vigorous tour of persuasion in the United States, Ben-Gurion for the rest of the year pressed the inner Zionist executive to re-define and clarify the goals of the movement. The idea of Jewish statehood was now increasingly affirmed by his more hesitant colleagues and they ratified his plans to prepare the people, and particularly the youth, for the coming struggle.

In effect Ben-Gurion had come round to a view of Zionism essentially the same as Jabotinsky's. By taking statehood as such to be the only guarantee for unhampered Jewish immigration he was endorsing the most essential part of the revisionist policy. Not yet anticipating the nearly total extermination of Europe's Jews the Zionist leaders saw the problem as that of providing the means of rescue for several million refugees at the end of the war. Clearly only an independent Jewish government could implement such a policy in Palestine. But while the purpose of statehood was understood then to be the rescue of Europe's Jews, its adoption as a political goal, in time, subtly relegated rescue to secondary status, since the requirements of the political struggle were not necessarily identical with those of rescue. Once the achievement of statehood became the overriding goal of the movement the Zionist *realpolitik* developed a rigorous logic and a momentum of its own in which humanitarian considerations were subordinate. Thus it was at the end of the war, when it was already clear that it was too late to rescue the Jews of Europe, for they had perished by the million in the Nazi gas chambers, that statehood had become an end in itself. The myth of sovereignty had gradually supplanted outrage and compassion as the emotional source of the movement's energies and of its increasing attraction for the Jewish masses.

In the spring of 1942 Ben-Gurion's persistence was rewarded. The American Zionist movement endorsed the goal of Jewish statehood in a manifesto known as the 'Biltmore Program' (after the name of the New York hotel in which the conference took place). When a number of Zionist federations in other countries followed suit it remained only for the Palestinian population to ratify the Biltmore programme as the aim of Zionism.

It was the issue of statehood that occasioned the first formal split in Mapai. From the mid-'thirties, when Mapai became increasingly responsible for shaping and implementing macro-Zionist policies, its concentration on national interests inevitably modified and diminished its socialist concerns. As a result, Mapai's role within the Histadrut increasingly identified it in the line of succession to Hapoel Hatzair rather than Ahdut Ha'avodah, its originally dominant left-wing component. The format of controversy within the labour movement now shifted leftwards, from the original nationalist critique (Hapoel Hatzair) of Ahdut Ha'avodah, to a new socialist critique of

Mapai's nationalist pursuits. Hashomer Hatzair now emerged as the main centre of opposition to the Mapai leadership in the Histadrut. But at the same time new centrifugal tendencies within Mapai itself arose with the growth of an internal socialist opposition to the official leadership. Initially Ahdut Ha'avodah as the dominant partner in Mapai had fostered the growth of centralized control of the Histadrut while Hapoel Hatzair had resisted the transfer of jurisdictions from ancillary institutions to the centre. But as the Mapai leadership veered gradually to the right, the left wing of the party, especially the United Kibbutz federation associated with the former Ahdut Ha'avodah, resisted the integration of the Histadrut and the enhancement of its authority over the agricultural settlements. The United Kibbutz did not, however, limit itself to matters of immediate concern to the agricultural workers, but developed views on all the wider issues of the movement, becoming a centre of socialist leadership for a sizeable portion of workers in the cities, and especially in Tel Aviv, where the faction became a majority in the local labour council.

The potential of the United Kibbutz faction became apparent as early as 1934 when, although agricultural workers accounted for no more than a quarter of Mapai's active members at the time, the group secured a majority veto over an attempt by Ben-Gurion to negotiate an agreement with the revisionist trade union movement. The underlying issue was essentially the allowable degree of class collaboration: for the left wing of the party this should be restricted to the absorption by the labour movement of the bourgeois investments pumped into national development. The socialist critique within Mapai quickly spread beyond issues of class contention to penetrate the larger issues of the future of the Jewish community, such as relations with the Arabs and, eventually, the major issue of the political succession to British rule.

The left opposition within Mapai opposed partition and later the target of statehood on both socialist *and* nationalist grounds. From a socialist standpoint the goal of Jewish statehood must await socialist control of all positions of power in the country; and from a nationalist standpoint it must await the further extension of national boundaries through colonization, and also the attainment of a level of development which would render British tutelage unnecessary.

In a Mapai conference called in October 1941 to discuss statehood the left wing emerged as a full-fledged opposition group, known as Faction 'B'. Ben-Gurion won a sufficient majority within the party to ensure the ratification of the Biltmore programme by the inner Zionist executive. On 12 November 1942 the creation of a Jewish state became the official goal of the Zionist movement.

But Ben-Gurion did not rest there. Placing the goal of a Jewish state single-mindedly at the centre of his endeavours he was determined, for 'educational' as much as for political reasons, that the mass of the Palestinian community should do likewise. He felt that a showdown within Mapai was absolutely necessary to clarify the full significance of the new Zionist programme, even at the price of a formal split in the party. The guarantee of Mapai's continued tenure of national leadership lay in its absolute majority within the Histadrut. Ben-Gurion correctly judged that the myth of sovereignty would be sufficiently powerful amidst the rank and file to leave Mapai in control of the Histadrut even after shedding its left-wing faction. It was in the Histadrut forum that Ben-Gurion staged his showdown with the left. In a meeting of the Histadrut executive in 1944 he insisted on a party whip on the issue of accrediting delegates to an international trade union conference, with a binding mandate to represent on behalf of the Histadrut the demand for a Jewish state. The left faction thereupon seceded from Mapai to form a separate party, Le'Ahdut Ha'avodah ('For Labour Unity'), intending by the name to convey the implication that it alone remained true to the tradition in which Mapai had originated. In the subsequent election to the general convention of the Histadrut in the autumn of 1944[1] Ben-Gurion's Mapai won fifty-four per cent of the votes, enabling it to carry on applying the power and momentum of the Histadrut as a whole to the furtherance of its own policies.

Just before the Histadrut elections a long-deferred general election to the Jewish community organs (the Elected Assembly and the National Council) was held. Here too the issue o statehood was a central concern of the election campaign. In this case the Biltmore programme obtained the support of parties commanding two-thirds of the total vote. The first meeting of the new assembly at the end of 1944 confirmed the demand for a Jewish state as the official policy of the Palestine Jewish population.

Apart from the internal Mapai opposition the most vocal and articulate opponents of the statehood doctrine were the elements associated with the bi-nationalist movement. These groups came together again in the autumn of 1939 to form the League for Jewish-Arab Rapprochement and Co-operation, which sought to establish a new centre from which to exert pressure on the Jewish Agency to make greater efforts towards reaching understanding with the Arabs. The League published many pamphlets and its leaders carried on discussions with the official Zionist leadership, as so often before, but to no avail. After the ratification of Biltmore the League had no more opportunities to present the bi-nationalist case within official Zionist circles. Hashomer Hatzair formally joined the movement and sought to expand its links with the Arab left.

In August 1942 Magnes for the first time associated himself with an organization to propagate the bi-nationalist opposition to the statist movement. This was the Ihud ('Union', referring to union between the Jews and Arabs of Palestine and between Palestine and the neighbouring Arab world) Association which embraced many of the League's members and obtained added support in the United States through the personal following of Magnes there. It was this latter circumstance threatening the unity of American Zionism that activated the full force of official Zionist energies against the Ihud, with the result that Magnes and his circle were virtually ostracized from the political community in Palestine and abroad. The Ihud members and Hashomer Hatzair continued tirelessly throughout the war to conduct discussions with such Arab leaders in Palestine and in the neighbouring countries as would lend an ear to bi-nationalist ideas. But their efforts were unavailing so long as the official leadership on both sides looked on them with disdain.

Also opposed to the statehood programme was a new party Aliyah Hadashah (New Immigration) formed in 1943 by immigrants from central Europe of a liberal persuasion. But the majority of the Jews in Palestine, by the time the war was over and the enormity of the Nazi holocaust had become apparent, were accustomed to the slogan of statehood. Ben-Gurion had won his battle to make this slogan the heritage of the world-wide movement and of the population in Palestine, however vague the means and however utopian the goal itself had seemed a few years earlier.

Jewish Palestine in the world war

The White Paper of May 1939 inaugurated a decade of conflict between the Zionist movement and the British government. The White Paper policy was to limit immigration to ten thousand a year for five years, in addition to providing an immediate allowance for twenty-five thousand refugees; to restrict further land purchases by the Jews to a small area in which they already owned most of the land; and to prepare for the establishment of an independent Arab state within ten years. The Jewish population of Palestine was deeply divided on the appropriate means of resistance to implementation of the White Paper policy. Ben-Gurion led the activists who wished to impair the administration of the country by every form of passive and if necessary active resistance, while at the same time initiating underground preparation for armed struggle to secure political independence in the long term. Ben-Gurion felt that only radical expressions of opposition could prevent the White Paper policies from becoming an acceptable norm for the appropriate level of Zionist aspiration. He therefore proposed to use not only the conventional means of protest and pressure but to generate a pattern of tension, instability and provocation in order to bend the administration. He found little support for this line even within his own party and he bowed to the majority, although it refused to accept his resignation. Mass demonstrations on the occasion of the promulgation of the White Paper were organized but the administration made a muted response and the activist line was thereby weakened. The outbreak of the general war in Europe necessitated a reformulation of the official policies of Palestine Jewry. Even after the outbreak of the war Ben-Gurion continued to advocate an activist approach. Speaking as chairman of the Jewish agency executive he declared that the movement would 'fight with the British against Hitler as if there were no White Paper, and fight the White Paper as if there were no war'. The more restrained policy favoured by his colleagues came into its own in the early summer of 1940 when the war came closer to the middle east and the Churchill government, more friendly to Zionism, was installed in London. By this time Ben-Gurion had himself changed his view and came to the conclusion that waging the war against Hitler must be given priority over all else.

On one issue the Jews of Palestine were united: that illegal immigration must be conducted ceaselessly for the rescue of Jews from Europe. Already in 1937 when the administration began to apply political criteria for the regulation of immigration the revisionist movement started to organize illegal immigration. The Histadrut followed suit in 1938, in conjunction with the Haganah, by establishing its immigration bureau (*Mossad Aliyah 'B'*) for this purpose. Under the auspices of the two organizations some twelve thousand illegal immigrants were brought into the country before the war. This activity was the first collective Zionist commitment to breaking the law.

The British authorities quickly became adept at intercepting illegal craft. Then in the summer of 1939 the London government suspended the legal quota and announced that all illegal immigrants apprehended would be charged against the official annual quota. The Zionists responded with determination to bend the policy by rapidly exceeding the quota through intensified rescue efforts.

During the war the British government naturally wanted to put the Palestine problem on ice and hold the *status quo* until the war was over. But for the Zionists there was no *status quo*, since the position of the Jews in Europe worsened from day to day.

From the Zionist standpoint Palestine was a haven for persecuted Jews, to which they had a natural right to come. The national home and the Zionist movement at large were bound up with the problem of the Jews in Europe, and could not be understood in any other light. The British policy, however, was to separate the two problems. The plight of European

Jewry was seen as part of a wider refugee problem with which the powers would have to deal after the successful conclusion of the war. The situation in Palestine was an entirely separate problem of colonial administration which had to be dealt with on its own political merits. As it stood at the beginning of the war the problem in Palestine was to appease the Arabs and thereby prevent the Zionist issue from propelling them into the Nazi war camp. The first step, as formulated in the White Paper policy, was to assuage Arab resentment at the influx of Jews under British protection. If this could be done, the London government felt, the Palestine problem would be contained for the duration of the war and the foundation for a long-term solution would be laid. In this perspective the Zionist pressure for rescue of Europe's Jews was an extraneous nuisance threatening the balance of British imperial interests. As for the Arabs, in their eyes the Zionist contention that the Jews had nowhere else to go but Palestine was without merit. If the European civilization which was responsible for the Jewish plight was unable to afford any refuge,[2] why should this burden be imposed on the Arabs? Palestine was the 'only place the Jews could go', only in the sense that the Arabs were too weak to defend their borders from intrusion as every other country did. The British therefore saw it as nothing more than their duty to supply the strength that the Arabs lacked to stabilize the situation in Palestine.

The Zionist leaders associated the White Paper policy with the appeasement doctrine of the Chamberlain government, and they expected, once the war broke out and became total in scope, that the policy would be reversed. They were appalled at the determination with which the Palestine administration implemented the policy. Particularly in the early years of the war, when rescue on a large scale was still possible while the Mediterranean was a relatively open sea, the Jewish community in Palestine was embittered by what appeared to them to be a callous attitude on the part of the authorities comparable to the Nazi savagery.

The Haganah and the Irgun hired scores of unseaworthy vessels at great expense and attempted to run the British blockade to land thousands of refugees in Palestine. A number of major disasters in the early years of this traffic raised anti-

British sentiment among the Jews of Palestine to a high pitch of intensity. The *Patria* and *Struma* were two cases which became an emotion-laden legend and contributed to a lasting deterioration of Zionist-British relations. In November 1940 the British navy off Haifa intercepted two broken-down old tubs, the *Pacific* and the *Milos*, carrying nearly two thousand refugees between them. The administration refused the refugees permission to land and proceeded to transfer them to the *Patria*, a larger vessel which happened to be available, with the intention of transporting them to Mauritius for internment. When its pleas to allow the refugees to land were unavailing the Jewish Agency executive ordered the Haganah to disable the vessel and so prevent its departure. The Haganah action misfired and the ship sank with the loss of about two hundred and fifty lives. Making propaganda of the incident (the truth of which was unknown to the public until several years later) the Jewish Agency announced that the refugees had perpetrated mass suicide rather than leave the shores of Palestine. The distress of the Jewish public was alleviated when the incident led to the survivors being granted permission to immigrate, but anti-British sentiment was immediately exacerbated when the passengers of another ship, the *Atlantic*, were willy-nilly deported to Mauritius.

Among a multitude of lesser mishaps which befell the refugee traffic the *Struma* disaster contributed most to the deterioration of relations between the Zionists and the British regime. The *Struma*, a cattle boat over a hundred years old, at the end of 1941 set out on the Danube from Rumania with a cargo of 769 refugees. The vessel headed for Turkey where it was hoped to receive immigration certificates from the Palestine administration. The Turkish authorities, fearful that there would be no certificates, refused permission to land there and ordered the craft to leave Turkish waters. A message from the Palestine government to Turkey indicating willingness to receive all passengers under sixteen years of age came too late. The vessel sank in the Black Sea in unknown circumstances, possibly as the result of a torpedo or a mine, with only one survivor. The fury of the Jewish population in Palestine was once again directed at the administration, and the high commissioner was portrayed in Zionist propaganda as a mass murderer.

In the five years following the promulgation of the White Paper the official quota of immigration was not filled. War conditions soon rendered large-scale rescue all but impossible. The Zionists' struggle against the White Paper therefore faltered, but was nevertheless vindicated in that such rescue as it accomplished was additional to rather than at the expense of legal immigration. Up to the end of March 1944 some fifty thousand official certificates were issued, of which twenty thousand were charged to illegal immigration.

To implement the White Paper restriction on Jewish land purchase the administration in February 1940 issued the Land Transfer Regulations. These regulations were stringently applied and offered few loopholes. Although nearly fifty new strategic settlements were established by the Jews during the war, purchases of new land were limited to a paltry acreage. (One side effect of the regulations was a rapid inflation in the price of saleable rural land.) The administration was thus on the whole successful in implementing the White Paper policy during the war years, but only at the cost of building up a swell of rancour and adding to the appeal of the dissident Zionist terrorist movement in the post-war years.

The Jewish economy of Palestine received a tremendous boost during the war due to the expansion of production geared to the needs of British forces in the middle east. At the outbreak of the war the economy was in a state of deep crisis and unemployment reached record proportions. When military operations brought the middle east into the sphere of war a dramatic change occurred in the economy. The British military authorities did not share the political hesitation of the civil administration about promoting Zionist enterprise. Although higher food prices assisted the Arab peasantry to raise its standard of living, the Arab sector of the economy lacked the sort of advantages that enabled the Jewish sector greatly to increase its relative strength in the country. The Jewish sector contained a significant pool of skilled labour and scientific manpower in addition to liquid capital, and it was much more readily exploitable than the Arab sector ravaged by three years of rebellion. Military camps, fortifications, hospitals, airfields and roads and fresh food supplies on a large scale were urgently needed. Only the Jewish enterprises were able to supply these at short notice. It was in this period that the institutions of the labour economy (the enterprises controlled by the Histadrut) came to dominate the Jewish economy. Combining political power with organizational strength the labour-owned firms secured the most lucrative contracts, not only in Palestine itself but also in other countries of the middle east. By the middle of the war the number of Jews employed in industry had doubled over the 1936 figure. Agricultural production rose to an extent which reduced Jewish dependence on food imports from two-thirds of needs at the beginning of the war to less than half at the end of the war.

Much more effective than its struggle against the White Paper was the participation of Palestine Jewry in the war against Hitler. If fighting the White Paper meant in the main persisting in illegal rescue activities, fighting the war meant mobilizing the people for military service in the allied cause and turning the Jewish economy into an arsenal against Hitler. Important by-products of the Jewish war effort, which were never far from the minds of the Zionist leadership, were the acceleration of the development of the Jewish sector of the economy, the growth of a local armaments industry and a general raising of the level of training and military capability of the country's manpower. Zionist war aims included the preparation of the economy to undertake large-scale absorption of refugees after the war, training the Haganah for the most modern warfare, and securing recognition of the Jewish war effort as that of a distinct national entity in the hope that this would strengthen the Zionist hand at the peace settlement.

At the very beginning of the war the national organs of the Jewish community made it clear to the London government and to the authorities in Palestine that they wished to place all the energies and resources of the Jewish community at the disposal of the British war effort. During the first months of the war when the British war commitment was less than total, the Zionist offer was politely filed. Not until 1941 when the middle east became a theatre of war, with the German army threatening Suez, was Palestine put on a war footing. In the meantime the Zionist institutions in Palestine on their own initiative organized voluntary mobilization. Within the first month of the war over a quarter of the Jewish population, including over two-thirds of the adult males, had registered to place themselves at the disposal of the community organs for any service that the British military authorities might request. The Irgun announced the cessation of its anti-British terror and maintained the truce for three years.

At first the administration responded coolly to the Zionist volunteer movement, seeking to maintain a balance between Arab and Jewish participation. But this policy was dropped as the Arab response proved negligible and Jewish help vital for the defence of Palestine itself. By the end of the war some twenty-six thousand Palestine Jews were under British arms while a slightly lesser number were involved in home guard duties within the framework of the supernumerary police which was augmented and placed under military command.

The Jewish volunteers were at first organized within a Palestine regiment formed of separate Arab and Jewish battalions. The Zionists pressed the London government to form a fighting force carrying the Jewish national flag. Churchill was favourable to the idea and gave his agreement in principle, but there was strong opposition in colonial service circles mindful of Arab resentment. The plan was postponed again and again and shelved at the end of 1941. The Jewish Agency then directed its pressure away from the London government and appealed to public opinion in several allied countries. Committees for a Jewish army were formed in the United States, Britain and elsewhere, seeking support for the creation of a force on the lines of the Jewish Legion of the first world war. The aim was eventually narrowed down to the creation of a Palestine Jewish force. The movement channelled the anger of the Zionist leaders in Palestine at the British refusal to install conscription in Palestine. The idea was tenaciously pressed against all official opposition until in the autumn of 1944 the Zionist agitation was rewarded by the formation of the Jewish Brigade. This was a unit of the British army carrying a Zionist flag, made up mainly of Palestine Jews but also including stateless refugees and British Jews. The Brigade took part in the Italian campaign and participated in the liberation of several concentration camps in central Europe. Many Brigade members maintained underground links with the Haganah and assisted with the organization of illegal rescue and immigration of refugees to Palestine. The Brigade, in addition to gaining significant experience in modern warfare, gave the ring of familiarity to the Zionist national idea and undoubtedly enhanced the Zionist claim for Jewish statehood.

In addition to regular service with the British forces the contribution of Palestine Jewry included a number of important missions of intelligence and sabotage behind enemy lines in Europe. In the early stages of the war the Zionist leaders drew up ambitious plans for many such actions and several were approved by the British military authorities. The British agreed at the same time to allow underground agents to give a part of their time and attention to specifically Jewish concerns such as rescue work and assisting Jewish resistance activities. As a result of political opposition in London, however, many of these plans were abandoned or reduced in scope, and it may be that several opportunities to exploit the daring and linguistic expertise of these volunteers were missed. Whether or not this greatly affected the military conduct of the war, it certainly hampered the Jewish rescue effort and caused much bitterness among the Zionists. In the event several Palestinian volunteers were parachuted into Europe and achieved some successes against the Nazi occupation at the cost of their own lives.

While the military participation of the Zionists in the war against Hitler yielded some satisfaction, the Jews of Palestine experienced a traumatic sense of rage and impotence in the face of the Nazi campaign of extermination. First reports of the massacre of millions of unarmed and helpless Jews in eastern Europe were disseminated by the free Polish government in exile early in 1942, but were met with disbelief. When the reports were verified beyond all doubt within a few months it dawned on the Palestinian community that six million of their brethren were doomed to extinction, and, as it appeared, the rest of the world was turning a blind eye. An Anglo-American conference held in Bermuda in April 1943 to discuss measures to alleviate the plight of the millions of persecuted refugees in Europe was in fact in no position, in the midst of the war, to discover effective solutions. But to Palestine Jewry the most striking aspect of the deliberations was that the British representatives had agreed to an American condition that the talks should not touch on American immigration laws, in return for which the Americans agreed not to raise the possibility of rescue by immigration to Palestine. The Zionists felt the sense of abandonment more keenly than they appreciated the undoubtedly formidable obstacles that stood in the way of effective intervention to foil the incredible grand design of the Nazi butchers.

The heroic uprising of the Warsaw ghetto in April 1943 inspired the Jewish youth of Palestine with fervour for action. Aiding resistance had a more powerful appeal than rescuing the helpless. But frustration was doubly intensified, for any effective action depended on partnership with the British forces, and these were engaged in savage total war with little to spare for rescue or heroics. At the same time circumstances confirmed the Zionist view of events and greatly reinforced the belief in political independence as the imperative solution for the Jewish plight. The movement for Jewish statehood received from Hitler an irresistible spark of fanaticism which Ben-Gurion had been unable to impart to it, at just the time when a Jewish state had become irrelevant to the masses of European Jewry for whose salvation it had been conceived. In the meantime it had become the crux of the political identity of the Jews of Palestine.

CHAPTER 10

THE STRUGGLE FOR THE SUCCESSION: THE STATE OF ISRAEL ESTABLISHED (1939-48)

Wartime development of the Haganah – the establishment and the dissidents – the collapse of British rule – partition and British withdrawal – declaration of independence

Wartime development of the Haganah

The political crisis of the Zionist movement in 1939 was reflected within the Haganah command in the process of re-defining the role of the organization in its new political context. Ben-Gurion, at the head of the labour wing, now saw the Haganah as the primary political instrument of Zionism in its struggle with the British power, while the right-wing spokesmen (led by Smilansky and Rokach)[1] opposed the expansion of the Haganah's role beyond protecting the Jewish population from Arab attack. The struggle for control of the Haganah continued unabated for fully two years until the overhaul of the organization was implemented to the satisfaction of both camps.

Ben-Gurion succeeded in instituting a general staff in September 1939, and Yaacov Dori was appointed its first chief.[2] The field force created to replace the field squads did not take firm root, partly on account of opposition by local commanders who feared losing their best men, but mainly for lack of funds to maintain a mobilized force on a full-time basis. The failure of the field force gave an impetus to the creation of the special squads, a new unit with responsibility for the most dangerous illegal operations.

Ben-Gurion wished to maintain a clear line of demarcation between the legal force of the supernumeraries and those units that might be engaged in operations directly aimed at the administration and its laws. As he pointed out, the Haganah had hitherto been illegal but had nevertheless operated for the most part within the spirit of the law. Now it would be obliged to work for the frustration of the law. In spite of the White Paper the right wing wanted no part in any activity directed against the administration and wished, if any such operations were undertaken by the leadership, that they should be conducted by a separate organization altogether removed from the Haganah. Ben-Gurion, while wishing for separation of command to take special operations beyond the political reach of the right wing, nevertheless was adamant that such activities must be organizationally integrated within the illegal Haganah in order to preclude its degeneration from lack of action or inspiration. The solution was the creation of the special squads subordinate solely to the head of command (and therefore in effect to Ben-Gurion) and outside the jurisdiction of the parallel command.

The special squads, being completely removed from the local framework of command and also from the parliamentary structure of the national command, were the nearest approach yet achieved to an army formation. But they too were short-lived. They undertook retaliatory actions against Arab terrorists, trial and execution of Jewish informers, preparations for intensification of illegal immigration and some acts of sabotage against British installations involved in implementing the White Paper. In the summer of 1939 they thus made a start in the development of the activist struggle that Ben-Gurion envisaged against the administration. But the outbreak of the general war brought an end to their operations and once again presented the issues of policy, organization and control that had exercised the Haganah throughout all its years.

In September 1939 the voluntary Zionist manpower muster proceeded, and the thoughts of the public were directed at the general question of the military role of Palestine Jewry in the world war. Meanwhile the administration, displaying little interest in that question, inaugurated a campaign of harassment, searches and arrests in the hope of liquidating the Jewish military underground. In 1940, just when this external pressure brought the Haganah to the brink of dismemberment, its internal contest for control reached the peak of its intensity. The right-wing elements to all intents and purposes withdrew from active participation in the national command. But the labour leadership continued to sustain the network of organization and even developed the Haganah throughout this time of its greatest stress.

The continued functioning of the Haganah network and its ability to conduct illegal immigration and maintain training, in spite of the interminable struggle for political control which paralysed the national command, was due in large measure to the firm evolution of the general staff under its first chief, Yaacov Dori. The general staff concentrated on developing technical and professional military expertise. In its first year it drafted a new constitution to clarify the line of command at the sub-political level and to improve the means of supervision and military effectiveness throughout all levels of the organization. The general staff maintained a number of separate bureaus divided by function and staffed by experienced young specialists. Its secretariat headed by Israel Galili[3] maintained liaison with the political command and ensured the implementation of policies compatible with the predilections of the labour camp. Around Galili and Itzhak Sadeh there emerged a circle known as the 'young Turks', composed of about fifty youngsters of the United Kibbutz movement who had served in Wingate's Special Night Squads or Sadeh's field squads. These young activists met every few months for discussion and kept alive the idea of a national army. In the absence of right-wing participation they were able to bring their aim to fruition in May 1941.

Syria had come under Vichy control, a pro-Nazi coup had taken place in Iraq, and Rommel's army stood at the gates of Egypt. The possibility of a German assault on Palestine sharpened the urgency of the demand for an independent Jewish force for the defence of Palestine with or without British sponsorship or co-operation. The Jewish agency executive authorized the establishment of a commando strike-force (*Plugoth Machatz* known as the Palmach) to be held in readiness for mobile action as an independent Jewish army in the event that the country came under German attack. Itzhak Sadeh was appointed commander of the Palmach but to avoid conflict with the regional Haganah commanders the initial constitution of the commando units placed them under the formal control of the local commands in whose sphere they operated. From this beginning the Palmach soon evolved into an independent standing army with its own separate general staff, though it was subject to the same ultimate political control as the Haganah command. It was intended to raise nine companies of hand-picked youngsters to be in constant readiness under the Palmach command, but this level of mobilization was not achieved for several years.

The imminence of the German threat to Palestine restored political unity to the Haganah. In June 1941 the Haganah leaders were able to thrash out an agreement to resolve their perennial political conflicts. The left wing made all the concessions demanded by the right, but the labour group nevertheless retained effective control through the predominance of Mapai personnel in key positions. A broad public security committee was set up to supervise the financial management of the Haganah. The national command was re-established on a broader basis with three members from each of the two main wings in addition to a representative of the religious parties and a neutral head of command. Moshe Sneh[4] was appointed to this position. Although he was formally a member of the General-Zionist party at that time his views were closest to those of the Mapai activists. By agreement a right-wing member was included in the military general staff. The middle-class leaders reluctantly made their peace with the existence of the Palmach which they discovered only on their resumption of Haganah participation.

The first two units of the Palmach were formed in the summer of 1941. By this time the British authorities were no longer concerned with legal proprieties and the Palmach units were attached to the British force which invaded Syria in August 1941 in a successful campaign to depose the Vichy regime. The Palmach men assisted as guides and behind enemy lines as intelligence agents and saboteurs. Jewish help was also used to depose the pro-Nazi regime in Iraq. These were among many instances of co-operation between the illegal Haganah and the British military authorities during 1941 and 1942 when the fate of the region hung in the balance.

By the end of 1942 the best-trained young members of the Haganah were serving in the Palmach in various parts of the country. During the period of German threat to the security of Palestine these were placed on full-time mobilization to be available for any contingency. It was in this way that the Palmach evolved as the Hebrew standing army. During the crisis the British even helped the Palmach with money but after the German defeat at el-Alamein co-operation ceased. The atmosphere of goodwill and co-operation was completely dissipated after the British authorities took back weapons they had supplied to the Palmach and the Palmach in turn successfully raided a military depot to regain possession of these arms.

When the middle-eastern military crisis passed, the Haganah and the Palmach were again pressed by an acute shortage of funds. It seemed inevitable that the Palmach would have to be dispersed and the standing army would be a thing of the past. The right-wing element in the Haganah in any case wished for the liquidation of the Palmach, which was nothing less than the dreaded independent military force under labour control. Kibbutz leaders, and particularly Tabenkin among them, found a solution which gave the Palmach a reprieve. In May 1942 a council of the United Kibbutz movement resolved to integrate the Palmach within the kibbutz network on the basis of two-thirds time working on the land to earn its keep and one-third for military training. The Palmach organization would remain intact and its members would not be members of the kibbutzim in which they were posted. The kibbutz would, however, guarantee their maintenance and also train its own youth for recruitment to the Palmach. The national organs gave their approval to the arrangement and a one-year contract was undertaken between the participating kibbutzim and the Palmach. The members of the Palmach did not like the arrangement and morale was low. They wanted much more intensive training, particularly to enable them to achieve their goal of familiarity with every inch of the terrain of the country. The national organs of the community were meantime conducting an intensive campaign for recruitment to the British forces and many Palmach members felt that this was the more vital challenge. Their morale was not helped by the high prestige attached to enlistment with the British and the many benefits enjoyed by the regular soldiers, such as uniforms, support for dependents and other privileges. Scores of Palmach members left its ranks for the British army, but the majority remained and the Palmach structure was tightened and strengthened. The general staff under Sadeh and his appointed deputy Yigal Allon[5] streamlined the military network and firmly established its independence and its virtual control by the left-wing kibbutz movement.

During the mobilization campaign the Haganah leadership and the Jewish Agency executive were much exercised by the issue of finding an appropriate balance between enlistment in the British service and retaining organized manpower within the country. It was desired to achieve the maximum possible national participation of the Zionist movement in the general war, with all the likely political benefits that might accrue later and indeed also for the military experience this would bring. At the same time there was concern lest the organization remaining in Palestine would be depleted to the point of atrophy. The issue was sharpened during the regional military crisis of 1942 when the chief of staff of the Haganah, Yaacov Dori, himself came to the conclusion that enlistment in the British forces was the imperative challenge, on the grounds that the national goal of a large independent army was incapable of achievement at the time. Instead, the Haganah should be maintained as a small trained cadre, but no further efforts should be made to enlarge it while the opportunities for military service with the British army continued. Dori's view was not shared by his colleagues in the Haganah command, and the 'young Turks' in particular pressed harder for the maintenance of a strong Haganah throughout the war period. Risking the opprobrium attached to opposing enlistment for the war, the Haganah leaders persisted in a campaign of persuasion to retain its most capable manpower. Although the organization did indeed suffer depletion it was able to maintain its firm nucleus by carrying on the activities of procurement, arms manufacture and maintenance of stores, illegal immigration and training activities among the young.

The development of military training for the younger age-groups gave a new lease to the faltering field force, although it was unable during the war to compete effectively with the Palmach and the British forces as a magnet for recruitment. The field force at the end of the war reached only half of the nine thousand that was its planned complement. At the same time, in competition with the growing dissident movement (the Irgun), some twelve thousand youths below military age were brought within the Haganah cadet force for training.

The majority of the Haganah membership was organized within the guard force ('*Chel Mishmar*', '*Chim*') responsible for static defence. At the end of the war these numbered over thirty thousand (of whom only four thousand were fully trained and armed) as against some six thousand engaged in the mobile Palmach and field force formations.

At the end of 1942 the Palmach units, after depletion due to recruitment to the British army, numbered some eight hundred organized in six companies distributed among a score of kibbutzim. Another two companies were formed within a year or so when numbers surpassed a thousand with increased enrollment by young recruits from the cities. During the war the Palmach command gradually raised the level of tactical deployment until by the summer of 1944 it was organized in three battalions each made up of three companies. The total enlistment in the Palmach at the end of war was about fifteen hundred in addition to a general staff of about thirty.

During the middle years of the war the Palmach conducted a continuous debate on its proper role within the wider Jewish self-defence movement. Sadeh initially conceived the force as an elite corps reminiscent of the old Hashomer but the view came to prevail that it should be broad-based in membership, with a rotation of service enabling it to maintain its own reserve of trained veterans. It sought to combine the maintenance of a rigorous standard of training with the broadest possible enrollment in the event of full mobilization. It nevertheless retained something of an elitist flavour in that its standards of training and leadership made it a natural pool for the provision of junior officers to other branches of the Haganah.

Amongst the important wartime developments within the Haganah was the evolution of a professional intelligence branch. Hitherto intelligence work had been informal and haphazard. The need for an improved intelligence service became apparent when the British searches and arrests early in 1940 confirmed that British intelligence had penetrated the Haganah. The first step towards a professional intelligence arm was taken in response to this, with the formation of a counter-intelligence network to anticipate British plans. From this evolved a full-fledged intelligence service with three units specializing respectively in British, Arab and Irgun activities. The Arab section had the most difficulty of the three in reaching a high level of penetration and expertise. By the end of the war the intelligence branch of the Haganah as a whole had become a highly professional arm of vital military importance.

Advances were also made in weapons procurement. The proximity of battle facilitated this in the early years of the war. When the Vichy forces in Syria began, following the British invasion, to defect to the Free French, they habitually sold their Vichy weapons before crossing over. Jewish agents, assisted by the Palmach soldiers on the scene, procured these weapons either directly from the French officers or by trading with the Arabs also engaged in this traffic. Weapons were also brought in quantity from Egypt and North Africa, both by purchase and by theft from abandoned stores. The quality of weapons was, however, for the most part defective, particularly in the case of the Vichy haul, since the French workers obliged to manufacture these often gently sabotaged their product. By the end of the war the Haganah arsenal was still relatively small and insufficient for the fifty or sixty thousand men linked to the underground organization. The total useable armoury of the Haganah at the end of the war barely exceeded six thousand rifles and a few hundred machine guns, sub-machine guns and mortars.

During the war the Haganah also developed its own weapons industry though it was handicapped by the constraints of working underground. *Ta'as*, the Haganah industry, managed to produce some two hundred thousand grenades and several hundred mortars with ammunition. These were distributed in underground stores around the country. Over half of the light weapons available to the Haganah at the outbreak of the war with the Arabs in 1947-8 consisted of these stocks built up during the world war.

The establishment and the dissidents

When half of the Haganah 'B' members returned in 1937 to the fold of the parent Haganah, the remainder, then numbering a few hundred associated with the revisionist movement, decided to continue their dissident military organization under the name of the Irgun. The Irgun represented a defiant opposition to the official community organs, refusing to accept their political leadership or to be bound by any of their decisions made on behalf of the community. Although Jabotinsky lent his name to the Irgun he did not control the organization and was unable to impose his view that restraint was the correct response to the Arab revolt.

During its first few months the Irgun lacked funds and was unable to establish firm central leadership. Local commanders had wide discretion in planning and implementing retaliation against the Arab population. By mid-1938 the central leadership of the Irgun achieved tighter control and conducted a terrorist campaign against the Arabs which matched the Arab terror in intensity. The Irgun activities played havoc with the Haganah policies and threatened the successful growth of the co-operation with the British authorities on which the future of the legal supernumerary force depended. Relations between the two movements became more than tense and each was involved in direct actions against the other. It was in these circumstances that Golomb sought an agreement with the Irgun. The Irgun for its part was amenable on account of its lack of resources and facilities for training. An agreement was outlined and secured Jabotinsky's endorsement, allowing for Irgun acceptance of Haganah discipline while its members would retain a separate identity within the Haganah framework. The Irgun followers would be permitted to enlist in the supernumerary force (whose recruits were screened for the British by the Jewish Agency). The agreement was vetoed by Ben-Gurion, then in London, who wrote to Golomb: 'I agree to negotiation with the revisionists on only one basis: acceptance of the political discipline of the Zionist Organization.' Ben-Gurion had come to see the defence movement in a broad political perspective transcending immediate military considerations. He felt that the inclusion of the Irgun elements within the Haganah framework would undermine its political potential while at the same time it would gratuitously enhance the political strength of the revisionist opposition.

Other attempts to procure unity between the Haganah and the Irgun followed in quick succession but failed. After the publication of the White Paper the Irgun acquired an unaccustomed prestige within the population which prompted it to raise its demand for influence in the Haganah above the level at which agreement might have been possible.

The Irgun itself during the first years of the war was disturbed by internal political disunity. While the main rationale of Irgun separatism in the pre-war period was its rejection of the policy of restraint in the face of Arab terror, many of the Irgun leaders were equally at odds with the Haganah leadership in their estimate of Britain's role in relation to Zionism. Some Irgun leaders saw Britain as the foremost enemy of the Zionist movement. The effective harassment of the Irgun by the administration fostered the anti-British animus. This sentiment was most strongly held by Abraham Stern, an Irgun leader who had not grown up in the ranks of the revisionist youth movement and who did not share the reverence with which Jabotinsky's followers submitted to his will. Stern cultivated a personal following among the more radical youths in Poland and directly challenged Jabotinsky's leadership. When the European war broke out Jabotinsky and Razi'el,[6] the Irgun commander, called a truce with Britain and gave emphatic priority to waging the war against Hitler. In 1940, immediately following Jabotinsky's death, Stern broke completely from revisionist discipline and took the majority of Irgun members in Palestine with him into a new dissident terrorist movement which subsequently adopted the name 'Lehi' (*Lochamei Herut Israel*, the 'Freedom Fighters of Israel', familiar to readers of the British press as the Stern Gang). The Irgun recovered its lost support from Stern when he elaborated his programme, which was to assist Germany to conquer Palestine in return for the transfer of Europe's Jews to its shores. Stern believed that a deal with Hitler offered better hope for Jewish independence than a truce with Britain.

In the early period of the European war the Irgun was under the control of the revisionist party headed in Palestine by Aryeh Altman, who followed Jabotinsky's new line of strong co-operation with the British. During this period the Irgun even established close rapport with the Criminal Investigation Department to the detriment especially of Stern's followers. Once again in December 1940 negotiations for unity took place at the highest level between Mapai and the revisionists. On this occasion, in view of the quiescence in Irgun activity and the similarity of aims, there seemed little to prevent unity and a broad agreement for a military and political merger was outlined and initialled. It was not, however, ratified. There was much opposition in Mapai circles and Ben-Gurion himself remained obdurate even although the lines of the draft agreement seemed to meet his requirements. Following the failure of the unity attempt bad feeling between the organizations recurred and was intensified.

Stern was killed by British police in February 1942, but not before his activities had greatly exacerbated disunity and tension within the underground movement. Stern's group did not have the means to carry out its grandiose plans for general terror aimed to remove British rule, and had to make do with a campaign of personal assassination of policemen. Many of Lehi's victims were Jews. The Irgun, Lehi and the Haganah closely spied on each other and on occasion each passed information to the British authorities to forestall actions by its rivals.

The year 1943 marked a low point in Zionist relations with the administration and between the rival underground organizations when the atmosphere of despair for the fate of European Jewry favoured the spread of extremist opinion. Anti-British passions were renewed within the Irgun when Menahem Begin (b. 1913), one of Stern's original followers in Poland, arrived in the country in 1942 and was appointed commander of the Irgun in 1943. At the time the Irgun had some five hundred members. The Irgun, with some success, now sought to spread its influence among the Haganah rank and file. When the Haganah command at the end of 1943 held in check the growing anti-British activism amongst its members, Begin

H

decided to go it alone and call an end to the truce with Britain. Begin cut the Irgun's ties with the revisionist party and in January 1944 announced the launching of a revolt against British rule. The Irgun was now its own master, answerable to no political authority but the judgement of Begin. He resolved that as long as Britain was still fighting Hitler the British army in Palestine would not be a target. At that time, in contrast with Lehi, the Irgun also sought to avoid personal injury, restricting its targets so far as possible to installations.

In the first months of the revolt the Irgun destroyed many British administrative buildings, and also established a press and radio to disseminate terrorist propaganda and information forbidden by the censorship. Many Irgun members were arrested and sentenced heavily under the emergency regulations devised in the 'thirties to cope with the Arab revolt. The renewed terror greatly agitated the official Zionist leadership.

At the end of 1943 a debate took place within the Histadrut on the role of the Haganah in the light of the political outlook. There was a discernible growth in activist sentiment, but the moderate view prevailed that although Britain might well need some violent prodding to constrain its anti-Zionist preferences, it would be mere fantasy to attempt to depose British rule enforced by an army of seventy thousand then in the country. Concessions must be sought by diplomatic means. If a general revolt of the Jewish population took place in the midst of the world war it was clear that Britain had the means and might well regard it as necessary to crush the Jewish society built up through half a century of sacrifice. The wanton irresponsibility of the Irgun seemed a bigger threat to the Zionist project than the British obstacle. The Haganah leaders were now torn by their wish to crush the Irgun while yet avoiding civil war or slipping into the role of aides to the British executioner.

'Nihilists, maniacs, charlatans, Fascists, murderers, bandits were the familiar terms used in the spate of speeches, articles and resolutions that poured out throughout 1944 against the Irgun and the Lehi.'[7] The revisionist party was no less fulsome than official Zionism in its vituperation of the Irgun. Apart from the terrorism itself great concern arose in the Jewish

Agency over the Irgun practice of raising funds by extortion and intimidation. Gangsterism or the dictatorship of a military junta seemed to be the logical culmination of this development which threatened the structure of representative democracy.

Begin, as leader of a tiny minority group in the country and himself only recently arrived in Palestine, did not hesitate to seek to dictate to the great majority of the people who had built the country inch by inch. To appreciate the primitive political understanding of Begin it is necessary to take account of the fact that the revisionist ideology had taught him little respect for the constructive efforts of the Palestine settlers. The fantasy of millions of immigrants inspired by statehood was more precious to the radical youth in Poland than the achievements actually realized in Palestine by the veteran settlers. From the depths of despair in Jewish Poland at the onset of the Nazi holocaust it was easy for Begin to identify Britain as the arch-enemy of Zionism. The myriad little building blocks of the national home cemented together under British protection were as naught to the dreamers in Poland who in their hour of despair saw only the needs of millions for refuge and Britain barring the doors of Palestine. Begin believed that he was justified in defying the preferences of the great majority since he considered that only through the experience of warfare would the general public come to realize that warfare against British rule was necessary and possible.

In its political ineptitude the revolt resembled nothing more closely than the Arab revolt of the 'thirties led by the Mufti with such disastrous consequences for his people. In April 1944 the Zionist leaders, appalled by Begin's clumsy timing of the revolt and fearful of the possibility that the Jewish population might come under the dictatorship of a terrorist junta, discussed measures to put a stop to the Irgun actions. There were many, especially within the religious and other non-socialist groups, who opposed taking any action against the Irgun. Ben-Gurion was the most vehement in denunciation of the Irgun which he regarded as the Achilles heel of the Zionist movement, and he called for the use of force against the Irgun. It was resolved to step up counter-Irgun propaganda and to provide Haganah protection against intimidation or extortion. The public was called on to isolate and ostracize known Irgun members. The Haganah did succeed in limiting the spread of extortion but did not succeed in preventing growth in the Irgun's support.

From May to September 1944 a new wave of Irgun operations directed at British police stations earned the Irgun admiration for its daring, and galvanized the Zionist establishment again to consider taking more vigorous action. The leadership was now pressed not only by the political dangers posed by Irgun operations but also by an ultimatum from the administration demanding that the official Jewish organs cooperate with the CID in its efforts to suppress the Irgun. There was nearly unanimous reluctance within the Agency to become informers for the CID. At the same time there was a sense of urgency about the need to crush the Irgun just at the time, in October 1944, when negotiations in London for the establishment of the Jewish Brigade hung in the balance. Golomb, who had been among the most constant in his efforts over the years to reach agreement with the Irgun, now returned from London and called for the use of force against the Irgun's 'demented and damaging deeds' which were subverting the Zionist diplomacy. It was decided to make one last attempt to persuade the Irgun to conform before embarking on the risk of civil war.

On 8 October Sneh, the head of the Haganah command, was assigned to meet Begin whom he had known in Poland. The two men had a long conversation.[8] Sneh pointed out that the elected leadership was well aware that the time might arise when it would be necessary to engage in military struggle against British rule or indeed against other powerful forces, and tried to persuade Begin that the time had not arrived for this strategy. Asserting that the Irgun operations were most damaging to the Zionist interest, he emphasized that the people could not allow a dissident minority to dictate its future. Begin responded that he was willing to submit to Ben-Gurion's leadership if Ben-Gurion would place himself at the head of a national liberation movement and form a provisional Jewish government. So long as Ben-Gurion failed to give leadership in that vein the Irgun would be obliged to continue its own war until the majority of the people followed it.

It was clear that Begin would accept nothing less than the imposition of his will as the price for terminating the terror.

Begin considered himself a visionary whose martyrdom was to suffer execration until everybody realized that he alone was right. His political judgements were simple, lucid and profoundly ignorant. Again and again he slipped into the fallacy, whenever the Agency or the Haganah adopted a policy resembling the Irgun line, of assuming that his view had triumphed rather than that it had found its moment. When Ben-Gurion in the immediate pre-war period had adopted the essential statist philosophy of Jabotinsky this was not to concede that Jabotinsky was right. (At that time, in 1939, Jabotinsky did not believe that there would be a war in Europe.) What had been wrong twenty years previously could become right in new circumstances. The seasoned leaders, who intimately knew how every Jewish plant in Palestine had been nursed to fruition within the choking constraints of the triangular conflict, saw a great difference between 1943 or 1944 and 1945. And if many of his colleagues were excessively subtle or cautious, this could hardly be said of Ben-Gurion. Begin made up in integrity what he lacked in wisdom. If civil war did not break out among the Jews of Palestine in the next four years of their ten-year crisis, it was in no small measure due to Begin's determination to avoid it.

The Agency resolved to issue an ultimatum to the Irgun, which was ratified by the National Council, warning that it would put the Irgun down by force if it did not cease its campaign of terror. One more attempt was made to use persuasion. On 31 October Golomb now accompanied Sneh at a meeting with Begin (who was with Lankin, one of his lieutenants). In the meantime the Irgun had suffered a telling blow. On 21 October the authorities deported to Eritrea 251 Irgun suspects. But the same impasse was reached. Begin refused to yield and Golomb put him on notice that the community would now act forcefully against the Irgun.

Ignoring the explicit strictures of the administration, the Agency now decided to take direct action against the Irgun rather than co-operate with the CID. This decision was reversed when on 6 November 1944 two Lehi agents in Cairo assassinated Lord Moyne, the British minister of state in the middle east, who as colonial secretary had previously evinced hostility towards Zionist aims.

Moyne was a close personal friend of Churchill, and the assassination proved costly to Zionism. Churchill immediately announced that he would reconsider his lifelong friendliness towards Zionism. At just that time he had been assuring Weizmann of a post-war settlement most favourable to Zionist aims in Palestime. For the next few years, during the peak of the Zionist struggle with the London government, Churchill maintained a studied silence.

The shock of the assassination reverberated throughout the public and crystallized the conviction of the great majority that the act was incompatible with the spirit of the Zionist movement no less than with its interest. People now felt that the struggle with the dissidents was a battle for the soul of the movement. Lifting the Jewish taboo on informing (which had deep roots in eastern Europe) was now seen as a lesser stigma than harbouring assassins.

Although Lehi was responsible for Moyne's assassination the fury of the public was directed towards the Irgun. (The Irgun itself condemned the assassination.) Lehi, now led by Yellin-Mor (a maverick with political intelligence much superior to Stern), had been relatively ineffective, and at its peak mustered no more than about two hundred armed men serviced by an additional two hundred supporters. Some personal links with the Haganah had developed and the Stern group avoided becoming a primary target of Agency concern. There was an informal understanding that it would cease its activities and the brunt of the Agency anti-terror campaign fell on the Irgun.

The Agency now called on the public to refuse shelter to Irgunists, to stand firm against intimidation and to give every help to the British authorities in suppressing the dissidents. The religious leaders and others still opposed co-operation with the administration. Y. Gruenbaum, a radical progressive leader much revered by all parties, resigned from the executive when it refused to excise 'to the authorities' from its proclamation. It was with the greatest reluctance that the Agency determined to help the CID. The socialist leaders were more vigorous than the others in supporting this measure.

At the sixth convention of the Histadrut in November 1944 speaker after speaker denounced the Irgun and speech after speech justified co-operation with the administration. Ben-Gurion summed up the discourse, calling for the hounding of known terrorists and stressing that the public should co-operate with the administration and put aside its qualms. The newly formed splinter party Ahdut Ha'avodah exceeded all others in anti-Irgun sentiment but baulked at co-operation with the British on the grounds that the administration might begin by suppressing the Irgun and end by suppressing the whole of organized Jewish society. Although Ben-Gurion had sufficient support to commit the Histadrut officially to co-operation with the administration, in practice in the months to come the influence of Ahdut Ha'avodah was felt in the conduct of the anti-Irgun operation. For the execution of the project devolved on Palmach members for whom Ahdut Ha'avodah's voice was paramount.

In consideration of susceptibilities of conscience in the matter of informing on the authorities, the Haganah decided to avoid imposing mandatory duty, calling instead for volunteers. A special unit for counter-Irgun action was formed for this reason, subject to the Haganah general staff but not to the command. Members of the Haganah intelligence branch and about twenty other volunteers already engaged in this work were added to a special unit of one hundred and eighty Palmach volunteers. The task was divided into three functions carried out by separate units: shadowing and detection, protection (of potential Irgun targets) and arrest. The detection unit succeeded in laying hands on the Irgun list of financial contributors. To the general amazement it was found that the seven hundred names of persons and institutions included many remote from the Irgun, whose contributions were elicited by intimidation. The list was passed to the police to enable it to give protection to those named.

The most sensitive part of the operation was the arrest of Irgunists. Special units kidnapped suspects, and after verification of their identity by the detection squad they were placed in confinement in improvised prisons in various Haganah kibbutzim. The captured Irgunists were found to be more co-operative in interrogation by the Haganah than when apprehended by the British, so that the Haganah was able to penetrate to the roots of the Irgun. Only leaders were handed over directly to the British, but on the basis of information supplied the authorities were able to make some three hundred arrests. The entire Irgun high command except Begin himself and one aide were captured by the authorities.

The Haganah found it impossible to maintain adequate confinement conditions underground, and rather than accede to the British demand that all Haganah prisoners be turned in, they were released within a short time and subjected to continuous Haganah surveillance. By the spring of 1945 the Irgun was virtually silenced without bloodshed. The 'season' (as it was known) then came to a close in a welter of contrition.

The chief rabbinate condemned the kidnappings. Middle-class leaders denounced the whole operation as a socialist conspiracy to destroy opposition to the labour hegemony. Against the wishes of the Haganah general staff and the left-wing members of the command, who considered the operation incomplete, the Jewish Agency called a halt to the 'season'.

At the conclusion of the war in Europe in May 1945 it became apparent that the counter-Irgun campaign had achieved a somewhat illusory success. Begin escaped capture and new young enthusiasts flocked to the Irgun to fill the ranks depleted by arrests. Begin, confident that it would not be long before the official leadership embraced Irgun policies, insisted that his followers show restraint in response to Haganah interference. Civil war was thus avoided and the Haganah acquired the image of tormentor of the underdog.

The administration was less than grateful to the Jewish Agency for its co-operation. The authorities merely complained that the counter-terror campaign had ignored Lehi. Relations cooled to freezing point when it became known that the police were pressing Irgun prisoners to inform on the Haganah. With the end of the war and the absence of any change in the White Paper policies such as many had expected would come with the installation of the Labour government in London, Zionist-British relations settled into a frame of overt mutual hostility.

From the point of view of the Zionist establishment it proved to be an expensive error to call off the anti-Irgun campaign before it had eliminated the dissident organization. By the spring of 1945 there did not appear to be much left of the Irgun but it immediately recuperated. The very hostility of the authorities to official Zionist aims, which accounted for the Haganah retreat in the anti-Irgun struggle, benefited the Irgun, increasing its power of attraction. The Irgun was merely driven deeper underground by the 'season' and its organization was strengthened rather than crippled.

In the remaining three years of British rule it appeared that the authorities were more concerned to coerce the official Agency leadership than to liquidate the Irgun. For the British policy, the most powerful threat came from the organized forces of Palestine Jewry with its growing world-wide support. The Irgun was a nuisance which could be expurgated if the will was found, but the Agency was a threat to the entire British position in the middle east.

The collapse of British rule

With the conclusion of the war in Europe it was no longer possible to use the war itself as an argument for deferring rescue measures. The extent of the Nazi holocaust, the devastation of Jewish life throughout Europe, became apparent at the end of the war. Only one hundred thousand Jews had survived the concentration camps, while nearly double that number were displaced all over Europe and caught up in a process of random migration. Agents of the Haganah gave the movement direction towards the Mediterranean ports, and the pressure and clamour for refuge in Palestine rose in intensity, while illegal rescue efforts continued unabated. The issue of the refugees in their appalling camp conditions became a rallying point for Jews throughout the world, bringing them into the orbit of the Zionist movement. The plight of the refugees now lent to Zionism an unprecedented emotional strength. Pressure on the London government from diverse sections of international public opinion was now exerted not on the basis of a romantic nationalist myth, but on urgent humanitarian grounds.

In the meantime, however, the White Paper policy had become the indispensable key, in the view of the British foreign office, to the position of Britain in the middle east. During the war Britain had prepared its plan for middle-eastern dominance on the basis of an Arab nationalism subservient to British interests. The strategy was formalized with the establishment, on British initiative, of the Arab League united by anti-Zionist sentiment in March 1945. Britain also expelled French influence from Syria and seemed set fair to maintain its dominant political power in the region as a whole.

Zionist hopes were raised by the election of the Labour government in London in July 1945, since the Labour party in opposition had taken a consistent pro-Zionist line on the Palestine issue. It soon became clear, however, that the new government would continue the policies of its predecessor and pursue the same line of cultivating Arab friendship by opposing Zionist aspirations. A Zionist conference in London just after the British general election issued a warning that Palestine Jewry would take up arms against British rule if the White Paper policy was not abandoned. Weizmann at this meeting made an unsuccessful plea for restraint and for diplomacy to restore the alliance of Zionism with Britain.

When it became clear that the new Labour government did not intend to reverse the White Paper policy the leaders of Palestine Jewry resolved to step up illegal rescue to a level which would make nonsense of the policy. Many immigrants were infiltrated under Haganah guidance overland from Syria and some hundreds were brought in by sea escaping detection. But it became increasingly difficult, and within a few months virtually impossible to evade the coastal patrols. The result was the filling up of detention camps in Palestine, where illegal entrants were held. At the beginning of October 1945 a Palmach unit specially trained for the operation successfully released some two hundred detainees from an immigrant camp at Athlit and brought them by night with few mishaps to various kibbutzim and to Haifa.

The Haganah leadership now began to feel that the time had come to challenge British rule. Although many still saw the problem in terms of prodding the administration to become a better partner to Zionism, the more activist view prevailed in the context of the desperate situation of the remnant of European Jewry. Within a year of initiating its 'open season' on the Irgun the Haganah formed a working alliance with the two dissident organizations.

It was not easy for the Haganah leaders to negotiate with

the Irgun given all the bad feeling that had been generated in the recent past. Many, especially within the left-wing camp of the Palmach, felt that an agreement was unnecessary, that the Haganah should itself conduct an anti-administration campaign without Irgun help. But the stronger feeling was that the separatist activities would endanger the effectiveness of the militant policy, and must therefore be terminated by agreement. Irgun activities at the time did not help those who advocated negotiation. The Irgun continued to raise funds by intimidation and the Lehi by armed robbery, and also attacked installations in which Jewish employees were involved and endangered. In one incident in mid-October 1945 the Irgun raided a Jewish Brigade depot for arms, making off with over two hundred rifles, which resulted in the imprisonment of eight of the Brigade members on duty.

Agreement was reached at the end of October 1945 with the formation of the 'Hebrew Resistance Movement'. The Irgun and Lehi accepted Haganah discipline in the conduct of all armed operations, although they maintained their separate identities and their own separate political authorities. Since the dissidents did not recognize the committee of eighteen which was ultimately responsible for Haganah policy at the top level, a new committee was formed to give policy guidance. Known as 'Committee X', this body included many who were not enthusiastic about working with the Irgun, a fact which hampered the growth of harmony in the resistance movement, and made it difficult for the Haganah to co-ordinate actions with the dissidents and to allocate the various tasks amongst the available units.

The newly united resistance movement immediately attacked British communications throughout the country. Fifty Palmach units totalling eight hundred men were involved in the sabotage of the railway line at a hundred and fifty-three points, while Irgun units were assigned to destroy the railway station and installations at Lod. Lehi conducted an abortive sabotage attempt at the Haifa oil refineries without authorization by Committee X. This was the first of a series of incidents in which the discipline of the agreement was less than perfect. Some coastal patrol boats were also sunk, and the whole campaign was executed with little loss of life.

In November 1945 the British foreign secretary Ernest Bevin issued a long-awaited clarification of policy. Bevin announced the formation of a joint Anglo-American Committee of Inquiry[9] to study the refugee problem in Europe and all aspects of the situation in Palestine, and make recommendations to both governments. Bevin wished to draw the United States into sharing direct responsibility for the Palestine problem, hoping in this way to reduce the effectiveness of Zionist pressure on the American government. Pending the publication of the committee's report fifteen hundred Jewish refugees would be allowed monthly into Palestine. Bevin was silent on the third (constitutional) article of the White Paper which envisaged the transfer of power to an independent Arab state. It now appeared that Britain intended to use the conflict between the two national groups as a pretext for continued British rule.[10]

For most of the war period relations between the Jewish and Arab populations were relatively quiescent. The Arabs were pleased enough with the implementation of the immigration and land transfer restrictions, and with the attitude of the wartime High Commissioner Sir Harold MacMichael who held office until replaced by Lord Gort in 1944. Arab agitation grew when the five-year term of the White Paper came to its conclusion without any effort by the administration to prepare the ground for implementation of the third article. However, the pattern of the triangular conflict of the pre-war period was virtually suspended. The Palestine Arabs were crippled as a political force, and the presence of the ex-Mufti at the side of Hitler during the war added to their weakness the onus of having backed the losing side. The neighbouring Arab states had earned a new respectability under British sponsorship when one by one they were brought into the United Nations Organization and thereby enabled to recover the political ground they had lost by having favoured the losing side. The Arab League rather than the Palestine Arabs now made the running in anti-Zionist diplomacy. Although Arab agitation added somewhat to the level of tension in Palestine, it was the Jewish population now ranged against the administration that carried the struggle for liberation from foreign rule.

The Anglo-American Committee of Inquiry, reporting in April 1946, unanimously recommended the immediate transfer of one hundred thousand Jewish refugees from Europe to Palestine. The committee was unable to overcome differences of opinion about the long-term solution of the Palestine problem and made only vague general recommendations in this respect. But all twelve members were agreed on the need to transfer the survivors of the concentration camps, who had told them in testimony that they were determined to reach Palestine in any case, whatever the obstacles. President Truman immediately welcomed the committee's findings, and announced his support for the transfer of the hundred thousand. The British government was taken aback, since it had not expected a unanimous report, and Bevin had committed himself publicly to implementing any unanimous recommendations. The government announced that it was unable to implement the recommendations (after receiving military opinion that this would require an additional division of soldiers) unless and until the Arabs and Jews surrendered their weapons and the Jewish Agency took full responsibility for eliminating the terrorist movement. This was clearly an evasive diplomatic formula since on past experience it was obvious that the Haganah would not give up its arms, and that even if it did the Arabs would certainly not do so. The Zionist leaders responded with the statement that weapons would not be surrendered and the promise that if Britain's concern was for security, the Jewish population would guarantee complete abstention from violence if the refugees were brought to the country.

The committee thus failed in its purpose of bringing the United States and Britain into line in resolving the Palestine issue. If the London government had with American help brought the hundred thousand to Palestine (against Arab opposition) the Jewish state might never have come into being. The militancy of the Jewish Agency and the appeal of the terrorist movement would undoubtedly have dwindled, and Zionism would have lost much of its emotional force if the survivors of the holocaust in direst need had been given shelter. Britain's repudiation of the report sustained intact the alliance between the Haganah and the Irgun and brought the

Jewish Agency for the first time to the conclusion that it must work for the removal of British rule. To any who had doubted it, it was clear by the summer of 1946 that the Palestine conflict could not be resolved without violence. The longer the conflict was allowed to fester by the indecision of the London government, the greater would be the appeal of extremist opinion on all sides and the greater the eventual bloodshed.

In May 1946 Britain recognized the independence of Transjordan and its elevation from an 'emirate' to a kingdom. The ex-Mufti of Jerusalem escaped from his detention in Paris[11] to Egypt, and resumed his active leadership of the Palestine Arabs. The Arab states met in conference at Blaudan in Syria and announced that they would intervene militarily if necessary to prevent a Zionist solution in Palestine. Britain in the meantime was engaged in re-negotiating its 1936 treaty with Egypt, and had begun to look on Palestine as a replacement site for its main military base in the region. During the investigations by the Anglo-American committee of inquiry the resistance movement called a temporary truce, which was violated several times by Irgun actions. When it became clear that the government was not going to carry out the recommendation for the transfer to Palestine of the hundred thousand, the resistance leadership decided to carry out its biggest action. Bevin had remarked that to carry out the recommendation would involve several divisions of soldiers. The Zionist leaders were determined now to demonstrate that it would be just as costly in divisions *not* to carry out the recommendation. They also wished to demonstrate that Palestine would not be a suitable location for a British military base.

On 17 June 1946 the Palmach executed a carefully planned operation for the destruction of eleven vital road and rail bridges, many of them heavily guarded. Ten were successfully blown up, but as a result of defensive action in one case fourteen lives were lost. At the same time eleven members of a Lehi unit were killed in an attack on the British railway works in Haifa Bay.

In response to the various armed actions of the underground the authorities invariably retaliated with searches, curfews and arrests with a steady toll of life. After the 'night of the bridges' (as it was dubbed in Haganah lore) the administration decided to carry out a long-planned action aimed at crippling the underground and paralysing the Jewish leadership. Seventeen thousand British soldiers took part in the action on 29 June conducting searches for arms and mass arrests of Palmach members and Jewish Agency officials. Some two thousand seven hundred were placed in prison camps built for the purpose. Although Sneh eluded arrest and Ben-Gurion was abroad on a mission, most of the top leaders of the Agency, including Moshe Sharett, were imprisoned.

For the first time intervening in this way in the immediate affairs of the Palestinian leaders, Weizmann asserted his authority as president of the movement and ordered Sneh to call a halt to further armed actions until a meeting of the Agency could be arranged to decide policy. Weizmann considered that continued armed action against the administration would be tantamount to waging war on Britain, and that this would be likely to endanger the whole Zionist project. Committee X yielded to Weizmann, who had threatened to resign if his wishes were not met, and Sneh reluctantly ordered the suspension of all planned operations. Sneh, among the most militant of all the Haganah leaders, now resigned from the headship of the Haganah command, although he remained a member of the command. (Sharett, from his prison, appointed Ze'ev Shefer acting head of command.) Before escaping to Paris for a meeting with Ben Gurion and other leaders still at liberty, Sneh pleaded with the Irgun to observe the order not to carry out further actions for the moment, but to no avail.

Although the Irgun had abandoned its concern for the loss of life and Lehi had not typically shared this inhibition, British casualties until this time had been relatively minor. The situation changed on 22 July 1946 when the Irgun, ignoring the official resistance committee's order to refrain, blew up a wing of the King David Hotel in Jerusalem in which were housed the offices of British administrative and military personnel. Nearly one hundred were killed, including Jewish and Arab employees in addition to British officials. The operation had been planned in co-operation with the Haganah but apart from ignoring the order to desist for the time being, the Irgun in its execution also failed to meet a Haganah condition that the offices should be evacuated before the explosion.[12]

The rump of the leadership still at liberty condemned the act and there was a sense of outrage among the public, which assisted the advocates of greater restraint. The delicate balance of co-operation between the Haganah and the dissidents was now irreparably damaged and to all intents and purposes the united resistance movement came to an end. But the tone of anti-British passion had in any case by this time reached such a pitch that Zionist publicity directed anger at the administration rather than at the Irgun. In imprisoning the Agency personnel the authorities apparently hoped to be able to install a new, more moderate leadership to act for the Jewish population. In the event the act merely mobilized greater support for the dissidents.

The struggle over illegal immigration sharpened as the administration sought once and for all to put a stop to the rescue movement, which was still bringing refugees to Palestine by the thousand. At the end of July 1946 the arrival of the ship *Haganah* with nearly three thousand passengers, followed by several other boats in quick succession, brought the struggle to a climax. The administration announced that all refugees without legal entry certificates would henceforth be deported to Cyprus (then under British rule) for detention. In the aftermath of the King David Hotel outrage the administration launched a new series of searches for illegal immigrants and arms. Twenty-seven thousand troops were now engaged in this activity and in imposing curfews and civilian identification parades. Considering the level of tension and provocation, the British soldiery on the whole behaved decently, although there were a growing number of incidents of unruliness, sometimes instigated by officers.

The administration certainly harassed the Jewish population but its response did not compare with the repression unleashed on the Arab revolt from 1936 to 1938. Paradoxically, the British brought the full power of military repression to bear on the Arabs just when they were developing policies in line with Arab demands, while they refrained from military action against the Jews at a time when they were doing their utmost to defeat the Zionist policies. An atmosphere of near-anarchy prevailed throughout the country and the administration had clearly lost control over events. The Irgun had gained prestige from its long association with the Haganah and it continued to attract new young followers. With the disintegration of the united resistance movement the Irgun acted more freely and in the autumn of 1946 achieved a peak of terror and sabotage activity in the face of the most stringent military controls deployed by the administration.

At the same time as a mood of greater restraint spread among the official Zionist leaders the London government began to seek a compromise solution that would have American support. The American and British foreign policy establishments came momentarily together in the Morrison-Grady Plan, a proposal for provincial autonomy of Jews and Arabs in a federal Palestine administered by Britain, upon the acceptance of which it was promised that the hundred thousand concentration camp survivors would be allowed into the country. This proved unacceptable to the Arabs and the Jews of Palestine, though the Arab League representatives came to London for discussions with the government. The Zionist leaders meeting in Paris issued a call for the partition of Palestine providing for a viable Jewish state. On 4 October 1946 President Truman, under Zionist pressure in the midst of the Congressional elections, repudiated the Morrison-Grady plan sponsored by the State Department and endorsed the Zionist partition proposal, thereby sweeping the ground from under the British diplomacy bent on securing American co-operation towards a solution consonant with Britain's imperial interests.

In Palestine the administration prevailed on the Zionist leaders to denounce the dissident organizations as a price for the release of the imprisoned officials. On 5 November they were released from prison and the government announced that it no longer sought the arrest of Ben-Gurion and Sneh. In effect the administration conceded that it could not replace the elected Zionist leadership. The establishment condemned the Irgun and Lehi and called for their isolation, but there was no talk this time of co-operation with the administration in hounding them.

In December 1946 the twenty-second Zionist Congress convened at Basle. The movement had grown to over two million and America had replaced Poland as the largest centre of membership. The revisionist party had returned to the Zionist Organization in the spring with the rise of activism. As a result of these changes Mapai lost its formal predominance to the General-Zionists who united for the occasion and represented the great majority of the Americans. The American leader Abba Hillel Silver joined with Ben-Gurion across party lines to secure the adoption of an activist line against Weizmann's pleas for moderation. Weizmann was not re-elected president on account of his commitment to continued cooperation with Britain. Ben-Gurion was re-elected chairman of the executive and assigned the portfolio of defence. Shertok (Sharett) was placed in charge of international diplomacy to co-ordinate activities with the American leaders. The congress condemned terrorism but made clear at the same time that its programme was the establishment of a Jewish state, with or without partition.

The Arabs in Palestine during 1946 increased their political activity under the direction of the ex-Mufti in Cairo. The Arab Higher Committee was re-established early in the year but was unable to overcome chronic disunity. With the arrival of the ex-Mufti in Cairo a new Arab Higher Executive was installed under his chairmanship. The Husaini faction regained control of the Palestinian national movement and stiffened organizational and underground military preparations. But while the Arabs of Palestine had been dormant during the war the Zionists had developed organizational, economic and military strength, in addition to international support. And in the post-war months the Jewish population had been energized and mobilized in the struggle against British rule, giving them a momentum which the Arabs in Palestine lacked. The Arab League states, potentially very much more powerful than Palestine Jewry, carried the hopes of the Palestine Arabs.

In the early months of 1947 the strife in Palestine continued without relief. Tension was increased when the ex-Mufti renewed his old campaign of intimidating political opponents, but agitation and political murder among the Arabs was a minor irritant compared to the havoc of the Irgun and Lehi terror. The authorities resorted to flogging captured terrorists and carried out a series of death sentences by hanging. The Irgun and Lehi kidnapped British hostages and retaliated in kind. Britain was plunged into deep economic crisis by the severest winter in memory. The British public was sick and tired of the Palestine involvement. By the beginning of February the government had practically given up efforts at a solution. Bevin resolved to place the whole issue in the lap of UNO. In Palestine the administration now fought a losing battle for the rest of the year to maintain a semblance of order in the absence of clear policy directives from London.

In May the Irgun carried off a daring coup, breaking into Acre prison and releasing some thirty Irgun and Lehi captives in addition to about two hundred other convicts. There were nine Irgun fatalities in the action, followed by three more when those captured in the escapade were executed. This sort of action, costly in life and of doubtful political value, had become typical of Irgun actions. They damaged the prestige of the authorities but had no effect on the political balance. Irgun actions in 1947 did not endanger Zionist aims so much as in the previous period during the European war, but they did cost the Zionists a good deal of sympathy abroad. The official Zionist leadership, although hampered by the stigma of terrorism, were at their most effective in the propaganda war abroad, by means of which they had created the formidable alliance with American Jewry and the skilful manipulation of American domestic politics. The greatest propaganda opportunity in its struggle with Britain came to the Zionist movement in the summer of 1947 when the British deported over four thousand refugee passengers of the *Exodus 1947* to their port of embarkation in southern France, rather than to Cyprus. The refugees, apart from a few score who were too weak, refused to disembark, whereupon Britain incurred international opprobrium by shipping them to Hamburg to the land where their torture had begun. The whole process took several weeks, enabling the Zionists to bring together the issue of rescue and the clamour for statehood in a telling emotional appeal to world opinion while the problem of Palestine was under investigation by UNO.

Partition and British withdrawal

Meeting in special session at the request of Britain, the General

Assembly of the United Nations Organization early in May 1947 set up the United Nations Special Committee on Palestine[13] (UNSCOP) to investigate and make recommendations on the Palestine issue in all its aspects. In the discussions the Arab spokesmen made it clear that the Arabs would not feel bound to accept any UNSCOP recommendations that violated the principle of Arab sovereignty in Palestine, and that war would likely follow any attempt to impose such a solution. The British delegate made it equally clear that Britain would not assist in the implementation of any solution that was not accepted by both sides. The committee held its first hearings in Jerusalem in mid-June and spent five weeks in the country sounding opinion, after which it briefly visited Lebanon to hear the spokesmen of the Arab states and then went on to Geneva to examine the problem in its European aspects and prepare its report.

The conclusions of UNSCOP were drawn up at the end of August. While the committee achieved unanimity on a number of basic principles its specific recommendations were divided between a majority and a minority report. The committee was unanimous in its view that the Mandate should be terminated and replaced by an independent Palestine, and agreed also on the necessity of maintaining an economic union of the country. The majority recommended the partition of the country into a Jewish and an Arab state in a geographic pattern resembling the Peel Commission proposals of 1937 with Jerusalem as an international enclave, while the minority made up of the delegates of India, Iran and Yugoslavia recommended a federal solution.[14] The majority report envisaged a two-year period of UNO trusteeship, to be administered in the main by Britain, in which the transition to independence would be effected. The minority report instead recommended a three-year transition towards a federal state with Jerusalem as the shared capital of both components of the federal union. The majority report designated a larger area for the Jewish state than the minority allowed for the Jewish part of the union.

The Arab spokesmen immediately rejected both reports absolutely. The Zionist leadership then meeting in Geneva rejected the minority report but welcomed the majority report in principle while reserving its final judgement till the General

Assembly of UNO came to a decision. The socialist left opposed the majority Zionist view. While welcoming the recommendation that the mandate be terminated the dissident labour parties called for the establishment by UNO of an interim international administration of the country to work towards a bi-national solution. The revisionists also opposed partition, claiming that the whole country should be immediately placed under Jewish sovereignty.

Arab and Zionist diplomacy now concentrated on the UNO arena as the General Assembly prepared to meet in mid-September with the intention of reaching a decisive resolution of the fate of Palestine. Before the assembly met the British government had taken the decision to withdraw from Palestine though it had not yet decided on the time-table of its new policy. The colonial secretary opened the Palestine deliberations at UNO towards the end of September 1947 with the announcement that Britain accepted the UNSCOP recommendation that the mandate be terminated. At the same time the British representatives continued to make it clear that Britain would not assist in the implementation of any scheme, such as partition, that was not acceptable to both sides. This refusal would extend also to co-operation in a gradual transfer of power, whether with a UNO trusteeship set up to conduct a transition to independence on the basis of partition or directly with the provisional organs of successor governments.

Zionist political pressure within America in conjunction with Soviet determination to hasten the collapse of the British position in the middle east brought about a momentary convergence of American and Russian policy in support of partition. Diplomatic competition between the Zionist and the Arab supporters concentrated on persuading the representatives of the small powers, especially those of Latin America. In view of the dependence of many of these upon the United States the balance of advantage lay with the Zionists. Pressing its advantage with great effectiveness the Zionist lobby secured the necessary two-thirds majority in favour of partition when the issue was brought to a vote in the assembly plenum on 29 November 1947. The assembly resolution endorsed a version of the UNSCOP majority report that included slight modifications favouring the Arabs in an attempt to win the acquiescence of Muslim states.

The Zionist effort was conducted to its successful conclusion in New York by a professional team of high calibre led by Moshe Shertok (later Sharett) and assisted personally by Weizmann and by influential sympathizers in the United States. In the thirty years that had passed since Weizmann secured the Balfour Declaration the capacity of the Zionist movement as a political force had been enlarged beyond recognition. In the meantime the European holocaust had greatly widened Zionist support, especially in the United States.

There is no gainsaying the importance of the UNO intervention as a factor in the creation of Israel as an independent state, nor the importance of Zionist diplomacy in securing that intervention. It could nevertheless be argued with considerable force that the facts that had been established in Palestine by the Jewish settlers provided the indispensable minimum basis for the diplomatic success. And just as Ben-Gurion could argue at the time of the Balfour Declaration that what would be done in Palestine would be the crucial determinant of the Zionist future, so now he could argue with equal cogency that the UNO resolution was a scrap of paper unless and until the Jewish population in Palestine could be fully mobilized to put it into effect. It was no less difficult now for Ben-Gurion to persuade his colleagues of the urgency for full mobilization of resources to prepare for war on a large scale, than it had been thirty years earlier to persuade his colleagues that the Zionist charter was the beginning rather than the consummation of the movement's struggle. The Jews in Palestine received the news of the partition resolution with great celebration and euphoria. A decision by the powers in New York, in which America and the Soviet Union were able to concur, was a most substantial international charter for independence. With the two largest imperial powers now committed to partitioning Palestine the British and the weak and disunited Arabs were the only obstacles to the successful culmination of a half century of world-wide Zionist effort, providing that the population in Palestine had the will and the leadership and organization needed to realize the opportunity.

Not accepting that the British really intended to withdraw from Palestine the Zionist diplomacy had regarded British influence as the most formidable obstacle to the legislation of partition, and now the British presence in Palestine was seen as the main obstacle to its implementation. Scepticism and uncertainty about British intentions continued right up to the very eve of the British withdrawal in May 1948. While it may well be that in its initial referral to UNO Britain still expected to be asked to carry on with the mandate, as the only possible peaceful solution, by the time the General Assembly reached its decision it is likely that Britain too had come to the conclusion that it must withdraw completely. Public opinion within Britain, exercised by the constant terror and the casualties uncompensated by any obvious political reward, certainly desired total withdrawal. The British government announced its formal decision to withdraw on 18 December and soon after made clear that the date for termination of its responsibilities would be 14 May 1948. The British role in the country now became one of trying to influence the outcome of the expected war in favour of the Arabs and there is little doubt that the assessment of the situation made by the British government and its advisers was that the Arab states would quickly crush the Zionist state by military means. The British administration ignored the increasing chaos in the country. It no longer even appeared concerned about the disorder occurring under its formal writ, and it intervened only sporadically where it seemed possible to throw some advantage to the Arabs. War had to all intents and purposes begun at the end of November and the Arab flight from the country also began at that early date. It was already clear then that the local Arab population was not inclined to fight either against partition or for sovereignty. The issue lay with the surrounding states, and even the Mufti found himself unable to maintain the initiative or achieve political control of the Palestine situation.

Declaration of Independence

The UNO partition resolution of 29 November 1947 specified in some detail the institutional arrangements for the transition from mandatory rule to Jewish (and Arab) sovereignty in Palestine, and also the constitutional requirements to be fulfilled by the new state upon its accession to independence. The British government, opposed as it was to the partition plan, declined to co-operate in effecting an orderly transfer of power, thus by default leaving the initiative with the Jews to prepare for their own independence. Accordingly, the Jewish leaders unilaterally adapted their quasi-governmental institutions so far as possible to conform to the UNO blueprint.

In November 1947 the executive of the National Council (*Va'ad Leumi*) of Palestine Jewry together with the Jewish Agency Palestine Executive sought to reduce duplication of effort and responsibility by forming themselves as a joint contingency committee (*Va'adat Hamazav*) with a small executive arm for the organization of military mobilization and the provision of needed services as the British administration began to deteriorate. At the same time they started discussing plans for the assumption of sovereignty in anticipation of British withdrawal.

The diffusion and overlap of responsibility among the various agencies of the quasi-government was in practice diminished as a source of confusion by the ubiquity and growing forcefulness of Ben-Gurion's personal leadership. By mid-April 1948, in no small degree as a result of his persistence and persuasive power, formal control of the armed forces and all Jewish policy-making institutions was detached from the Zionist organs with external sources of authority and vested in Palestinian organs responsible solely to the Jewish population living in the country. On 1 March 1948 the National Council resolved to replace the contingency committee by a more broadly based authority, including leaders of parties such as the revisionists and communists not hitherto represented in the official quasi-government, with the status of a pilot provisional government to succeed to the powers of national administration on the lines envisaged in the partition plan. Following close discussion and negotiation between the political parties dissidence was virtually eliminated and all political power was reposed in a thirty-seven-member People's Council (*Mo'etzet Ha'am*), with a thirteen-member executive, the People's Administration (*Minhelet Ha'am*) drawn from among its members. Early in April the Zionist General Council ratified the initiative of the Palestine leaders, abdicated its own presumptive jurisdiction and formally designated the People's Council and the People's Administration as the prospective provisional government of the Jewish state which would come into being immediately upon termination of the mandate.

The People's Council was composed through inter-party negotiation in rough correspondence with the estimated political strength of the various groups within the country. Ben-Gurion's Mapai received ten seats, enough together with its allies in the centre to command a majority against criticism from the left and right. The revisionists were allocated three places, though active Irgun leaders were excluded. The executive group of thirteen included four from Mapai but no revisionists. Ben-Gurion's immediate Mapai colleagues in the smaller committee were Eliezer Kaplan,[15] David Remez,[16] and Moshe Shertok (Sharett). These supplied the core of the country's leadership on all matters other than security, defence and military procurement, which occupied the major part of Ben-Gurion's own time and concentration.

During the months between the passage of the UNO resolution and the termination of the mandate there was much uncertainty within the Jewish leadership about the wisdom of declaring the independence of the state immediately upon the withdrawal of the British. Many thought it best to rely on the possibility of a truce with the Arabs as mooted in UNO circles, involving postponement of the assumption of sovereignty and the establishment of a transitional regime under international trusteeship. Others feared that this would forever let slip the opportunity to achieve independence. Argument was intense and opinion closely divided right up to the eve of British withdrawal, though this was not allowed to impede the preparation of machinery for a smooth accession to independent government. Such machinery was in any case needed to protect Jewish life and fill the administrative void left by the accelerating disintegration of British rule. Britain's refusal to co-operate in implementing partition and the failure of the mandatory administration to maintain peace and order undoubtedly hastened the crystallization of support within the Jewish population for immediate independence. Opinion amongst the Zionist leaders gradually swung towards the consistent view of Ben-Gurion in favour of declaring Jewish statehood, so that by early March the leadership was able to pursue this policy on the basis of near unanimity among the general public.

Meeting for the first time in mid-April the Committee of Thirteen (as the People's Administration was popularly known) completed details of the plans for installation of the provisional government and discussed the terms of the announcement to be made asserting Jewish independence. By 12 May all lingering uncertainty had given way in the Committee of Thirteen to a determination to proclaim Jewish independence with effect from midnight of 14 May, the appointed moment for the formal vacation of power by Great Britain. After deciding by a majority of those present (in a vote of five to four) to exclude from its terms any specification of the boundaries of the new state in view of the obvious likelihood that these would be determined by military results, the thirteen delegated to a committee of five the drafting of a proclamation of independence. The wording of the proclamation was the object of intense argument right down to the last minute before the deadline imposed by the fall of Sabbath on Friday eve of 14 May. The point of wording that occasioned the greatest difficulty in securing agreement was the precise term for the invocation of divine auspices. While the secularist representative on the drafting committee wished to eschew any such language whatsoever the religious spokesman pressed for a robust expression of official trust in 'Israel's Rock and Redeemer'. The compromise negotiated in the nick of time by Ben-Gurion retained the formula initially sponsored by the drafting committee expressing trust in the 'Rock of Israel'.

On the afternoon of 14 May the People's Council convened in Tel Aviv and issued the Declaration of Independence[17] as rendered vocally on its behalf by Ben-Gurion. Following a brief statement of the Zionist theory of Jewish history and the grounds of the legitimacy of the state, the proclamation announced the establishment of 'a Jewish state in Palestine, the State of Israel', and intimated that the People's Council would function until the ratification of a constitution as the provisional council of state, whose thirteen-member executive arm would be the provisional government.

PART III

THE NATION IN THE MAKING (1947-67)

*People cherish the footprints of history
rather than the direction of advance.*
J. B. *Agus*

CHAPTER 11

WAR, ARMISTICE AND
IMMIGRATION (1947-51)

*Ben-Gurion the leader – the war of independence – armistices
and boundaries – mass immigration*

Ben-Gurion, the leader

Just as the Balfour Declaration was Weizmann's personal
monument, the proclamation of Israel's independence was the
culmination of a personal *tour de force* on the part of Ben-
Gurion. Unfashionable though it is to attribute decisive weight
to the impact of individual genius in history, the study of
Israel's history ineluctably forces the conclusion that Ben-
Gurion will endure for posterity, cherished or reviled, as the
indispensable creator of the state, the terms of its existence
and the image of its being.

Surrounded throughout his political career by men of great
ability, he nevertheless rose to dominate them at crucial
historical junctures. Invariably ahead of his colleagues in his
sense of the direction of events and in his appreciation of the
opportunities latent in circumstance, he also displayed the
boldness of decision needed to translate his insights into
realities. The caution and timidity of his immediate colleagues,
a product often of excessive subtlety, held sway so long as
events flowed slowly. His vigour and decisiveness, his single-
mindedness and lucidity overwhelmed opposition when the
velocity of events rendered these qualities invaluable. To his
right the terrorists displayed greater daring but not a modicum
of political insight, while to his left the idealistic culture was
too easily enmeshed in labyrinths of abstraction. Only the

devotees of Ahad Ha'am and the Magnes-Buber-Hashomer Hatzair circles displayed an equally profound understanding of Zionism as a historical force, but Ben-Gurion was easily able to relegate them to the academic periphery of the movement by means of an occasional rhetorical gamble negating their detachment. Only Jabotinsky more incisively sounded the national spirit, but Ben-Gurion silenced his voice as an alternative centre of leadership within Palestine by adopting his political strategy in all its essentials. Towering above those of his colleagues who shared his views he was able to drive them and the people to grasp independence from the political and military flux while perhaps only few among them understood its implications and especially its terms.

His foresight and his knowing choices imposed upon the people in their political innocence, and evoking their enthusiasm, created a distance between him and his people. He was a stranger to the Jews and the Zionists abroad, and even to the Israelis in the aftermath, a hallowed presence rather than a personal peer. Marked out from the first amongst his contemporaries as neither typical Jew nor Zionist nor even pioneer-farmer, he was in touch with the future and in search of its levers while they wrestled with diurnal chores and hoped. Moving from stage to stage with the times he left his colleagues anchored to their past commitments while he picked up new helpers in each successive arena. From countryside to the Histadrut, from Mapai to the diplomatic world of the Jewish Agency and the British power structure, from there to the global Zionist and alien forces from which he hoped to elicit recognition of the independence of a new nation, he came finally into the capacity of military leadership.

Ben-Gurion was able to comprehend the secular *realpolitik* of the twentieth century and the historical opportunities for creating the new state while yet he lacked the comprehension of foreign cultures possessed by such as Weizmann and Sharett. He grasped their sources of power without ever being charmed by their cultures, except for a latent sentimentality in regard to England as typified for him by Oxford. He could not for a minute assimilate to the alien as could his cosmopolitan contemporaries. The obverse of his fanaticism was his provincialism. America for him was a perennial enigma except in respect to its macro-political potentialities. His only resource for grasping the gentile world was his immersion in Greek philosophy and Buddhism. The Soviet giant was a magnet for his hatred mingled with respect for its power. Reversion to its archaic sources enabled him to place the Zionist ideology in a millennial perspective transcending the immediate Jewish tradition and experience. By making a radical break with Jewish history he was able to fit Zionist needs into the mould of contemporary world history.

He preferred to work with handpicked youngsters, the children of his contemporaries. In this way he expressed his affinity for futures in contrast with his contemporary colleagues who were a generational in-group restricted to those who had shared in the primeval Ottoman and post-Ottoman experience. Ben-Gurion made quick judgements about people and used them up, leaving them stranded if and when he discovered, as he often did, that he had been mistaken about them. He never rewarded service with personal favours. Not a good judge of individuals, he could nevertheless mobilize them. In choosing his lieutenants he was incapable of intuiting their temperament or their calibre. But he was constantly aware that his lieutenants were the people's generals, and would closely monitor their performance to discard the inadequate. Rather than insight into human nature, he relied on the stereotype of their backgrounds when assessing their potential. Capable of great vindictiveness and personal pettiness, he never forgave nor forgot personal enmity and displayed great ruthlessness in pursuit of his prey. He appeared not to realize the pitiful vulnerability of lesser men to his Olympian spleen because of his democratic temperament: a form of flattery in which he placed his most humble adversaries on a par with himself. He always retained respect for his victims in the throes of their humiliation.

His greatest blind spot was a deliberately worn eyepatch: the Arabs. He understood their peril better than any of his associates who evinced greater compassion for their fate in the conflict with Zionism. Occasionally he revealed sorrow for their weakness and always showed a respect for their humanity which had a more authentic resonance than the lament of others claiming to be more moved by the issue of justice for the Arabs. Only Hashomer Hatzair and the Ihud circles could claim an equally genuine appreciation of the Arab plight, and Ben-Gurion sensed this. His own colleagues within Mapai, committed to the same *realpolitik* and to his leadership, were easily contained and domesticated. Knowing this, Ben-Gurion concentrated with absolute determination on the Jewish problem, leaving the Arabs to take care of themselves. As for Magnes and Buber and the others, he resorted to every device including ridicule to prevent the essential truth of their position from becoming the doctrine of the movement. He isolated them and made his choice for war with a profound grasp of its implications for the course of Zionism and the social personality of Israel. Believing that thus alone could Zionism bear fruit and knowing full well that this would determine the character of the state and the terms of its existence for generations to come, he resolved on a military resolution. While not welcoming the implications, he appreciated their self-fulfilling and irreversible nature, and the creative energies they could release.

The war of independence

The Zionist Congress in December 1946 assigned to Ben-Gurion the portfolio of defence. This enabled him to take the initiative in military planning and to gather under his own command the various elements of partisan military organization. At the age of sixty and at the peak of his powers, he now added to the political tasks to which he had long been accustomed the new responsibility of directing the military strategy of Palestine Jewry.

Ben-Gurion was unable to persuade his colleagues to accept his view of the impending challenges. While his political associates looked to the international arena as the primary battlefield in which the future of the Jewish state would be determined, Ben-Gurion and his advisers in the Haganah anticipated the need to prepare for war with the armies of the neighbouring Arab states. When the convergence of Soviet and American views on Palestine became apparent early in 1947 Zionist leaders tended to assume that Britain and the Arabs would have no choice but to accept a *fait accompli*. Ben-Gurion, on the other hand, while he considered that the

Arabs of Palestine would not offer effective resistance to partition, foresaw that the neighbouring states would intervene with military force and also that it would be necessary to counter British attempts to create conditions for Arab victory.

The Haganah commanders concurred in Ben-Gurion's political assessment but they nevertheless found it difficult to appreciate its implications for military planning and organization. Their military imagination had been formed by the defence doctrines that had evolved in response to paramilitary attacks on settlements. Although the Palmach had familiarized the Haganah with the functioning of a mobile army, experience was more or less limited to company-strength operations against limited non-military targets. There was still great difficulty in grasping the concept of a modern army capable of destroying enemy power in the field. Ben-Gurion was determined to convert the organization and psychology of the underground forces into those of a modern army organized in brigades and even divisions deploying heavy equipment. Like the political leaders, his military colleagues were unable to see that the Haganah might ever have any use for heavy armament.

Already in the summer of 1945 Ben-Gurion was alert to the opportunity to acquire weapons when the major armies of Europe would gradually scrap their armour. He set up a team in Paris for the clandestine procurement of artillery, tanks and aircraft. At Ben-Gurion's insistence (and against their better judgement) the Jewish Agency provided some three million dollars for this purpose. The mission was on the whole successful, hampered less by financial stringency than by British vigilance in Europe and at points of entry in Palestine. France and Czechoslovakia were the main sources of supply. Much of the equipment had to be kept in secret storage in Europe until the British withdrawal from Palestine.

After a close countrywide review which he personally conducted in the spring months of 1947 Ben-Gurion came to the conclusion that the Haganah was not making sufficient use of the military knowledge and experience accumulated by the thousands who had served with the British forces in the European war. He considered that the Haganah of itself did not have the inner momentum to provide the basis for a modern army. For this it would be necessary to activate the entire Zionist movement, mobilize the population in Palestine and infuse it with his own sense of urgency and imminent danger. His efforts were to little avail until the passage of the UNO partition resolution at the end of November triggered the first violent Arab reactions.

At a Mapai meeting in January 1948 Ben-Gurion spoke in a manner which revealed how even at that late date he felt he had to struggle against the complacency of his colleagues:[1]

'Many important and precious things which comrades are speaking about and about which I too spoke some time ago do not penetrate my ears now and I no longer know their significance. Just now I heard X speaking about the state, and it seemed to me that I had forgotten the meaning of this word. I heard him say that the wisdom of Israel is the wisdom of redemption, and neither do these words mean anything to me, for I feel that the wisdom of Israel now is the wisdom of war, this and nothing else, this and this alone. Without this wisdom both the word "state" and the word "redemption" are emptied of their content ... The eight months before us are not like any eight months we have known in any other year, nor perhaps like any eight years or any eighty years, and I have no hesitation in saying – nor like any eight hundred years that have passed or that will come. For there is a clear feeling that into the seven or eight months before us and into which we have already entered, is compressed the whole of Jewish history: that which has continued for over three thousand years and on which will depend the Jewish history to come, perhaps for hundreds or even thousands of years. So I am not able nor do I wish to see beyond the next seven or eight months, for in my eyes they determine everything, for during them the war will be decided, and nothing exists for me now but this war.'

At the end of November 1947 when the first phase of the war began, the Haganah network embraced about forty-five thousand men and women in settlements and cities throughout the country. Of these some three thousand comprised the highly trained Palmach units, two-thirds of which were mobilized and the remainder in reserve. Nearly ten thousand were organized in the field force units, while the rest, numbering about thirty-two thousand, consisted of the static settlement units. In addition to the Haganah there were a probable three thousand or so followers of the Irgun (and a few hundred in Lehi), of whom but a small proportion were combat-trained. A shortage of infantry weapons reduced the effectiveness of the Haganah forces at that time.[2]

In November a campaign of mobilization was instituted, leading to full mobilization of the fit population by the early spring. By the time the state was declared in mid-May the Haganah was able to field some thirty thousand men in addition to a slightly larger number in the units responsible for defence of their own settlements. By this time many consignments of lighter weapons and ammunition that had been purchased in Europe had been brought into the country, and some heavy armaments had also arrived, eluding British interception. Although the mobilization was of necessity voluntary, social sanctions were sufficiently powerful to ensure a response equivalent to conscription. Thousands were being trained at the same time under Haganah direction in the detention camps in Cyprus and in refugee centres in Europe. Several hundred volunteers from abroad added to the complement of officers and technicians who had good training and experience in the European war. The limitations of the Haganah as a fighting force were in good measure balanced by its advantages over a standing army. Its voluntary basis and democratic ethos made for toughness and initiative in battle, while its intimate connections with the local communities under its protection made for a spirit of stubborn defence. On the other hand, of course, its underground existence impeded training and movement in the early weeks of the war when the British forces still exercised some control.

The Arab states made preparations to invade the country after the British withdrawal. Until that time the British force of seventy-seven thousand troops and several thousand armed policemen formally controlled the country. Although they were theoretically neutral there is little doubt that the British policy was to assist the Arabs, and particularly Abdullah of Transjordan, to obtain strategic advantages. The Arab Legion, British officered and trained, with a fighting strength of over four thousand was the best-equipped force in the Arab world. Britain allowed it to take control of Arab areas of the country and to press on the Jewish position in and around Jerusalem while the British administration still remained in the country. The administration also turned a blind eye to the infiltration of a volunteer army from Syria (The Arab Liberation Army) mustering a strength of about five to seven thousand including irregulars. These combined Arab forces, in addition to the deployment of the Palestinian Arabs themselves, were no match for the Haganah. The local Arabs had the topographic advantage of control of the high ground in nearly every part of the country. The Arabs had quantities of light arms, but no organization of any military consequence. Two rival paramilitary forces had evolved in the cities. In the countryside military organization was still based, as in the Arab revolt of the 'thirties, on small bands formed round the leadership of local notables. On the whole the Arab population showed no strong disposition to fight against partition, nor did they respond with enthusiasm to the charms of sovereignty embellishing the UNO partition plan.

Initially the Haganah staff had plans for the static defence of settlements and Jewish population centres. Arab attacks were met with strong local reprisals, but in order to avoid a direct confrontation with British troops it was thought best to avoid strategic movements. Ben-Gurion was not satisfied with this militia approach and the Haganah staff needed little persuading to change its strategy when the nature of the threat to the Jewish population became clearer after a few weeks. Violence erupted throughout the country at the beginning of December 1947. Although direct Arab attacks in force on Jewish settlements were repulsed with heavy losses, Arab sabotage and terror in the cities and the roads inflicted heavy casualties. At the end of March, after four months of intermittent strife, Jewish casualties included nearly a thousand killed. The main danger to the Jewish population was the Arab ability to strike at vital communications by ambush and sabotage from the high ground. Jerusalem was cut off from the rest of the country and placed under close siege. Arab forces pressed on the Etzion block of settlements to the south of Jerusalem and in the surrounding Judean hills, tightening the noose around the city.

Assuming the intervention of Arab armies after the British withdrawal, it became clear that the prospective Jewish state would be dismembered unless the Haganah took control of the tenuous communications linking the Jewish cities and settlements. If the Arabs had accepted partition and a state of peace had prevailed the territories allocated by partition to the Jewish state would have been viable. But in the face of attack the topography of the proposed Jewish state rendered it indefensible from within. Accordingly the general staff of the Haganah, pressed by Ben-Gurion, prepared a detailed offensive plan ('Plan D') to capture key positions from which to maintain strategic defence in the face of invasion on several fronts. The plan was ready early in March and was due to be executed immediately upon British withdrawal. It provided for the capture of all cities of mixed population in which Arab attacks on civilians were taking a heavy toll of life. These and other Arab settlements within the boundaries of the prospective Jewish state would come under military rule, while within the territory allotted to the Arab state forward positions designated for capture would be held so long as the requirements of defence of the Jewish population made this necessary.

As the situation of Jerusalem worsened and elsewhere casualties rose steadily Ben-Gurion pressed for an immediate offensive regardless of the British presence. It had become politically urgent to demonstrate the Jewish military capacity to defend the borders of the proposed state, since the apparent Arab successes in the first four months of hostilities had contributed to a movement in UNO to retreat from the partition recommendation. With supplies of food and water in Jerusalem running out, relief of the siege was the first objective of the Haganah offensive. Early in April the Haganah after heavy fighting in the hills opened a way for three convoys of supplies to the city. On 10 April, the Irgun, acting with Lehi and without full Haganah approval, although at the time it was just concluding an agreement for co-operation with the Haganah, attacked the village of Deir Yassin near Jerusalem and wantonly massacred some two hundred and fifty of its civilian inhabitants.[3] Two days later the Arabs retaliated by ambushing a Jewish medical convoy in the city, killing seventy-seven doctors, nurses and students. Atrocities like these had become mutually habitual.

During April and early May the Haganah took control of Tiberias, Haifa, Safed and Jaffa, the first three of these being cities of mixed population within the area designated for the Jewish state. In spite of their great inferiority in men and arms, the Arabs had the advantage in the first four months of the war so long as the Haganah limited itself to local defence, however active. The second phase of the war from the beginning of April to mid-May, with the Haganah on the offensive, demonstrated its overwhelming superiority in manpower and military capacity in the field, in spite of the shortage of weapons. Jewish losses in the six weeks of fighting on the offensive exceeded one thousand two hundred and fifty killed.

An event of great political importance which occurred during the first two phases of the war was the mass flight of some three hundred thousand Arabs from their homes in Jewish-controlled areas.[4] The Arab exodus began gradually in December and January with the departure of about thirty thousand of the wealthier elements as disorder mounted in the country. By the early spring general panic spread among the Arabs wherever the Haganah arrived in force. As each of the cities of mixed population was captured by the Haganah the Arabs fled *en masse*. In part this was the result of the atrocity propaganda issued by the Arab media (with the probable intention of increasing mobilization). Exaggerated propaganda of this sort reached a high pitch after the Deir Yassin outrage. In part the flight was the result of the disorder and lack of leadership within the Arab community. In this phase of the war the Zionist leaders, fearful of adverse political trends at UNO and anxious to rebut the prevalent view that the Arabs would be unwilling to live in peace with the Jews under partition, made efforts to persuade the Arabs to remain in their homes. These efforts were to no avail in the face of the contagious panic. Civilian efforts of this kind, which were particularly vigorous in Haifa, were in any case counteracted by psychological warfare in the streets by the Haganah personnel. Many of the fleeing Arabs left for other parts of Palestine, rather than for Syria and Lebanon, in the belief that their absence would be brief, until the armies of their neighbours would come and remove the Zionist threat to their way of life. [5]

When the pre-state phases of the war were concluded and the Jewish state stood intact the ambiguous Zionist policy was changed. The flight had not been anticipated by the Zionists but its occurrence generated the aspiration for a homogeneous state. In the expansive phases of the war after the Arab invasions the Haganah now encouraged, sometimes organized, usually prodded and occasionally coerced the Arabs to leave the territories coming under Israeli control. By the war's end in January 1949 a total of some seven hundred thousand Arabs had become refugees in the neighbouring countries. [6]

In the first months of the war before Israel asserted its independence Ben-Gurion was concerned about the slackness and diffusion of political and military control, and the inadequacy of the quasi-governmental organization to conduct a total war effort. He pressed for the speedy establishment of a provisional government centralizing control in a ministerial pattern, to supersede the authority of the Jewish Agency by organs solely responsible to the Palestine population. He was at the same time concerned at what he had begun to see as the dangerous dispersal of command functions in the Haganah. He was worried about the continued practice of local and municipal autonomy in defence matters, about the separate command and sectarian ethos of the Palmach, about the political party pressures within the Haganah high command and about the continued dissidence of the terrorist organizations. He had also begun to suspect that Galili was not the right man to head the Haganah, [7] and had come to the conclusion that the command as a whole, and certainly the post of head of command was redundant from the moment the Agency transferred its authority to the provisional government at the end of April.

The Agency formally acknowledged the transfer of all its executive functions to a new national executive (the People's Administration) of thirteen which was in effect a pilot provisional government. Ben-Gurion made it known to his colleagues (not yet publicly but as a 'trial balloon') that he now considered the Haganah command and its headship abolished, and that he would deal directly as 'minister' with the military general staff. There ensued a furore of protest by the left-wing spokesmen. Galili was a member of the new Mapam party made up of a merger between Ahdut Ha'avodah and Hashomer Hatzair, and he was popular with the Haganah and Palmach commanders and rank and file. There was a strong suspicion that Ben-Gurion wanted a political purge for partisan (Mapai) reasons. In fact Ben-Gurion was indeed preparing the ground for the termination of the Palmach separate command, which he knew would be fraught with opposition and tension when the time came. In his view it was the Palmach that by its partisan psychology and elitist myth endangered the idea of a national army. Some of the socialist leaders (though not Galili himself) argued that the army was an instrument of class and that it should remain under labour control. Ben-Gurion conceded that the state might be a class institution but argued that the army was nothing but the lifeline of the country as a whole, and must therefore be above class or party considerations. On failing to secure support, and on discovering widespread resentment and uneasiness within the Haganah leadership in reaction to his proposal, Ben-Gurion relinquished his pressure for the time being and conceded Galili's formal reinstatement. But he made it clear to the Haganah staff, without delay, that it was he who intended to direct the war strategy. The force of his leadership and his undoubtedly acute grasp of the military problems facing the country, particularly in their political aspects in which the staff was not so well-versed, soon created the atmosphere in which he was able to implement Galili's removal from the leadership of command.

Of equally great concern was the termination of dissident activities, which in the first phase of the war had become a greater threat than ever before not only to the political prospects of the community but to its very security and defence. Preliminary negotiations faltered on the insistence of the Irgun that it would maintain its separate identity, even under Haganah command, until a Jewish state was declared, and the equally firm determination of the Haganah leaders that only a single army rather than a merger of parts would meet the needs of the hour. An agreement was drawn up early in March 1948 along the lines desired by the Irgun, the conditions of which resembled those underlying the united resistance movement of 1945–6. The agreement was ratified by the Zionist executive in mid-April by a slender majority secured against the fierce opposition of the labour groups. The Irgun undertook to dissolve itself upon the declaration of statehood and to act only with Haganah approval until then. After a false start the agreement was put into operation only at the end of April, two weeks before the establishment of the state. The Irgun units were now at the disposal of the central military machine, but there was some dismay in these circles when it was discovered that, contrary to its propaganda, the Irgun was unable in fact to field any considerable numbers for combat. Lehi formally relinquished its independence a few days later.

Ben-Gurion insisted, just two days before the declaration of statehood, that he would continue to carry on the responsibility for defence only if a single national army subject to the single authority of the ministry of defence was set up without delay. The Israel Defence Forces were established formally in this spirit by order of the provisional government on 26 May 1948. The order provided for universal conscription and proscribed all armed organizations outside the framework of the new national army. For some weeks this remained merely formal rather than actual. Ben-Gurion still had to struggle against dissident habits on the part of Irgunists and former Lehi members even although the law proscribing these activities was that of Israel rather than the British writ.

Immediately following the declaration of Jewish statehood the expected Arab invasion took place. Armed forces from Egypt, Transjordan, Syria, Iraq and Lebanon attacked in the south, the Jerusalem corridor, the central front facing Tel Aviv and the northern areas from the Jezreel Valley through the Galilee to the borders of Syria and Lebanon. The combined Arab forces numbered less than those of the Haganah,[8] although at first they had greater fire power and the advantages of initiative in attack. The new Israeli army was able to overcome its deficiencies in vehicles and fire power as the armouries assembled in Europe and also the United States were now brought in without interference. The numbers at the disposal of the Israeli forces grew from month to month with the immigration of young men trained and ready for combat. The Israelis began with superior forces and increased their superiority as the war proceeded. From the outset the Arab regimes, with the exception of Abdullah of Transjordan, underestimated the strength of the Israeli manpower and failed to appreciate that it would not remain static. Apart from these purely material considerations there was no comparison between the combat spirit of even the tiredest Israeli units (which had already been in battle for five months before the invasion) and the poorly motivated Arab soldiers. The Egyptian units had not even been led to expect combat, and thought they were moving in to occupy a collapsing society offering the prospect of easy loot. These military factors aside, the main weakness of the Arab attack was its shaky political foundation.

From the point of view of inter-Arab politics Palestine was seen as a vacuum upon the withdrawal of the British forces, and the Arab interventions had the aspect of a contest for the spoils. If the Arab states had aimed to assist the Arabs of Palestine to take control of the country and had they worked in unison towards that end, they would in all probability have succeeded in foiling partition or in making some inroads on the Israeli boundaries, in spite of their military weakness. The rout of the invasion was in large part attributable to the fact that the Arab heads of state were fighting each other for control of Palestine, rather than fighting Israel on behalf of Palestine.

The leading Arab antagonists were the ex-Mufti of Jerusalem, Hajj Amin al-Hussaini, whose aim was to expel the Jews, re-assert his authority in Palestine and establish there his own independent government; King Abdullah of Transjordan, who aimed to annex the Arab-designated portions of the country in addition to Jerusalem and as much of the Jewish state as possible, and then to negotiate peace with a rump Jewish state or enclave; King Farouk of Egypt, whose main concern was to prevent Abdullah's aggrandizement; and the Syrians, who sought to annexe the northern regions of the country before Abdullah's Arab Legion could reach them. The Iraqi contingents were not enthusiastic for battle, while Lebanon had no wish for battle at all, but was anxious to prevent the extension of Syrian hegemony near its borders. The Palestinians themselves were not mobilized nor united on any clear aim. The battle was fought over their heads. At first Egypt was the most reluctant to become involved and also opposed the intervention by others. Only when Abdullah's ambitions began to appear capable of realization did Hajj Amin and the Syrians prevail on Farouk at the last minute to commit his forces.

The decisive phase of the Arab-Israel war was the four-week period from mid-May to 11 June 1948 when the UNO succeeded in imposing a truce. With the initiative of simultaneous attack on several fronts, the Arab armies in these weeks, in spite of poor training and defective equipment (in every case except the Arab Legion), might with better leadership have posed a serious challenge to the security of the Jewish population and to the boundaries of the Jewish State. In the event the attack was routed and Israel was able to extend its borders considerably beyond those recommended in the partition proposal. Although much overextended by the need to cope with battle on several fronts, the Israeli forces made up in tenacity, brilliant improvisation and extraordinarily brave and able leadership in the field, what they lacked in experience, firepower and logistical resources.

In the north the main thrust of the Syrian attack was checked. Israel lost the important power station in the Jordan valley, but held the attacking Iraqi force which joined the Syrians in pressing on settlements in the region. On the central front the Iraqis established control of the Arab areas but did not make inroads on the Jewish coastal plain.

The greatest Arab threat was that posed by the Arab Legion in the Jerusalem area. While one Egyptian column advanced along the coast to within twenty miles of Tel Aviv, where it was obstructed by the stubborn resistance of Israeli settlements, a second column moved through Arab territory to link up with the Arab Legion in the Jerusalem area, aiming to keep an eye on Abdullah rather than to reinforce him. The kibbutzim of the Etzion bloc to the south of Jerusalem fell to the Legion shortly before the proclamation of statehood. This was the most serious dent the Arabs made in Ben-Gurion's policy of holding all rural settlements at all costs, whether in the territory of the state or in the area allocated to the Arabs. Against the advice of his generals Ben-Gurion accorded top priority to the Jerusalem front. He believed (as did Abdullah on his side, in dispute with his advisers) that to hold Jerusalem was the key to holding the rest of the country, while chief of operations Yigal Yadin and others on the general staff argued that holding the rest of the country would secure Jerusalem. Ben-Gurion prevailed and every effort was bent to relieving the city, again under heavy siege, and maintaining Israeli control over both the larger Jewish and the smaller Arab quarters of the new city. On being rebuffed again and again in their attempts to break open the road to Jerusalem in the vicinity of the Arab stronghold at Latrun the Israelis by night built a new rough road over the hills and brought relief to the city. A major Israeli disaster was the surrender of the Orthodox Jewish quarter in the walled Old City. However in the new city the Israeli civilian resistance, assisted by a small military contingent, sufficed to withstand the Legion attack and hold the Jewish and Arab sections. In the meantime the few isolated settlements in the south, with very limited help from the mobile forces, sustained heavy losses under constant Egyptian bombardment and intermittent direct attacks. With great tenacity they succeeded in blocking further Egyptian advance towards Tel Aviv.

At the end of four weeks of heavy fighting following the invasion, the Israeli position in the country as a whole was strategically secure within the boundaries of the state. The Arab Legion had succeeded in taking the Old City of Jerusalem and Mount Scopus (the site of the Hebrew University), while the Syrian forces in the north had captured an important settlement and a stronghold on high ground overlooking others. As against these Arab successes the Israeli forces were in control of small but significant necks of land in the Jezreel Valley, the Jerusalem corridor and to the south of Tel Aviv, that had been designated for the Arab state in the partition plan. Israeli losses in the four weeks included nearly twelve hundred killed. During this period of the war, shipments of heavy equipment from abroad and increased supplies of local manufacture relieved the chronic deficiency which had restricted the Israeli potential in the previous months.

Meeting in special session in the middle of May the general assembly of the UNO appointed a mediator for Palestine, while the security council explored the possibility of imposing a cease-fire. Political differences among the powers, reflecting their orientation towards the combatants, delayed the evolution of an acceptable formula until 29 May. On that date the powers agreed to issue a call for a four-week truce, during which the movement of fighting men or war material within or into all countries involved would be suspended. (Israel was to be permitted to admit immigrants but not to mobilize or train them during the truce.) The mediator, Count Folke Bernadotte, negotiated with the parties in Palestine and overcame their reservations, securing agreement on all sides to a month's truce beginning on 11 June.[9]

Over a hundred observers were quickly despatched to supervise the truce. The cease-fire, after a false start, held good, but the provisions designed to restrict military movements that could yield an advantage to any combatant were not effectively implemented. The Israelis managed during the truce to bring in considerable quantities of heavy equipment, including aircraft, forwarded by capable purchasing agents abroad. On the Arab side(s) too material supplies were brought to the several fronts. Apart from resting, re-grouping and military preparations for a resumption of battle, there was also much political recrimination in both the Arab and the Israeli camp. Abdullah toured Arab capitals in an abortive attempt to persuade them to accept a resolution of the Palestine issue on lines favourable to Transjordan. In Israel the truce was punctuated by a crisis which brought the country to the brink of civil war.

After the formal establishment of the Israeli army at the end of May the Irgun was permitted to maintain a temporary headquarters subordinate to the general staff in order to facilitate the absorption of its members into the national forces. The Irgun was required to cease its activities in the procurement of arms abroad and their manufacture locally, and to turn over its facilities and contracts to the defence ministry.

On 20 June 1948 it was reported to the cabinet (the provisional government) that the Irgun had independently arranged for its ship, the *Altalena*, to arrive off the coast with eight hundred volunteers together with a consignment of five thousand rifles and two hundred and fifty machine guns with ammunition. According to accounts by the Irgun principals, they understood that the government welcomed the speedy arrival of the ship in spite of the truce, and that spokesmen authorized to act for the government had discussed with them the distribution of the weapons.[10] Although they had not reached agreement about distribution they thought that they were engaged in an amicable negotiation in the matter and that they were in a position to proceed with the unloading. If he himself indeed knew otherwise, Ben-Gurion did not disabuse his cabinet colleagues of the belief that the Irgun was bent on defying the authority of the government and arming its own men in the face of the law. After the passengers had disembarked (together with a small portion of the arms) the army was ordered to secure the surrender of the ship, if necessary by force. Shots were fired. Begin boarded the ship and ordered it to make for the shore twenty miles southward opposite Tel Aviv. There again it was met with fire and sixteen Irgunists were killed in addition to scores wounded. The ship with its load was burnt out and remained grounded as a monument to the crisis which had brought the public close to the brink of civil war.

The public was very agitated by the *Altalena* affair. People were shocked at the spectacle of the army firing on the Irgunists and were not inclined to give credence to the official rumour that the Irgun had planned an armed revolt against the government. Tempers soon subsided, however, and in the aftermath it appeared that Ben-Gurion had won the victory he sought, whatever the cost in goodwill. For the legitimacy of the state and the authority of the government were effectively dramatized, with a salutary effect on morale. Scores of Irgunists were arrested after the affray and their leaders went into hiding as in the old underground days. Ben-Gurion intended an amnesty but wished if possible to capture Begin and his lieutenants to shatter once and for all the appeal and glory of dissidence. The Irgun did not recover from the blow and lost little time in disbanding and creating a new political party, Herut, to carry on its opposition in the conventional manner.

The identity of the organization was still maintained for a time in Jerusalem.

Since Jerusalem was designated an international zone in the partition resolution the Israeli government did not yet claim sovereignty in the city. The UNO truce supervisors and a committee of foreign consuls tried to maintain the semblance of international authority. In this context the Haganah, Irgun and Lehi continued to exist in form, although the Haganah contingent in the city clearly took its instructions from the army. The Irgun refused to work under Israel army control in the Jerusalem area so long as the government failed to declare the city an integral part of Israel and indeed its capital city.

During the truce the UNO mediator Bernadotte explored the possibility of a political solution to the conflict in the hope that the military events might have influenced the parties to change their political outlook. Towards the end of June he presented the Arab League and the Israeli government with a set of new proposals for a settlement along the lines that had long been favoured by the British and Abdullah. Not surprisingly the proposals were turned down on all sides. As the truce drew to the end of its four-week term the Israeli government responded positively to a call by the security council for its prolongation, and many of the Arab states were similarly inclined. But Egypt and Syria had by now become more than ever fearful of Abdullah's aggrandizement and insisted on carrying on the war. It also appears that the Egyptian government had come to believe its own propaganda to the effect that easy victory lay within its reach and only the truce imposed by the UNO had prevented them destroying the Jewish state.

Ten days of heavy fighting now took place on all fronts. By this time the Israeli forces mustered sixty thousand men under arms and wielded much heavier firepower than before. In this phase of the war, between 9 July and 18 July, Israel wrested from the Arab armies the initiative that had favoured them as attackers. Israeli military control was extended to several additional Arab areas. The loss of small pockets of territory was amply compensated by large gains in Lower Galilee (including the cities of Ramle and Lydda with its airport, although once again Latrun eluded capture) and the areas around settlements that had been under Egyptian duress

261

south of Tel Aviv. At the end of this round of battle the Arabs were only too glad of a truce, though the military commanders on the Israeli side chafed. On this occasion the security council threatened sanctions, and Israel accepted the truce which was to be of indefinite duration pending a peaceful solution.

Israel now took stock of its situation. Many men had been fighting almost continuously for seven months and were at the point of exhaustion. Huge debts for arms had been incurred and the economy was on the brink of failure for want of essential manpower. The Negev was isolated by Egyptian control of its roads, although it was an integral part of the Jewish state as delineated in the partition plan. Jerusalem was still vulnerable and its population had suffered a good deal of hunger and demoralization. Syria still held a bridgehead in Israeli territory. None of the Arab armies had been decisively defeated, so that their threat was not dispelled. On the other hand some two hundred Arab villages in the Jewish area had been occupied, and a hundred more in the Arab part of Palestine. A huge airlift of arms from Czechoslovakia was under way and additional heavy equipment was also being brought in from other centres in Europe. Militarily there was confidence that the new state could take care of itself, but there was great uncertainty about the political struggle which could be expected during a prolonged truce.

Reporting to the cabinet at the beginning of August on the military and political situation, Ben-Gurion presented his view that a prolonged truce would bring about a worsening of Israel's situation. Continued truce-supervision by international agents who 'do not even require our visas' would undermine the image and the standing of the state before a world which had not yet become accustomed to its existence. The need for continued military preparedness coupled with inaction would undermine morale and be financially ruinous. Politically therefore it was necessary to obtain peace or remove the invaders from Israel's borders. An indefinite truce would bring only the disadvantages of war without the benefits of peace. Sanctions would be less damaging than the continuation of the present situation. With sufficient training and readiness the army could send all the invasion forces packing within a month to six weeks. The truce must therefore be terminated by about the end of August or mid-September at the latest. The UNO must be told that if the Arab armies had not gone by then the Israeli army would throw them out.

Ben-Gurion now took advantage of the truce to focus on army problems. Plans were drawn up for the expulsion of Egyptian forces from the Negev, and on other fronts planning was advanced to supersede the customary improvisation. The army was reorganized logistically into three frontal divisions better adapted to the scale of available manpower than the previous pattern based on individual brigades. Mobilization was stepped up to free men needed in the civilian economy and to replace the wounded and battle-weary. By the end of August some seventy-eight thousand were under arms. Immigration helped to bring the total to about ninety thousand by mid-October. Although they had been reinforced the combined Arab armies apart from a few thousand Palestinian irregulars were by then no more than half of the Israeli strength. Desertion was reduced by better provision for the families of those on active service.

Ben-Gurion now felt that the time had come to eliminate the separate command of the Palmach. About ninety per cent of the Palmach commanders were members of the Ahdut Ha'avodah faction, which had merged with Hashomer Hatzair to form Mapam. Throughout the rest of the army the labour movement also contributed a major share of the commanders. But the general staff itself was free of any homogeneous political influence. (Ahdut Ha'avodah actually complained of discrimination in this respect.) Even after the army had been established to succeed the underground movement, the partisan psychology continued to be reflected in indiscipline, desertion and voluntaristic habits at all levels. Ben-Gurion felt that there was a failure to appreciate that the army was not an extension of the Haganah but an instrument of state sovereignty, new to the Jewish experience which included no military tradition. While he did not equate the Palmach with the dissident terrorists he felt that its separate command was no less a threat to the nurturing of a modern army under civilian control. He attributed many military setbacks in the previous months to the duplication of command in operations and administration.

In mid-September he called a meeting of the sixty-four Palmach commanders to air views. It was clear from the discussion that his fears about the attitudes fostered by separatism were well-grounded. Many Palmach spokesmen apparently saw the brigade as the only guarantee for the avoidance of civil war, as a vital socialist instrument to counteract a fascist coup by Begin. This was radically contrary to Ben-Gurion's own view that the struggle against the dissidents was an act of *government* authority, and not a political squabble between rival parties free to operate on their own terms, as might have appeared during the underground period.

At any rate Ben-Gurion had no difficulty procuring agreement within the general staff to the termination of the Palmach command. The chief of staff, Dori, acting on the defence minister's explicit instructions, on 7 October issued an order abolishing the Palmach command and bringing its three brigades on an equal footing with the others within the framework of the frontal divisions. The Palmach officers obeyed without demur but Mapam leaders agitated within the Histadrut for a restoration of the Palmach and it was some time before political tension subsided on the issue.

The issue of the Irgun was still not satisfactorily resolved. The provisional government had announced that Israel's laws would apply in Jerusalem, although the formal status of the city was not yet determined. Israel was now claiming that territory under its control would be the basis of its political boundaries, but the continued existence of the Irgun and the apparent inability of the government to exercise its authority in the city weakened the diplomacy aimed at securing international recognition of Jerusalem as an integral part of the state. Efforts were made to negotiate with the Irgun in Jerusalem for its disbandment, and the government was considering the use of force. Matters came to a head on 17 September when a group of former Lehi members, who had refused to accept the disbandment of the Lehi in May, assassinated Count Bernadotte and his aide in Jerusalem. The government ordered the general staff to present an ultimatum to the Irgun requiring its members to disband, give up their weapons and join the army on an individual basis within twenty-four hours. The Irgun submitted and the chapter of dissidence was closed.

Before his death Count Bernadotte had submitted a new plan for Palestine along lines similar to his earlier proposal in which he suggested an exchange of the Negev for western Galilee. This reinforced Ben-Gurion's view that any political settlement would be based on confirmation of the military *status quo*. He therefore resolved urgently to expel the Egyptians from Israeli soil before discussion along these lines could be far advanced at the UNO. The Egyptians had repeatedly violated the truce by interfering with legitimate Israeli attempts to maintain supplies to its besieged settlements in the Negev. Plans were drawn up for a resumption of battle in mid-October on the assumption that Egyptian forces would again interfere with a convoy and thereby free the Israeli forces to take action, an option that had been approved in such circumstances by the truce observers but not previously exercised.

There was concern in the general staff about the possibility that any renewal of fighting in the south would trigger simultaneous action by the Arabs on other fronts. By this time, however, Arab disunity had reached its peak as the contours of the new map of Palestine were beginning to become apparent. The Mufti on 20 September installed in Gaza the 'Arab Government of All Palestine'. Immediately a congress of Palestinian notables meeting in Amman denounced the Gaza government and pledged allegiance to Abdullah on behalf of the people of Palestine. The risk to Israel of co-ordinated Arab action appeared less than overwhelming.

Egypt provided the pretext for a general attack as expected, and the Israeli forces managed to relieve the isolated Negev settlements, encircle the best units of the Egyptian army at Faluja and capture Beersheba. The attack met with heavy resistance and it was not possible for the Israelis to bring the action to a decisive conclusion for the Negev as a whole in the few days available before the UNO reimposed the truce.

Shortly after the action in the south, truce violations by Kaukji's Liberation Army in Galilee gave Israel the needed pretext for a general action. Within hours the Israelis captured the whole of Upper Galilee and completely routed Kaukji's force. As in the south, the new truce on this front required Israel to remove its mobile forces but allowed it to maintain a garrison, thereby enabling it to retain effective control of the newly won territory.

In mid-November Israel prepared plans for the total expulsion of the Egyptian forces. At the end of November a Palestinian congress at Jericho proclaimed Abdullah king of all Palestine, while at the same time an understanding was reached between Israel and Transjordan securing a cease-fire in Jerusalem. On 23 December 1948 Israel launched a full-scale assault on the Egyptian positions while simultaneously rapidly moving southward through the Negev. The rump of the Egyptian force was hemmed in within the narrow Gaza 'strip' while the Israeli advance reached into Egyptian territory in the Sinai peninsula. Britain's whole middle east policy now appeared to be in ruins, and it brought pressure on Israel to withdraw from Egypt on pain of having to fight the British forces. Resisting the pleas of his generals who wished for time to complete the consolidation of Israel's hold in the southernmost parts of the Negev, Ben-Gurion bowed to the British threat. Israeli pilots had just shot down five British aircraft reconnoitring the battle zone, and Ben-Gurion was unwilling to risk any further offence to the former mandatory power. Since the other Arab armies had done nothing to assist Egypt during the Negev campaign it appeared clear to the Egyptian government that its battle for control of southern Palestine was lost. It now sued for peace. Israel's military struggle for independence was over, at a cost of six thousand killed, including two thousand civilians. Arab casualties were higher.

Armistices and boundaries

The Palestine Arabs as a body had not been a belligerent nor were they a party to the Israel-Arab negotiations by which the war was concluded. The Palestine Arab state envisaged in the partition plan did not arise. Those areas of the country remaining outside Israeli control were taken, on the basis of their military presence, by Transjordan and Egypt. Owing to their military failure Syria and Lebanon did not receive any of the Palestinian territory. Armistice negotiations were conducted separately with each of the four Arab governments. Iraq signed no agreement but undertook to abide by any arrangements made by its neighbours. Saudi Arabia, which had sent a token military force in the later stages of the war, also refrained from entering any agreement. Thus the armistices were concluded between Israel and its immediate neighbours. Applying great diplomatic acumen and skill the acting UNO mediator, Ralph Bunche, succeeded in bringing the parties to agreement in spite of the gulf of hatred dividing them.

It was widely believed in Israel (and there was a similar view in some Arab circles) that the armistices might provide a bridge for a transition towards a peace settlement. Such hopes were fully dissipated by the summer of 1949 when the last agreement was signed with Syria. The agreements included a rhetorical gesture towards peace, and sought to stabilize the *status quo* rather than to resolve the issues in conflict or correct anomalies. Borders were thus delineated without prejudice to claims that might be put forward in the context of a peace settlement. The demarcation of boundaries corresponded with the configuration of military control. These boundaries became the legitimate boundaries of Israel and its neighbours as recognized by states outside the Arab world. Thus the armistices confirmed the law of conquest, and the partition of Palestine in effect was implemented by Israel, Abdullah and Farouk, with the UNO seal of approval.

With its army in a state of defeat and collapse Egypt was the first to negotiate. Proceedings began on 12 January 1949 on the island of Rhodes with the signing of a cease-fire. Demarcation of boundaries in the Negev presented the most difficult issue. Egypt clung to its war aim of controlling at least a part of the Negev, while Israel to the contrary demanded Egyptian withdrawal from the Gaza strip. The population of Gaza had been swelled from about seventy thousand by the addition of some two hundred thousand refugees. Agreement was reached on 24 February, providing for boundaries following the military disposition; the establishment of a civilian Egyptian administration in Gaza; the demilitarization of a contested zone at a strategic road junction in Israeli territory giving access to the Sinai peninsula (el-Auja); and the repatriation of troops surrounded in the Faluja pocket. The agreed boundaries conformed approximately to the original partition plan, except that Egypt took the Gaza strip which had been allocated to the prospective Arab state in Palestine.

Lebanon followed Egypt in negotiations. There were few difficulties in this case since both sides had already come to an informal understanding allowing for mutual withdrawal of forces from border villages on each side of the traditional international boundary. Signing of the armistice was delayed pending the withdrawal of Syrian troops from Lebanon and from the north-eastern portion of Palestine where the borders of the three countries met. The agreement was signed on 23 March 1949, on the basis of the former Palestine boundary, with a reduction of forces on both sides of the demarcation.

Simultaneously with the Israel-Lebanon talks the negotiations with Transjordan began at the beginning of March. They had been preceded by secret direct meetings between Israeli officials and Abdullah in his palace. There is no doubt that Abdullah looked forward to an eventual peace settlement with Israel and it was on this basis that many problems and anomalies were built into the armistice as though temporary. The peace prospect was foiled by a multitude of Arab pressures on Abdullah, culminating in his assassination. The result was that the complex armistice agreement contained festering sources of tension in the years ahead.

While the talks went on Israeli military forces were racing to take control of undecided stretches of land in the south-eastern portion of the Negev down to the Gulf of Akaba. Transjordan had hoped by a token military presence there to establish a claim, but the Israelis succeeded in occupying the area down to Eilat (on the Israeli side of the Gulf of Akaba) and holding it sufficiently firmly to take the matter out of the realm of discussion. At the same time the Iraqi forces withdrew from the Arab areas on the central front. The existing cease-fire line gave Israel a long border, at some points only eight miles from the sea. As a price for acceptance of Transjordan's annexation of the Arab areas vacated by Iraq, Israel insisted on having this line pushed back a few kilometres along its entire length. Transjordan, not caring for a resumption of battle, had no choice but to accede, although this meant the demarcation of borders dividing many villages and separating people from their lands.

As for Jerusalem (Transjordan holding the walled Old City and Israel the extensive new city) the two sides had a common interest in recognizing each other's status there in order to forestall active UNO intervention for internationalization of the city as envisaged in the partition plan and again endorsed by the security council as recently as December 1948. Transjordan held the area of Mount Scopus on which stood the Hebrew University and Hadassah hospital. Israel was enabled to police these buildings, but agreement to resume their use was not implemented, nor were understandings about Jewish access to holy places. The armistice was signed on 3 April 1949. Transjordan annexed the 'western bank' area of Palestine and became the Hashemite Kingdom of Jordan.

Immediately after the Israel-Jordan agreement was concluded negotiations with Syria began. These were the most difficult of the series and talks were broken off for several weeks. The armistice was not signed until 20 July. Alone among the Arab armies at the end of the fighting the Syrians held parts of the territory which the partition plan had allocated to the Jewish state. Since Israel itself now held many areas not included in its territory by the plan, Syria insisted not without logic that it should retain its bridgehead on the basis of the military *status quo*. It also challenged the international boundary that had been drawn by Anglo-French agreement nearly thirty years before. But the underlying military reality was undoubtedly much more favourable to Israel, and Syria was bound to yield in the end. Bunche found a formula which made agreement possible but contained the seeds of future strife. Syria agreed to withdraw its forces, and the disputed areas near the Huleh swamp were demilitarized and placed under local administration subject to supervision by the UNO Mixed Armistice Commission, on which, as in the case of the other armistices, both sides were represented.

The security council recorded the formal termination of Israel's war of independence by liquidating the office of acting mediator on 11 August 1949. Israel in the meantime had already secured recognition by about fifty governments, including all the major powers, and on 11 May 1949 had been accepted into membership of UNO. The state had firmly established its sovereignty in a territory exceeding by more than a third that allocated to it by the partition plan. The UNO had proved incapable of implementing the plan, although it did make a contribution to ending military hostilities.

Israel emerged from the war and the armistice with long convoluted boundaries. Of about ten thousand square miles of mandated territory west of the River Jordan, Israel held about eight thousand square miles bounded by almost six hundred miles of land frontier, in addition to a hundred and fifty miles of coastline.

The hilly Galilee is bounded by Lebanon to the north and to the east by Syria, with an average width of about forty miles. The range of hills is interrupted to the south by the Valley of Jezreel (Esdraelon, or Armageddon of old) stretching thirty miles from Haifa to the Jordan Valley south of the Sea of Kinneret (familiar also as Lake Tiberias or the Sea of Galilee). The Mediterranean coastal plain in which is concentrated the greater part of the population stretches from Haifa southward to Tel Aviv, with a varying width of from ten to fifteen miles. A corridor from Tel Aviv leads up to Jerusalem atop the Judean hills, which decline abruptly to the lowest point on the earth's surface at the Dead Sea. Over half the area of the country is made up of the arid southern desert, the Negev, seventy miles at its widest and reaching the Gulf of Akaba at the port of Eilat which links the country through the Red Sea to the far east. The longest border is that with Jordan, hemming in the coastal plain in the north and bounding the Negev to the east all the way down to the Gulf. To the west the Negev shares a boundary with the Egyptian Sinai Peninsula and the short Gaza strip jutting up the coastline.

Mass immigration

The British withdrawal in 1948 bequeathed to the provisional government a chaotic situation in banking, fiscal administration, communications and supply. In February the London government announced the exclusion of Palestine from the sterling area and the 'freezing' of sterling balances amounting to about £100 million held in London for the credit of Palestinian institutions. The British-owned oil refineries at Haifa, the largest enterprise in the country, were closed down in April. The mobilization of manpower for the war and the sudden complete separation of the Arab and Jewish sectors of the economy also disrupted normal production.

For the financing of the war Jewish sympathizers abroad came to the rescue of Israel with the greatest financial effort yet tapped by Zionism. As a result of this support the shortage of foreign currency during the war was not in fact such a severe problem as the transportation of supplies to the country. In the face of great reluctance on the part of commercial carriers and insurers to service the region at war, arms mainly from Czechoslovakia, supplies of fuel from Rumania and grain from various ports were maintained throughout the year by the most primitive improvised means of transport.

Pending the establishment of an adequate fiscal administration the government arranged with the National Council to use its existing machinery to levy the communal tax as in the past, and supplemented this revenue by raising three new loans from the public to a total of £13·5 million. But these revenues were quite inadequate to cope with the provision of daily supplies for the masses of new immigrants flooding into the country. The government resorted to deficit financing on a large scale. On 9 August 1948, after months of secret preparation, the government issued a new Israeli currency to replace the sterling Palestine pound. The old money was repatriated to London to join the frozen Palestine assets, while the new money in effect represented large-scale government borrowing. It was inevitable that a rapid growth in purchasing power not matched by increased production engendered inflation.

In spite of rampant inflation and widespread economic dislocation due to the war the government unhesitatingly upheld its commitment to rescue the Jews in the refugee camps of Europe. Unselective mass immigration brought to the country thousands who were in need of immediate medical care, food and shelter and for several months would be unable to contribute to production. Many of the younger immigrants had been given military training in the camps and were able to participate effectively in the prosecution of the war. But most were a burden on the economy from the moment of their arrival. Even overseas Jewish support of over two hundred million dollars in 1949 and 1950 was hardly sufficient to put the economy on an even keel while the mass immigration continued.

The establishment of the state inaugurated a period of mass immigration which continued unabated until the end of 1951. In the first three and a half years of the state the Jewish population was more than doubled by immigration alone, and the character of Jewish Palestine was transformed almost beyond recognition. From the beginning of Zionist immigration in 1882 until the proclamation of statehood in 1948 upwards of four hundred and fifty thousand Jews, allowing for re-emigration, settled in Palestine. The Jewish population at the establishment of the state was close to six hundred and fifty thousand, of whom about sixty per cent were the survivors of these immigrants and forty per cent their native Palestinian offspring.

Immediately upon asserting its independence Israel brought to its shores the refugee remnant of European Jewry. In addition to those housed in the displaced persons camps there came over a hundred thousand from Poland and a hundred and twenty thousand from Rumania, along with smaller numbers from Czechoslovakia and Hungary and the entire Jewish community of Bulgaria numbering nearly forty thousand. Although these had escaped incineration by the Nazis their lives were totally dislocated by the war and they were only too glad to take advantage of the freedom to emigrate that the east European countries maintained for a short time. Over a hundred thousand came in the year 1948 alone. By the end of 1951 some three hundred and twenty thousand new immigrants of European origin had arrived in Israel. The festering problem of Jewish displacement in Europe was thus liquidated.

In the same period, as the result of Israel's establishment in a state of war with the Arabs, many Arab regimes initiated a severe persecution of their ancient Jewish communities, thus creating a new refugee problem and an un-anticipated major new source of population for Israel. Almost the whole of the Iraqi Jewish population, over a hundred and twenty thousand, came to Israel when the Iraqi government overcame initial hesitations and compelled them to emigrate, allowing the Jewish Agency to carry out their transfer. Their property in

Iraq was expropriated so that, like most of the immigrants of the period of mass immigration, they came to the country destitute. The entire community of Yemen, nearly fifty thousand in number, were flown to Israel in a massive airlift via Aden. From Libya and north Africa, Turkey and also Iran came most of the Jews whose ancestors had lived there for centuries. Between May 1948 and the end of 1951 there came a total of some three hundred and twenty-five thousand from the countries of the middle east, matching in scale the influx from Europe. Apart from the majority who were victims of the new persecution, those from Yemen, Turkey and Iran were motivated by Zionist sentiment inspired by Israel's creation.

Besides those from Europe and the middle east there came a net addition of about fifteen thousand from other parts of the world, bringing the total net influx in the period of mass immigration to approximately six hundred and sixty thousand. Natural increase of about ninety thousand in this period brought the total Jewish population at the end of 1951, when the mass migration concluded, to approximately one million and four hundred thousand.

The diminution of the Arab population as a result of the mass flight of 1948 was proportionally even greater than the growth of the Jewish population through mass immigration in the first three years of statehood. Within the territory held by Israel at the time of the census conducted in November 1948 the Arab population was estimated as one hundred and fifty-six thousand, including fifteen thousand Druze, compared to over three-quarters of a million before the war. As a result of Jewish immigration the Arab population was reduced from about eighteen per cent of the total at the end of the war to about eleven per cent at the conclusion of the mass immigration in 1951. Of the Arabs some seventy per cent were Muslim, twenty per cent Christian and ten per cent Druze.

The most pressing immediate problem of the greatest magnitude was that of housing and feeding the immigrants until they could be absorbed into productive economic life. The Arab flight during the war was a crucial factor reducing the problem of housing to manageable proportions in the first year of mass immigration. In the first phases of the Arab flight

273

abandoned land and property were brought into the Jewish economy by haphazard looting, squatting and military confiscation unguided by any clear central policy. Immigrants swarmed into the abandoned zones. In the first year of the state about a hundred and twenty thousand new immigrants found homes in abandoned Arab accommodation. A proportion of these, in the rural areas, were immediately inducted into agriculture on abandoned lands, and were thereby enabled to contribute directly to alleviation of the food shortage. Thereafter the immigrants were given shelter in hastily improvised camps, in tents and temporary structures, which sprang up all over the country. In 1950 the planning for absorption of immigrants was improved, and transit centres were built near the main cities where employment could be found, enabling the immigrants to become independent while still awaiting permanent housing. Nearly a quarter of a million immigrants were housed in such centres by the end of the period of mass immigration. The government and the Jewish Agency, with the help of the army, maintained supplies to those who continued in need of public support. Conditions were extremely crude for some years and great sacrifices had to be borne by the veteran population as shortages of food and clothing and every amenity became general throughout the country.

The period from 1948 to 1951 is remembered in Israel as the austerity regime. The government sought to suppress inflation by stringent price controls and physical rationing. But it did not succeed in mopping up the excess purchasing power arising from heavy government borrowing. Consequently, black markets proliferated with devastating effect on efforts to control the allocation of resources. With the conclusion of the war in 1949 the economy was in the throes of an acute crisis. The balance of payments presented the most pressing symptom as overseas Jewish support waned with the cessation of fighting. The citrus industry, the main earner of foreign exchange, was extensively damaged in the war. Apart from a much reduced citrus crop and the proceeds of diamond polishing, the country had little earning power in foreign markets. A loan of a hundred million dollars from the Export-Import

Bank of the United States was earmarked for machinery and did not ease the problem of immediate supplies.

In September 1949 the government devalued the currency, thereby temporarily stemming the inflationary pressure. But the situation deteriorated within months as immigration continued unabated. Short-term relief was procured by successful negotiation with Britain for the release of blocked sterling in 1950. But again by the end of 1951 rampant inflation had all but destroyed the credibility of economic transactions. Once more rescue came in the nick of time in the form of a loan from the Export-Import Bank and a grant-in-aid from the American government, together totalling a hundred million dollars. It was not till the beginning of 1952, when immigration subsided, that the government was able to introduce coherent policies to bring the economy under control.

CHAPTER 12

CONSTITUTIONAL TRANSITION (1948-53)

*The provisional government – the 'Small Constitution' –
citizenship and personal status – subordinate governments
and the state*

The provisional government

In the weeks preceding statehood the People's Council and the People's Administration commanded wide popular support amongst the Jewish population, and their administrative competence was firmly established before the British evacuation. Although they convened only a few times before the independence deadline of mid-May these bodies managed quickly to master the levers of power and administration, and they prepared detailed plans for the smooth operation of independent government.[1] The manner of the British withdrawal in conditions of war in conjunction with an incessant flow of immigration resulted at first in an atmosphere of administrative chaos. But this disorder was relatively superficial, concealing a basic firmness and efficacy of control. It was in this period that the characteristic Israeli style of government by improvisation in a spirit of absolute patriotic devotion emerged and received its most pronounced vindication.

While the shell of administrative practice was inherited from the British structure of government, the bureaucratic ethos informing it derived from the culture of eastern Europe in combination with the pioneering ethic. The existing machinery of quasi-government, including the departments of the Jewish Agency executive and those of the National Council, was modified as necessary to incorporate functions hitherto performed by the British administration. The experienced officials, albeit in short supply, were able under the auspices of Jewish sovereignty to continue operating much as before notwithstanding insecurity of tenure and a crippling lack of resources. By the end of 1950 a Civil Service Commission was formally established and the rationalization of conditions of service was inaugurated. In the meantime the quasi-government had been translated into the provisional government of the new state and that in turn into the constitutional government with relatively little mechanical disruption. The thirty-seven-member People's Council, the legislative organ, was designated the provisional council of state, while its executive arm, the People's Administration, became the provisional government.

The first official instrument of the state of Israel was the Declaration of Independence announcing its own establishment and confirming the status of the provisional government pending the introduction of a definitive constitution. The provisional regime itself, in effect, through its political decisions and practices established the basic constitutional framework of government which was to have a decisive impact on subsequent constitutional development. During the provisional regime, which continued until 14 February 1949, the main outlines of Israel's administrative institutions and the relations between them were shaped and the conventions of government crystallized.

The Declaration of Independence may be regarded as a rhetorical manifesto rather than a major constitutional source. Immediately following the reading and signing of the proclamation the provisional council of state issued its first formal decree, composed of three clauses. The first announced that the Council was the legislative authority, with the discretion to delegate this power to the government in case of emergency. The second clause cancelled all regulations arising from the British White Paper of 1939 and also specific clauses of the Defence (Emergency) Regulations of 1945 relating to immigration and land transfers. The final clause of the decree announced the 'reception' of all law in operation at the accession to statehood, subject to compatibility with this and future Israeli laws and with any changes resulting from the establishment as such of the state.

The inaugural decree met the need for immediate public guidance as to the validity of the laws in force at the accession to independence.[2] It was followed on 19 May 1948 by the enactment of the first formal constitutional instrument, the Law and Administration Ordinance (*Pekudat Sidrei Ha'Shilton Ve'Hamishpat*), which incorporated the substance of the decree while amplifying it and elaborating in greater detail the constitution of the provisional organs of government.

In stipulating that the provisional government would implement the policies laid down by the provisional council of state, report to it and be accountable to it for its actions, the ordinance gave formal effect to parliamentary supremacy while at the same time in practice establishing effective cabinet government. The cabinet was authorized to appoint the prime minister and to define its own ministers' jurisdictions, subject to the obligation to publish these decisions in the Official Gazette. The legislature alone could authorize the budget of the government, and alone could impose taxes by law. However, the legislature was empowered to declare a state of emergency,[3] in which circumstances the government could authorize the prime minister or any other minister to issue emergency regulations with the effect of suspending or amending existing legislation on any matter, including taxation, for periods up to three months and subject to publication. Immediately following the promulgation of the ordinance the provisional council of state declared a state of emergency, which has continued in force ever since, enhancing the initiative of the government and securing its effective dominance over the legislature.

The ordinance also provided that local authorities and the courts would continue to operate within their historical jurisdictions pending further legislation. At the end of June 1948 the Supreme Court was established, completing the machinery for the smooth reception of existing law. The government was charged with the appointment of its members, upon nomination by the minister of justice, subject to ratification by the Council. In addition to the reception of laws in force under the mandate, the ordinance endowed with legal validity any measures published after 29 November 1947 by the Jewish Agency, the National Council or the People's Administration in connection with the maintenance of vital supplies and services.

On 16 May the provisional council of state co-opted Chaim Weizmann and designated him its president. No formal provision for the office of president of state was made until early 1949, but in the meantime, although he had no constitutional standing nor any powers, Weizmann as President of the Council was regarded as head of state. Ben-Gurion was determined that the office would be merely honorific and ceremonial, and helped to ensure this by himself enjoining the Council at the outset to accord this high tribute to Weizmann. He thereby presented an altruistic façade while forestalling any move to bring Weizmann into active government. Although Weizmann himself had expected an energetic political role and was bitterly disappointed to find himself relegated to the periphery, there is no evidence to suggest that his expectation of influence rather than honour was well-founded. Ben-Gurion certainly had no intention of sharing the top leadership of the country with one whose efforts for three decades had been concentrated in the external arena he so despised. The ascendancy of the Palestine-centred branch of Zionism and Ben-Gurion's dominant influence within it were eloquently manifest in the exclusively Palestinian composition of the provisional government.

The 'Small Constitution'

Following the transitional procedures recommended in the UNO partition resolution, the provisional government made preparations for the election of a Constituent Assembly with authority to draw up a definitive constitution, under which in turn a legislature and government would be duly elected to supersede the provisional organs. The provisional council of state in July 1948 had appointed a constitution committee to explore the problems connected with a constitution and to prepare a draft proposal for the consideration of the prospective Constituent Assembly. The committee received several proposals from various personages but concentrated its attention on a thorough detailed draft prepared by Dr Yehuda Leo

Kohn (1894–1961), a political scientist engaged for this purpose by the Jewish Agency immediately after the passage of the UNO partition resolution.

The discussions in the provisional constitution committee revealed the relative rigidity of the ideological differences between the established political parties in regard to social ideals and their political expressions deemed worthy of national emulation. The foremost political cleavage predictably concerned the place of religion in the constitution, and there were also divided opinions about the technical arrangements of government, and especially the method of election of representative organs. The orthodox spokesmen envisaged theocratic rule to be arrived at by the gradual assimilation into public law of the main tenets of traditional Jewish jurisprudence as and when political circumstances allowed. In the meantime they would be satisfied with a basic minimum of religious standards in public life and exclusive religious jurisdiction over personal status. The secularists were for the most part inclined to concede the importance of maintaining links with traditional Judaism in the public life of the state, but were not unanimously disposed to preclude all possibility of civil marriage. Mapai pressed strongly for an electoral system that would tend to assist the crystallization of a two-party system, but not surprisingly the spokesmen of the smaller parties rejected this. Working closely to Kohn's draft the committee was able after several months to draw up a sophisticated working document for consideration of the Constituent Assembly as soon as it would convene.

On 19 November 1948 the provisional council of state enacted the Elections to the Constituent Assembly Ordinance in which it adopted a method of election closely resembling the procedure that had operated in *Knesset Israel* during the mandate. The membership of the Constituent Assembly was fixed at one hundred and twenty, to be elected by direct secret ballot on the basis of proportional representation of party lists. The eligible voters, with a minimum age of eighteen and no disqualification on account of short residence, were determined on the basis of a census that was conducted for this purpose on 8 November. The country as a whole was to form a single constituency and voting was to be for the party list as a whole, with the order of candidates on the list being the order of election when proportions were determined. This provision reinforced the power of the party leaders who controlled the nomination of candidates and their ranking in the list.

At least amongst the leaders of the provisional government if not amongst the people at large enthusiasm for the project of a written constitution gradually waned throughout 1948. The preparation of a draft constitution had been prompted in the first place by the desire to conform to the recommendations of UNO. But the standing of UNO as an authoritative source of constitutional law was much diminished by the incapacity of the organization to implement partition with suitable machinery for an orderly succession to the mandatory. In the meantime the improvising style of government had become prevalent and appeared efficacious and widely acceptable to the people. Whether with the intention of abandoning or undermining the commitment to a written constitution or not, the provisional council on 14 January 1949 passed the Transition to the Constituent Assembly Ordinance providing that the Constituent Assembly, unless it should otherwise determine, would succeed to all the legislative powers vested in the Council and that the provisional government would continue to function in a caretaker capacity until a new executive organ was formed under the authority of the Constituent Assembly. Thus, although the constituent function was not formally withdrawn from the Constituent Assembly, it was nevertheless clear to the electorate that it was to choose a legislature and a government rather than a constitutional convention.

The transition to independent statehood had remarkably little effect on the pattern of party politics. The political parties originating in the ideological culture of the veteran settlers were a significant institutional vehicle of continuity linking the politics of the pre-state period and post-independence Israel. With the exception of the communist party and a number of competing electoral alliances formed by the Arabs in their new minority status, all the parties in Israel had their roots in the Zionist movement and in their various visions of the structure of the future autonomous Jewish society. The Communist party alone, combining dissident Arabs and Jews, stood apart from the nationalist ethos stimulated by independence, and in this they were fully consistent with their previous posture in regard to the Zionist movement in the pre-state period. The Arab lists were a link between those Arab notables who remained in the country and the Jewish power structure, rather than the kernel of a new political movement arising out of Israel's establishment. In return for needed favours the Arab leadership supported Mapai and could usually be relied upon to behave as Mapai's clients in matters remote from Arab concern.

Apart from ephemeral minor groups only three new parties were added to the spectrum in 1948 and these were directly descended from the politics of the pre-state period, projecting new labels rather than new political movements: Mapam (*Mifleget Poalim Meuhedet*, the 'United Workers' Party'); Herut (short for *Tenuat Herut*, 'Freedom Movement', named after *Herut*, the underground newspaper of the Irgun); and the Progressives.

Mapam was founded in January 1948 as a political coalition of Hashomer Hatzair and Ahdut Ha'avodah-Poale Zion, the group which had broken from Mapai's discipline in the early forties. The respective kibbutz movements of the two groups, Hakibbutz Ha'artzi and Hakibbutz Hameuhad, were not combined nor was there any integration of the various services undertaken by the two movements for their members. The new party was conceived in a spirit of socialist optimism and enthusiasm as the political arm of the militant left, determined at least to be the keeper of Mapai's conscience if not itself swept to power by events.

Herut was founded in June 1948 on the initiative of the Irgun, under the leadership of Begin, as a consequence of the impending dissolution of the Irgun under the new circumstances of independence. Hounded by the provisional government and Ben-Gurion personally, the Irgun could not expect to continue as an underground movement in defiance of the legitimate government and accordingly it surfaced as a political party dedicated to opposition to the labour establishment. Although its links with the external revisionist movement were severed Herut was supported by the great majority of revisionist followers living in Israel, and it formally identified itself with Jabotinsky's political programme. With its strident nationalist rhetoric and its vehement antipathy to the Histadrut, Herut succeeded in attracting those new immigrants, especially from the countries of the middle east, who felt dissatisfaction or nursed concrete grievances in the experience of assimilation to their new life.

At its conference in August 1948 the General-Zionist 'A' faction split from its parent movement and formed the Progressive Party together with Oved Zioni ('Zionist Worker'), the liberal groups within the Histadrut, and Aliyah Hadasha ('New Immigration'), the organization representing in the main immigrants from central Europe who had found it difficult to penetrate the leadership based on the old east-European generation. The party was marked by the strength of its appeal to professional people and by its critical and principled liberal attitudes.

Of all the parties Mapai and the religious factions seemed to undergo the least change over time. Mapai's loss of the support of its more radical socialist members in the early 'forties was compensated by its attractiveness to immigrants, for many of whom it was identified with the state and with the legendary figure of Ben-Gurion. Its control of the Histadrut, in which it retained an absolute majority even after the formation of the Mapam opposition, greatly aided Mapai in organizing and mobilizing electoral support.[4]

The general election, the first to be held in Israel, took place on 25 January 1949 and the Constituent Assembly convened on 14 February. Eighty-seven per cent of the half million eligible voters participated, and accorded Mapai a plurality of thirty-six per cent, yielding forty-six seats in the assembly. Mapam led the other parties with nineteen seats, the United Religious Front, an electoral alliance of the four religious groups, received sixteen, and Herut obtained fourteen seats. The General-Zionists followed with seven and the Progressives with five seats, the remainder being distributed amongst half a dozen minor parties. That the major parties were broadly satisfied with the outcome may be inferred from the fact that none insisted on the Constituent Assembly calling new elections under a constitution.

On 16 February without delay the Constituent Assembly passed the Transition Law, based on the work of the provisional constitution committee, under the terms of which it formally assumed the legislative function and constituted itself a unicameral legislature, the first Knesset. While formalizing many of the practices and arrangements devised during the provisional regime the law also filled some gaps and to some extent clarified the pattern of inter-governmental relations. The Transition Law came to be known as the 'small constitution' and in effect comprised the core of the uncodified constitution of the state.

The Transition Law provided for the election of a president by a majority vote of the Knesset and outlined his powers, confirming their essentially ceremonial and symbolic nature. Immediately after the promulgation of the Transition Law the Knesset proceeded to elect Chaim Weizmann President, his tenure to be coterminous with the Knesset with the addition of three months after the convening of a new Knesset. The law did not actually provide for the termination of the first Knesset but in effect allowed for its continuance as long as it could supply a government enjoying its confidence. Since the law provided no other basis for such a decision, it was to be assumed that the Knesset alone could implement its own dissolution and arrange for elections to its successor.

The Transition Law left it to the Knesset itself in the course of time to develop its own rules and procedures, and except for supplying the skeletal framework for cabinet-Knesset relations did not stipulate in any detail the pattern of inter-governmental relations as a whole. The capacity of such an unrefined constitution to support effective government in a time of great stress and crisis attested to the legitimacy of the leadership and the efficacy of its style of improvisation.

The law left to the government itself the determination of its size and its departmental organization and except for the prime minister did not confine the appointment of ministers to the membership of the Knesset. However, the practice of drawing the government from amongst the Knesset membership was early established and subject to only occasional exception. The prime minister had a free hand in forming his team and the cabinet would bear his personal stamp, since the law stipulated that in the event of the prime minister resigning the entire cabinet must fall with him. The law provided for the 'collective responsibility' of the government but did not clarify the concept, which proved to be a point of great difficulty in the context of coalition politics in succeeding years.

In accordance with the new law the provisional government submitted its resignation to the president, while continuing to act as a caretaker government. Although theoretically unbound in this matter the president was expected to consult all major leaders and to call upon the leader of the largest party to form a new government, as indeed he did. Ben-Gurion negotiated a coalition agreement with the religious parties and the Progressives and presented his first cabinet to the Knesset on 8 March 1949, receiving the necessary vote of confidence two days later.

The small constitution in its first months of operation proved more or less adequate to the requirements of effective government and detracted from the momentum of the movement for a written constitution. The revised Kohn draft prepared by the provisional constitution committee was referred immediately to the newly formed Constitution, Law and Justice Committee of the Knesset. In committee discussions over a period of weeks it soon became apparent that a consensus on the terms of a definitive written constitution was politically unattainable and that expenditure of political energies to this end was neither necessary nor perhaps desirable.

The direction of the committee discussions confirmed that a change in atmosphere had taken place since the time of the establishment of the state. From the outset the committee focused on whether to adopt a written constitution at all rather than on the politically complex problems presented by its formulation. The committee failed to reach any conclusion and in February 1950 after nearly a year of work it brought the matter before the Knesset plenum, where it was then sporadically debated for several months.

The debate followed party lines, with the coalition groups rejecting and the opposition groups supporting the early adoption of a complete constitution. Mapai appeared reluctant to place its coalition under the stress that a majority decision on the role of religion might place it. Its main partner in government, the religious front, was unwilling to risk a political resolution of the issue along secularist lines and preferred to operate from the relatively tolerable *status quo* bequeathed by the mandatory regime. The opposition groups feared that failure to adopt a written constitution might place the Mapai-dominated government beyond the reach of democratic constraints. On 13 June 1950 the issue was brought to a final vote in the Knesset on three alternative resolutions: one sponsored by the religious groups calling for the regulation of constitutional relations by statutes in the form of fundamental laws; the second, favoured by the opposition parties, calling for the enactment of a full constitution within a specific time; and the third proposal, a compromise put forward by Mapai, which was adopted by a hairbreadth majority, in the following terms:[5]

> 'The first Knesset charges the Constitution, Law and Justice Committee to prepare a draft constitution for the state. The constitution shall be built chapter by chapter in such a manner that each in itself shall comprise a fundamental law. Each chapter shall be brought before the Knesset as and when the committee completes its work, and all the chapters together shall be assembled as the constitution of the state.'

The question whether the constitution should be completed and written all at once or be composed piecemeal as each section passed through the legislative mill was really of secondary importance. Under the sway of the government led by Mapai and the religious parties the adopted resolution evaded the major issue of the status of fundamental law, both as to the conditions of its enactment and as to whether it would require a constitutional jurisprudence to maintain its supremacy over ordinary legislation. The fundamental laws passed by the Knesset over the years under the terms of the 1950 'chapter by chapter' resolution were in fact, apart from their titles, indistinguishable in status from other laws, subject as they were to passage and amendment by simple majority (and even to amendment by laws not themselves entitled fundamental), while at the same time ordinary laws enforced by the judiciary were not subject to review in the light of fundamental laws.[6]

The preparation of fundamental laws simultaneously with other pressing affairs proved to be a slow process, the first such measure being passed only in 1958. Many laws of constitutional or fundamental purport were passed without being singled out and designated as such and some originated with the government itself rather than in the constitution committee as provided for under the 'chapter by chapter' resolution. Thus the constitutional flexibility aimed for in the 1950 resolution was in practice achieved in the very process of constitution-making, which essentially took the form of piecemeal codification of current practices as these were established.

Citizenship and personal status

On 5 July 1950 the Knesset passed the Law of Return, giving to Zionist doctrine its most forceful legal expression. As indicated in its title, the law characterized the immigration of Jews as a return to their homeland. The law therefore accorded every Jew the right to immigrate and in principle entitled any Jew, whatever his citizenship and wherever resident, to exert a claim on Israel's courts for enforcement of this right. Exception was made for those engaged in activity directed against the Jewish people and for those likely to endanger public health or security. An amendment to the law in 1954 added past criminals to those excepted. The same right of 'return' was accorded to any Jew who initially came to the country without the intention of settling but who later wished to do so. Jews who immigrated or those born in the country before the law came into effect were deemed also to have immigrated under the doctrine of return. The term 'Jew' was not defined in the law. An intending immigrant declaring himself a Jew would normally be accepted as such by immigration officials processing visa applications in their countries of origin.

The Law of Return in Zionist theory was regarded as the formal corollary of the termination of Jewish 'homelessness' by the establishment of the state. Taken on its own the law merely accorded to Jews abroad the right to immigrate to Israel. Its effects were amplified when taken in conjunction with the Nationality Law passed by the second Knesset on 1 April 1952, which came into force from 14 July 1952.

With the transition from the Palestine regime to Israeli sovereignty the issue of citizenship came under a cloud of confusion. Judicial opinion was divided as to whether tenure of Palestinian citizenship under the British dispensation automatically conferred Israeli citizenship under the new regime, or whether the whole population was technically stateless pending new legislation. The balance of legal opinion favoured the latter unsatisfactory conclusion, which was duly corrected by the Nationality Law.

Under the Nationality Law citizenship was automatically granted to any Jewish immigrant by virtue of return, unless being over eighteen years of age and a citizen of another country he expressly declared against receiving citizenship. Acquisition of Israeli citizenship by a Jewish immigrant thus required no positive act on his part, while opting out of citizenship did not impair the right of immigration under return. In its application to non-Jews, that is for the most part Arabs, the Nationality Law provided for acquisition of citizenship by residence, and additionally, for both Jews and non-Jews by birth or naturalization. To obtain citizenship by virtue of residence Arabs had to have been Palestinian citizens immediately before the establishment of the state, registered as residents on 1 March 1952 and resident in fact on 14 July 1952. They were also required to furnish documentary proof of meeting these conditions or of having legally entered the country during the time between the establishment of the state and implementation of the law. Children born during those four years and two months to parents entitled to citizenship by virtue of residence acquired it through that of their parents, while children born before the establishment of the state were subject to the same requirements as adults.

As to citizenship by birth, having one Israeli parent was sufficient condition for its acquisition by children born after the law came into effect, whether Jewish or non-Jewish and whether born in Israel or abroad.

Conditions for the acquisition of citizenship by naturalization were relatively liberal, and included three years' residence out of the five years previous to the application, and, except for those who were Palestinian citizens immediately before the establishment of the state, having some knowledge of Hebrew. Marriage to an Israeli national might serve as ground for exemption from the conditions though not from the process of naturalization. The granting of citizenship by naturalization was placed in the absolute discretion of the minister of the interior.

The Nationality Law combined the aim of promoting the acquisition of Israeli citizenship by Jews with that of regulating its acquisition by Arabs in such a way as to curb their illegal entry into the country. The law was thus clearly discriminatory on ethnic grounds, favouring in effect the Jewish immigrant over the Arab resident who had lived in the country all his life. The debate in the Knesset revealed much doubt about the propriety of the terms of citizenship for Arabs. In the event, however, the vast majority of Arabs living in the country were able to secure citizenship in virtue of residence quickly and easily. The apparently formidable impediments were administered leniently and aimed at the detection and exclusion of infiltrators rather than at diminishing the status of legal residents.

Although on account of security considerations Israeli legislation in its practical effects often infringed equality of status under the law, the doctrine of equality as an ideal was firmly embedded in the constitutional tradition that had evolved prior to statehood. The legal foundations of personal status inherited from the mandatory regime were subjected to less substantial modification than any other branch of Israel's constitution, although their initial adaptation to the new Israeli conditions was marked by considerable difficulty and uncertainty involving frequent individual hardship.

Not only the basic constitutional law of the mandatory administration as laid out in the Order-in-Council of 1922, but also the text of the mandate for Palestine itself in regard to civil and religious liberties and personal status remained in force after the establishment of the state, subject of course to consistency with Israeli statutes as provided in the Law and Administration Ordinance of 1948.

Article 15 of the mandate expressly guaranteed freedom of conscience and forbade governmental discrimination amongst citizens on grounds of race, religion or language. Israel's Declaration of Independence reaffirmed these guarantees while adding sex to the proscribed criteria of discrimination. The Order-in-Council of 1922 guaranteed internal autonomy to every legally recognized religious community. Under the Religious Communities (Organization) Ordinance of 1926, which in substance remained in force in Israel, religious communities were endowed with legal personality as public agencies of the state dispensing legal powers enforceable by the state.

The Supreme Rabbinical Council headed jointly by the *Ashkenazi* and *Sephardi* Chief Rabbis was carried over from the mandatory period as the highest rabbinical authority at the apex of a network of local religious councils formed by periodic election. Each local rabbinical office was constituted as a court (*Beth Din*) responsible for all the administrative and judicial affairs assigned to it by law. The Supreme Rabbinical Council constituted the highest court of appeal in the rabbinical jurisdiction.

By receiving mandatory practice Jews in Israel at the accession to independence were subject to exclusive rabbinical jurisdiction in all that pertained to marriage, divorce, maintenance and probate. In all other aspects of personal status the rabbinical courts shared their jurisdiction with the secular civil courts, their competence being contingent on the consent of the parties. The legal situation was marked by extraordinary confusion. Under the mandate membership in a recognized religious community was voluntary and contingent on enrollment in an official register. Individuals who opted out of the official community could settle all their affairs in the secular courts. This sometimes occasioned uncertainty as to the validity of religious jurisdiction in hard cases during the British administration.[7] After Israel's establishment the confusion was magnified since the official community register had to all intents and purposes lapsed in the early 'forties and did not incorporate the masses of new immigrants since then. Furthermore, even this defective legal basis was weakened upon the presumptive termination of Knesset Israel as a legal personality when the National Council dissolved early in 1949.

Working under a multitude of extraordinary pressures in its first years, the government of Israel was unable immediately to introduce order into the constitution of personal status. Improvisation was maintained until the issue was settled for the Jewish population, at least for the time being, by the enactment of the Rabbinical Courts Jurisdiction (Marriage and Divorce) Law in September 1953. As a result of this law issues of maintenance and probate were given over to concurrent jurisdiction with secular courts, the range of exclusive rabbinical jurisdiction being narrowed to matters of marriage and divorce. At the same time the application of the jurisdiction was extended by inclusion of foreign nationals within its purview, and also by an important change in the criterion by which persons were brought under its sway. The law abandoned the mandatory criterion of registration in the Jewish community as the basis of rabbinical jurisdiction over a person's status, and replaced it by the criterion of *being* a Jew. This reflected a shift in the status of the Jewish community resulting from independence.

Hitherto in Palestine, as indeed elsewhere in the world where Jews enjoyed autonomy in the regulation of personal life, the community was the source of administrative power whether exercised by laymen or rabbis. Now the sovereignty of the state had become the source of this power and the community of Jews as such lapsed as a political entity. Being a Jew in this new context ceased to be contingent on affiliation with the community but became a personal attribute of individual identity. The law simply referred to 'matters of marriage and divorce of Jews in Israel' without supplying any definition of Jews. The effect of the change was in practice to install the rabbinical law itself as the authoritative source for determination of its own subjects. The importance of the changed criterion lay in the exclusiveness of the rabbinical jurisdiction based upon it over those aspects of personal status assigned to it by the law. In matters connected with marriage or divorce the rabbinical law, so far as Jews recognized by that law were concerned, was the exhaustive civil law of the state. Since the rabbinical law claimed as its subjects all persons born of a Jewish mother, the professed atheist no less than the devoutly orthodox Jew was subject to its writ. The law taken in conjunction with the parallel legislation applicable to non-Jews had the effect of ascribing a religious identity to every Israeli. The individual could choose as between recognized religions but marital affairs could not be arranged outside the clerical sphere, which meant in effect that mixed marriages were ruled out since none of the religious jurisprudences permitted them. However, marriages conducted abroad under whatever auspices were recognized as valid in Israel, a necessary consideration in view of the immigrant character of the population. Under this law more than under the Law of Return, which merely established a right without exerting any compulsion, the problem of the definition of 'Jew' emerged recurrently and often acutely in the political arena. The processing of immigrant applications under the Law of Return was conducted by secular officials following loose secular criteria of judgement regarding the claim to be Jewish. So too the registration of population required for administrative and statistical purposes was operated by secular criteria. However, the judgements of immigration officials or population registrars were in no way conclusive in determining Jewish identity, which was within the sole jurisdiction of the rabbinical authorities.

Under the mandate the Muslim community was organized on similar lines to the Jewish but exercised a much wider range of exclusive jurisdiction covering the whole field of personal status. The Muslim religious courts and the Supreme Muslim Council dissolved in the conditions of war and Arab flight. The Supreme Muslim Council was not restored but the minister of religious affairs directly intervened to re-establish the Muslim religious courts on an improvised basis later retroactively validated by law. While subjected to considerable changes in their organizational forms the Muslim courts continued as under the mandate to exercise their customary jurisdictions.

The organization of the Christian communities continued in Israel without interruption along the lines evolved within the Ottoman juridical system and maintained by the mandatory administration. Each of the several recognized denominations had its own distinctive institutions and all had religious courts of the first instance, though only the Greek Orthodox had a resident archbishop and its own court of appeals. For other denominations appeals from the lower courts were processed with the participation of higher religious authorities not resident in Israel. This procedure, even if it involved nationals of Arab countries, was fully honoured by the Israeli authorities and decisions emerging from external sources were enforceable as Israeli law. The Christian ecclesiastical jurisdiction corresponded with the rabbinical and was not so extensive as the Muslim in the range of its exclusiveness.

The constitutional transition consequent on statehood thus gave institutional form to the paradox of Jewish identity as derived from the secular national ideology. The Jewish community ceased to exist but all residents of Jewish origin were assigned a Jewish identity by ascription. Whereas in the diaspora and in mandatory Palestine to be Jewish was a voluntary act comprising a complex choice at various levels of identity, now in the name of a national theory of Jewish identity it became an involuntary status defined by religious criteria.

Subordinate governments and the state

Among the most difficult problems of the transition from colonial status to independence were those presented by the multitude of activities that had been carried out by the Jewish population of Palestine in voluntary frameworks but which now became the direct responsibility of the state. The most crucial struggle for state authority against the vestiges of pre-state partisan psychology was the showdown with the dissident terrorist movement and the Palmach. Ben-Gurion attached greater importance to this than to any other domestic issue in 1948. In successfully bringing these movements under firm government authority, albeit at a great price in goodwill, he greatly enhanced the credibility of the state and attracted to it the legitimacy which he saw as vital to its consolidation.

Although the issue was most sharply joined where the bearing of arms had been involved, there occurred many other instances and forms of resistance to the exclusive exercise of governmental authority. Those executive departments of the Jewish Agency which were exclusively Palestinian in composition were easily enough assimilated by the new state bureaucracy. But what of the external wing of the Zionist Organization? What was to be the status of Zionist leadership abroad, accustomed to holding the purse strings and sharing in the making of the movement's policies in the Palestinian arena?

293

Rivalry between the Palestinian leaders and those of the Zionist Organization living abroad, especially the Americans, had been a normal feature of the policy-making process within the movement during the period of the mandate. But when Jewish independence came into view the issue assumed a new value. As early as November 1947, before the partition proposal had been approved at UNO, friction arose on the structure of the prospective Jewish sovereignty. When officials of the Zionist general council at that time began to discuss convening a plenary session of the Jewish Agency executive to elect a provisional government, strong objections were raised in Palestine on the grounds that this must be the exclusive prerogative of residents of the country. Meantime discussions within Palestine proceeded towards enlarging the representative structure of the national organs and preparing for the transition. At the end of December Remez pointed out that it would not be logical to include foreign residents in Israel's government but at the same time said that no decision had yet been made on this. As preparations further evolved it became clear that the initiative was fully with the Palestinian leaders. In mid-July 1948 the Jewish Agency executive itself called upon those of its members living abroad to come to Israel to settle. In August the American leaders Silver and Neumann shifted the focus from the question of possible external influence in Israel's domestic affairs, which by then was clearly not going to be countenanced, and raised the question of Israel's influence within the external organizations. They demanded that members of Israel's cabinet should automatically resign from the Jewish Agency executive and expressed resentment that the Israeli government was effectively in a position to take decisions affecting the Zionist movement as a whole. The American view was widely supported by the leaderships in other countries and by the political parties other than Mapai, most of which were relatively stronger abroad than in Israel. A clear majority within the Zionist Organization was formed in favour of the American view but there was reluctance to settle the matter firmly against Mapai opposition, which was tantamount to opposing the view of the Israeli government.

With the termination of the British mandate the constitutional status of the Jewish Agency in relation to government formally lapsed. While unwilling to allow the Agency to continue under Israeli sovereignty as a state within the state, the Israeli leadership nevertheless wished to maintain the semblance of Agency autonomy in conducting its immigration and settlement operations, in order to sustain the fiction of the representative 'national' character of world-wide Jewish participation in Israel's development. The government wanted an understanding with the Zionist Organization which would enable it effectively to control not only Agency activities within Israel but also indirectly Zionist activities within Jewish communities abroad, while avoiding language which might imply an Israeli claim to privileged status in regard to the citizens of foreign countries.

At the twenty-third Zionist Congress held in Jerusalem in 1951, the first since the establishment of the state, the issue of the relation of the organization to the new state was explored and resolutions were adopted pointing the way to a formula of agreement with the government. The Knesset formally regulated the relationship in November 1952 by enacting the World Zionist Organization-Jewish Agency (Status) Law. The law confirmed that the Zionist Organization, while being recognized by the state as the 'authorized agency' for this purpose, would continue to organize immigration and settlement activities within Israel. The law provided that the details and forms of co-operation with the government would be determined by a covenant between the Israel government and the Zionist executive. The covenant was implemented in 1954, providing for a co-ordinating board (already in existence since 1951) through which the government was effectively able to exercise control.

The World Zionist Organization-Jewish Agency (Status) Law complemented the Law of Return, but had greater substantive effect given the involvement of a major bureaucracy. The significance of the law from the constitutional point of view was that it provided a formula for continuing the link between Israel and the Jewish people abroad in the manner that had earlier been acknowledged in the League of Nations mandate in accordance with the demands of Zionist ideology, while yet ensuring that claims such as those that had been made by the Jewish Agency on the mandate could not be exerted on sovereign Israel. The law enabled Israel to sustain its own myth in which it regarded itself as representative of the Jewish people, while protecting its own independence from interference by the Jewish people, and at the same time securing its own power of interference in Jewish affairs abroad without explicitly asserting this power. The transition to independence thus involved a re-definition of relations between Jewry and Israel which perpetuated the myth of Israel as a 'colony' of the Jewish people while at the same time promoting the fact of the Jewish people as a 'colony' of Israel.

The Jewish Agency and its subsidiaries had sustained a measure of general unity within the national home. Below this level of formal quasi-government, intense ideological rivalry between competitive voluntary movements had produced a corresponding pattern of social cleavage dividing the population into distinct groupings many of which maintained virtual private governments. Before statehood these groupings attracted the primary loyalty of their members, who played their part in the struggle for independence first and foremost as devotees of the various movements. It was as a member of a political party or of the Histadrut or the Irgun that the individual asserted his political identity and it was within such groups that his social needs were requited. Independence thus presented a challenge to habit. The state now claimed primary allegiance and required the movements to adapt their roles to fit the framework of participation in state power rather than competition to establish statehood in particular preferred forms. Providing as they did for the social welfare, education, housing and employment of their members in addition to ramified communal and cultural services, the sophistication of these movements contributed greatly to the very attainment of independence, and thereafter to the relative orderliness with which the transition to independent administration was accomplished. At the same time the pre-state institutional matrix influenced the political style and constitution of the state, in subtle and informal ways forcing its design and constraining its government.

The legislative power of the state enabled the government to impose new norms but did not of itself suffice to establish immediately an attitude of acceptance of the primacy of the state domain by private governments accustomed to exercising extensive authority over their affiliates. The habit of intense competition in seeking to mould the ideal image of the state before its incarnation did not readily give way to the more prosaic demands of competing for influence within its framework as a given political environment. Nor did the habit of opposition to authority, nourished in the colonial arena but in the case of the east-European Jews already ingrained in the more remote past, quickly succumb to the realization that the new authority was neither alien nor hostile to the aspirations of the people. It need not therefore be a matter for surprise that an element of federalism characterized the constitutional configuration of Israel in its first years of transition.

The political parties best exemplified the protogenic federal aspect of Israel's constitution. Rather as the labour parties by dint of their prior existence had determined the way in which the Histadrut functioned politically, the political parties at large in their historical priority to the state and in their extensive reach into the lives of their followers, resembled and regarded themselves as corporate proprietors of statehood. Whether involved in the government coalition or on the sidelines in opposition the parties shared a common attitude to government, that the extent of its jurisdiction derived from their own prior authority and the effectiveness of its authority from their own political constituencies. As creatures of the parties the state and its government were accorded ascendancy only at their will. The parties tended to preserve for themselves paternity rights in delineating the content of state autonomy. It is as though the political parties in collusion had entered into a federal bargain relinquishing certain of their prerogatives to the new government, but retaining power to manipulate and regulate the boundaries of federal jurisdiction. This attitude, as though playing host to the state, characterized all the parties and was associated with an implicit secessionist threat. Mapai, straddling as it did all the key points of control, was the effective umpire of the federal bargain, and together with the Histadrut saw itself as the indispensable backbone of the state.

CHAPTER 13

IDEOLOGICAL AND POLITICAL TRANSITION (1948-56)

Labour, nation and state – political participation, parties and issues – the stable coalition – civil-military relations – Israel, Judaism and Jewry

Labour, nation and state

In common with other national movements the Zionist movement had been deeply exercised by the social issues whose resolution would give content to the framework of national independence. That the leadership of Zionism within Palestine fell to the labour movement was due in part to the explicit conviction of the pioneers that the national and social struggles were identical or at least inseparable. This point of view enabled the labour movement more effectively than other groups to articulate the rhetoric of commitment and to select its tactics and policies. Accustomed in ideological discourse to elucidating the range of choice in terms of national-social dialectics, the labour movement as a whole was better prepared than other institutions to adapt to independence without experiencing a marked break with its own past. The sense of continuity prevalent in Mapai and in the Histadrut was a most important stabilizing factor during the constitutional transition in the first few years of statehood. At the same time the sense of continuity of historical role and habit acted as a brake upon change and exerted a conservative pull on its direction.

In the decades preceding statehood socialist ideas and doctrines had suggested to the labour leaders their approaches to national issues. Building a socialist society was seen as synonymous with building a sovereign nation. Socialist pursuits were measured against nationalist purposes, nationalist strategies were answerable to the socialist conscience. The range within which the two sets of values could be comfortably synthesized determined the horizons and boundaries of the Histadrut's sphere of operation. At the same time the tension between the two poles of commitment constantly tugged at the foundations of consensus.

As the succession to the British mandate became a palpable issue in the late 'thirties the socialist-Zionist conjunction was attenuated and its relevance as a guide to policy was subjected to its severest challenge. The socialist-Zionist consensus had served the Histadrut well in the guidance of day-to-day policy, but the synthesis itself, as distinct from the consensus, tended to break down when confronted with the choice between national and social objectives as an actual terminus rather than a floating hypothesis. The labour movement had to opt for either an early national solution or a putative socialist solution to the issue of succession. Ben-Gurion had firmly subordinated socialist considerations to what he regarded as national imperatives and he became increasingly impatient of questions of socialist propriety. While the majority followed Ben-Gurion in the nationalist policy the opposition had crystallized within the Mapai left (Ahdut Ha'avodah) in the demand for postponement of independence until both nationalist and socialist goals could be realized at a higher level, and in the 'outside' left (Hashomer Hatzair) in the endorsement of a purist socialist alternative. In the case of Ahdut Ha'avodah it was as though the practical impossibility of simultaneously obtaining ideal national and social conditions was compensated by the aspiration for greater purism in both directions, in preference to a potential approximation in one direction alone. Hashomer Hatzair, on the other hand, saw national fulfillment as necessarily a derivative of socialism. Thus in both cases the socialist-Zionist synthesis was flawed no less than in the case of Mapai.

It may be that the crisis in ideology reflected a discrepancy between the vocabulary of policy and the actuality of circumstance. The issue of sovereignty in the manner in which it emerged was extraneous to the semantic models of European nationalism and socialism in which the labour-Zionist world-view had been framed. Their European vocabulary rendered intelligible the actions of the labour pioneers in the context of such European national and class institutions as had been transplanted to Palestine. It was, however, inadequate to cope with the issues of colonial reality in the degree that these deviated from European patterns of experience. With the gradual development of the Jewish economy elements of European national and class institutions were imported into Palestine, lending relevance to nationalist and socialist doctrines of European origin. At the same time, the British imported elements of the national and social relations characteristic of societies under colonial rule. The two discrete processes could be reconciled in the vocabulary of socialist-Zionism only as long as Britain maintained its protective attitude towards Zionism. The changed British policy of the late 'thirties, in forcing the labour-Zionists to grapple with the issues of independence, carried the labour movement through a transition from a European type of nationalism reminiscent of the nineteenth century to an anti-colonial nationalism more typical of the southern hemisphere in the twentieth century. But the transition was not symmetrically reflected in the ideological culture. The changed circumstances had not been anticipated by the labour-Zionist theory nor was their meaning fully appreciated by the labour-Zionist movement, except for Ben-Gurion, until the late 'forties.

In following Ben-Gurion's national policy in the mid-'forties the nationalist majority within the Histadrut had to sacrifice the indulgence of its socialist alter ego. Having abandoned the synthesis of national and social goals to throw all its energies into the national struggle as newly defined, the Histadrut then found itself in 1948 up-staged by the sovereign government as the new centre of national leadership. The new state and its bureaucracy, and particularly its army, were now the legitimate claimants of national loyalty. The Histadrut was thus deprived of its habitual jurisdiction in the formulation and leadership of the national cause.

The Histadrut had close links with the government through its Mapai majority and had a strong sense of the continuity of its role, but the Histadrut's place in the political life of the country was nevertheless transformed by the fact of statehood. The organization now needed to recapture its lapsed socialist persona and redeploy its ideological and material resources in a new perspective *vis-à-vis* national life. Hence a conservative tendency began to manifest itself within the Histadrut allowing that what it sought to conserve was an innovative socialist undertaking against radical statist tendencies inherent in the new nationalism galvanized by independence.

The adaptation of the Histadrut to its new public status was eased by its key part in the absorption of immigrants. This national challenge enabled the Histadrut for some years to maintain the myth of its essential national capacity, while obscuring the reality of its increasingly sectarian role. The transition was eased by the fact that a great increase in its membership due to immigration enhanced its power as a sectarian social force. Paradoxically, the Histadrut attained the peak of its power in the mid-'fifties at the very time when its own ideological bearings forced it to contemplate its possible redundancy as a primary vehicle of national development. Its power, in order words, was augmented in its aspect as an interest group in a pluralistic democratic polity at the cost of its diminution as the most dynamic author of its political environment.

The pattern of transition of the Histadrut from its dominance in the anti-colonial nationalist movement to its subordination as custodian of the socialist heritage of a segment of the independent nation was pre-figured in the initial response within the Histadrut to its abandonment of the nationalist-socialist synthesis in the early 'forties. The socialist conscience of the Histadrut was then institutionalized in the political parties and kibbutz movements of the left, whereas now the Histadrut as a whole edged into this position in relation to the state. In the meantime, however, the context had changed in such a way as to turn the radical-conservative axis upside down. For then the socialist response had been radical, rejecting the nationalist embrace of the social *status quo* in favour of a creative vision of the future society which would be worthy of independence. Now it was conservative, protecting the socialist sphere within an environment in which the institutions of the state were the most dynamic radical factor. Pending independence it had been possible to dream of creating a new society, whereas following independence it became necessary to accept the configuration of society as more or less given. The pursuit of independence had endowed existing social relations with promise and fluidity whereas its advent had rendered them concrete and vested them with fixity.

Just as Mapai had been the primary vehicle of continuity and stability in conducting the transition to independence for the country as a whole, so within the Histadrut sphere Mapai supplied the indispensable regulating mechanism ensuring a smooth passage. Its control of the Histadrut by an absolute, if slim, majority enabled Mapai to give full recognition to the Histadrut's core values while rendering these compatible with the national or statist interests for which Mapai in government held responsibility. The pattern of transition and Mapai's key role in the process were exemplified in an organizational crisis within the kibbutz movement originating in the fateful choice of the early 'forties and culminating in 1951.

As Mapai took the nationalist high road in 1944 the kibbutz movement on the 'inside' left, Hakibbutz Hameuhad, found itself increasingly politicized much as Hakibbutz Haartzi on the 'outside' left had been since the mid-'thirties. These two movements thus became a socialist opposition rather than instruments of Histadrut pioneering as originally conceived, and their respective political parties, Ahdut Ha'avodah (initially Faction 'B' of Mapai) and Hashomer Hatzair (the two groups which united in 1948 to form Mapam), became essentially the political arms of their kibbutz movements. Mapai had already become a broadly based national party whose kibbutz members (in Hakibbutz Hameuhad and Hever Hakvutzot) were but a minority segment among the many elements of organized labour and non-labour groups from which the party drew its support. Thus in the case of the left-wing, the kibbutzim 'owned' their parties, while in the case of the Mapai-oriented kibbutzim the party 'owned' them.

Academic and journalistic discussion of the place of the

kibbutz in Israeli political life invariably points to their extraordinary and proportionately excessive influence within the political leadership of the nation. In fact it was their *lack* of influence in the counsels of the nation that pushed the left-wing kibbutzim into opposition. The kibbutzim that remained within the Mapai orbit were not in fact influential in the making of high policy in their capacity as kibbutzim. It is true that a great many of the Mapai leaders and its functionaries in a wide span of public institutions had personal links with the kibbutz, but it was as Mapai leaders that they found themselves in the kibbutz movement rather than as kibbutz leaders that they had any peculiar influence within Mapai. Had there been a pronounced kibbutz influence in shaping national policy this would have been reflected in a socialist determination of the national strategy, which would have sought an accommodation with the Arabs other than a military resolution and other than partition. The kibbutzim had failed to have this influence when Ben-Gurion legitimized and pressed ahead the implementation of Jabotinsky's nationalist policy. To question the extent of its political influence is not of course to derogate the inspirational power of the kibbutz movement as a diffuse cultural force.

Following the attainment of independence and the mass influx of immigrants the kibbutz movement experienced a crisis of adaptation which was sharpened by a rapid decline in its prestige, due to the emergence of a whole new range of national challenges beyond its competence. In the course of adjustment to the new situation, in which the nationalist and socialist functions were dispersed, Hakibbutz Hameuhad found itself unable to continue embracing the followers of both Ahdut Ha'avodah and Mapai. The movement split on party lines in 1951. The left-wing kibbutzim now affiliated with Ahdut Ha'avodah and the remaining Mapai-oriented groups joined with Hever Hakvutzot to form a new federation, *Ihud Hakvutzot Ve'Hakibbutzim*. Not only did the organization as a whole split in this manner, but individual kibbutzim including some of the oldest and most venerated split up physically to eliminate political diversity within them. The physical dismemberment of several kibbutzim, involving the dismantling and distribution of assets and occasioning great personal acrimony amongst lifelong colleagues and friends, indicated that political party allegiance had become a stronger identification than the kibbutz social life. It was as members of their party that the left-wingers now saw themselves bound together rather than primarily as comrades sharing a specific form of communal life. It was their lack of influence in national politics that impelled the kibbutzim to reorganize to procure political homogeneity within them. Only the Mapai members were able to fit into the broader nationalist framework because only they were willing to accept their lack of influence as a movement.

The Mapai kibbutzim contributed personnel to the leadership in their individual capacities. If they exerted any kibbutz influence as such then it was only as a pressure group on behalf of agriculture and specifically often as a counter to the claims of the moshav movement. Mapai thus mediated the adjustment of its own kibbutzim to the wider national arena as newly defined by independence, in which many other elements besides pioneering labour had a crucial role. The non-Mapai kibbutzim then became the exclusively socialist sectarian interest.

Having achieved clear-cut political separatism the socialist kibbutzim were now able to exert considerable influence within the Histadrut arena, increasing labour militancy in the trade union sphere and pressing harder the Histadrut's claims to the major share of public investment resources. Mapai in its Histadrut context rather than in its kibbutz aspect now came to represent the socialist wing of the party while the government and the civil service became the agents of the party's nationalist persona. The Histadrut as a whole now functioned conservatively as an anchor of Mapai's ideological heritage rather than merely its convenient instrument as in the pre-state period.

During the mandatory period the Histadrut and its agrarian wing in particular had been successful in attracting the lion's share of public funds, deemed as they were to be the vanguard of national development. The Mapai-led Jewish Agency had favoured labour institutions. As long as the various ideological movements before independence were in contention for the type of society to be established it was possible for the executive organs to show favouritism of this kind and thereby advance their own blueprint for the hypothetical state. When Mapai became the responsible governing party of the independent state it had to take a broader view. While indeed continuing to favour its own followers so far as possible, it was now unable to ignore other elements of the population. For the purposes of defence and development every dynamic resource had relevance, whether of socialist persuasion or not. From the point of view of government the relative importance of different interests changed from the assessment arising in conditions of the struggle for independence.

Political participation, parties and issues

The major change in the political ethos of the Jewish population, which was formalized by the armistice agreements, was its translation from a minority settler community in a colonial context to a majority-enjoying sovereignty. Veterans and new immigrants alike for the first time became masters in their own country.

By comparison with the period preceding independence the most striking change in the quality of political life after 1948 was a paradoxical conjunction of increased political power with reduced voluntaristic initiative in shaping society. The *praxis* of the veteran settlers was in large part the initiative they exercised in the creation of new institutions. Under colonial rule the settlers were in a way freer to make their own lives than they were after the growth of power that came with independence. The veteran elites now exercised power for the whole society, but their new situation offered less scope for new initiative. They now faced the challenge of adapting what had become relatively stable institutions to the new circumstances of a society in rapid change and flux. For the masses of new immigrants, on the other hand, all was still new, and the experience of initiative now became theirs: the oldtimers had the power and the newcomers the *praxis*! Not that the immigrants wielded the spontaneous initiative that had characterized the efforts of the early settlers, but they nevertheless had a sense of freedom and creativity through their identification with and participation in the institutions administered on their behalf by the veterans.

The euphoria of political independence in a population which in its various countries of origin had known only subjugation or persecution, helped perhaps more than any other factor to sustain morale and the patient acceptance of austerity and disorder in the first years after the establishment of the state. It was the intoxicating sense of *praxis* and political access, rather than Zionism, which quickened the national spirit. The sense of shared identity and belonging was nourished by the common participation in intelligible institutions of state power rather than by common Zionist or Jewish sentiments. From the perspective of the new population, with its background of colonial status in the autocracies of the middle east or the concentration camps of Europe, independence in their new state was a profoundly liberating experience. The veterans now operated the levers of central power with a corresponding loss of 'federal' freedom in their communal concerns, while the new immigrants under the administration of the oldtimers felt themselves part of a free system with which they could identify and which was building the framework of their lives anew.

The country was sufficiently small and its participatory institutions at the grassroots sufficiently penetrating to yield a widely diffused sense of shared endeavour in the exercise of available power. While the small size of the country undoubtedly favoured the centralization of power and limited the relative influence of local organizational concentrations, it also had the effect of rendering national policy-making concerns quite intimate. From the institutions of street-corner democracy up through the bureaucracies of the political parties and the Histadrut with their patronage, to the upper reaches of national leadership, the threads of political integration were woven in the fabric of felt sovereignty. The state was the primary nation-making force and the common membership was widely experienced as a vivid domestic autonomy.

Inevitably under the conditions of independence, as the political parties adapted to their role as competitive interest groups in the pluralistic political arena, their ideological continuity with the past became increasingly rhetorical.

(Nevertheless their ideological habits and myths were an important stabilizing factor in the transition from inchoate Zionist state to Israeli nation.) For the veteran generation, 1948 was the climax of its lifework, and it wished heartily for some of the fruits of its lifelong sacrifices. The first years of the state were marked by tension between the psychological demobilization of the veteran generation, as reflected in a gradual atrophy of its ideologies, and the need to mobilize the masses of new immigrants who were innocent of ideological pretensions. The pioneering practice and its rhetoric which had formed the political vocabulary of the veteran generation for half a century now seemed irrelevant to the new immigrant masses. Without Zionist indoctrination, these could be assimilated and their energies mobilized only by means of machine politics and patronage. Thus, from having for long been communal service agencies for their devoted ideological adherents the parties now gradually became machines for the induction of nominal followers in the electoral marketplace.

The spirit of communalism characteristic of the labour parties in the period before independence had been responsible for the proliferation of cultural, social and economic responsibilities under political party auspices. The non-socialist parties had found it necessary, in the competition to survive and grow, to adopt similar practices to those derived from various socialist doctrines and predilections. Social life in every aspect was thus highly politicized in the pre-state period. The rapid doubling of the population by the influx of immigrants who had shared neither in the established ideological allegiances nor in the informal machinery of their federal integration, but only in the direct exposure to the institutions of national sovereignty, brought about the gradual displacement of the communalist rationale of party life by that of electoral competition for the control of government.

The masses of immigrants quickly learned that their votes were highly prized by the veteran party officials. The agents of the political parties, whether in their capacities as government or Jewish Agency or Histadrut officials or officers of local government or the religious bureaucracy, competed vigorously at the grassroots to secure the support of the newcomers on the basis of the manifold services that their respective parties could offer. In giving allegiance or the promise of his vote to a particular party the new immigrant expressed a newly acquired sense of his personal worth, rather than commitment to a particular concept of economic organization or social justice. The political integration of the new population was thus crucially mediated by the veteran political parties. Immigrants for the most part did not secure a significant foothold on the ladder of political promotion, but remained subservient to the veterans and their Israeli-born heirs who controlled the political parties and centres of power. Although they were thus clients of the parties rather than an influential political force within them, the immigrants' experience of assimilation was, by their association with the parties, bound up with the hectic issues of national life and development. While the desire for electoral success was the driving force of party competition, for the immigrants the vote was a somewhat abstract secondary vehicle of participation. The parties came across to them as grassroots providers, assisting their assimilation and giving them a stake in the more remote reaches of institutional power.

In the quest for employment, housing, educational or religious facilities, assistance towards settlement in agriculture or vocational and Hebrew-language instruction, immigrants encountered officialdom in various guises, but they apprehended the political party labels as cutting across institutional boundaries. The consumer of assistance would be shuttled from bureaucracy to bureaucracy, from the Histadrut to the municipality to the religious council, from the Jewish Agency to this or that ministry, always to meet the ubiquitous party signposts which alone seemed to point a clear route through the official maze.

For nearly three decades the distribution of official jobs at all levels in the major bureaucracies had been based on the application of an informal proportional party 'key', revised from time to time as elections to the organs of the quasi-government registered changes in public sentiment. This procedure, given the dependence of new immigrants on official assistance of every kind, brought about the assimilation of the masses of immigrants to electoral politics in a pattern closely resembling the pre-state configuration. Rather than forming a powerful new political movement counterposed to the veteran population which they outnumbered, the immigrant masses latched on to the veteran parties. The relative strength of the parties determined their capacity to absorb newcomers to their respective banners, so that the pre-existing pattern was reinforced rather than undermined by the influx of new voters. Mapai, for the multitude, was the most lucid symbol of state power, and it held the most plausible key to personal participation and assimilation. Only the religious parties exerted a comparable immediacy of appeal. The loyalty of its appointees enabled Mapai, with the lion's share of official jobs, to exercise influence in all the minutiae of public life and to promote national integration by the diffusion of state symbols throughout all the bastions of lingering feudalist mentality which it controlled.

In contrast to old-established states in which political life turns on matters analogous to the choice of furnishings and interior decoration, the conflicts in new nations tend to be about foundations and architecture. Although political issues in established societies may tap similar depths of feeling and belief, they do not as a rule, short of revolutionary politics, involve choices with the same degree of importance as those facing new societies. Israel within a short span experienced both conditions. The basic structure of the society was shaped with phenomenal speed during the first few years of statehood. Within about five or six years after independence the foundations that had taken fifty years to build were bearing the weight of a firmly set social order.

The speed of change accentuated a discrepancy that became apparent during the transition from Zionist state-making to Israeli nation-making, between the language of politics and its practice. The language continued to be about 'architecture' long after the politics were about 'decoration'. It was as though the structure had suddenly sprung up around the elites while they argued about blueprints. While they discussed the future as though its possibilities remained wide open they acted in the political arena within the narrow boundaries set by the *fait accompli*. While the parties continued to elaborate the issues in terms of first principles they were busy adapting to the consequences of the policies implemented by Mapai. Given the embryonic status of national development in Israel's first years the policies of the government had a crucial influence on the whole range of social relations and on the very content and quality of the evolving national culture. But given the vigour of government and the speed of change under Mapai's stewardship the time was quickly past when government policies could exert this determining impact.

As the parties adapted to their new role, becoming political machines geared to the mass electorate, their ideological heritages became the preserve of their elites. The party leaders defined issues in the vocabularies of their old myths while in daily practical affairs they jostled for position in accordance with new pressures. Thus the conventional characterization of Israeli political issues in terms of basic choices between capitalist or socialist directions, secular or theocratic norms, western-oriented or neutral foreign policy, conciliation of the Arab world as against a militaristic diplomacy, may fail to appreciate that the choices had soon ceased to be actual. Decisive and probably irreversible commitments were made in the first years: the capitalist economy run by the labour bureaucracy was chosen rather than socialism; the secular society with a dash of mysticism and sentiment, always making allowance for the minimum proprieties in deference to religious sensibilities, quickly ruled out theocracy; the full-fledged western orientation due to the pressing need for capital to underpin mass immigration ruled out neutralism; and reliance on force soon superseded the option, if it ever existed, of conciliation of the Arab world. Thus Mapai talked the language of social democracy while promoting the capitalist economy; the religious parties deployed the imagery of theocracy while indulging in petty clerical politics; the parties of the left elaborated socialist doctrine while protecting the market interests of their kibbutzim; the middle-class groups expressed themselves in the language of classical liberalism while pressing for government protection and a greater share of largesse for its members; and the right-wing of politics cultivated the rhetoric of chauvinist hysteria while nurturing a populism of the dispossessed. In fact the issues of politics were blurred as much by the deficiencies of its traditional vocabulary as by the complexity of multi-party debate.

In Israel as elsewhere the multi-party structure of politics tends to impede the crystallization and resolution of issues through the electoral process. But the multiplicity of parties is the effect rather than the cause of intractable differences of interest and outlook. Divergent conceptions of social norms and also of the country's proper place in the international jungle divided people in several directions at once, so that politics traversed a great variety of possibilities. Rather than agreeing to differ on a number of well-defined basics, people had not yet reached agreement upon what to differ about. On some concerns groups would overlap in broad consensus but the same groups would be pulled apart on other issues. In this context election campaigns could not clarify the issues in the form of a two-way choice. The indecisiveness of elections on matters of policy meant that Mapai, as the strongest party holding the centre ground, retained the initiative in formulating and directing policy. In effect, multi-party politics produced one-party rule.

Immigrants were made immediately eligible to vote in general elections. Elections to the Knesset were held in 1949, 1951 and 1955. Although twenty or more party lists were put before the voters at each election the number securing representation in the Knesset remained steady at around a dozen. Voter participation was at its highest in 1949 when the proportion of recent immigrants was smallest, reaching a level of eighty-seven per cent of those eligible; in 1951 seventy-five per cent used their vote, while in 1955 participation stabilized at eighty-two per cent. As may be seen from the returns summarized in the following table[1], only minor changes took place in the distribution of electoral sentiment, in spite of the induction of several hundred thousand new voters during these years. The only notable change registered in the 1951 election was the shift within the right wing of the ideological spectrum, in which Herut lost ground to the General-Zionists. This swing proved to be temporary and was substantially reversed in 1955. In 1951 it appears that

Party	1949 % vote	1949 Knesset seats	1951 % vote	1951 Knesset seats	1955 % vote	1955 Knesset seats
Mapai	35·7	46	37·3	45[a]	32·2	40
Herut	11·5	14	6·6	8	12·6	15
General-Zionists	5·2	7	16·2	20[b]	10·2	13
Mizrahi-Hapoel Hamizrahi	12·2	16[c]	8·3	10	9·1	11
Agudah-Poale Agudah			3·6	5	4·7	6
Ahdut Ha'avodah					8·2	10
Mapam	14·7	19	12·5	15[d]	7·3	9
Communists	3·5	4	4·0	5	4·5	6
Progressives	4·1	5	3·2	4	4·4	5
Arab parties (Mapai)	3·0	2	4·7	5	4·9	5
Others	10·1	7[e]	3·6	3[f]	1·9	—
Total:	100·0	120	100·0	120	100·0	120

a. Before the conclusion of the second Knesset's term two defectors from Mapam were added to the Mapai support.

b. Before the conclusion of the second Knesset's term three members elected on oriental ethnic lists joined the General-Zionists.

c. In the first election the four religious parties formed an alliance, running together as the United Religious Front.

d. Mapam underwent a number of splits during the second Knesset term, losing two members to Mapai, two to the communists, and in 1954 with the total defection of Ahdut Ha'avodah it lost the support of an additional four members.

e. In the elections to the first Knesset the Sephardim, an oriental ethnic list, secured four seats, two of which later joined the Mapai. Other seats were obtained by a Yemenite list, and one each by the Fighters (ex-Lehi) and WIZO (Women Zionists) groups which were later liquidated.

f. These were the two remaining Sephardim and one Yemenite representative, all of whom joined the General-Zionists before the conclusion of the term of second Knesset.

Mapai probably gained some ground on its left from Mapam and lost on the same small scale to the General-Zionists on its right. In the 1955 election Mapai suffered a setback, presumably losing in the main to the newly established Ahdut Ha'avodah and in some measure to the General-Zionists. Geographic analysis shows that in the 1955 election Mapai, Mizrahi-Hapoel Hamizrahi and the Communists gained most in the new towns with concentrations of new immigrants,

while the General-Zionists recorded their weakest impact in this constituency. In Israel's multi-party system it is not possible to obtain a clear picture of the place of policy concerns or issues in the minds of the voters, nor indeed to resolve such questions by electoral means. Mapai's losses in 1955 do suggest an element of public dissatisfaction with its performance in government, a possibility confirmed by the simultaneous loss of support for the General-Zionists who had participated in the government coalition for the first time. Since the religious support was steady it may be presumed that its followers did not hold the religious front responsible for the secular performances of government.

The stable coalition

Its lack of an absolute majority made it necessary for Mapai from the time of the formation of the first government and ever since to work in coalition with other parties. At the same time its formidable electoral plurality ensured that any government would bear an indelible Mapai stamp. Since its rise to dominance in the 'thirties Mapai had worn its ideological mantle ever more lightly. Always retaining a spontaneous social-democratic bearing, it acquired the pragmatic aspect of a governing party, its reputation nourished by its successful record of national leadership.

Given stability of public opinion, the logic of multi-party politics in Israel appeared in effect to install one-party rule. The authority of the governing party was enhanced by its alliances, while opposition remained fragmented as long as the government coalition was based on the ideological centre. Ben-Gurion's desire for a broad-based coalition capable of generating national unity virtually necessitated working in close conjunction with the religious groups. The pattern imprinted on the first elected government became the most durable aspect of Israeli coalition politics: an alliance between secular social democrats and orthodox religious interests occupying a centre ground on social and economic issues, with co-optation of additional representation on the near left or right as circumstances allowed. The relationship formed in the early period between Mapai and the religious parties was quickly institutionalized, becoming the anchor of coalition government and of its relative stability over many years.

It is probable that the strength and success of Mapai's association with the orthodox groups was sustained by an element of illusion. Secularist to the core, Mapai perhaps misunderstood its religious partners. The Mapai leaders felt sentimental fellow-feeling for the exponents of theocracy while yet regarding them as an archaic vestige of the east-European small town, reminiscent of their own religious education, but surely fated to disappear and assimilate to the new secular national culture. They did not perhaps appreciate the vigour of orthodoxy as an inspirational movement capable of transcending its new geography and withstanding the formidable secularist influences playing upon the young generation. The orthodox leaders on the other hand displayed shrewd political judgement and an unerring instinct for the realities of power. Mapai might have illusions about the eventual demise of orthodox Judaism in Israel, but this did not interfere with the assessment of the religious parties that Mapai was the main repository of public power and the necessary lever for securing the irreducible minimum of orthodox demands on the population. If Mapai was given to shallow sentimentalism in regard to Jewish tradition, then so much the better. This at least afforded the orthodox parties a finer opportunity than might have been available through association with the socialist left or the nationalist right.[2]

The first coalition government formed in March 1949 exemplified the constitutional origins of Israel in an essentially federalist political milieu. The negotiated coalition agreement resembled a federal bargain whose signatories were its umpires and whose interpretation was susceptible to the vagaries of political circumstance. Coalition crisis was predictably attendant on any exogenous departure from the political *status quo* and equally predictably the same government would emerge intact from any crisis on the basis of a suitably modified bargain. Thus the instability of government was more apparent than real, a reflection of rapid change in the society rather than an index of constitutional frailty.

In composing his first government Ben-Gurion conducted talks across what he regarded as the spectrum of constructive parties, from Mapam to the General-Zionists. He was unable to bridge the ideological gulf between these two and was forced back on the narrower base of Mapai-National Religious Front. Bargaining focused on the distribution of ministerial portfolios as much as on the policies to be pursued. Both the General-Zionists and Mapam were unbending in their claim to a share of portfolios in excess of their share of the popular vote. Mapam moreover insisted on a substantial share of administrative patronage, particularly in defence and foreign policy. Mapai reached agreement with the religious parties, joined by the Progressives and the Sephardim, to form a government on the basis of a programme reflecting Mapai's predilections in every particular, but not precluding religious influence in matters of importance to its partners. Given its dominant electoral position Mapai was able then and in subsequent coalitions to retain for its own nominees the most important ministries, including the premiership and defence, finance, foreign affairs and education. Mapai also secured the chairmanship of the Knesset and, after Weizmann's death in 1952, the presidency.

The need for new legislation in every sphere enhanced the role of the Knesset in its first few years. However, the institutional and moral primacy of the government in conjunction with the fragmentation of the party system precluded the Knesset from occupying the central position that its designers may have intended for it or that its formal status might have imparted to it. Debates in the legislature were sometimes of high calibre and often exhaustive in range, but legislative output seldom revealed any great indebtedness to the debates. What was done depended on the leaderships of the main parties and on the balance of coalition politics rather than on any crystallization of public opinion around concrete issues.

Ben-Gurion more than ever exerted personal initiative, and his leadership gave firm direction to the government from the first. His personal prestige had been enhanced by his successful conduct of the war. Increasingly the public looked to him to provide clarity amid the welter of confusion and flux of the period of mass immigration. Never short of words, Ben-Gurion devoted himself to the building of the army and to the issues of foreign policy and education, while at the same time delivering inspirational speeches magnifying the consciousness of Israel's links with the ancient past. As though helping the people to forget the horrors of the recent Jewish past he increasingly reverted to the glories of ancient Israel, the biblical prophets and the Macabees.

The first major coalition crisis occurred about a year after the installation of the first cabinet on the issue of education in immigrant camps. In accordance with the Compulsory Education Law passed in September 1949 parents were entitled to opt for enrolment of their children in one of the recognized 'trends' (politically based), in default of which children were to be placed in the school nearest to their place of residence. As a result of hectic competition between political party agents in the immigrant camps and frequent instances of coercion of parents, the law was amended in March 1950 to exclude the immigrant camps from its provisions on the registration of children, and to place education in the camps directly under the control of the ministry of education. The religious parties contended that the ministry, controlled by Mapai, was using its powers to bring children from orthodox homes into labour-oriented schools, securing parental acquiescence by providing religious instruction. Attempts to eliminate malpractice procured for some months a postponement of the disintegration of the coalition, but did not suffice to restore mutual trust between the parties. A Knesset debate in February 1951 revealed that the core of the conflict was the claim of the labour 'trend' school system to conduct religious instruction under the guidance of the Histadrut's own religious faction,[3] as against the insistence of the Mizrahi-Agudah front that it alone was responsible for religious education. As pointed out by Ben-Gurion, the law said nothing about religious schools and secular schools, but only about the choice of parents as between the four recognized 'trends', any of which in principle could offer religious or secular instruction. The religious parties, however, suspected that religious instruction as practised in the labour schools might well be spurious and more likely based on the recruitment interests of Mapai than on divine revelation. Ben-Gurion designated the issue one of confidence, and upon his defeat in the Knesset on 14 February 1951 he announced his resignation. Thereupon the first Knesset voted to dissolve itself, calling a general election for 30 July 1951.

The first Knesset had not been legally limited in its term of office. With the transition to the second Knesset peaceably effected, the constitutional foundations of government could be seen to have been firmly laid. The second elections were conducted under closely similar regulations to those enacted by the provisional government for the first elections. As with many measures of the provisional regime these had been seen at the time as a transitional expedient, but equally with other such measures the election procedures became a precedent vested with an aura of conservative propriety influencing subsequent constitutional development.

The second Knesset convened on 20 August 1951 and once again Ben-Gurion negotiated in an attempt to include Mapam and the General-Zionists in a broad coalition. Again he failed in this, and in the event formed a government closely resembling its predecessor in party composition. Ben-Gurion attributed the rigidity of Mapam and the General-Zionists in negotiation to the legacy of an obsolete mentality formed in the period before statehood. As he saw it, the failure of these parties to make the compromises necessary for their participation in a Mapai-led coalition was due to the prevalence of a sectarian habit of mind that needed to be overcome by the diffusion of statist values. Concerned above all to hold the centre ground, Ben-Gurion was reluctant to swing Mapai into close association with either Mapam or the General-Zionists to the exclusion of the other. The new government which took office in October 1951 was based on a coalition agreement maintaining the tenor of Mapai doctrine. The coalition platform now included a commitment to legislate for the replacement of party control by state control of the school system, with the possibility of parental choice and a guaranteed religious education for the children of parents who wished it.

A cabinet crisis arose in September 1952, when the Agudah and Poale Agudah factions withdrew their support from the government in opposition to military conscription of females. The government attempted to carry on with its reduced support in the Knesset, but this became impossible when in December Hapoel Hamizrahi also left the government, once again on the issue of religious education. President Weizmann died on 9 November 1952 and was succeeded by the Mapai nominee, Yitzhak Ben Zvi. On 19 December the government resigned and the new President called upon Ben-Gurion to form a new government. On this occasion Ben-Gurion succeeded in bringing the General-Zionists into the coalition. The considerable strengthening of the General-Zionists in the 1951 election and the corresponding decline of Mapam may have been the factor which weighed with Ben-Gurion in accepting partners on the right while Mapam remained in opposition. As soon as this negotiation was successfully concluded the representatives of Hapoel Hamizrahi rejoined the coalition.

Ben-Gurion had become very tired of the constant coalition bargaining, which he felt was a result of the long Jewish history in which participation in responsibilities of state had been lacking. The new coalition agreement incorporated the aim of reforming the electoral system to reduce fragmentation and stem the proliferation of parties. The project was dear to Ben-Gurion, with his growing distaste for petty politics, and to many of his Mapai associates who saw its obvious advantages for the party. It was also agreeable to the General-Zionists who saw in it the prospect that they might become the main centre of opposition and the most likely alternative government. The aim was not realizable on account of the veto-power of the smaller parties, which were unwilling to contemplate political suicide. Electoral reform remained on the agenda as a perennial issue.

In the autumn of 1953 Ben-Gurion resolved to withdraw from active politics for a year or two. He took two months' leave to enable him to make a close study of defence problems to satisfy himself that security needs would be properly met during his extensive, if temporary, retirement. Moshe Sharett was appointed acting prime minister and Pinhas Lavon acting minister of defence. In November Ben-Gurion informed the President of his intention to retire, and on 7 December 1953 he submitted his formal resignation.

Since the proclamation of statehood Ben-Gurion had grown

greatly in public esteem and popularity. His political stature was now widely acknowledged and he gripped the imagination of the people, whereas in previous years he had been something of a politician's politician. The new immigrants took him to their hearts. He had become a vivid father figure, accessible and closely identified in the minds of the people with the state itself. Amongst his own colleagues and the population at large he had begun to appear indispensable to the conduct of public life.

In explaining the reasons for his retirement Ben-Gurion emphasized the psychological fatigue that overcame him after nearly a score of years under constant pressure. He made it clear that his intention was to withdraw for a year or two rather than to retire permanently. Ben-Gurion and his wife became members of Sdeh Boker, a pioneering settlement in the heart of the Negev, and took up residence there immediately after his resignation. Ben-Gurion hoped by his action to dramatize the challenge of developing the southern wilderness and to inspire the youth to follow him and regenerate the pioneering spirit of the country. In this he failed. To his great disappointment it appeared that pioneering had become a national legend and at best a slogan, rather than a vibrant movement.

Sharett became the new premier while retaining the foreign ministry, and Lavon became defence minister. Sharett formed a government on the same coalition basis as its predecessor. Sharett was popular, gifted and experienced. People quickly became accustomed to his relaxed, somewhat dowdy leadership, and many felt relieved to be rid of the excitements generated by Ben-Gurion's more abrasive and tempestuous conduct of government.

Before his retirement Ben-Gurion appointed Moshe Dayan chief of staff and Shimon Peres director-general of the defence ministry. Ben-Gurion himself picked Lavon for the defence portfolio. It is probable that he expected the new defence trio to isolate Sharett in any efforts he might make to develop conciliatory policies in relation to the Arab world. Some would go further, to assert that Ben-Gurion positively hoped to prove the bankruptcy of Sharett's alternative leadership, and that he fully expected to be recalled to government by popular demand as being indispensable to the country's security. This is indeed what happened, if not quite in the way that Ben-Gurion is alleged to have anticipated. However, even if it be held that Ben-Gurion's political stewardship was indispensable, the formal transfer of authority to his successors demonstrated that the system of government was constitutionally firm.

Civil-military relations

When Ben-Gurion withdrew to his desert retreat he thought that he had firmly settled the manner of military decision-making and the pattern of civil-military relations. He believed that he had eliminated partisan psychology from the military ranks and that he had instituted a reliable distribution of functions between the defence ministry and the army. His close attention to military matters over many years had nurtured the evolution of military doctrines consistent with his own political understanding of security needs. The army revered him and its generals shared his strategic orientation and political views. The balance of civil-military relations was, however, excessively dependent on the personal affinity between Ben-Gurion and his top military advisers. This was revealed to the top echelons of government, if not to the general public, during the abortive tenure of Lavon as minister of defence.

Lavon brought to the office a brilliant theoretical mind, great dynamism and a powerful and exciting 'presence'. It was for these qualities that Ben-Gurion considered him a potential successor as leader of the country, in spite of an almost total absence of background in defence and military matters. Lavon had been associated with the Hapoel Hatzair wing of Mapai, and throughout the pre-state period he had sided with the cautious leaders of this wing, such as Sprinzak and Kaplan, in opposition to Ben-Gurion's more daring and risky political programmes. Under Ben-Gurion's influence after 1948, Lavon had become more 'activist' in outlook and became one of the most dedicated of the Premier's supporters.

Perhaps owing to his very lack of experience in defence affairs as much as to any instability of personality, Lavon pursued personal dominance in the military sphere to a degree in excess of that which even Ben-Gurion had cared to assume. Lavon was not satisfied with merely filling Ben-Gurion's shoes. Wishing rapidly to acquire the personal authority in defence which he lacked, Lavon sought to establish himself as a defence leader in his own right and to surpass Ben-Gurion as the pre-eminent custodian of the country's military security. In the initial transitional years of independence the ministry of defence and the army had supplanted the labour movement as the most important power base in the society. Ben-Gurion had developed a pattern of policy-making in which the minister concentrated on strategic political issues and military doctrines, while the chief of staff and the army high command developed the tactical concerns contingent on high policy. Lavon sought to extend ministerial control to the very details of tactical planning. Dayan and Peres, sharing the activist outlook of the new minister, hoped for close co-operation with him in the rivalry that had developed within the cabinet between the conciliatory policy favoured by Sharett and supported by the socialist left, and the more activist line laid down by Ben-Gurion. But Lavon disturbed the political balance by going it alone, seeking neither consultation nor goodwill amongst cabinet colleagues nor hesitating to interfere in military jurisdictions. He soon earned the resentment of Dayan and the army officers in addition to that of Peres and his own ministry staff, while at the same time occupying an aloof and isolated position within the government. He did not hide his scorn for the Premier, and did not trouble to confide in Sharett the most elementary outlines of military developments. He hoped to carve out a personal following within the ministry and the army which would not depend on the goodwill of Dayan or Peres.

Lavon's attitude brought Dayan and Peres into a close personal alliance aimed at his ouster. As tension increased between Lavon and his military colleagues he took to rationalizing his personal ambition in terms of the broad principles of civilian control of the military. He now spoke in terms of reorganizing the entire military-industrial complex to bring it under closer civilian control. If he had troubled to cultivate a political alliance for the advancement of this line, his views, containing considerable merit in themselves, might have carried more weight. The left-wing politicians undoubtedly found these ideas congenial, but Lavon's identification with extreme activism, the posture by which he hoped to secure a personal following amongst the military, ruled out the political promotion of his views on the left. As it was, the issues of principle which Lavon adumbrated were apprehended as an irresponsible personal crusade endangering army morale and national security. The acrimony of Lavon's relations with the top military elites threatened the very survival of Sharett's government. These tensions were concealed from the general public, but sooner or later, if allowed to fester, they were bound to come into the open and threaten the public confidence in defence institutions which Ben-Gurion had painstakingly built up.

An opportunity to oust Lavon from office arose in connection with a disastrous sabotage operation conducted by Israeli intelligence in Egypt in the autumn of 1954. The action, known in Israel as the 'security mishap' (or 'fiasco' or 'scandal'), was intended to exacerbate Egyptian relations with the western powers, just as Britain was preparing to withdraw its military forces from the Suez base.[4] Clumsily conceived and implemented, the operation led to the capture and execution or life-imprisonment of members of an Israeli spy-ring in Egypt. The Israeli public was not at the time informed of these matters. (The Egyptian trials of the captured agents were portrayed as show-trials arranged for propaganda purposes.) The government was concerned about the conception, mismanagement and responsibility for the operation. Sharett set up a two-man inquiry committee, the Olshan-Dori committee to investigate the circumstances.

A cabal of intelligence officers, seeking to protect their own position, forged documents and committed perjury to place the responsibility for the fiasco in Lavon's lap.[5] Dayan (who had been abroad at the time of the operation) and Peres muted the issues of competence and command within the intelligence unit, and broadened the inquiry into a general review of relations between the minister and the army. Their testimony called in question the fitness of Lavon for the office. The Olshan-Dori committee was unable to get to the bottom of the matter. Concerned for the reputation of the army, they presented Sharett with an evasive report, which, although it did not give conclusive evidence for Lavon's involvement, nevertheless implicated him in responsibility for the fiasco. Lavon found himself isolated not only within the military arm, where his attempts to conduct a personal investigation came up against a wall of disloyalty, but within the cabinet as a whole. Sharett was unwilling to support Lavon who had given him nothing but trouble and discourtesy, and refused Lavon's request for the dismissal of Peres and the insubordinate junior officers. In the atmosphere of crisis and ill-will within the defence community, neither would Sharett contemplate Lavon's far-reaching reform proposals. Lavon was compelled to resign. Pressed by agitated Mapai ministers, Ben-Gurion now came out of his retirement in February 1955 and resumed office as defence minister in Sharett's government.

Although an aura of failure surrounded Lavon, Ben-Gurion was careful to avoid putting him into political disgrace. The public was quite unaware of the crisis which did not come to light until the 'Lavon Affair' broke in 1960 (see below, pp. 394ff.). In the meantime, there was a sigh of relief in the army at Ben-Gurion's return. Lavon was soon re-instated in a position of power as general secretary of the Histadrut. That the headship of the Histadrut represented a demotion from the defence ministry neatly summarizes the transition that had taken place in political life since the accession to sovereignty.

Ben-Gurion gave the most cursory consideration to Lavon's reorganization proposals and lost no time in restoring the morale of the army. While arranging for the removal to other posts of the army officers whose integrity was called in question by the sabotage episode and its sequel, Ben-Gurion decided to refrain from further probing. Not sure in his own mind as to the degree of Lavon's responsibility, he preferred to let the matter rest. He immediately restored the pattern of civil-military relations in which the lines of authority were blurred, but mutual personal respect and loyalty were absolute.

Israel, Judaism and Jewry

Although their prolific interaction with the public agencies of assimilation gave the immigrants much common experience and generated a shared consciousness, this did not contain anything specifically Jewish. While for many oriental immigrants their new life in Israel represented a fulfilment of their Jewish heritage, for most of the refugees from the west it represented the repudiation of their Jewish past. Neither Zionism nor Judaism, so far as the adult generation was concerned, matched the power of political independence itself as an inspiring and unifying dynamic of national life. For the younger generation it was necessary to develop a positive Jewish dimension of national life. The school system was the key institution for regulating the ferment of national consciousness to give uniformity, direction and continuity to the collective fellowship. The elements of Jewish consciousness that were built into the school curriculum reflected the bargain between Mapai and the religious parties which had become the crux of the country's political stability.

The prominence of bible studies in the curriculum of the secular schools reinforced the tendency to identify with the ancient past on Israel soil. The bible was taught as national history, geography and literature. This did not strengthen links with the Jews abroad where the bible belonged to religious education for orthodox and non-orthodox alike. In the mid-'fifties an inspector of schools raised the issue of specific Jewish consciousness as a problem for the secular schools. Active discussion followed within the ministry of education and among the public at large, leading to the formal inclusion of 'Jewish consciousness' as an explicit component of the curriculum.

The Mapai leaders, and among them the succession of secularist ministers of education, retained pleasurable memories of their own early religious upbringing, and considered themselves authorities on Judaism. They tended to adopt a patronizing attitude to their orthodox religious partners, seeing their religious practice as merely a decorative version of Mapai's own nostalgia. As secularists the Mapai leaders tended to assume that religion would gradually atrophy. But in the light of its commitment to Zionist doctrine envisaging the state as Jewish the government had a special responsibility for the definition of the Jewishness of the non-orthodox majority of the population. Of course religious choices would remain in the personal sphere, but the state as Jewish had to provide some general norms giving substance to this doctrine.

The teaching of Jewish consciousness was not notably successful. At first the socialist left opposed the formula, accusing the education minister, Aranne, of introducing religious education to the secular schools. Initially the religious parties also opposed the course, suspecting a Mapai ploy to induce religious children to enrol in the secular schools. Tension over the issue declined when it became apparent that, under secular auspices, the teaching of Jewish consciousness could have little religious significance. Religious practices were presented as exotic rituals that people used to perform. There was no attempt to pose religious belief as a viable choice facing young people in the modern world. Mapai was not in fact interested in enlarging the religiously educated population. The course gradually evolved as a special aspect of the history of modern Israel, in which Jewish consciousness and Zionism were conflated to become virtually synonymous.

The difficulty of establishing a substantial sense of allegiance to Jewry abroad was due in part to the traumatic nature of the Nazi holocaust which supplied the most vivid memory held in common by Jews in the west and in Israel. (For the increasing oriental segment of the population this was a remote and unintelligible episode, in itself a factor augmenting the difficulty.) People were not able, either abroad or in Israel, to face and unravel the implications of the genocide in Europe. They were not willing to probe the failure of Jewish agencies, Zionist and non-Zionist, to rescue their brethren, nor to investigate the failure of the gentile world to prevent the catastrophe. Not that the Israelis wished to forget. Ubiquitous public monuments and ceremonies commemorating the millions who perished kept the memory alive almost beyond tolerance. But the memory was present as a pervasive hysteria, formative indeed, but ambiguous in its bearing on the evolution of the national identity of the young generation born in Israel.

In this context Zionist education, as a critique of Jewish

life in the diaspora, inculcated disrespect for the martyrological burden of Jewish history. Official history as taught in the schools gave an almost morbid prominence to the holocaust and its appalling details. This tended to evoke a response of rejection rather than identification on the part of the children. Rather than the acute sorrow and compassion felt by their parents as they contemplated the incredible Nazi slaughter and mourned its victims, the Israeli young would tend to react to the fate of European Jewry with feelings of shame and disgust, relieved by a touch of *hubris*. The holocaust tended to confirm for the young the validity of the Zionist repudiation of Jewish peoplehood unconfined and unsupported by territorial trappings. Gradually in the schools a greater emphasis was placed on the heroism of Jewish resistance, perhaps magnifying its extent and significance. The inconsistency was resolved by linking the spirit of resistance with Zionism. Thus instead of a link with Jewry abroad, the Zionist interpretation of the holocaust yielded merely an affirmation of Israel's historical rationale. This effect was indeed intended by the political leadership, but the ambivalence inherent in the differential perspectives of the generations imparted some superficiality to formal attempts to locate Israel's own identity in relation to the European trauma. For the older generation the issue was much too painful to bear definition and scrutiny. For the young, there was evident reluctance to identify in any way with the people whose victimization reflected the pathology of a world negated by the very testimony of Israel's existence.

For the Israeli leaders and survivors of Nazidom a gnawing sense of guilt was perhaps their most painful personal burden. Did the Jewish Agency and other organs do all that had been possible to save the Jews of Europe from extermination? Were the various wartime negotiations with the Nazi executives of death morally impeccable? Also, while Jewish statehood was theoretically an instrument of rescue, in the event it came too late to avail the millions. Did the concentration on attaining statehood itself impede rescue? Did Zionist statecraft contribute to the toll of Jewish life? These and other questions involving the historical and ideological relations of Israel with world Jewry were submerged in the unconscious mind of the nation like the reservoir of a chronic nightmare. From time to time they came to the surface, demanding precise elucidation in the courts of law, as in the 'Kastner case'.

Dr Israel (also referred to as Rezso or Rudolf) Kastner was a senior Mapai official who during the war had been a Zionist leader of Hungarian Jewry. On behalf of the Jewish rescue committee of Budapest he had in 1944 conducted negotiations with Eichmann and other Nazis for the release of a portion of the country's million Jews from their impending slaughter. In 1953 Malkiel Gruenwald, the right-wing editor of a private newsletter, circulated an accusation that Kastner had collaborated with the Nazis in the murder of hundreds of thousands of Hungary's Jews (two-thirds of whom were incinerated) in return for the escape of a few hundred of his own relatives and Zionist friends. The Kastner episode had ramifications reaching the top levels of the Jewish Agency in Palestine, for whose wartime diplomacy Sharett had been responsible. The government of 1954, headed by Sharett, was not only sensitive to the painful implications of Gruenwald's allegations for the wartime history of Zionist diplomacy, but also anxious on account of Kastner's political standing as a high government official and prospective Mapai leader. Collaboration with the Nazi plan of extermination was a capital crime under Israeli law. The attorney-general instituted a suit for criminal libel against Gruenwald. To the government's dismay the district court substantiated the validity of Gruenwald's charges, in effect thereby incriminating Kastner, and dismissed the case. The attorney-general immediately filed an appeal to the supreme court. On a motion of no confidence in the government, presented by Herut and separately also by the Communists in the Knesset on the issue of the government's handling of the case, the General-Zionists abstained even though they were partners in the coalition. Sharett resigned, bringing the government down just before elections for the third Knesset. Public emotions were greatly agitated during the trial. A wave of recrimination swept the community of Hungarian survivors in the country and other immigrant groups from Europe. The verdict of the court had opened a gaping wound in the fabric of Zionist moral and social cohesion. Kastner was assassinated as though in proof of the intolerable tension which the probing of holocaust history could engender. The supreme court, by the smallest majority, delivered its judgement posthumously restoring Kastner's honour.

In the early 'fifties, in the aftermath of the mass immigration and under the unrelenting barrage of terror on the borders, before economic buoyancy began to mitigate the universal hardship and austerity, the Israeli public was not ready squarely to confront the Jewish trauma. The people could not yet retrospectively formulate a lucid national response to the elemental horrors in the grip of which the birthright of the state had been contrived and delivered.

CHAPTER 14

ECONOMIC AND SOCIAL DEVELOPMENT (1952-64)

Resources and population – economic growth and structure – economic and social absorption

Resources and population

As a result of the war and the armistices the territory of Israel was augmented by more than a third in excess of that allocated to it by the UNO partition plan. Before the establishment of the state every acre of land for Jewish settlement had to be dearly bought from its Arab proprietor. On the eve of independence the Jews held some four hundred thousand acres comprising about seven per cent of the total land area of Palestine. Following the armistices over five million acres, nearly four-fifths of the area of Palestine west of the Jordan, came under Israeli jurisdiction. Over half of this consisted of the uncultivable Negev desert in the south while the remainder comprised land that was potentially cultivable by means of dry farming or irrigation. Official estimates considered over two million acres potentially cultivable, of which in the short term some eight hundred and fifty thousand acres could be brought under irrigation given an adequacy of water resources, while in the longer term a further half million acres would be suitable for irrigation.

Nearly nine-tenths of Israel's eight thousand square miles came into the public domain. The state inherited all land that had belonged to the mandatory, consisting mainly of roads, railways and forests and also some formerly German-owned urban and suburban tracts that had been impounded by the British as enemy property during the war. The entire southern Negev wilderness, regarded as ownerless, became state land. The state also appropriated some four hundred thousand acres of marginal land in the northern Negev to which putative title, regarded as unsound, had been held in the main by absentee Arabs. The major part of the increment accruing to Israel from the war consisted of a million acres of fertile land in the northern and central regions which, together with the fabrics of several hundred villages, were abandoned by the Arabs in their headlong flight.

The government in the midst of the war did not have a clear policy in regard to the Arab property. The policy of appropriation was determined by the pressure of immigration, which resulted in an urgent need for shelter at a time when mobilization for the war ruled out large-scale construction. It was the mass immigration that shaped the policy rather than political considerations in the context of Israel-Arab relations, although it was indeed in that context that the official rationale of the episode was later formulated.

Legal means were gradually improvised under the emergency regulations to absorb the abandoned lands into the public sector, a process culminating in the enactment of the Absentee Property Law in March 1950,[1] followed at the end of July by the establishment of the Development Authority for this purpose. Under the law the custodian of absentee property, working from within the ministry of finance, was authorized to transfer Arab lands and property to the Development Authority, which was in turn empowered to sell or lease it to the state or to the Jewish National Fund. Apart from relatively minor urban or suburban stretches, this land could not be passed to private ownership. Those immigrants or settlements that had established tenure of houses or lands in the period of flux before the completion of legislation were for the most part confirmed in their occupancy, but rent contracts were drawn up and they became lessees of the national agencies rather than owners. The fiction of absentee ownership was maintained but the rights of ownership were converted to a potential claim on the revenues of property or their equivalent rather than a resumption of access. To all intents and purposes the absentee assets were nationalized, for the most part by a process of gradual transfer by sale to the Jewish National Fund.

The evolution of the law in its various improvisations after the outbreak of hostilities reflected a shift in the official view of Arab assets from 'enemy' to 'abandoned' and finally to 'absentee' property. The crystallization of the latter concept in the law of 1950 involved a broadening of the scope of appropriation to include any property vacated for any period and for any purpose during the time of fighting by Arabs who nevertheless remained within the territory controlled by Israel, and who were now Israeli subjects. Under this rule the state confiscated a considerable portion of land owned by Arabs living in Israel who were under suspicion of association with enemy forces bent upon the state's destruction, in addition to that of the Arabs who had taken flight beyond Israel's borders.[2]

A gradual process of legislative rationalization brought the state domain into a single administration, the Israeli Lands Authority, which was set up within the ministry of agriculture in 1960 under the supervision of a public council chaired by the minister. Some ninety-two per cent of all land eventually came under government ownership or control through the authority. In joining the new administrative structure the Jewish National Fund to all intents and purposes ceded control of its holdings to the state, and as the need for new acquisition lapsed its functions were reduced to land amelioration and afforestation. During the 'fifties legislation was also enacted to bring all natural resources under state ownership.

Given the aridity of much of Israel's soil the main limitation on the expansion of agriculture was the supply of water. It is estimated that the potential supply based on the mean replenishment rate of water sources amounts to about fifteen hundred million cubic metres annually. Some eighty per cent of supplies were brought under development and exploitation by the mid-'sixties. From the establishment of the state to the mid-'sixties the area under irrigation was increased five-fold from seventy-five thousand to three hundred and seventy-five thousand acres, while dry cultivation was doubled in the same period to bring the total area of land in agricultural use to about one million acres. Although the scale of agricultural development is limited by the water ceiling, the favourable climate of Israel is a resource providing opportunities for the export of exotic fruits, vegetables and flowers.

As a scarce and vital natural resource water was brought under state ownership and control. In 1959 the Water Law was passed vesting all water rights in the state and empowering a water commissioner in the ministry of agriculture to issue licences for exploitation, set tariffs and allocate resources amongst the various consumers. Agriculture, taking over four-fifths of supplies, was by far the largest consumer.

Apart from local and regional measures, the development of water resources included two national projects for the transfer of water from the major sources in the north to the arable land in the south. The first project, begun in 1952 and completed in 1956, consisted of a network of pipelines, pumping stations and reservoirs carrying water from Rosh Ha'ayin at the sources of the River Yarkon near Tel Aviv to the northern Negev. The second project, the largest water undertaking, was begun in 1956 and completed in 1964, carrying water from the Jordan at Lake Kinneret to the headworks of the Yarkon project.

With the exception of building materials, of which there was a plentiful supply of high quality, Israel was faced with a paucity of natural resources. However, mineral deposits had a potentially important role as earners of foreign currency. Government was involved in this field from the outset, not only as 'owner' of the resources but as direct investor and exploiter, in the absence of private interests capable of undertaking the risks of development.

Israel's primary mineral reservoir is the Dead Sea, with estimated reserves totalling over forty thousand million tons of various chlorides and other chemicals. The Dead Sea concession had originally been granted to the Palestine Potash Company in 1937. When the major installations of the potash works at the northern end of the Dead Sea came under Jordanian jurisdiction in the war the company sold its interests at the southern end to the government in 1952. In 1961, upon the receipt of a capital loan from the International Bank for Reconstruction and Development conditional on the majority ownership being in private hands, the government once again leased the exploitation rights to the Dead Sea works. The Mining Ordinance of the mandatory government issued in 1922 formalized the procedure of concession and remained in force in Israel. This was superseded in their areas of application by the Petroleum Law of 1952, the Submarine Areas Law of 1953 and the Water Law of 1959.

A new road was constructed from Beersheba to the Dead Sea works at Sodom and expansion of potash production was put under way in the early 'fifties. From a zero point in 1952 production rose by stages to over half a million tons by the mid-'sixties. Almost all the product was exported. Another resource which came to light in 1953 was petroleum and in 1963 natural gas. Commercially exploitable reserves were estimated as two million tons of crude oil and an amount of natural gas equivalent to over one and a half million tons of liquid fuel. Output of oil by concessionaries, including private and quasi-public companies, grew tenfold from the mid-'fifties to the mid-'sixties, to reach an annual level of over a quarter of a million tons of liquid oil and natural gas. This output comprised approximately eight per cent of domestic consumption. At Timna, near the site of King Solomon's mines, copper deposits of relatively poor quality were developed. Usable reserves are estimated at between twenty to thirty million tons. Production began in the mid-'fifties and within a decade reached an annual level of about ten thousand tons, all for export.

The limitation of Israel's economic potential by the aridity of the soil and the paucity of natural resources was counterbalanced by the steady growth of population due to immigration. Also the gradual formation of a pool of technologically advanced skills made possible the development of exports geared to the lucrative markets of highly industrialized countries.

In February 1952 the government introduced policies based on a longer-term view than had been possible during the hectic immigration of the first three and a half years. With a series of measures dubbed the 'new economic policy', including a further devaluation of the currency and the levy of a compulsory ten per cent loan on all notes and deposits, a disinflationary trend was established. The General-Zionists now joined the government coalition as policies more to their liking took shape. Physical controls and rationing were gradually dismantled and market forces given freer rein in regulating the allocation of resources. Greater incentives to private initiative and greater confidence in the future of the economy were established. The immediate impact of the new policies was to lower levels of personal consumption. It was not for some years, however, that reserves of foreign exchange were built up.

With the introduction of the new economic policy and the completion of mass rescue the Jewish Agency for the first time applied a policy of selection in order to avoid further economic stress arising from immigration. At the same time the governments of eastern Europe imposed restrictions on emigration. In this way immigration was reduced to a trickle in the years 1952-4. Re-emigration also grew in this period, and in the year 1953 exceeded the influx. Immigration on a moderately heavy scale resumed in the years 1955 and 1956, swelled by a new tide originating in north Africa, where the Jewish Agency had been actively propagating immigration to a population with no Zionist background. The Suez-Sinai war of late-1956 triggered new persecutions of Jews in north Africa. At the same time the Soviet suppression of the Hungarian uprising occasioned a sizeable flight of Jews. These events were reflected in a large tide of immigration in 1957, followed by a lull till the end of 1960. The years 1961-4 were once again marked by heavy immigration, accounted for in large part by the invidious position into which the Jews of north Africa were thrown by the attainment of Arab independence.

By the end of 1964 the Jewish population had grown to almost two and one quarter million as a result of immigration exceeding one million since the establishment of the state, in addition to natural increase of over half a million. (See the table of statistics on opposite page.) The Arab population with its high fertility grew to over a quarter of a million by the end of 1964. Migration was a negligible factor of change in the level of Arab population. The Arab rate of natural increase approximately matched the Jewish immigration and natural increase taken together, so that the Arab proportion of eleven per cent of the whole remained more or less steady from the end of 1951 at the conclusion of the mass immigration of Jews. The population of the country thus totalled approximately two and a half million at the end of 1964.

Jewish Population Growth, 1919–66

Period	Initial population	Net immigration	Natural increase	Total increase	Population at end of period
1919–48	56,000	426,500[a]	167,500	594,000	650,000
1919–23	56,000	29,500	6,500	36,000	92,000
1924–31	92,000	57,000	26,000	83,000	175,000
1932–38	175,000	195,000	42,500	237,500	412,500
1939–45	412,500	89,500	62,000	151,500	564,000
1946–48[b]	564,000	55,500[b]	30,500	86,000	650,000
1948–66[c]	650,000	1,093,500[d]	601,500	1,695,000	2,345,000[e]
1948–51	650,000	666,500	88,000	754,500	1,404,500
1952–54	1,404,500	20,000	101,500	121,500	1,526,000
1955–57	1,526,000	136,000	100,500	236,500	1,762,500
1958–60	1,762,500	46,500	102,000	148,500	1,911,000
1961–64	1,911,000	193,500	134,500	328,000	2,239,000
1965–66	2,239,000	31,000	75,000	106,000	2,345,000

Sources: Adapted from tables in annual statistical abstracts of the Central Bureau of Statistics of the Government of Israel; Zion Rabi, *Hahit-pachut Hademographit be'Yisrael, 1948–1966*, 2nd ed., Hebrew University of Jerusalem (1968); and M. Sicron, *Immigration to Israel, 1948–1953*, Falk Project for Economic Research in Israel and Central Bureau of Statistics (Special Series No. 60) (Jerusalem 1957).

a. Emigration during the mandatory period totalled some 59,000 or 12 per cent of the number of immigrants.

b. Up to 14 May 1948.

c. From 15 May 1948.

d. Jewish emigration between 1948–66 totalled approximately 164,000 or some 13 per cent of the number who immigrated in the same period. This figure includes nearly 100,000 declared emigrants, the remainder being residents abroad who had not returned to the country after one year's absence.

e. Population counts up to the year 1961 are based on *de facto* population, including tourists and excluding residents abroad, while after that year the population is measured *de jure*. Thus the official sources display minor discrepancies between immigration statistics and population counts up to 1961. See explanatory notes in CBS *Statistical Abstract of Israel* (1966), pp. XXXIII–IV.

Apart from the Arab flight and the magnitude of the Jewish immigration which correspondingly reduced the proportion of the remaining Arabs, a transformation took place in the demographic and cultural configuration of the population between 1948–64. Within the Jewish population the proportion of Europeans, and particularly east-Europeans, was much reduced by the scale of immigration from the countries of the middle east and by the growth of the native-born Israeli generation. From about ten per cent of the Jews in 1948, those born in Asia and Africa rose to over twenty-eight per cent by the end of the mass immigration in 1951, and remained at about that proportion until the end of 1964. Those born in Europe declined from about fifty-five per cent of the whole in 1948 to little over thirty per cent at the end of 1964, while at the same time the Israeli-born grew from thirty-five per cent to about forty per cent. By 1964 those of the Israeli-born with parents from the middle east outnumbered those with European parents. By the end of 1964 the number raised in an oriental cultural background thus approximately matched the number from European homes.

While the age structure of the European immigrants was relatively old those from the middle east were relatively young, and the indigenous Arabs even younger, so that the overall age structure of the population was not much affected by the immigration. A high birth rate amongst the immigrants from Asia and Africa was gradually reduced as they assimilated to the country. Over the years a decline of fertility among the Jews, attributable to a reduction in the number of women of child-bearing age, contrasted with an opposite trend amongst the Arabs. However, the population as a whole contained a high proportion of children, so that the economy was manned by a small labour force relative to the size of the population.

Economic growth and structure

Two salient features of Israel's economy crystallized in the first years of the state: the magnitude of the population increase and the steady flow of foreign investment capital into the country. Given the weight of mass immigration and the delayed impact of investment on growth and absorption, it is not surprising that the first of these features was more obvious than the second, at least until the mid-'fifties. But in the early period the basis was laid for the approximate matching over time of the requirements of absorption and the inflow of investment funds.

The policy of mass immigration decisively affected the style and structure of the Israeli economy. The socialist aspirations of the veteran leaders were in effect sacrificed to the imperatives of rapid economic growth. Doubling the Jewish population within three years and tripling it within twelve could only be accomplished if the economy grew at great speed. Rapid development was necessary to provide the basic necessities of food and shelter for a new population for the most part destitute or of very limited means. The population was without Zionist or socialist background and was not prepared for rigorous pioneering. The successful absorption of the immigrants depended above all on massive capital imports from whatever source.

The growth of the Jewish economy of Palestine had been sustained first by the import of immigrants' personal assets and later by the military requirements of the allied powers during the second world war. After statehood, by contrast, the main sources of capital were those generated by strenuous diplomacy in foreign capitals and energetic fund-raising within Jewish communities abroad. The major sources were outright Jewish donations without strings; German reparations and personal restitution payments; loan capital from foreign governments, banking institutions and investment companies; private loan capital raised by the sale of Israel Bonds; private investment; and the personal assets and remittances of immigrants. Direct grants-in-aid from the American government were a relatively minor source.

The mass immigration made necessary the rapid importation of both consumption and investment goods. Exports were negligible in the first few years owing in the main to the damage inflicted by the war on the citrus plantations. The growing foreign trade deficit could only be defrayed by the mobilization of funds abroad on an unprecedented scale.

The following table summarizes the capital import figures over an eighteen-year period, showing the respective shares of the public and private sectors of the economy.

Although he understood little of economics and was not interested in its finer points, Ben-Gurion appreciated the scale

Net Capital Imports, 1950–67 (in $ millions, rounded)

Years	Loans and investments^a		Unilateral transfers^b		Total		
	public	private	public	private	public	private	total
1950–4	289	168	751	109	1040	277	1317
1955–9	288	81	778	433	1066	514	1580
1960–4	353	642	718	967	1071	1609	2680
1965–7	422	235	527	623	949	858	1807
1950–67	1352	1126	2774	2132	4126	3258	7384
Annual average	75	63	154	118	229	181	410

Source: State of Israel, Prime Minister's Office, Economic Planning Authority, *Israel: Economic Development*, Final Draft (Jerusalem, March 1968), p. 173, adapted from table 23.

a. Includes Israel Bonds.
b. Includes German reparations and restitution, and outright Jewish donations.

of the need for foreign capital to underpin the policy of mass immigration. At the end of 1951 he personally launched the sale of Israel Bonds in the United States, establishing a major source of capital for the future by harnessing Zionist sentiment to the country's investment needs. At the same time he lent his personal energies and prestige to preparing the ground for negotiations with West Germany for reparations to Israel on a large scale, in spite of tremendous emotional opposition to this policy on the part of large segments of the public who felt that the acceptance of financial compensation diminished the memory of the victims of Nazism.

The stormiest debate in the history of the Knesset took place in January 1952, on the issue of negotiations with West Germany. Only Mapai itself and the religious parties were in favour of negotiating the claim. The strongest opposition came from Mapam and Herut. The Mapam spokesman likened an earlier negotiation for a loan from the American government to the sale of Israel's body, while the proposed deal with Germany, he suggested, was like the sale of its soul. Herut staged a mass demonstration using violence within the Knesset precinct and introduced rowdy behaviour into the assembly. Begin portrayed agreement with Germany on compensation for the victims of Nazism as the greatest abomination in the millennia of Jewish history. The government's case, which won the day by a narrow majority, was based on the cost of absorbing immigrants. Estimating the cost of absorption at three thousand dollars per immigrant, the claim was put forward for one and a half billion dollars. This was to enable Israel to provide for half a million surviving victims of Nazi persecution, including not only the post-war refugees but also those who came to the country before the war.

The German Reparations agreement, concluded with the German government in September 1952 and ratified by the Bundestag six months later, provided for the payment of some $820 million to the state of Israel over a twelve-year period, and also outlined the basis for subsequent German legislation to implement personal restitution payments to the individual victims of Nazism. Such restitution in the event brought larger amounts of capital into the country than the reparations. The agreement allowed for the import of raw materials from other countries at German expense, but the major part of the reparations was to be used for the purchase of goods in Germany. An Israeli purchasing mission was set up in Cologne. The first consignment of goods reached Israel in the summer of 1953. Between then and 1967 Israel received in reparation some $775 million net and an additional $1,200 million in personal restitution payments, some of this in the form of individual pensions. West Germany fulfilled its undertaking to the letter. The credit was devoted mainly to the purchase of capital stock such as machinery, ships and rolling stock, in addition to fuel and other raw materials.

Jewish donations were elicited in response to annual appeals devised by Zionist activists under the guidance of Israeli officials. Campaigns were institutionalized in Jewish communities throughout the world in a pattern which assured Israel of a major share, usually about two-thirds, of the proceeds of philanthropy in competition with local causes. Especially in the English-speaking countries of which the United States was by far the most important, the response was consistently generous, reflecting the skill of Israeli propaganda in achieving a dominant position for Zionism throughout the network of Jewish communal institutions. While using incidental crises and events with great effect the appeals were mainly based on the principle of sharing the burden of absorption of immigrants in Israel. Between 1950 and 1967 the amounts provided from this source (which included direct contributions to various public institutions in addition to the main sums channelled through the Jewish Agency for housing and land settlement) totalled approximately $1,735 million.

The gross sale of Israel Bonds, the third major source of foreign capital, totalled some $1,260 million up to 1967, though redemptions totalling nearly $500 million began in the early 'sixties.

Additional capital was made available over the period in the form of loans from governments (especially the United States and West Germany) banking institutions and investment companies, amounting to $2,100 million gross or a net balance of about $685 million (allowing for repayments and debt service incurred during the period). Direct American grants totalled about $320 million. Private foreign capital investments increased steadily after a slow start and by 1967 reached a total of about $1,000 million. The personal assets of immigrants and personal remittances in cash and kind, although not relatively a large source by comparison with the pre-state period, added some $885 million to the total capital import of the period.

These figures show how Israel managed to absorb the masses of immigrants without undergoing economic disintegration or a drastic decline in living standards. Capital imports were equivalent to about $3,600 per capita of the average population over the eighteen-year period. If those who came in the years 1948 and 1949 are included in the calculation, the import of capital per immigrant totalled approximately $6,000 in that time. Corruption was almost entirely absent in the administration of these funds, and on the whole they were used with telling effect. Capital imports promoted rapid economic growth. A steady increase in labour productivity resulted both from the rise in capital intensity and the diffusion of new skills accompanying the induction of immigrants into unfamiliar occupations.

The crisis of the mass immigration period in the three years following the establishment of the state abated with the implementation of the disinflationary policies of 1952. But acute shortages of consumer goods and austerity of living standards persisted until towards the end of 1954 when the effects of the inflow of foreign capital began to be registered in the economy. The first instalments of German reparations and initial sales of Israel Bonds inaugurated a period of sustained expansion which continued without major interruption from 1955 to 1964. Gross national product rose during this period at an average annual rate of about ten per cent, with a per capita growth exceeding five per cent.

The rate of increase in per capita consumption almost matched that of per capita growth. Thus the increase in production was insufficient to close a chronic gap between imports and exports. In effect the economy depended on unilateral transfers of foreign capital to make up a chronic deficit in the balance of payments. About seventy per cent of the deficit in the balance of payments current account was usually met by unilateral transfers. Imports comprised about a third of the total national product, and grew at an average rate of more than ten per cent every year. Although exports grew relatively faster at an annual average rate of over seventeen per cent, the absolute import surplus increased from a low point of two hundred and thirty million dollars in 1954 to a peak of five hundred and seventy million dollars in 1964. The steady expansion of incomes during the years of growth built up the pressure of domestic demand in a way which threatened reserves of foreign exchange painstakingly built up after 1958. The ten years of expansion were followed by an economic crisis beginning in 1965.

During the first five years of statehood living standards in Israel were lowered or at best held steady. Then during the decade of growth from 1955 to 1964 the annual per capita increase in consumption averaged over five per cent in real terms. This was paid for by the continued dependence on capital imports, since the resources consumed could otherwise have been invested in the export industries to reduce this dependence. The preference for increased consumption was in part the consequence of the relative youth of the population and also the destitution of newcomers at the time of their arrival. The persistent inflation of the early years undoubtedly enhanced the propensity to consume. The increased living standard represented by the absolute increase in consumption was reflected also in a change in its composition. The share of food in total consumption dropped and that of various services, consumer durables and housing rose. By the mid-'sixties over ninety per cent of the population owned a radio, and more and more people acquired refrigerators and cars. Per capita private consumption in fixed dollar equivalents rose from about five hundred dollars a year at the height of the economic crisis in the early 'fifties to over a thousand dollars in the mid-'sixties.

The construction of dwellings for the immigrant population was one of the most pressing challenges to the economy, and at the same time the most dynamic lever of economic growth. A large portion of new housing was built by means of public finance for sale over a long period on easy terms for low-income families. For several years immigrants were housed in temporary transit camps of a very crude standard. Residential construction absorbed a third of gross investment in the economy as a whole. Between 1948 and 1967 some six hundred and fifty thousand dwellings were built, including temporary structures amounting to about a tenth of the total. Dwelling units were small, with less than three rooms on the average, and amenities were fairly crude.

In spite of the steady growth in consumption about a quarter of total resources was nevertheless invested. Domestic savings grew gradually in the 'fifties until they comprised nearly half of the total available for investment. Government assisted investment by the direct commitment of capital on its own account and also by providing incentives and guidance to private entrepreneurs. The activities of government absorbed an average of about a fifth of total resources over the years. The largest items of civilian public expenditure were health, education and the administration of central and local government. Half of the funds spent by the government, or one-tenth of total resources, comprised acknowledged military expenditure. Although it is not possible to measure the exact amounts of defence expenditure it is clear that they were a major component of the economy.

The fact that the sources of external funds were largely

public gave the government a decisive influence over the allocation of investment and reinforced a habit of state interventionism congenial to the Mapai leadership. This circumstance helped to sustain the pattern of economic organization formed in the pre-state period, in which government and quasi-governmental agencies, the labour co-operative movement and private enterprise each commanded a sector of the economy. Little change in the relative size of the three sectors took place over the years, with the government and the Histadrut sector each contributing about a fifth of the total domestic output and the private sector about three-fifths. An increase in the scale of defence industries was balanced, from this point of view, by a willingness on the part of government to relinquish its direct holdings and encourage the relative growth of the private sector. Although it lost some ground to private enterprise, particularly in the industrial branches, the Histadrut maintained a strong position by using its Mapai connection to attract a considerable share of public resources.

In addition to land, natural resources and defence industries, the public sector included the railway, posts and communications services, a controlling share in air and sea transport, aircraft manufacture, shipyards and ports, power production and public utilities, housing construction companies and a host of minor enterprises. Ownership in many government concerns was shared with the Jewish Agency or the Histadrut and sometimes with private interests. The Histadrut sector was dominant in agriculture in which it occupied about three-fifths of the field; in construction in which, with about a quarter of those employed, it contributed about a third of the net product; and in road transport in which its affiliated co-operatives had a near monopoly of passenger services. The Histadrut's share in industry was of the order of about fifteen per cent of the whole, and it also had interests in trade, banking and insurance. The Histadrut had a major share of the basic metal industry and other such enterprises involving great risks and deferred returns.[3]

The organization of the economy under varied auspices produced considerable diversity in the forms and styles of management. Government concerns were naturally on a large scale and in a monopolistic position, while those of the

Histadrut included hundreds of relatively small co-operative units alongside large bureaucratic corporations. Arab farming was a major component of the private agricultural sector. Although rationalization gradually increased the typical scale of operation in private industry, and production was dominated by a few firms in each branch of manufacture, there nevertheless remained a tendency to dispersal amongst small family-owned workshops. Under the conditions of protection and the limited domestic market exports were often encouraged by means of approved cartelization, and the major portion of private industry escaped the pressures of competition. Efforts to attract foreign private investment were increasingly rewarded as the expansive phase of the economy sped to its culmination in the early 'sixties. Private enterprise thrived in most branches of trade and industry, although in nearly every field it encountered competition from labour-owned concerns.

Israel's economy is perhaps unique in the capitalist world in that it is controlled by a labour bureaucracy. The strength of the labour movement, both in respect of its own direct economic activity and its influence over government, ensures the application of constraints on private capital as a price for its freedom to pursue profit. The labour movement, in the interest of mass immigration, was willing to abandon its favoured socialist design for the economy and to hold its peace with the dominant petit-bourgeois pattern of relations, so long as it retained effective control of the steering wheel.

Tendencies apparent in the structure of the Jewish economy of Palestine were accentuated in the development of Israel's economy. A high concentration in services and a small agricultural base relative to the scale of industrial growth are characteristic features, which resulted in part from the scale of unrequited capital imports. The expansion of health and education services in pace with the increase in population accounted for a steady rise in investment in public institutions. The magnitude of housing need for the expanding population resulted in the growth of a relatively very large construction industry. Transport industries also grew large in this context. Agriculture experienced a gradual decline relative to industry, while the overall share of primary production remained relatively small. A rapid expansion of agriculture was needed in the early 'fifties to meet the enlarged population's pressing demand for foodstuffs. But as investments in the development of water resources and machinery raised agricultural productivity it became possible to maintain a steady rise in output without significantly increasing the numbers employed. Towards the end of the 'fifties it then became possible for industry to absorb the larger share of new hands entering the labour force. Manufacturing developed more slowly than other branches in the early 'fifties and then as heavy investment in equipment bore fruit industrial output grew relative to other sectors during the decade of expansion from 1955 to 1964. In the early 'sixties industry experienced a chronic shortage of skilled workers.

In terms of output and employment, manufacturing accounted for about a quarter of the economy and government services nearly as much; agriculture and fishing declined from nearly a fifth of the economy at the beginning of the 'fifties to about an eighth in the mid-'sixties; nearly a tenth of the working population was engaged in construction activities throughout the years. Although the basic structure of the economy remained unchanged over time, with its relatively high concentration in services and construction and its relatively small primary production sector, significant changes occurred within the primary branches. These were of importance in increasing the country's export capacity or in minimizing the import surplus by substitution.

Within agriculture the share of proteins such as milk, eggs, meat and fish grew and stabilized at about half of the total agricultural product. The most marked change in the composition of agricultural output was a doubling of the relative share of meat production within a decade. Another major development was the introduction and expansion of industrial crops such as cotton and sugar beet. The acreage under industrial crops was increased eightfold in the period of fifteen years. The share of citrus fruits, the major agricultural export, declined relative to other fruits which also began to reach foreign markets. From about a half of all exports at the beginning of the 'fifties, the share of agriculture in export earnings declined to less than a fifth in the mid-'sixties. By the end of the 'fifties agricultural supply saturated the domestic market and the country reached approximate self-sufficiency in all foodstuffs except for grain, meat and sugar. As the standard of living rose and the share of food in total consumption declined accordingly, the rate of increase in domestic demand slowed down, while exports did not increase sufficiently to compensate. It became clear that the further expansion of agriculture, given sufficient water, would only be possible through the development of exports. Agricultural exports grew in dollar value to a hundred millions annually in the mid-'sixties. A beginning in the export of raw cotton was made in 1962 and fruits, vegetables and flowers also began to penetrate foreign markets on a small scale.

Following the initial period in which the government accorded top priority to agriculture, it then promoted industrialization as the best means of expanding employment and reducing the trade deficit. Industry as a whole was much diversified, often as a result of investment decisions based on political or social considerations rather than calculations of profitability. Protection and the limited size of the local market helped to sustain small-scale ownership and fragmentation of production. In addition to the small size of the domestic market the main limitations on industrial development were the scarcity of indigenous raw materials and sources of energy. This meant that, with the notable exception of chemicals, development was linked to the pattern of imports and the means of payment rather than to the exploitation of natural resources. Energy, of which industry consumes a third of the available supply, is generated from fuel-oil. Generating capacity was increased tenfold between 1950 and 1967.

Over the long period the relative share of basic consumer-goods industries such as food processing, textiles, footwear and furniture declined as the standard of living rose, while relative expansion took place in rubber, plastics and chemical industries, and also in metalworking, machinery and vehicles. In the mid-'sixties, at the conclusion of the expansive phase in which internal structural shifts took place within industry, food processing, textiles and the manufacture (or assembly) of vehicles were the largest branches, together comprising over two-fifths of industry as a whole in respect of employment and output. The combined share of metalworking, machinery and chemicals, often taken as an index of industrialization, stood at the relatively low level of one-third.

Industry's contribution to exports grew rapidly from about $18 million in 1949 to $375 million in 1966. The net contribution to foreign earnings in terms of added value grew from $5 million to $170 million. The greatest increase took place in diamond processing which rose from some $9 million or about half of the total in 1949 to some $165 million in 1966, of which about $40 million represented added value. Of other industrial exports the most important were textiles (cotton and synthetic yarns), processed foods, mining products (mainly copper cement), chemicals (potash and phosphates), refined petroleum, rubber tyres, edible oils and plywood. Europe provided the market for over half of all industrial exports.

Economic and social absorption

That the doubling of its population by the intake of nearly three-quarters of a million destitute immigrants within four years did not result in the disintegration of Israeli society attests to the viability of the institutional fabric created by the east-European Zionist leaders and settlers during the preceding half century. The newcomers, like their predecessors mostly refugees from persecution rather than committed Zionists, found a coherent social order to which they must assimilate. At the same time the new immigration, comprising as it did at the end of 1951 over half of Israel's adoptive population, itself became a formative component of Israel's social personality no less than the veteran community of settlers who had laid the foundations. The mass immigration transformed the demographic and cultural contours of Israel and introduced an atmosphere of fluidity and creativity which became a fixed part of the reality to which subsequent immigrants would in turn assimilate.

In order to increase the supply of foodstuffs and also to develop outlying areas in the interest of security, the government favoured settling the maximum possible number of immigrants in agriculture. Inducements included housing on easy terms and an immediate livelihood in building the settlement and ameliorating the land at public expense. Capital assistance was made available by the settlement authority of the Jewish Agency. These facilities did bring a portion of the immigrants to the land, but did not suffice to counteract a tendency to drift to the cities which had marked Jewish settlement since the beginning of the century.

Unlike the veteran settlers of the labour movement who had founded the kibbutz and moshav movements on their own initiative, and who willingly undertook the hardships of pioneering, the new immigrants had to be settled under paternalistic bureaucratic auspices. They had to be guided, directed, cajoled and trained to become farmers. Given the attitudes of the new population the kibbutz model of settlement was clearly unsuitable. An adaptation of the moshav, the smallholders' co-operative, proved to be the type of settlement most acceptable to the newcomers. In the first decade of the state about three hundred new settlements of the moshav type were founded for new immigrants, in addition to about a hundred kibbutzim established for the most part by Israeli youth groups or by Nahal, the army agricultural corps.

New settlements were at first sited in the coastal plain where auxiliary employment was available in the cities pending agricultural self-sufficiency. Some villages were established without any prospect of making a living by farming, but were engaged in public works such as afforestation and road-laying, with auxiliary small farms as an additional source of income. The Jewish Agency and the Histadrut supplied teachers, health services and vocational training, surrounding the settlers with official guidance. Not all the settlements survived their early vicissitudes, and there was a high turnover of population even in those that took firm root. Of about twenty-five thousand households settled in the moshav in the first decade, some sixteen thousand remained and adapted to their new way of life.

Up to 1960 about one-eighth of the new immigrants were engaged in agriculture, a proportion similar to that of the population as a whole, four-fifths of which lived in the cities or large towns. Although this was somewhat disappointing to the planners, the achievement was considerable in that these people without previous farming experience became rooted on the land, not as a depressed class or even a tenant class, but within the egalitarian order of the co-operative movement.[4]

About sixty per cent of the new farmers were from the countries of the middle east, bringing with them a patriarchal social system and traditionalist habits of mind. In their countries of origin they had lived at the level of subsistence with no capitalist motivation. Their economic aspiration had been to expand leisure rather than profit. To become integrated in their new economic and social environment therefore involved a major adjustment.

The authorities initially sought to achieve rapid integration by bringing together within each individual settlement people of diverse cultural origin. It was found that this created tension within the village and contributed to a flow of people away from the land. In 1954, when the period of hectic improvisation began to give way to more careful planning for absorption, a new concept of settlement was instituted. Ethnically homogenous groups were now formed as the basis of the individual village, and the settlements in a region, each with a population of different origin, were linked to each other through a regional centre. This proved to be a more effective approach to social absorption and also had great economic advantages. In the Lachish region of the northern Negev a group of settlements were established to raise industrial crops (sugar beet, cotton and groundnuts) and the urban centre of the region, Kiryat Gat, was planned as an industrial processing centre for the crops of the surrounding settlements. Advantages of scale were achieved in social services such as health and education, and cultural contacts between groups of different origin were enabled to develop on the basis of cohesive settlements within which social tension was at a minimum. The approach proved very successful and was grafted on to existing settlements elsewhere in the country which had lacked central institutions at the regional level. In this way the isolation of new settlements was overcome and economic, social and cultural contacts with the rest of the country were much enhanced.

It was on the cities and on the urban economy that the main brunt of absorption of the mass immigration fell. In the initial period of absorption, before the effects of new capital investment began to be felt, unemployment then rested at a level of about eleven per cent of the labour force. By the mid-'fifties it was reduced to seven per cent and as the growth of the economy was set in motion it was brought down to little over three per cent in the early 'sixties. The shortage of highly skilled workers accounted for an uneven distribution of unemployment. In outlying development areas where the initiation of new enterprise was not always matched by the geographic dispersal of the population and its skills, unemployment sometimes ranged as high as twenty to thirty per cent even in periods of high employment in the country as a whole. Also, immigrants from Asian and African countries with a lower educational level than the rest of the Jewish population were at a marked disadvantage in the labour market. Within this group unemployment persistently stood at more than one and a half times the average for the working population as a whole. Especially vulnerable within this social group were those between fourteen and seventeen years of age for whom the level of unemployment stood as high as fourteen per cent while the national average, in the early 'sixties, stood at around three per cent.

Economic absorption for many immigrants involved adapting to new occupations. By the year 1954 nearly sixty per cent of those immigrants who had worked abroad had to change their job in the process of settling in Israel. This was particularly common among those who had formerly engaged in trade or sales or clerical occupations. The relatively low level of technology before investments began to bear fruit in the mid-'fifties also necessitated large numbers of professionals adapting to occupations below the level of their qualifications. As economic expansion brought about an increased demand for professional and technical skills in the early 'sixties, those of Israeli birth secured a higher share of such employment than recent immigrants. There was also a marked discrepancy between the share of highly skilled jobs taken by immigrants from Europe and those from the middle east. A greater proportion of the latter were absorbed into the unskilled class. The occupational patterns of Jews and Arabs also differed markedly, the latter being much more heavily concentrated in agriculture and the building trades, with relatively very few in professional and administrative capacities.

The Histadrut exercised a vital influence in absorbing the immigrants into economic life. Determined to defend the living standards of veteran members against the threat of devaluation by cheap labour which was inherent in the mass immigration, the Histadrut energetically organized the newcomers within its trade unions. The Histadrut had traditionally been committed to an egalitarian wage policy in which differentials were limited to correspond with need as measured by the number of dependants maintained by the wage-earner. The policy of unregulated mass immigration, which the Histadrut fully supported, brought about a change in the approach to wages. Without Zionist or socialist predispositions, the newcomers could not be expected to give their best efforts to production except by means of financial incentives. In the midst of the rampant inflation of 1949 the Histadrut resolved that wages should be directly linked by incentive pay to productivity. Norms and premiums were gradually built into the wage structure, while restraint was applied to claims for all manner of increase other than those underpinned by increased production. Even cost-of-living allowances, which had been a basic feature of collective bargains since 1943, were regulated by restraint. The policy was successful in contributing to disinflation in the early 'fifties, but by 1955 it came asunder on the issue of differentials.

In 1950, as the Histadrut began to implement its productivity policy, differentials within the working population and between employees and the self-employed were in all probability narrower than anywhere else in the world. The introduction of productivity as a key element in wage determination favoured the skilled over the unskilled. Shortages of skilled labour, which became acute as the economy began to expand, also accounted for a widening of differentials between skilled and unskilled workers. The Histadrut modified its traditional egalitarian approach in the interest of expanding job opportunities and thereby assisting the rapid absorption of new labour. In exposing labour in this way to free market forces the Histadrut policy contributed to income stratification on the basis of duration of residence, since the immigrants were on the whole less skilled than the veteran population. Thus, while the Histadrut was adamant that newcomers should be assimilated through the trade unions on equal terms with veterans in the labour market, the simultaneous endorsement of skill differentials had the effect of placing the immigrants at a disadvantage. But while the skilled workers were moving up in the income scale, professionals were gradually losing their narrow differential, such as it had been, in relation to industrial workers. As a result of inflation, cost-of-living allowances by the mid-'fifties made up over half of the wage packet. Since these allowances were subject to a ceiling and were free of tax, this had the effect of narrowing differentials for those earning the highest incomes. This process took place just as the demand for professional skills was increasing as a result of economic growth. Doctors, engineers, teachers and higher civil servants successfully bargained for a restoration of differentials to the 1950 levels.[5] This brought about considerable strain in the relations between the intellectual and manual occupational groups. For some years the Histadrut had to grapple to save the unity of the labour movement from the consequences of its own policies. During the pre-state period in which the pioneering ethos embraced the professionals and brought them willingly under the socialist leadership of the labour movement, the unity of workers by brain and hand was a characteristic achievement of the movement. But following the immigration, when all policies were governed by the imperative of growth and rapid absorption, the pioneering culture gradually succumbed to that of the marketplace.

If the Histadrut abandoned its vision of a socialist economy, it continued to use its power to hold income stratification as between workers and other sections of the community to a minimum. In the late 'fifties, when the bulk of the immigrants were already absorbed into the economy and social patterns had stabilized, the most prosperous half of the urban families received three-quarters of the total income while the poorer half earned one-quarter.[6] The degree of stratification was steeper, if allowance is made for the rural population and also for the fact that the lower earners supported larger families. Even so, Israel was still among the least pyramidic societies in the industrial world. Stratification nevertheless gave rise to social tensions which were exacerbated by a conjunction which came about, due to a variety of factors, between income and ethnic differentiation.

Duration of residence in the country, level of education and skill, age distribution and instability of income due to job insecurity at the lower levels all conspired to hold the immigrants from Asia and Africa at the bottom of the social scale. Thus the processes of integration in Israeli society were accompanied by a countervailing process of cleavage, the more pronounced as ethnic differentiation and social stratification came into close correspondence. European immigrants were differentiated from those from the orient, and the generation of immigrants from the Israel-born. Integration was assisted by political, educational and welfare institutions, the army and intermarriage, but was insufficiently rapid to preclude cumulative processes of cleavage.

It was not until September 1949, with the enactment of the Compulsory Education Law, that the government took direct responsibility for education. The law required school attendance of all children from the ages of five to thirteen, inclusive, and of adolescents aged fourteen to seventeen who had not had previous elementary education. Although the government supplemented the existing network by the addition of 'official' schools, most elementary education continued to be conducted under the auspices of the ideological 'trends' controlled by the political parties anxious to secure the future allegiance of their offspring. Friction and abrasive competition between the trends plunged the education system into the volatile political arena.

After months of negotiation between the various interests the Knesset succeeded in August 1953 in enacting the State Education Law. The ideological 'trends' were abolished, and government responsibility for curricula replaced political party control. The state now provided official religious schools for those wishing an alternative to the majority secular system. Uniform minimum standards were applied throughout the secular and religious schools, as well as privately supported schools outside the state system. The extremely orthodox Agudah opted out of the state system and had to supplement partial state support by private funds. At the time of enactment of the law a little over a quarter of schoolchildren were enrolled in religious schools, including both the official and Agudah establishments. Within a few years this proportion increased to a third, reflecting the high reputation that these schools earned among the general public. The law did much to accelerate the integration of the younger generation in spite of the cultural diversity of their homes. It was not fully implemented so far as the schools of the kibbutzim were concerned. The prohibition of political indoctrination on party lines was evaded in these schools, and the labour-dominated ministry turned a blind eye so long as the standards of the kibbutz schools continued to stand comparison with the system at large.

Secondary education was neither compulsory nor free, but was operated by various private and public agencies with some support from local government. Gradually from year to year an increased measure of state support was afforded to secondary schools, and scholarships were made available in increasing volume to make secondary education more accessible. The ministry conducted a matriculation examination for secondary school-leavers, as a selector for higher education. The institutions of higher education received a significant portion of their budgets from the government, but were obliged to conduct their own fund-raising campaigns abroad to enable them to grow in pace with the demand for places. The government, the Histadrut and other public agencies also devoted considerable resources to the expansion of vocational and adult education.

If the common schooling did not suffice to establish unity of national outlook within the younger generation, given the cultural diversity of its immigrant parentage, the process of social integration was assisted by military conscription. The Defence Service Law of 1949 laid the foundation for the army to play an important educational role. Apart from the provision of school buildings and teachers for the children of hundreds of thousands of new immigrants, the problem of education included that of training young adults and mature adults who lacked the Hebrew language. A high proportion of the immigrants came to the country with no formal education whatever. The army undertook to teach conscripts the language, topography and history of the country as part of their military training. It was hoped also to generate pioneering sentiment among the young conscripts who had no preparation for life in their new society. Nahal, the agricultural corps of the army, was set up in 1949 to enable conscripts to combine their military service with agricultural training by participation in the creation of new border settlements. The army also provided special courses during their period of service for all who had no previous elementary education. The egalitarian legacy of the Haganah was maintained by the army in spite of the introduction of formal insignia and hierarchical ranks. Officers and men shared the same conditions and were on terms of intimacy. The democratic atmosphere of the army did much to hasten the confident intermingling of young people of unequal civilian social status, and to create a sense of unity which was not only of military value but also contributed to dissolving social barriers on the return to civilian life.

As to the long-standing gulf between Jews and Arabs, it remained as before, with the Arabs now a bitter minority. Concentrated in a cultural and economic enclave in Galilee and along the extensive border with Jordan, the Arabs did not become integrated with the majority immigrant society, nor did they desire to do so. Exposed by radio and television to the excitements of the nationalist movement in the surrounding countries, the Arabs in Israel glowered with hostility at the Jewish immigrants who had taken over the country. Resentful of their new minority status in their ancestral homeland, they had no alternative but to submit to the rule of the newcomers.

The Jews for their part were barely aware of the existence of the Arab minority in their midst. The local Arabs entered their consciousness only as a threatening shadow on the countryside. The Jewish population as a whole was ignorant of government policy in relation to the Arab minority and had little knowledge of the disabilities inflicted on the Arabs in the name of security. The hundreds of thousands of new immigrants who came in the years after the period of war and mass immigration were quite unfamiliar with the episode of the disposal of Arab lands and its implications. Official policy was to accord equality of rights to all citizens, Arab or Jewish. But in practice the majority of the Arab population, living near the borders, came under military rule and were subject to restrictions on their freedom of movement under the defence (emergency) regulations of 1945. These regulations had been sharply denounced by the Zionists, at whom they were originally aimed by the British administration. There was near-unanimity among spokesmen of all parties in the Knesset that the British legislation should be superseded by new measures less harsh in their incidence, but to no avail. The government continued to view the Arab minority as a potential fifth column, and it was not until the mid-'sixties, ten years after violent tension on the borders had subsided, that military rule was relaxed. By that time military rule itself had become the main source of Arab disaffection. In practice military rule had become an instrument for the suppression of Arab political opposition, particularly as fostered by the Communist Party. The ballot-box symbolized official equality but concealed the threat of withdrawal of work-permits. While supporters of the Mapai client-parties might find the military restrictions inconvenient, others found them more than merely cumbersome.

The underlying basis of relations between the two communities was most crudely unveiled on the night of 28 October 1956. The peaceful villagers of Kfar Kassem were massacred as they returned home from the fields, unknowingly violating a curfew that had been hastily imposed on the eve of the Sinai war. The officers responsible for the killing were indeed court-martialled, but were later amnestied.

CHAPTER 15

THE ROAD TO WAR (1948-57)

Israel and the Arab world – regional power politics – deterioration of the armistices – security versus peace – towards Sinai – the Sinai war and aftermath

Israel and the Arab world

The circumstances of Israel's creation were most unfavourable to the evolution of a foreign policy capable of winning peace with the Arabs. Until the decisive events of 1948 Zionism had been the dynamic factor in Palestine, directed towards a radical change in the *status quo*. Initiative was with the Zionists, and with them lay the responsibility for accommodation with the Arabs. In these conditions Arab policies were reactive, and Arab responses were consistently inadequate to counter the thrust of Zionist initiative. After 1948 the Zionist state was committed to the new *status quo*, the Arabs bent on transforming its very basis. Thus, although from the point of view of the Arabs the Zionists continued to wield the initiative as the prime factor of disturbance in their own political milieu, Israel after 1948 became essentially reactive in posture. Israel's policies in protection of the *fait accompli* of the Jewish state were now determined by Arab hostility. The Arabs continued after 1948 to view Israel as expansive although Israel only wished to secure the new *status quo*. From the Israeli standpoint the Arabs now held the key to peace.

The inability of UNO to implement its own partition plan had left the way open for a military determination of the status of Palestine. The Arab assumption that the Jews would be unable to defend the portion of the land allocated to them placed the whole of Palestine in contention among the Arab states. This had its effect on the attitude of the Zionists. They too came to view the whole country as open to military contention. Thus, they were unwilling to renounce the territory gained in battle and revert to the boundaries laid down in the partition resolution. The Israelis did not even conceive of renunciation of captured territory as a policy alternative. Israel wanted the territory won at such great cost in the race with the Arab armies, and felt that the law of conquest was valid since it had been adopted by the Arabs themselves in preference to a settlement imposed by the superpowers under cover of United Nations' legality. The victorious Israelis could not give credence to an apparent readiness of the Arab states in defeat to revert to the partition plan and recognize its boundaries, since at the end of the fighting the Arabs were no nearer agreement on the disposal of the Arab portion than they had been at the outset in relation to the country as a whole.

Israel's creation in the face of obdurate Arab opposition gave the country a view of security which enveloped the issue of survival itself. The trauma of near-extermination of the Jews in Europe added an apocalyptic dimension to the security perspective. Mass Jewish immigration and economic development came to be seen not merely as measures of Zionist fulfillment but as vital means of survival. Foreign policy was thus subordinated to the requirements of increased military strength and manpower, which aggravated Arab hostility and in turn reinforced the policy.

The Arab refusal to accept Israel's existence as a Jewish state called in question the very legitimacy of the state in international intercourse. Foreign policy thus involved the persistent cultivation of international support no less than in the pre-state period. Given the extent of foreign interests in the Arab world Israel had to resist any tendency to impose restraints on its sovereignty or to tamper with its boundaries as delineated in the armistice agreements. Apart from territorial integrity, the issue of sovereignty was bound up with the policy of mass Jewish immigration, which was at the same time the primary ideological rationale of Jewish statehood and the primary underlying source of Arab resentment. In the context of pressure for the repatriation of Palestinian refugees the ethnic homogeneity of the Jewish state came to be regarded as a first principle of Zionism rather than merely a derivative of the security considerations on the basis of which the principle was argued in the diplomatic arena.

Before the conclusion of the 1948 war the general assembly of UNO appointed the Conciliation Commission for Palestine, composed of the representatives of the United States, France and Turkey, to mediate between Israel and the Arab states in an effort to procure a peace settlement. In the spring of 1949 the commission convened to indirect talks at Lausanne representatives of Israel and the four armistice signatories, Egypt, Lebanon, Jordan and Syria. Representatives of the Palestinian refugees were not invited to the talks.[1] The refugees were politically disorganized and the Arab states supposedly acting in their interest did not consult them. The war had been between the Zionist movement and the Arab states about the disposal of Palestine, and the Palestinian people were ignored as a political entity by the Arab regimes no less than by Israel. The Arab states did not share with the Palestinian victims of the war a direct interest in peace.

To the Arab governments the situation of the Palestinian refugees appeared no worse than that of the masses of population in the Arab states and indeed in many respects materially better after international assistance was brought to bear. Thus the humanitarian aspect of the problem did not appear as a matter of high priority. With the exception of Jordan the Arab governments had nothing much to gain from a settlement, and much to lose. The Palestinians were the victims of the war, not the Arab states. These had lost no territory nor anything else recoverable by making peace, but in the main had suffered a loss of pride. Their humiliation by the Zionists threatened the survival of their unstable and corrupt regimes. A peace settlement would accentuate rather than ameliorate their plight, since it would necessitate admitting defeat. The only ways of avoiding such an admission would be to induce Israel to abdicate its sovereignty, clearly an unattainable goal, or to maintain belligerency. By holding the conflict open the Arab governments could entertain the prospect of a second round against Israel and thereby persuade their people that the war was not lost because the war was not over. It was clear enough that Israel was in no position to dictate peace by threatening to resume war at that time.

King Abdullah of Jordan, the country most affected by the influx of refugees and also by the territorial issues, was willing to sue for peace. This made clear that the underlying issue of inter-Arab conflict about the political succession in Palestine, rather than refugees and boundaries, was the stumbling block to a settlement between the Arab states and Israel. (Of course such a settlement would not have terminated the conflict if it had failed to satisfy the claims of the Palestinians. But it is conceivable that a settlement with Jordan, if it made provision for the refugee problem, might in time have become acceptable to the majority of Palestinian refugees.) A secret agreement between Israel and Abdullah was negotiated but aborted.

When peace began to appear remote, Israel in the summer of 1949 concluded that relations with the Arabs would hinge on the attitude of Egypt, the strongest of the Arab states. Israel therefore became reluctant to follow through its peace diplomacy with Jordan, fearing that any agreement would not withstand Egyptian opposition. For a time therefore Israel hoped to reach an understanding with Egypt by adopting a hostile attitude to Jordanian annexations in Palestine. When it became clear that Egypt was not game for such collusion with Israel, peace discussions with Abdullah were resumed. Early in 1950 Abdullah, who continued to enjoy British backing for his plans, proposed a five-year non-aggression pact based for the time being on existing boundaries. Sharing with Israel a desire to forestall UNO intervention for the internationalization of Jerusalem (for which Egypt, in a reversal of policy, was now pressing), Abdullah also proposed to settle differences with Israel over access to the holy places, and to restore co-ordinated municipal services between the Old City and the new. Open borders and free access to Haifa port were included in the draft agreement. After much hesitation Israel approved the plan in February 1950, against the better judgement of those leaders outside the conciliatory foreign office circles led by Sharett. Abdullah himself was unable to secure any support for the agreement within his own country or in the Arab world at large, and had to rest content with formally annexing Arab Palestine in April 1950 and riding out the storm until his assassination. Abdullah's policy brought about the total alienation of the Palestinian portion of Jordan's population. These now increasingly identified themselves with Cairo, from where they expected leadership towards recovering their lost inheritance.

The Israel-Jordan diplomacy did not reflect a conciliatory attitude on Israel's part so much as it confirmed that both parties wished to settle the conflict over the heads of the Palestinians. The Israeli appraisal was that even the most altruistic approach by Israel might have failed to secure agreement with the other Arab states; the interests of the Arab states simply did not coincide with those of the Palestinians on whose behalf they purported to act. By its fatal failure to revert to the UNO partition boundaries and repatriate the refugees, who had themselves fought neither Israel nor the UNO edict, Israel in 1949 may have lost the only opportunity for a possible long-term evolution of peace. Such an approach by Israel would have required not merely a conciliatory attitude but an exercise of statesmanship of egregious quality beyond the range of Ben-Gurion's classical *realpolitik*. In ignoring the displaced Palestinians as a political factor Israel merely took its cue from the Arab governments.

Israel's attitude to the issues in conflict with the Arab states was formed gradually and was not at first marked by the rigidity which soon came to characterize it. Its initial response to the demand for repatriation of the refugees was formed in the midst of war. During 1948, in the conditions of periodic truce, repatriation was precluded by the obvious military advantage it would confer to the Arabs. It was therefore determined that no refugees would be allowed to return while the Arab states continued to make war. Future repatriation was not foreclosed. Neither the Israeli public nor its government had thought deeply about the matter. All energies were concentrated in the military effort the results of which would determine the political future. Under American pressure Israel offered at the beginning of August 1949 to repatriate one hundred thousand refugees as a step towards an over-all settlement. By offering a counter-proposal the Arabs showed some willingness to discuss the Israeli offer. But in the meantime discussion of the issue in Israel had revealed that public opinion was vehemently opposed to any 'softness' on the part of Israel's negotiators. What was the logic of the Arab case if, as they said, they had made war to rescue the Arabs of Palestine from Israeli dominion, and now they sought to repatriate them under Israel's flag? Repatriation, it was felt, was merely a code word for the subversion of Israel's sovereignty. The Israeli offer was withdrawn and a policy of obduracy matching in intensity that of the Arab states was instituted.

The crystallization of Israel's inflexible approach to the Arab world coincided with completion of the occupation by new immigrants of the Arab properties and lands abandoned in Israel. From the summer of 1949 onwards Israel's view of the wider issue of relations with the Arabs was in large part shaped by the interest of economic absorption of the new immigrants, a process in which the assimilation of Arab properties into the national economy played a vital part. Repatriation now simply became impracticable in view of the demolition or occupation of abandoned homes. The relocation which would have been necessary in the event of a return of the refugees to within Israel's borders would presumably have failed to requite the tenacious desire of the Palestinians to return to their homes. Ben-Gurion intended no irony when he pointed out that on humanitarian grounds the refugees would be better off where they were than as objects of resettlement in Israel, yet away from their original homes. (It did not occur to him that the immigrant occupants of Arab properties and lands might more justly be relocated elsewhere in Israel, although implementation of such a policy would undoubtedly have produced overwhelming chaos and conflict.) Apart from minor adjustments made for the reunion of dispersed families Israel now buried repatriation as a live issue and substituted the offer of financial compensation as its basic diplomatic doctrine.

Apart from the more obvious strategic and economic considerations shaping Israel's attitude to the refugees, there appeared to be an underlying failure to apprehend the intensity of the attachment of the exiled Palestinians to their land. So far as the Zionist minority in eastern Europe was concerned, the pariah status of the Jews had precluded any comparable attachment to the land although they had lived for centuries in the Polish-Russian territory. As a migratory movement Zionism was founded on an *assumed* rootlessness and on the desire to strike new roots under national auspices. It was unintelligible to the Israelis that the Arabs might prefer to live in their own homes and lands under Israeli jurisdiction rather than under Arab government in territories not far from their own homes. This goes some way towards explaining the ease with which the Israeli authorities had appropriated the Arab properties as though they had been abandoned forever. The Palestinian migration was in geographic and cultural terms a very minor move compared to the relocations that the Zionists themselves had experienced from their very childhood to the time of their settlement in Palestine. The Zionists tended to view uprooting and migration as a normal feature of political life.

The Israeli view acquired a firmer structure in 1950 and 1951 when several Arab governments expelled their ancient Jewish communities in retaliation for the dispersal of the Palestinians. The ineptitude of this Arab policy, which greatly strengthened Israel by providing an unanticipated addition to its population from a non-Zionist source, is beside the point. In particular the behaviour of Iraq, whose government peremptorily expelled over a hundred and twenty thousand Jews and purloined their considerable property, buttressed the logic in which Israel now saw the wider middle-eastern issue as essentially a problem of population transfer. The Iraqi act also gave point and lent an aura of reasonableness to the Israeli demand thereafter that Palestinian claims for financial compensation must be balanced against the dispossession of the Jews in Arab lands, although of course the Palestinians were not responsible for that act.

Until the summer of 1949 Israeli policy in relation to the Arabs was fluid and the attitude of the public was uncertain about the future. Expectations of peace were widely held within the Israeli leadership and the general public. When it became clear that these expectations would not be fulfilled a new self-confidence informed the conduct of Israel's approach to the Arabs. It was now assumed that peace was only possible in the long run and that it would come about in time if Israel rapidly built the country's strength and demonstrated to the

Arabs that the *status quo* was irreversible. Time, it was widely believed, was on Israel's side.

The definitive policy of obduracy which Israel now implemented in relation to the Arabs generated its own validity, its assumptions favouring the perpetuation of the conditions which gave them birth. His colleagues and the wider public now grasped and came to share Ben-Gurion's consistently held view that Israel's foremost and most difficult challenge remained, much as before 1948, the task of persuading the Jews to come to live in Israel. In this perspective peace and foreign policy in general, and relations with the Arabs in particular, were of secondary significance. The solution of these problems was subordinate to and would be attendant on the completion of the Zionist mission to reunite Jewry in its ancient homeland. Arab hostility could indeed be turned to advantage by sustaining unity within Israel and generating spartan tendencies which would enhance the inspirational appeal of the country to Jews elsewhere. So long as the Arabs were weak and divided the hostility surrounding the country was a relatively minor problem by comparison with the internal challenges of development. As the Arabs progressed, it was believed, their militancy would decline and their acceptance of Israel would be assured. In the meantime Arab enmity would be met with a relentless display of Israeli strength. Exponents of conciliation, such as foreign minister Sharett, were now relegated to the fringes of policy-making in subordination to Ben-Gurion and his military advisers. The moderate specialists of the foreign office became the diplomatic apologists for the policies of the activists.

Regional power politics

The different approaches to the Arab world, as reflected in the belief in a policy of intimidation on the one hand and conciliation on the other, had their roots in the earlier divisions within the Zionist movement. The views of Ben-Gurion and Sharett on the Arab world logically flowed from their views of the historical process by which the state itself came into being. For Ben-Gurion the vital fact of modern Jewish history which led to the creation of the state was the immigration of

Jews to Palestine in the last decades of the nineteenth century and after. In his view the birth of the state began with the establishment of the physical Jewish presence on the soil of Palestine, and was a result of the devotion and daring of the settlers. The architect of the state in the historic moment of its fruition was the army. For Sharett, the re-awakened national will of the Jewish people in their world-wide dispersion was the driving force which created the state. This national will was formed by the inspiration of a powerful political vision in which many parts of the Jewish people shared, and for the fulfillment of which their contribution was no less important than that of the settlers. The creation of the state was part of a wider international process in which the political and diplomatic successes of the Zionist movement were the most crucial factor. For Ben-Gurion the army continued to be the sole guarantor of independence and national creativity, while for Sharett the fate of the state continued to be bound up with the political forces at play in the world at large. Ben-Gurion's view did not imply that Israel should 'go it alone' in its conflict with the Arabs. From the first he firmly believed in Israel's need for allies to help to sustain it in the face of Arab enmity. But these must be allies who would support Israel's policies, rather than dictate them or even influence them. Allies must be sought who would give their support by supplying arms. But Israel's policies would not be determined by the state of 'world opinion' or by the interests of potential allies.

Ben-Gurion shared with the great majority of his colleagues who originated in eastern Europe an intense hatred of Russia. This may have had some influence in directing his eyes westward, as might his early expectation, soon to be painfully shattered, that the Jews of America would come in their masses to settle in Israel. He quickly abandoned the 'neutralism' that had seemed a realistic starting point for foreign policy, seeking instead an intimate political or military alliance with one or more western powers. Sharett, who had come to Palestine as a small child and was raised in a Levantine milieu by parents of an earlier generation of settlers, did not have the same animus against the Soviet Union as most of his colleagues in Mapai. He clung more tenaciously to the neutralist approach. He showed greater imagination than Ben-Gurion in appreciating the political potential of the 'third world', taking initiative in cultivating relations throughout Asia and Africa even before the imperial powers authorized independence in these continents. Until the Korean war he retained an idealistic hope for rapprochement between east and west, in which he fondly believed Israel itself might play a part. But the neutralist approach proved to be untenable in the absence of peace with the Arabs. The chronic conflict with the Arabs stimulated imperial competition in the region, reducing the scope for local initiative.

The international constellation of events did not favour Israel in its first years. Early in 1950 Israel made a bid for arms from the United States, only to be turned down while incurring Soviet displeasure. The United States, Britain and France in May 1950 issued the Tripartite Declaration in which they undertook jointly to regulate arms sales to the region and to underpin the policy by guaranteeing the armistice boundaries. This was not quite the alliance Israel sought, but the declaration influenced Israel to commit itself all the way to a western orientation. Eighteen months after the tripartite guarantee Israel made known its willingness to participate in the (abortive) Middle East Defence Command which the United States was sponsoring as a barrier to Russian penetration of the region. This helped Soviet hostility to Israel to ripen into a re-assertion of the traditional anti-Zionist doctrine of the communist movement. The Soviet support for the partition of Palestine and its recognition of Israel had served their purpose of hastening the British decline in the region, and the Soviet government was now cautiously groping for Arab friendship.

A wave of official anti-semitism swept across eastern Europe towards the end of 1952. At the end of December the Slansky show trials in Prague, involving two prominent Mapam leaders then in the country, conjured up an international Zionist conspiracy aimed at the heart of the communist world. A month later Stalin, probably of unsound mind as his death approached, unveiled the doctors' plot in which Jewish doctors were supposedly planning the extermination of the Soviet hierarchy. In a protest demonstration in Tel Aviv the Soviet Legation was damaged, whereupon Russia immediately broke off diplomatic relations with Israel (to be resumed a few months later after Stalin's death).

Just as the Soviet Union became actively hostile to Israel the United States, seeking to inherit Britain's imperial control of the region and fearful of Soviet penetration, began actively to woo Arab friendship. In 1954 Dulles authorized military aid to Iraq in the hope of persuading it to join in a 'northern tier' pact with Turkey and Pakistan aimed against Soviet encroachment. The Baghdad Pact (CENTO) was formally consummated at the beginning of 1955. The pact had the effect not only of tempting the Soviet Union to adopt a more energetic diplomacy of penetration, but also of galvanizing Nasser to make a more energetic bid for leadership of the Arab world in competition with Iraq. Nasser's hostility to the pact brought him directly into close affinity with Soviet aims.

Nasser in July 1954 successfully negotiated with Britain for the evacuation of its military base at Suez on Egyptian terms. He then turned towards Russia for help in countering Iraqi ambitions and American designs. After some months of close contact a 'Czech-Egyptian' arms deal was concluded by which Russia supplied to Egypt quantities of high-quality armaments the like of which had not yet been seen in the region. Nasser's prestige rocketed throughout the Arab world in September 1955 when the arms deal was announced. Israel hoped for compensatory armament from the west and was dismayed when the western response turned out to be intensive courting of Nasser rather than an application of the tripartite doctrine of 1950. By early 1956 Ben-Gurion had concluded that Israel would have no choice but to go to war before Egypt could assimilate the new weaponry.

Deterioration of the armistices

Immediately after the war of 1948 the Arabs had no coherent plan for the resumption of hostilities against Israel. The neighbouring states were convulsed in political upheavals, accelerated and accentuated by their defeat, and were accordingly fully preoccupied with their internal problems. However, they asserted their verbal hostility in no uncertain terms and conducted a campaign of harassment against Israel which, if not strategically planned and co-ordinated, was nevertheless a constant and effective irritant. The most comprehensive measure involving some unity of action was the extension of the economic blockade instituted by the Arab League some years before Israel's establishment. Initially the boycott had been designed to eliminate trade between the Arabs and the Jewish economy of Palestine, but it was now gradually extended to third parties doing business with Israel. Pressure was exerted on firms in several countries to cut their economic links with Israel on pain of losing business in the Arab world. The boycott had some successes but failed to win the active support of foreign governments or many firms. It nevertheless contributed to the sense of siege which gripped Israel. The boycott was more effectively applied in the form of a shipping blockade in the Suez Canal and the Gulf of Akaba. The Suez ban was extended by Egypt to all ships doing any business with Israel, while the Gulf of Akaba was controlled by gun emplacements in the Tiran Straits, thwarting Israel's desire for trade with the east through the port of Eilat. This was particularly costly to Israel since it was thereby compelled to import oil from afar at greater expense than would have been possible from Iran, which was the nearest non-Arab source of supply.

In the armistice agreements Israel and the neighbouring Arab governments undertook to refrain from military action and also to prohibit violent action by residents of the border areas. The agreements were based on the assumption and expectation that peace negotiations would soon follow and accordingly they did not attempt to embody the outlines of a political settlement. It was therefore only to be expected that in the absence of peaceful intentions the armistice regime would gradually crumble under great strain. With the failure of the conciliation commission and following the vociferously announced intention of the Arab states to maintain a state of war the armistice agreements became the very form of the *status quo* which the Arabs were pledged to reverse, rather than a stabilization of the *status quo* as a step towards a political settlement.

The deterioration of the armistices was reflected in a debilitation of the United Nations machinery that was set up to implement them. The United Nations Truce Supervisory

Organization (UNTSO), chaired by its chief of staff who reported directly to the security council, was made up of a team of observers who worked with the separate Mixed Armistice Commissions (MACs) set up to police each of the four agreements, with the joint participation of representatives from the two countries involved. UNTSO degenerated into an ineffective verbal umpire unable to deter or diminish violence directed against Israel or to restrain the latter in its retaliatory policies. Israel came to see UNTSO as a nuisance hampering its self-defence. The MACs became puppets in the propaganda war of the belligerents. Complaints of infringements of the armistice were filed and investigated, then thrown into the battle of words at Lake Success. The Arabs successfully limited the MACs to policing the military cease-fire, preventing them from developing a political role in sorting out the multitude of non-military infringements involving property or the movements of civilians along the borders. As complaints proliferated in the interest of propaganda warfare the MACs became incapable of reconciling disputes or even investigating them. They became mere keepers of a scoreboard of the conflict.

The Syrian MAC was the first to collapse. Contact between the two sides was more or less limited to issues arising out of the armistice provisions for the demilitarized zones on the shores of the Sea of Galilee. Few people lived in the area, so that tension was a direct product of government policies rather than of haphazard civilian infringements of the armistice. The Syrians wished to impede Israeli development of the Jordan waters. The sources of the river were in Syria, Lebanon and Israel, in addition to a major tributary flowing into it from Jordanian territory. The river itself was entirely within the territories of Israel and Jordan, and was indispensable to the economy of both countries. Syria had little direct benefit from the river, but sought to use her geographic position to exert control over the riparian states.

The first difficulties arose from Israel's immediate plans to drain the Huleh swamp, near one of the demilitarized zones on the border with Syria. The project involved redeveloping some Arab-owned land in the zone. Terms of compensation were agreed with the Arabs who would be displaced by the development, but Syria succeeded in persuading these Arabs in Israel to withdraw their agreement and to resist the development. Thereupon Israel applied its powers of compulsory acquisition. Syria lodged a complaint with the MAC on the grounds that the Israeli project would alter the military balance and interfere with the restoration of normal civilian life in the zone, contrary to the armistice provisions. The chairman of the MAC, General Riley, called in question the basis of sovereignty in the demilitarized zones, a matter that had been left somewhat vague in the armistice agreement. Israel took the view that its sovereignty was absolute and decided to proceed with the drainage works. Discussions in the MAC were broken off early in 1951 and shooting incidents took place, followed by Israeli bombing of a Syrian military outpost. Syrian troops entered Israeli territory and heavy fighting ensued. The whole matter was then brought before the security council. The council passed a resolution in a sense favouring the drainage project but calling on Israel to delay work until the issues of property rights in the zone were satisfactorily settled. The matter was peaceably concluded for the time being when Israel found a way of completing the drainage of the Huleh swamp without impinging on the demilitarized zones.

The larger question of the Jordan waters proved to be a more recalcitrant problem. The United States sponsored a plan for co-operative development of the Jordan waters to the mutual advantage of the four states. Eric Johnston, a special representative of the state department, succeeded between 1953 and 1955 in obtaining agreement on the technical level for a plan from which all the states would derive some benefits, Syria and Lebanon on a relatively small scale, and Israel and Jordan to a degree which would determine the capacities of their agricultural economies. Syria refused its political consent and the plan was shelved. Israel proceeded to implement its own part of the regional plan. Syria wished to prevent this development, even although Jordan would stand to lose thereby as much as Israel. The issue remained a perennial source of tension until the mid-'sixties when the Israelis completed their plan for bringing water from the Jordan to the south of the country.

It was the Jordan MAC that had the heaviest load. The problems on the border between Israel and Jordan, populated largely by Arabs from Palestine, were the most complex. The abortive peace negotiations were followed by years of tension and bloodshed on the tortuous boundaries dividing the two countries. The internal political upheavals in the other Arab countries precluded their mounting a coherent policy of warfare on Israel. For the first four years or so after the armistices it was the Palestinians in Jordan who kept the tension simmering.

The Palestinian refugees, many of whom were separated by only a few yards from their former homes or lands on the Israeli side of the border, habitually infiltrated to steal crops or inflict sabotage. At first these intrusions were spontaneous but soon became an organized campaign of plunder and terror. Israel countered by killing on a greater scale. From time to time the Jordanian government tried to restrain the violence originating within its jurisdiction. Periodically the MAC functioned in an atmosphere of co-operation, but the Jordanian government, under constant pressure from the activist Palestinians who now comprised the major part of its population, often failed to back measures of control agreed to by its own MAC delegates. Tension mounted from year to year and became chronic.

During these years of mass immigration and austerity the Israeli public was not disposed to weather the border strife with serenity. Morale was low and emigration on the increase. The government came under constant pressure to take harsh measures and show the Arabs force. A hysterical note was sounded in public discussion, the more marked as Israel found itself in these years becoming isolated in the diplomatic world. The tendencies of power politics increasingly pushed Israel out into the cold. The patience of the public became exhausted by the insecurity on the borders as tension rose to a peak in the summer of 1953, after a series of killings by infiltrators from Jordan. By this time the government had evolved a definitive policy of retaliation with ruthless punitive force designed to intimidate the people of Jordan and its government. On 14 October 1953 a large Israeli force attacked and

371

all but destroyed the border village of Kibya, killing over fifty
civilians.

After the breakdown of the peace discussions with Abdullah
Israeli policy evolved in the overriding interest of security
rather than on easing a transition towards peace. The policy
of emphatic retaliation against border incursions took some
years in the making, sponsored by Ben-Gurion and his
military advisers against the stiff opposition of foreign minister
Sharett. The slaughter of civilians at Kibya brought upon
Israel a shower of diplomatic condemnation and also disturbed
a section of Israeli public opinion. As a result the more
moderate line favoured by Sharett gained some support,
enabling him to install a more restrained policy on his elevation to premiership. Punitive force was now limited so far as
possible to military targets and activism was modified to
minimize civilian casualties. The doctrine of retaliation, with
this refinement, nevertheless prevailed, and was applied by the
defence establishment sometimes without full governmental
endorsement. The retaliatory policy was reinforced by its own
effects, in that once the Arabs came to expect this response any
weakening of resolve on Israel's part would encourage them
to step up border harassment. The Kibya raid seemed to
have the desired effect in reducing border disturbances emanat-
ing from Jordan. The focus of tension now switched to the
Gaza Strip. Egypt rather than Jordan was now responsible
for further incursions from Jordanian territory, in addition to
those launched from Gaza. Relations with Egypt, in its first
years of rule by the new military junta, came to the fore again
as the crucial front in the issue of war or peace.

Seething unrest among the Palestinian refugees crammed in
the Gaza Strip inevitably led to violence on the border with
Israel. The refugees were to all intents and purposes abandoned
to their fate by the dying Farouk regime and were not even
allowed the elementary privileges of Egyptian citizens. Israel
aggravated tension in the summer of 1950 by forcing several
thousand Negev Bedouin into the Gaza territory, claiming
that they had fought with Egypt in the war. Israeli settlements
in the northern Negev came under constant harassment by
spontaneous infiltration of refugees bent upon plunder and
revenge.

And yet official provocations in the first years of the armistice were few and far between. Gaza was remote enough from Cairo to enable Egypt to relegate its human misery to oblivion. Interference with Israeli shipping was about as far as official Egyptian engagement went. Israel was sufficiently occupied with policing its Jordanian and Syrian borders to diminish any attempt to respond provocatively to violent incidents in the Negev. When Nasser came to power in the summer of 1952 he was fully occupied in consolidating his revolution and was in no haste to come to grips with the Israel conflict. His accession to power was welcomed in Israel, where a common line of reasoning was that a 'progressive' Arab regime would be more likely than a 'traditionalist' one to seek the benefits of peace and co-operation with Israel. Secret contacts between Israeli and Egyptian spokesmen lent support to this view and steps towards formulating a basis of agreement between the two countries were advanced. With Sharett's appointment to the premiership Nasser even expressed in public his hope that this portended an improvement in relations. Contacts between the two governments continued until the spring of 1954 and then broke down as Nasser reversed his initial judgement and resolved to renew the struggle with Israel. As Nasser's ambition to lead the Arab world to unity and freedom from western domination crystallized in actual diplomacy it became obvious that the Palestine issue was the best available instrument. Unlike Jordan, Egypt was strong enough to carry off a policy of rapprochement if it had wished. But the pan-Arab stakes were more attractive.

When Nasser succeeded in negotiating British withdrawal from the Suez zone a tremor of fear shot through Israel. One result was the ill-conceived sabotage operation which brought Ben-Gurion back to office. In the meantime the American diplomacy by which Iraq was elected to occupy the front line against the spread of Soviet power drove Nasser to seek alliance with the Soviet Union. In the autumn of 1954 Nasser began to organize Palestinian guerrilla units (*fedayeen*) in the Gaza Strip. These penetrated deep into Israel and wrought havoc among the embryonic settlements of the northern Negev. Public opinion in Israel became monolithically activist and Sharett's pleas for restraint no longer struck a chord of optimism. The spy trials in Cairo, which the Israeli public believed to be framed for propaganda, aroused a frenzy of excitement. Upon resuming office Ben-Gurion launched an assault on Gaza which inflicted heavy casualties. But Egypt was not to be intimidated as had Jordan. Nasser merely stepped up fedayeen actions, using the Gaza raid as a diplomatic rationale for more energetic battle. In the aftermath of the raid the toll of border murders increased beyond endurance. By the time Nasser announced the conclusion of the arms deal with the Soviet Union a general sense of siege gripped the Israeli population. Nasser's propaganda to the effect that Egypt was preparing for battle to crush Israel was now taken at face value. At the same time Nasser himself became a prisoner of his propaganda, which unleashed nationalist ferment throughout the Arab world.

Security versus peace

On the broader issues of foreign policy Ben-Gurion and Sharett held many assumptions in common and did not clash so sharply as to impede normal co-operation between them in government. Their divergence was most pronounced, and in 1956 led to a complete break between them, on the issue of Israel's posture and policies in relation to the Arab world. After the dissipation of the euphoria generated by the armistice agreements in the first half of 1949 neither of the two believed that peace with the Arabs was attainable in the short term. From the failure of the peace efforts of 1949 Ben-Gurion concluded that the conflict was irreconcilable since the Arabs did not need peace. From the success of the armistice negotiations Sharett concluded that peace and recognition could come about if an appropriate climate was fostered. Faced with mounting Arab militancy and threats of war in the early 'fifties Ben-Gurion advocated the emphatic use of force as a deterrent, while Sharett pressed for a conciliatory approach as a means of moderating the conflict.

The view of Ben-Gurion (popularly dubbed 'activism'), which throughout most of the time since 1948 commanded majority support amongst the general public, was infused with the messianic imagery in which Jewish history was characterized as a saga of the people's longing for the land, and Israel's existence as a culmination of Jewish destiny fraught with universal significance. The state was envisaged as a vehicle of great cultural potential and bearer of light for the rest of the world. From this standpoint, and also in the context of the capacious sub-continental Arab patrimony, the Arab claim to Palestine was but a minor irritant of little historic consequence. In any case the issue was not a matter of justice or morals, but a conflict of national interests which, like all such conflicts in history, would be settled by force. Gestures of conciliation, compromises or concessions were irrelevant to the conflict and would only encourage Arab intransigence by feeding illusions about Israel's weakness. They were irrelevant because it was not in Israel's power to restore to the Arabs what they had lost. The Palestinian's dream of return was a fantasy since the land they had left no longer existed, having been transformed beyond recognition by Israeli development. As to the wounded national pride of the Arab states in defeat, nothing short of Israel's elimination could assuage it. As long as Israel maintained and increased its strength the Arabs would eventually learn that Israel was indestructible. Then and only then would they come to accept its existence. Until that time, while the Arab world underwent its upheaval of modernization and its nationalism became increasingly abrasive, Israel would meet force with greater force. Security must be the starting point and centre of policy, and peace in the long run would be its derivative.

Ben-Gurion's *realpolitik* held that security must never be subordinated to peace. Sharett on the other hand considered that it was necessary to make short-term sacrifices of security, however painful, in order to create a climate in which the longer term pacific attitudes could be nurtured. In his view the policy of force, whether applied in punitive retaliation or pre-emptive attack, would merely exacerbate and deepen the conflict in the long term and evoke Arab militancy rather than persuade the Arabs that Israel was invincible. It would fester the scars of the conflict rather than persuade the Arabs to slacken their enmity. It would diminish the long-term prospects for peaceful relations without which the short-term gains in security would prove spurious.

It is an interesting paradox that Ben-Gurion, the consummate exponent of political 'realism', leaves a copious literary legacy replete with romantic messianic effusion often poetic in intensity. Sharett on the other hand, a man of extraordinary linguistic and aesthetic sensibility, inclined to verbosity, articulated his more idealistic political practice coolly and with logical precision.

The difference between the two views reflected a difference in the time-scales on which the two analyses were projected. Paradoxically Ben-Gurion, whose vision of Israel in the flow of history encompassed centuries and millennia, was the more concerned about immediate threats to Israel's security, while Sharett was exercised by the long-term pattern of relations with the Arabs. Ben-Gurion habitually projected his policy recommendations as conclusions drawn from the ramifications of centuries of Jewish history, but these conclusions referred to the weeks or months ahead rather than the years. Sharett, who was given to a less extravagant view of Israel in the perspective of contemporary world politics, thought in terms of the years, even the generations ahead. As violence rose to a peak in the summer of 1953 the issue became sharper. From then until 1956 relations between the two men deteriorated in a struggle for dominance between the moderate professional diplomatic establishment led by Sharett and the activist defence establishment composed of Ben-Gurion's devotees.

Sharett's was a losing battle from the first. The complexities of Israel-Arab relations in their historical development were lost on new immigrants, who looked on the Arabs as a foreign nuisance. Immigrants from the Arab countries, smarting from their recent persecution, held the Arabs in contempt and enjoyed their new membership in the ranks of the victorious. Ben-Gurion showed remarkable patience in countenancing Sharett's persistent critique of his approach. The conflict between the two men was reminiscent of the pre-state divergence between Ben-Gurion and Weizmann, for there was a marked continuity between Weizmann's view and that of Sharett. Ben-Gurion had the deepest respect for Sharett, sensing perhaps in the back of his mind that his own nationalistic world-view yielded the disadvantages of provincialism, in contrast with the shining virtuosity of Sharett in foreign intercourse. As a close party colleague for two decades Ben-Gurion was aware of the warm personal popularity that Sharett attracted. A solitary 'charismatic' figure, Ben-Gurion was deprived of this, and it is possible that his regard for Sharett was in some degree enhanced by its usefulness in affording him a vicarious link with the human warmth of party life. Ben-Gurion was now sufficiently in control of the country's destiny to allow himself the luxury of deference towards Sharett's criticisms. He knew that Sharett held him in deepest veneration as a leader of men. He appreciated Sharett's extraordinary diplomatic skill while yet clinging to his own view that the world abroad mattered but little in comparison to Israel's sovereignty. He respected Sharett's technical brilliance and was willing to allow him to develop a foreign policy establishment of great scope and calibre so long as it did not interefere with the foundations of his security doctrine.

Ben-Gurion may have been surprised at the coolness and poise that characterized Sharett's style as prime minister. It appeared that the business of the country could proceed without benefit of constant harangue from the centre of government. But Sharett came unstuck on his failure to master the defence elites. Had Lavon chosen to co-operate with Sharett the two in harness might in all probability have been able to modify Ben-Gurion's hold on the defence community. It was not that Lavon's arrogance and independence were unmanageable. Sharett could have put Lavon in his place and kept him there. But neither was able on his own to deflect the unswerving loyalty of the generals and civilian staff of the defence ministry to Ben-Gurion and his policies. Ben-Gurion might not be indispensable to the smooth running of the government nor even to the maintenance of public morale, but in the military view he was indispensable to the maintenance of public security and army morale. Sharett came to the same conclusion. It was revealing of the relationship between the two men that Ben-Gurion returned to serve under Sharett's premiership. But both men already then, early in 1955, realized that the days of continued co-operation between them were numbered. If the circumstances of Ben-Gurion's return were not in themselves sufficient to portend the break between them, Ben-Gurion wasted no time in pointing up the crux of their differences. A few days after re-assuming office Ben-Gurion launched the heavy assault on Gaza that put Nasser on notice that the Sharett interlude was over.

Institutionally, the conflict between Ben-Gurion and Sharett took the form of rivalry and often bad feeling between the defence establishment and the foreign ministry. The army leaders professed contempt for the foreign office as a 'talking shop'. They saw the function of diplomats as explaining to the world the actions of the defence elites, however embarrassing these might on occasion be. They believed that any action, provided it was successful, could be projected by diplomacy to obtain international acquiescence. Foreign policy was a subordinate branch of defence policy. Sharett did not on the whole dispute this but felt that close consultation on the likely repercussions of any action was vital and that closer co-ordination and dovetailing between the two forms of expertise was necessary in the preparatory stages of policy.

In their first years of operation the armistice agreements came within the responsibility of the defence ministry. Sharett succeeded when he became prime minister in bringing this within the foreign ministry's jurisdiction. But that was as far as Sharett was able to modify the institutional framework of policy-making. He was unable to exercise influence over military procurement by agents of the defence establishment, or even to persuade them that they should at least keep the foreign ministry closely informed. Peres in particular incurred Sharett's displeasure by pursuing a vigorous, and successful personal diplomacy. Peres procured arms and initiated a political partnership with France while Israel's ambassador in Paris was obliged to attend his round of cocktail parties in ignorance of the negotiations being conducted over his head. Sharett himself experienced this situation most painfully in December 1955 when he was deep in negotiation with the United States for arms, and Ben-Gurion, without informing him or consulting him, launched a reprisal raid on Syria (the Kinneret incident) which swept the diplomatic ground from under his feet.

During his tenure of office as premier, although there were several Arab provocations, Sharett managed to veto many retaliatory actions proposed by the military. In the cabinet he was often able to mobilize a majority on these issues. Whether in the long run a continuation of this policy of restraint would have had its desired effect on the Arabs is impossible to say; the Sharett interlude was too short. The dominant Ben-Gurion line more convincingly created its own justification, until eventually no other policy seemed possible. Even after Ben-Gurion returned to defence Sharett managed on occasion, by bringing his view before the cabinet, to obtain a veto on military action. Ben-Gurion was faced with the constant irritant that a 'dovish' majority in the coalition cabinet could be conjured by Sharett's force of persuasion. It was the fear that such a majority might arise to interfere with a plan of pre-emptive war that the defence establishment was drawing up in the summer of 1956, that brought Ben-Gurion to the point where he felt it necessary to break with Sharett and remove him from the government.

Sharett himself had wished not to be included in the new government formed in the autumn of 1955 following the elections to the third Knesset. He foresaw that his differences with Ben-Gurion would soon prove incompatible. Ben-Gurion wished to postpone the day of Sharett's resignation as long as possible. As he later put it, he wanted Sharett in the cabinet *because* of his opposition. By the summer of 1956, when the Sinai campaign was being planned, this was no longer possible. Early in June after a long general discussion between the two men, Sharett's resignation was decided on. To all appearances Ben-Gurion 'dropped' him from the government. In fact Sharett resigned wholeheartedly, if sorrowfully. He believed that Ben-Gurion's policies were profoundly mistaken but at the same time he felt that his gift of leadership was indispensable, and that he himself did not have the political support to provide alternative leadership that would unite the people in the face of the rising tide of Arab militancy. He deferred to Ben-Gurion, conceding him the victory in their long struggle. Golda Meyerson (Meir), regarded as a pliant and absolutely devoted follower of Ben-Gurion, succeeded Sharett as foreign minister.

379

Towards Sinai

The arms which poured into Egypt in the autumn of 1955 radically altered the balance of military forces in the region. The armour and aircraft now reaching Egypt were of much better quality than Israel's relatively antiquated equipment. Israel's efforts to obtain comparable weaponry were rebuffed in the west and the east. Its consequent vulnerability accelerated the evolution of a war psychology in Israel since Egypt, if given time, would absorb its new equipment and become capable of carrying out its threat to annihilate Israel.

In a speech at the Guildhall in London in November 1955, Eden, the British Prime Minister, evoked a frenzy of resentment in Israel by suggesting that it should make territorial concessions to the Arabs to avert war. Dulles did not have a reassuring effect when in February 1956 he advised Israel to rely on the UNO for its security. France maintained a cautious silence while pressing Nasser behind the scenes to abandon his intervention in support of the Algerian liberation movement which was then exercising the French regime.

The United States (together with Britain which had not yet made up its mind about Nasser) was closely courting Nasser with an offer to build the projected high dam at Aswan in which Egypt placed great hopes for its economic development. Meanwhile Nasser was borne on a high tide of adoration throughout the Arab world, encouraging him further to assert Arab pride in dealings with the arrogant west. In a deliberate affront to the United States he extended diplomatic recognition to China. The United States peremptorily withdrew its offer to build the Aswan dam. Nasser had anticipated this and was ready with his riposte. In July 1956 he announced the nationalization of the Suez Canal.

In the spring of 1956 the military situation changed in Israel's favour after several years of diplomatic isolation. The French despaired of keeping Nasser out of Algeria and so decided to supply modern arms to Israel in the hope that this would occupy Nasser enough to take the Egyptian sting from the Algerian revolt. Ben-Gurion had resolved on pre-emptive military action in the autumn of 1955 when the arms from eastern Europe became available to Egypt. A variety of plans were considered but vetoed by the cabinet which was still under the restraining influence of Sharett. The arrival of French arms now made possible military action on a large scale. Giving rather too little attention to the change in Israel's military capacity, Nasser stepped up the war propaganda asserting Egypt's leadership of the Arab world in its determination to destroy Israel. His own propaganda had practically made Nasser a prisoner of the street. The nationalization of the canal now brought about a political conjuncture which yielded to Israel the military power to devastate Nasser's forces. Britain and France were shocked by the nationalization of the canal. As the main shareholders in the Suez company they resolved to reverse the edict at all costs. Efforts by Dulles to defuse the crisis only alienated Britain and France. They decided to act on their own without American support in an attempt to topple Nasser from power and recover control of the canal. France now took the initiative in exploring the possibility of co-operative action with Israel. To the Israelis the opportunity was irresistible. Ben-Gurion was desperately anxious for an alliance with a western power. He and his military staff were preparing an all-out battle to clear the Egyptian army from Gaza and its bases in the north of the Sinai peninsula, and to secure control of the southern coastal strip of the peninsula commanding the approaches to the Gulf of Akaba. It was intended at first to maintain the appearance of mounting a large-scale reprisal action aimed at Gaza, but the central aim of the planned campaign was actually to traverse the peninsula and open the Gulf of Akaba to Israeli shipping. To deal with the border violence a local action in the Gaza area would have sufficed. But the political and economic damage inflicted by the Egyptian blockade of Israeli shipping was even greater than that of the unrelenting guerrilla pressure on the population. An attempt to break the Suez blockade by bringing international pressure to bear on Egypt had failed. In the autumn of 1954 Israel had sent one of its own vessels, the *Bat Galim*, to the canal in the hope that the arrest of the ship by Egypt would stimulate UNO intervention of sufficient weight to open the canal. Israel did not feel that any means other than diplomatic were appropriate in pressing the claim for access to the canal. But the Tiran Straits was a different matter. Bounded by four countries, Israel, Jordan, Saudi Arabia and Egypt, it could not legally be subject to the control of any one state. Israel needed the use of this waterway to develop its trade with the far east, which offered the main potential market for the minerals of the Negev desert. Military action could be applied to this end without impinging on Egyptian centres of population. It was for this reason that a full-scale battle in the peninsula was thought necessary. But Ben-Gurion was fearful of Egyptian air attack on Israeli cities in the event of a general war. He therefore needed not only hundreds of heavy vehicles capable of traversing the long desert tract down to the Tiran Straits, but also some assurance of air cover to protect the civilian population. France's overtures exactly fitted the need.

British diplomacy greatly complicated the unfolding of the general crisis in the middle east. Earlier in the year Jordan, in response to growing pro-Nasser sentiment within the population, had summarily dismissed Glubb Pasha, the British commander of the Arab Legion. Nasser had brought Syria into a unified military command under Egypt, and had isolated Jordan, preventing King Hussein from pursuing the tendency to gravitate towards Iraqi leadership that might have brought him into the Baghdad Pact. The rise of pro-Nasser feeling made it more difficult for Hussein to control violent Palestinian actions against Israel. Tension on the Jordan-Israel frontier reached a new peak in the late summer of 1956 as Israeli reprisals increased in volume, but appeared to have lost their effect in reducing belligerent action from across the border. Britain had lost prestige following the expulsion of its officers from the Jordan forces, and was now anxious to counteract the impression of hostility to the Arabs that its anti-Nasser diplomacy on the Suez issue was generating. Britain therefore sought to reassert its influence in Iraq and Jordan and to demonstrate to them that it was still their most reliable ally. Following heavy Israeli reprisals on Jordan, Britain encouraged Iraq to bring its forces into Jordan, well knowing that Israel might consider this an occasion for war, since Iraq had signed no armistice. Britain promised the two Arab countries that it would come to their assistance under their treaties of alliance if Israeli actions made this necessary. Thus, while it was ranged alongside France and Israel in the conflict with Egypt, Britain at the same time threatened Israel on its other Arab front. Ben-Gurion was most reluctant to reach a showdown with Britain. All the while his representatives were flying back and forth to France negotiating the co-ordination of the planned Anglo-French Suez campaign with the projected Israeli campaign in Sinai. In the event Israel made use of the tension generated by Britain on the Jordan front to provide a cover for the Sinai plans. While mobilizing the population for the major engagement with Egypt, Israel put on the appearance, deliberately spreading rumours to this effect, that its preparations were geared to the problems of the Jordanian front and especially the implications of a possible Iraqi intrusion. This made it possible for Israel to maintain the element of surprise on which the success of its Sinai operation would largely depend. So successful was this diplomatic deceit that the United States government, which Britain and France did not take into their confidence, was unaware of the nature of the impending war.[2]

Negotiations between Britain, France and Israel were not entirely smooth. The French and Israelis had reached a relationship of warm mutual confidence, but neither partner had equal confidence in Britain. Britain wished to use Israel's services in the effort to destroy Nasser, but at the same time it wanted to maintain a hostile attitude to Israel for the sake of its Arab friendships. Israel was not keen on exposing its forces to 'friendly' British bombing for the sake of Britain's interests. Late in October 1956 Ben-Gurion flew to a secret rendezvous near Paris for some tough bargaining.[3] Britain wished Israel to launch an all-out war against Egypt to provide the western powers with a robust pretext for occupying the canal. Ben-Gurion would have none of it. He wanted a limited war, if indeed on a large scale, and had no interest in the canal. Unknown to Britain, he secured the promise of French air cover in return for which he agreed to drop a paratroop force near the canal to enable Britain and France to pretend that their Suez intervention was aimed to protect the canal from damage by the combatants. This was the plan that was adopted and implemented.

Although he did not trust British intentions, and suspected

that British hesitancy might even foil the Anglo-French undertaking, Ben-Gurion nevertheless wished for British participation. Relations between Israel and Britain were cool by comparison with the warmth of the full-fledged alliance that had evolved between Israel and France. But Ben-Gurion felt that British participation on the Suez front would be the best assurance of avoiding a showdown with Britain on the Jordan flank. British threats on that front had lost their sting when a hasty election there confirmed that overwhelming Nasserite sentiment gripped the country. Iraq was virtually isolated in the Arab world, and Hussein late in October confirmed this development by bringing the Jordan forces together with those of Syria under Egyptian command. Ben-Gurion could not be sure that Jordan and Syria would not come to Egypt's assistance, but he hoped that a quick demonstration of Egypt's military weakness would be enough to paralyse its partners. In the meantime Jordan's act merely assisted Israel by giving greater substance to its cover for the Sinai plan, according to which the Jordan front was Israel's main concern. A war on two or three fronts certainly would not suit Israel, but Ben-Gurion felt that he must take a chance on this. The Israeli leaders had no doubt that they could rout all three Arab armies if necessary, but did not wish to be diverted by a general war from the main aim of freeing the southern waterway. The joint command excited Arab nationalist fervour and something of the intoxication of the Arab masses may have disturbed Nasser's judgement. He was not ready for war and his plan was to launch an attack on Israel in the spring of 1957. But his propaganda machine was carrying him to dizzying heights of popularity and it was too late to dampen the war fever throughout the region. Nasser might have done his utmost to call off the excitement if he had appreciated the magnitude of the change in the military balance brought about by greatly increased French aid to Israel.

Down to the last few days Ben-Gurion hesitated to authorize the Sinai assault. He was unsure whether the Anglo-French campaign at Suez would be carried through. Without it the Israeli plan of attack would have followed a more economical strategy. But he now had sufficient confidence in the promised French air support to risk battle even if the Anglo-French undertaking failed. In fact Nasser had already withdrawn part of his forces from Sinai to meet the Anglo-French challenge at Suez. Ben-Gurion was worried about the American reaction, in the midst of a campaign in which Eisenhower was running for re-election as a prince of peace. He detested having to deceive America, but Eisenhower's cables confirmed that the Anglo-French deception was intact and likely to divert some of the American wrath from Israel. He was less fearful of the Soviet reaction now that Russia was deeply preoccupied with the Hungarian revolt. He was confident at least of French political support when the issue came before the security council. He decided to go ahead and take the consequences. The assault began with the component devised for the benefit of Anglo-French hypocrisy. At dawn on the morning of 29 October 1956 Israeli troops dropped by parachute at Mitla Pass, within reach of the Suez Canal.

The Sinai war and aftermath

Israel had developed a modern army since 1948. Among the most important legislation enacted by the first Knesset was the Defence Service Law approved in September 1949. The law regulated military conscription, providing for two years' service for males aged eighteen to twenty-six, eighteen months for those between twenty-seven and twenty-nine, and twelve months for unmarried females. Reserve service of up to about a month each year was required to the age of forty-nine. (The periods of active and reserve service were revised from time to time in accordance with military needs and the availability of manpower.)

The law in effect created a citizens' army. The professional army was limited to a small officer corps whose members were obliged to retire at the ceiling age for reserve service. The forced early retirement of career officers created a leadership in tune with the youngsters in the ranks, and provided opportunities for promoting to the top commands talents still possessed of their youthful vigour. This made possible the evolution of the Israeli doctrine of leading from the front which, although it took a heavy toll of commanders, enormously enhanced battle morale and initiative in the field.

The reserve service kept the civilian population in fighting trim. This enabled Israel to wield great military capacity relative to the size of its population. The constant border tension had enabled many raw conscripts to obtain battle experience in reprisal actions. The reserve system was backed by techniques of speedy mobilization which, in addition to limiting the cost of delivering force, also helped the army to maintain the element of surprise. On the eve of the Sinai campaign Israel mobilized ninety thousand men within three days, formed in their units poised for attack. These were additional to the standing army of conscripts then numbering about fifty thousand. Civilian vehicles (which were also included in the reserve organization) were mobilized to transport men to the field of battle in the south. The needs of the economy, except for vital services, were practically ignored, since it was assumed that fighting would be over within ten days at most. About half the forces were deployed for the Sinai action while the remainder covered the other fronts in case Jordan or Syria, whose forces were both nominally under Egyptian command, came to Egypt's assistance.

The Israeli army was able to absorb its new equipment at great speed. Nasser had deployed his army in Sinai for an attack on Israel, probably intended for the spring of 1957, so that his forces were not well disposed for defence. His army was saturated with new equipment which the soldiery had not yet fully assimilated. In Israel, shiploads of French armour and vehicles, many without markings, were driven straight from port to the battlefield. Planes and tanks of modern vintage also arrived up to the last minute and were put into immediate service. The armoury of Israel had been transformed beyond recognition in the six or seven weeks before the assault. From the moment in early September when tentative understanding had been reached with France in the matter of air cover, the flow of supplies that had begun in the early spring was stepped up. The full integration of the Israeli land, sea and air forces under a single general staff facilitated the rapid assimilation of new equipment. Lines of command were hewn to a skeleton, with great stress placed on local initiative and solving problems at the level where they occurred without reference to higher authority. Following its experience of 1948 Israel was determined that any future action would take place on enemy soil. Backed by strategic frontier settlements geared for stubborn defence, the army was able to concentrate on making ready for lightning offensive action spanning great distances.

After the parachute drop at Mitla Pass Ben-Gurion waited for the expected Anglo-French reaction before fully engaging the Gaza front. If the western powers failed to keep their part of the bargain he could still withdraw from the Suez vicinity with the pretext that the action there was aimed at mopping up nearby guerrilla bases; plans could still be switched to localize battle to Gaza and the Gulf of Akaba. Britain and France rose to the occasion with a solemn ultimatum to both sides (!) to withdraw to within ten kilometres of the Suez Canal, and an announcement that Anglo-French forces (ready in Cyprus) would in any case occupy the canal to protect navigation! Of course Israel yielded to the ultimatum and Egypt rejected it. Britain and France hammered Egyptian airfields and communications preparatory to landing troops at Port Said. The withdrawal of Egyptian troops from Sinai to counter the Suez challenge generated a psychology of retreat. Although they were able to offer stiff resistance from some positions the Egyptian forces as a whole could not recover their balance when taken by surprise at the speed and strategic daring of the Israeli assault throughout the whole Sinai peninsula. Israel was not interested in destroying the Egyptian army but in demoralizing it. The withdrawal became a retreat and the retreat a rout. Before the week was over Israeli forces controlled the whole peninsula and took command of the Tiran Straits. Israeli fatalities numbered one hundred and seventy. The Anglo-French diversion, if not crucial to Israel's victory, certainly reduced the cost of the action, as did active French help in the air and in ground communications. Israel had not defeated the Egyptian army in equal battle. The achievement of the Israeli army, and its military originality, consisted rather in the lightning speed and superb organization which enabled it to take fullest advantage of the few days that political constraints allowed for warfare.

As soon as the war broke out the United States set about mobilizing diplomatic opposition to the aggressive action. Fast and furiously cease-fire calls issued from the UNO. The

Soviet Union, just then preoccupied invading Hungary, took time off to support the American initiative and topped it up with threatening letters to the three principals. Israel had attained its objectives before Britain and France had begun to land their forces on the ground at Suez. Although it had stopped shooting by 5 November Israel delayed its official acceptance of a general cease-fire to assist France, encumbered by a vacillating Britain, to sustain the rationale of Anglo-French occupation of the canal zone. Although Israel had no wish to become entangled in the Suez aspect of the drama, it was keen that the undertaking should proceed. Israeli speed in conjunction with Anglo-French dilatoriness gave Ben-Gurion the opportunity to project the Sinai campaign diplomatically in its full distinction from the Suez adventure. But since the collusion with imperial Britain and France had damaged Israel's standing at the bar of international opinion, Israel wished at least to reap the advantage of the collusion, that it would attract some of the political heat in the direction of Britain and France and lower the temperature in the vicinity of Israel.

Soviet threats sapped Eden's nerve. The Suez operation folded after a few hours of desultory action in Port Said. Britain and France, with Nasser, acceded to a cease-fire on 6 November. Israel now braced itself for the political storm. Ben-Gurion was not sure in his own mind what line to adopt in order to extract the maximum advantage from Israeli occupation of Sinai. Israel's campaign had led to the destruction or capture of enormous quantities of new Soviet equipment. For the moment Egypt was militarily supine. Jordan and Syria had not moved. Israel was not interested in holding the peninsula, but it relished the quiet on all borders. Opinion in the country favoured retaining the Gaza Strip to eliminate the threat of guerrilla attack. Israel was determined to keep control of the Akaba approach, and lost no time in passing ships through the straits.

It was very quickly apparent that the political climate was unfavourable to confirming Israel in the fruits of victory. The United States exerted heavy pressure on Ben-Gurion to evacuate all Egyptian territory. The Soviet Union brandished rockets. Britain resumed its position behind the United States, and amidst a furore of criticism of Israel only France stood firm in its support. Ben-Gurion felt that he had no alternative but to yield. He announced his willingness to withdraw from Sinai, indicating at the same time that he intended to bargain for guarantees. In spite of strong domestic criticism of his policy, Ben-Gurion stuck to his decision.

On 4 November the UNO general assembly had innovated, resolving to establish a 'United Nations Emergency Force' (UNEF) to police the Israel-Egypt borders. This gave Israel its opportunity to extract some security and freedom of navigation, from its otherwise hollow victory. Demand after demand by Ben-Gurion, including freedom of passage in the Suez Canal, failed to achieve the necessary political support. Ben-Gurion therefore evacuated Israeli forces from most of the Sinai peninsula, first dismantling all military installations and destroying fortifications, roads and airfields. He then dug in his heels, insisting that Egypt be not allowed to return to Gaza nor to the Tiran Straits. The elimination of guerrilla bases in Gaza and the freedom of passage in the Gulf of Akaba on which the development of the Negev depended had been Israel's main war objectives. Ben-Gurion was obdurate that Egypt should not be allowed to return to its positions there. But this too was politically unattainable. When in early February France suggested that the newly formed international force should be stationed at Gaza and at the approaches to the Gulf of Akaba, Ben-Gurion yielded, conscious that Israel was isolated except for the French help. He did not wish to risk the imposition of sanctions by UNO. On 1 March 1957 Israel announced its withdrawal from all positions beyond its frontiers. UNEF was installed at Gaza and at Sharm el Sheikh overlooking the Tiran Straits. UNO was now a party in its own right to the maintenance of peace. The UNEF presence, which Israel absolutely refused to allow on its side of the border, was a political defeat for Egypt, but at the same time the security it offered to Israel was somewhat flimsy, since it depended on Egyptian acquiescence. This held for ten years.

For a decade now Israel was able to expand its population and economy in an atmosphere of relative calm. Quieter borders relaxed the people. The war had resolved none of the basic issues of the Israel-Arab conflict, but it brought about many changes in the quality of life in the country. The new young generation of immigrants achieved a sense of equality with the old-timers by dint of their participation in battle. The legend of 1948 which imparted an aura of exclusiveness to the veterans now faded in the shadow of the brilliant military personality displayed by the modern army of Israel. Military *hubris* became an integral component of the national personality. The comradeship of battle also assisted social integration. Materialistic pursuits, competitive consumerism buoyed by the rapid economic growth, gradually relegated the pioneering mentality to the tedious gossip of the old. The new national identity began to take firm shape and the 'normalization' of Jewish life that Zionism had pursued ironically became the epitaph of socialist-Zionism.

CHAPTER 16

IDEOLOGICAL AND POLITICAL DEVELOPMENT (1955-66)

The Mapai succession – the Mapai split – from war to war

The Mapai succession

Bitter personal and factional conflicts in the decade following the Sinai war were the delayed political expressions of a process whose culmination the war institutionalized: the transition of the society from a voluntaristic co-operative community united by its dream of sovereignty, to a new nation formed and united by the ideology and machinery of the state itself. The classical institutions, the political parties, the Histadrut, the Jewish Agency, the kibbutz and moshav movements, had by 1956 more or less satisfactorily adapted to their new roles in the framework of the state and had come to accept the primacy of the state as claimant to national allegiance. The ideological struggles dividing the population before 1948 were now supplanted by personal and institutional rivalries in the struggle for control of the state apparatus. Elite rivalries began to cut across traditional ideological boundaries and assumed the character of a struggle between the generations for the political succession. In the first decade the old institutions came to accept the succession of the state, while in the second decade the elites of the old institutions battled for personal primacy in the state against the new elites to which the state had given birth.

The most bitter of the personal conflicts of the second decade took place within Mapai itself. Ben-Gurion, true to form, pioneered the issue of the generations. The teenage founders of Israel had become a gerontocracy. The 'old man', as he had come to be known, identified himself with the 'young guard' of Mapai and sought to wrest control of the party from its veteran elite in the hope that he could install the more youthful elements in power before he himself withdrew from the fray. Dayan and Peres became the symbols of the younger generation within Mapai which stood for the new values generated by political independence. Pragmatism against ideology, technocratic efficiency against cosy amateurism, merit against nepotism, 'etatism' against outmoded communalism, military clarity and incisiveness against civilian fuzziness and political chicanery: these became the slogans dividing the young from the old guard (and obscuring the underlying issues of policy). Ben-Gurion for the time being lost the battle of the succession. The old guard of the party, controlling the organizational machine and believing that new leaders should earn their spurs within it, adopted a tenacious defensive stance and succeeded in postponing if not resolving the determination of the succession.

Since 1951 the Mapai young guard had taken shape as a ginger group pressing on the veterans for a voice in policy-making. The struggle for power crystallized in 1956 at the heart of the party machine, with the installation of Giora Josephtal as general secretary. Though not formally associated with the faction Josephtal was a distinguished ally of the young guard. He brought many of the younger novices into the party administration for the first time, accelerating a process in which attitudes towards the young increasingly became the basis of political alignments within the party. Simultaneously Lavon took office as general secretary of the Histadrut and studiously excluded the younger aspirants from all positions in the Histadrut's administrative hierarchy. Nursing a bitter sense of grievance against Dayan and Peres dating from his abortive tenure as defence minister, Lavon quickly established his personal control of the vast Histadrut empire and developed its potential as a counterweight to the agencies of government. This personal background to the conflict engendered or at least converged with a tendency towards ideological rationalization in which the interests of the state (the young 'technocrats') were counterposed to those of the Histadrut (the veteran politicians).

The political prestige of the young guard was enhanced in 1958 when Dayan left the army and announced his intention of entering politics. Soon after, Peres, Eban and Josephtal all made it known that they would run for the Knesset in the elections due in 1959. All were close supporters if not protégés of Ben-Gurion, and he made it clear that he would in all probability introduce them into the cabinet, thereby ensuring them a prominent place in the party list.

Dayan set the pace of ideological warfare in a series of speeches attacking the Histadrut's industrial policies and the style and habits of the kibbutz movement. Lavon held his fire, concentrating on buttressing the Histadrut's influence within the party machine. Then in 1959 he mounted a blistering counter-attack on the young critics of the Histadrut. The first round in the struggle was won by the young guard when Mapai, after a campaign based largely on their personal glamour, won a resounding victory in the elections to the fifth Knesset, while at the same time Mapai ran without the help of the young in the Histadrut and lost considerable ground.[1]

Following the election Josephtal joined the government and was replaced at party headquarters by Joseph Almogi, a Haifa labour leader of great ability who was at that time personally identified with the veterans. Almogi sought to occupy a median position between the Histadrut and the government by gathering into the party secretariat some of the decision-making capacities that had tended over the years to become concentrated in the cabinet circle around Ben-Gurion. Relations between the Histadrut and the state became the most controversial issue within the party. Policies were no longer smoothly shaped by informal meetings of the inner circle behind closed doors. Dayan and Peres publicly pressed for the nationalization of the health insurance services of the Histadrut, which were the underlying basis of its great organizational strength. Lavon and his colleagues in the Histadrut saw this as an expression of the government's undue greed for power. Peres in 1960 voiced the most outspoken attack yet on the Histadrut, depicting it as a feudal barony intervening between the worker and his loyalty to the state, and ridiculing the concept of healing the sick as a prerogative of the labour movement. Ben-Gurion remained silent but at the same time hinted lucidly enough that Dayan and Peres had his backing on the issue. The party professionals who operated the machine called for the disbandment of the young guard which it felt had crossed the permitted boundary of ideological dissension to become a faction. Histadrut spokesmen accused the young guard of violating party discipline by taking a position contrary to the official party line on an issue as important as the health service. For the first time Histadrut leaders voiced direct criticism of Ben-Gurion. At the height of battle, in the summer of 1960, the Lavon affair broke, rocking the country and splitting the party from top to bottom.[2]

In spring 1960 Lavon came into possession of new material information relating to the fatal fiasco of 1954 that had led to his resignation as defence minister in February 1955. Owing to the censorship the public was quite unaware of the circumstances of Lavon's resignation, or that since that time Lavon had bitterly kept silence about what he believed had been a shady officers' plot to secure his ouster. In April 1960 Lavon passed his new information to the prime minister. The material implicated two officers in perjury and another in a forgery of documents executed to place the responsibility for the fiasco squarely on Lavon's shoulders. Lavon claimed that his new material conclusively cleared him of any responsibility, and demanded that Ben-Gurion publicly exonerate him. Ben-Gurion refused on the ground that since he had not accused Lavon neither could he exonerate him, and pointed out that since Lavon's 'rehabilitation' would necessarily involve the imputation of guilt to others, this could only be done by judicial means. Just then a Jerusalem court sitting in another matter issued a verdict throwing suspicion on one of the officers implicated by Lavon. Ben-Gurion thereupon ordered the chief of staff to initiate an inquiry into the conduct of the officers involved. For this purpose the Cohn Committee was set up under the chairmanship of Judge Haim Cohn of the Supreme Court. Lavon was infuriated when he heard of this investigation and persisted in his demand that he be 'cleared' without awaiting the results of an inquiry into the conduct of the others. Lavon now struck a blow at Mapai by bringing the matter before the foreign relations and security committee of the Knesset, in which opposition members participated. The blow became a thunderbolt when leakages to the press in September 1960 made it known to the public that Lavon in the secret committee proceedings had made allegations calling in question the integrity of Dayan and Peres. Ben-Gurion maintained an uneasy silence until 3 October 1960 when he issued a statement in the terms of his initial reply to Lavon's demand. Relations between the two men now reached breaking point. In spite of the shortage of facts heated public discussion ensued. The press and the public widely believed that Lavon had indeed been victimized. The Mapai leaders were greatly agitated by the implications for the party of the public mud-slinging which seemed to know no bounds. At a meeting of the Mapai executive on 19 October Ben-Gurion made it clear that he would not budge on the need for a judicial determination. The leadership was split, with many inclined to support Lavon. Eshkol was assigned the task of seeking a compromise solution that would bring the affair to a quick conclusion.

The Cohn Committee now submitted its findings which Ben-Gurion passed to the government's legal counsel for an opinion. Gideon Hausner gave his opinion on 24 October, to the effect that the Cohn Committee had not found sufficient proof of forgery but that investigation of the matter should continue. Pressed by Eshkol acting in his role as trouble-shooter, Sharett issued a statement that if the facts established by the Cohn Committee had been known in 1954–5 they would have carried sufficient weight to relieve Lavon of the guilt that had then been imputed to him of sharing in the responsibility for the fiasco. Eshkol hoped that Sharett's statement would suffice to quell the furore, and Lavon indeed declared that it was satisfactory to him. Ben-Gurion was not satisfied, however, and insisted that a judicial inquiry could not be waived on the point of Lavon's responsibility. Eshkol and others now pressed for a resolution of the conflict at cabinet level.

In Ben-Gurion's absence and in the knowledge that he was opposed to so doing, the cabinet appointed a ministerial committee of seven under the chairmanship of the minister of justice to study the issue and rule on the proper procedure for its resolution. Eshkol, representing the interest of the veteran Mapai leaders in a quick termination of the embarrassing imbroglio, dominated the committee proceedings. To the astonishment of Ben-Gurion, who was sure the committee would be bound to affirm the need for a judicial undertaking, the ministerial committee departed from its terms of reference to rule on the substance, concluding that Lavon was indeed free of responsibility for the fiasco. Eshkol and his colleagues were no less amazed at the ferocity of Ben-Gurion's reaction than he had been at the boldness of their conclusion. When the cabinet voted on 25 December 1960 to accept the committee's findings Ben-Gurion expressed dismay that the ministerial committee had implicated an officer without providing him with an opportunity to put his case, and demonstratively left on extended leave.

It was now clear that Ben-Gurion was close to submitting his resignation which would automatically bring down the government. There was no optimism within Mapai that the party could hold its own in a general election in the aftermath of the Lavon affair. Frantic efforts by his colleagues to hold Ben-Gurion in place were to no avail. Ben-Gurion took the view, not apparently well-founded, that his resignation and refusal to accept collective responsibility for the cabinet decision would render the decision nugatory. Now in a hectic round of party executive meetings Ben-Gurion and Lavon both raised the level of personal vituperation until it became necessary for the party to make an immediate choice between the two men.

Lavon's 'rehabilitation' by the cabinet proved to be a pyrrhic victory. It had come about in part as the result of anxiety about the possible cost of failing to appease Lavon, who, perhaps encouraged by the widespread public sympathy he had attracted, had shown that he would stop at nothing to have his way. Many party leaders were now equally agitated about the probable cost of a failing to appease Ben-Gurion. Quite apart from this consideration there were many who felt that Lavon had lost all eligibility to continue representing the party at the head of the Histadrut, on account of his wanton disregard for the elementary collegial proprieties incumbent on party leaders in their public utterance and behaviour. Eshkol once again acted as broker in a movement to oust Lavon from the headship of the Histadrut. When Lavon intimated that he would submit to no party tribunal Eshkol and his colleagues decided to push the issue through the party executive. While this process was under way Ben-Gurion on 31 January 1961 announced his resignation. The government fell. On 4 February, too late to forestall the old man's resignation, Lavon was deposed from the secretaryship of the Histadrut by a vote in the Mapai central executive committee. Ben-Gurion now saw the Lavon affair, to which he had not been a party, as concluded, and himself became a party to what he regarded as a more important affair, that of the committee of seven. He now determined to rectify what he saw as a gross miscarriage of constitutional propriety perpetrated by his colleagues in Government.

To the general public it seemed that Ben-Gurion had dictated Lavon's removal in a high-handed manner. His prestige sank to the lowest point in his long career. He was wounded to the core by the new public image in which he was seen as a ruthless autocrat. Leaders of the academic community rubbed salt in his wound by issuing a sequence of statements referring to the deterioration of public life revealed by the spectacle of the twice-wronged Lavon being hounded from office by a stubborn old autocrat. This, when he felt that he was defending a vital constitutional principle from abuse by sloppy irresponsible procedures. The public was inclined to be sceptical about his commitment to high principle, seeing this as a cover for his concern for the reputation of the army. Undoubtedly it was this concern that gave Ben-Gurion's conduct in the affair its exceptional intensity of tone.

The available evidence gave ample support to the suspicion that Lavon had been the victim of a conspiracy by his subordinates. At the same time the evidence was not conclusive. Ben-Gurion's view that only a judicial inquiry would be properly qualified to pronounce on the innocence or guilt of the parties to the affair was formally incontrovertible. And yet his insistence on judicial proceeding was in all probability based on a judgement that such an inquiry would be unable to get to the bottom of the matter. Both the Olshan-Dori Committee of 1954 and the Cohn inquiry of 1960 had failed to establish conclusively the guilt of the army officers implicated by Lavon. Ben-Gurion's main concern was most likely the good name of the army and the reputation of the young guard whom he wished to promote to the top leadership of the country. Alongside these considerations Lavon's personal grievance seemed trivial to him.

For six weeks efforts were made to prevent a general election by restoring the previous coalition or forming a new government. Ben-Gurion's attitude to his former coalition colleagues responsible for the ministerial inquiry precluded the success of his own attempt to form a new government. Suggesting to Mapai that he should withdraw to prevent an election in the aftermath of the affair, he nominated Eshkol as the party's candidate for premier. Mapai refused on the grounds that the coalition or opposition parties were not going to dictate to it who should be its leader. The party now braced itself for an election with Ben-Gurion at its head. Elections were set for August 1961. Mapai lost five seats in the Knesset.[3] The party achieved a fair degree of unity for the election campaign, losing only a small number of votes as a result of Lavon calling on his supporters to spoil their ballots.

The vote to depose Lavon marked a break by the veteran Mapai leaders from their umbilical attachment to Ben-Gurion. Not only Sharett, but also many old-guarders voted against the ouster. The rift between the young guard and the veterans now widened as Ben-Gurion's personal prestige declined, and with it his ability to bridge both tendencies in the party by force of his leadership. Golda Meir, who had long been one of Ben-Gurion's most loyal supporters, now joined Lavon as an antagonist of Dayan and Peres.

Tension between Meir as foreign minister and Peres as deputy defence minister (closely backed by Ben-Gurion) arose early in 1958 in a manner reminiscent of Sharett's experience some years earlier. After the Sinai war Peres carried forward his earlier successes in military procurement by developing a vigorous personal diplomacy in France and Germany. Rivalry between foreign ministry personnel in the European capitals and defence emissaries responsible to Peres greatly agitated Mrs Meir.

Although neither she nor the other veterans had any great affection for Lavon, the affair of 1960 helped to bring them for the first time to a point where they could contemplate the possibility of dispensing with Ben-Gurion's leadership. Thus, although Lavon's own political chances were squandered, he had driven a wedge between the old man and his long-time colleagues, thereby assisting the Mapai veterans to withstand Ben-Gurion's efforts to elevate the young guard to the pinnacle of power.

Except for the personal devotees of Lavon the party closed ranks to meet the challenge of the 1961 election. Lavon gathered round him a few score kibbutz intellectuals and academic socialists in a personal movement, *Min Hayesod* ('From the Foundation'), which sought by publishing a lively journal of that name to exert ideological influence within Mapai. While the young guard continued to propagate the values they felt to be more appropriate to an advancing industrial society, Min Hayesod gave expression to the views of the veteran politicians of the third immigration (who were far from friendly to Lavon or his movement), seeking to restore confidence in the socialist habits of mind rooted in the pioneer heritage. Although Lavon himself was eliminated from the succession his movement helped to bolster the image of the older politicians and to revivify the spirit of the Histadrut. Meanwhile, conscious above all of electoral considerations, the professional machine politicians rallied behind Ben-Gurion and for a time came into association with the young guard, suppressing their temperamental antipathy for its members.

Ben-Gurion's veteran colleagues now constrained his freedom of action to a greater degree than had been customary, prevailing upon him after the 1961 election to form a coalition with the left rather than with the liberals according to his taste. The Mapai old-timers began to see Ahdut Ha'avodah as a potential counterweight to the young guard. For the first time in a generation the leaders of that party, sympathetic to the ideological tendencies brought by Lavon to the forefront of Mapai, indicated their willingness to consider rejoining their old Mapai comrades. By lurching to the left Mapai could here pick up a ready-made young leadership with potential electoral glamour to match that of the Mapai technocrats. Combining ideological rectitude with tender years, the Ahdut Ha'avodah leaders could neutralize the Mapai young guard and enable the generation of the third immigration to carry on running the country when Ben-Gurion passed from the scene.

Much as he wished to pursue the matter further, his colleagues persuaded Ben-Gurion to let the Lavon affair, or as he would have it the ministerial committee affair, rest. He held his peace for the time being, stung by his new reputation for authoritarianism and misplaced obstinacy. He did not wish to be the cause of any more resignations by his colleagues, preferring to be their prisoner. In previous years he had been less considerate of their feelings, in the assurance of their implicit loyalty. After 1961 he could no longer depend on that.

To all intents and purposes Ben-Gurion was a defeated man. His party had learned to think of governing without him. He had been an electoral liability as a result of his obstinacy in 1961. He had failed to persuade the public to see and understand what he felt to be the profoundest issues in the Lavon affair. His support for Dayan and Peres had lost him the unconditional loyalty of the veterans. He had failed to deliver the young military technocrats to power, and had seen their reputation tarnished. He realized that it would take some years' work to promote them, but no longer felt up to this. Although he had always cherished labour unity he had no taste for the merger with Ahdut Ha'avodah that was being widely canvassed. He passionately believed that the traditional ideological culture in which the Mapai veterans and Ahdut Ha'avodah had their roots had become irrelevant, that the future security of the country called for a leadership schooled in the decade in which the modern army had been shaped under the sign of the state. As his mind turned to the Negev and his eye rested on the sidewalk cafes of Tel Aviv teeming with the 'normal' young generation, he felt again the tiredness that had overtaken him a decade before. Again he felt the urge to dramatize his personal vision. At the cost of his personal reputation he had failed to gain acceptance for his chosen heirs, but at least he had projected the issue of ideological adaptation. Now he must try again to bring the Negev into public focus, to bring the public, however dimly, to see the dangers and opportunities inherent in his own political legacy. In 1963 he announced his resignation, making it clear beyond doubt that it was final.[4] Talking of a university of the Negev, he made his way again to Sdeh Boker, this time to take up permanent residence.

Ben-Gurion wholeheartedly endorsed Eshkol, the choice of Mapai, as his successor. Eshkol as finance minister had always loyally supported Ben-Gurion's policies. Over the years he had become a useful troubleshooter in party squabbles or coalition tensions for which Ben-Gurion had little patience. Ben-Gurion felt that Eshkol had sound 'statist' instincts and was inclined to forgive him for his key part in the ministerial committee affair, assuming it to have been a lapse of judgement due to over-hastiness to bury the Lavon affair. Eshkol, who was the prototype of the sympathetic machine politician, was more or less acceptable to all elements in the party, including both the young and Lavon's supporters.

The Mapai split

As soon as Ben-Gurion retired the Mapai leaders of the third immigration took firm control, displaying none of the diffidence about taking full charge of the country that had characterized their response to Ben-Gurion's withdrawal a decade previously. Eshkol made it clear that he intended to retain the defence ministry with the premiership as had been Ben-Gurion's practice. The young guard had no choice but to mute their claims for the time being.

Eshkol wished quickly to establish a powerful reputation in his own right.[5] To this end he actively promoted the negotiation of an electoral alignment with Ahdut Ha'avodah. In 1960 Mapai's absolute majority in the Histadrut, on which ultimately the political power of the party was based, had sunk perilously low. Unity with the left would strengthen Mapai's position in the face of growing liberal and right-wing sentiment within Histadrut ranks.

In the absence of Ben-Gurion the young guard fiercely opposed alignment with Ahdut Ha'avodah, which could be expected to reinvigorate traditional ideology and threaten their long-term political prospects. They made a vain effort to persuade Ben-Gurion to return to office on their behalf. In fact, although he had left of his own accord, Ben-Gurion was no longer effectively leader of the party, and in any case was adamant about remaining in retirement. Meanwhile in his desert retreat Ben-Gurion had been preoccupied with the affair of the ministerial committee. This had become an obsession with him. He had resolved to bring the issue before the public again. Desperately anxious to secure his backing against the Ahdut Ha'avodah merger, Dayan and Peres, against their better judgement and at great political risk, associated themselves with Ben-Gurion's personal crusade.

The general public had heaved a sigh of relief at the conclusion of the Lavon affair. The spectacle of the country's top leaders joined in constant invective and public recrimination was not edifying. There was little appreciation for Ben-Gurion's technical critique of the ministerial committee or for his assertion that if not rectified the cabinet decision accepting the committee's findings would have devastating consequences for the standards of public life. Public opinion inclined more to the view that the old man's obstinacy was the real threat. Ben-Gurion had become obsessed by Lavon, whether on account of a well-founded visionary fear for the future of the country under its familiar cosy political leadership or whether, and this was more probably at the heart of the matter, out of fear for his place in history. Inherent in the public sympathy for Lavon was the implication that Ben-Gurion's obstinate refusal to endorse the removal of the cloud of suspicion from Lavon was merely a vindictive response to the first challenge to his personal authority that had been presented since 1948. Surrounded by adulation since 1948, when alone among his peers Ben-Gurion grasped the nature of the struggle facing the country, he had become used to receiving the benefit of the doubt on issues of policy that were in dispute within Mapai. Until Lavon exploded his bombshell in 1960 nobody had dared to cross him without so much as a gesture of deference. But, more important, the public's refusal to share Ben-Gurion's view carried the implication that it was willing to question the integrity of the defence establishment and possibly even the moral authority of Ben-Gurion's own leadership in the early fifties. This was not the way in which he wished posterity to view his career. He would prefer by his obsessive behaviour to gamble with his current reputation for egregious political insight, rather than permit that reputation to be shrouded in doubt in relation to his leadership in the first decade of the state.

The old man had come to see Lavon not only as a political menace, but as a more likely target of suspicion about his role in the 1954 affair than he had hitherto allowed. Ben-Gurion now assiduously probed the affair for himself with the help of devoted aides who joined him at Sdeh Boker. If the public was not agitated by the abstract injustice inherent in the ministerial committee's procedure then he would seek to prove either that Lavon bore more guilt than he admitted or that the implicated officers were innocent of framing him. His political judgement certainly faltered when he felt that his findings about the 1954 scandal would prove to be an irresistible challenge to Eshkol, the government and the leadership of Mapai.

While Ben-Gurion was busy preparing his case that the government should revoke the decision of its predecessor exonerating Lavon, Eshkol was busy preparing to revoke the Mapai decision disqualifying Lavon from office as a representative of the party. Ahdut Ha'avodah's new-found affinity for its parent party was a product of the defeat of Ben-Gurion and the young guard and of the ideological ferment which Lavon and Min Hayesod had introduced to Mapai. Ahdut Ha'avodah made it a condition for its joining Mapai in an electoral alignment that Mapai's decision of February 1961 censuring Lavon should be reversed. At the beginning of May 1964 the followers of Min Hayesod were meeting at Hulda, the kvutza with which Lavon was personally associated, to consider whether the faction should withdraw altogether from Mapai and establish a rival party. The Mapai veterans made haste to prevent such a split. Eshkol sent a letter, with their blessing, to the Min Hayesod conference declaring that all the rights of Lavon and his followers in the party were restored. Ben-Gurion reacted angrily to Eshkol's initiative. He turned on Eshkol with venom, resuming the stormy style of party politics which had agitated the country during the Lavon affair.

Ben-Gurion had never been a good party man. The historic issues that had absorbed his energies as national leader carried him some distance from the give and take of party management. On these issues his leadership usually prevailed by force of his historical insight and his gift for attracting mass support. He saw the issue of succession and the immaculate image of the army on the same plane of historical significance as any of the great turning points in the sixty years of his political career. He did not seem to see that the leadership was necessarily a *party* issue. His doctrine of 'statism' as symbolized by the army that always won had become part of the public consciousness by dint of his personal prestige and that of Dayan, but it lacked an institutional base at the grassroots outside the military-industrial segment of society. If the party would not be the vehicle of his political testament, which by reduction had now become completely bound up with Dayan and Peres, then he would break with the party of his own creation.

Eshkol well knew that Ben-Gurion intended to bring the matter of the ministerial committee before the government and that in so doing he would reintroduce the Lavon affair to the full glare of publicity. He therefore resolved to speed the discussions with Ahdut Ha'avodah, since only a broadening of party support in this way would enable the veteran leadership to withstand another assault by the young guard. Ahdut Ha'avodah in the circumstances was able to exert greater influence on Mapai. In return for an electoral alliance it now demanded that Mapai abandon its commitment to reform of the electoral system. If an alignment between the two parties could also draw Mapam into the fold the result would resemble the majority system that Mapai favoured, while retention of the existing proportional representation would leave Ahdut Ha'avodah with a safety net if the merger did not work out. As Eshkol built up acceptance for Ahdut Ha'avodah's demands and the secretariat of Mapai at the end of October 1964 reached the threshold of agreement, the tension with the young guard mounted. Since the 'Hulda letter' the young guard had successfully organized many branches of the party to oppose the leader's policies.[6] The abandonment of the commitment to electoral reform was the last straw so far as Ben-Gurion's followers were concerned. Dayan resigned from the cabinet. In October Ben-Gurion passed to the minister of justice the results of his personal investigation of the Lavon affair and the proceedings of the ministerial committee of 1960. In mid-November the Mapai executive ratified the secretariat's decision favouring the alignment. Ahdut Ha'avodah for its part would wait until the Mapai convention due in February 1965 before giving its final go-ahead to the alignment. The struggle now warmed up for the Mapai convention which would be called on to ratify either the alignment or the acceptance of Ben-Gurion's demand that the party direct its government representatives to repudiate the cabinet decision of early 1961 exonerating Lavon.

Ben-Gurion's specific request to the minister of justice was that a supreme court inquiry should be conducted into the government's actions of 1960 and early 1961. This had the aspect of a direct challenge to Eshkol's leadership, given the key role that he had played in the government's handling of the Lavon affair. Eshkol ruled against any inquiry whatsoever and brought the issue before the party by resigning the premiership and bringing down the government. In effect Eshkol was taking up Ben-Gurion's implicit challenge to his personal leadership. Eshkol's move was politically most astute, taking the ground from under Ben-Gurion's feet. Rather than a choice between the alignment and Ben-Gurion, Eshkol faced the party with the choice of having a government or having the Lavon affair. A determination in favour of Eshkol would itself clear the way for the alignment and put the Lavon affair to rest. At the same time, rather than battling against the alignment with some prospect of success, Dayan and Peres and the young guard were forced into supporting Ben-Gurion's unpopular crusade and opposing the popular Eshkol personally.

Ben-Gurion could not hope to win the showdown unless

he presented himself as an alternative head of government: he was certainly in no position at that point to install Dayan. The young guard was stranded. Mapai gave Eshkol a vote of confidence, instructing him to re-form a government of the same composition as the caretaker cabinet, and allowing Mapai ministers a free vote in the cabinet on the issue of the judicial inquiry. At the end of December the coalition cabinet voted to drop the Lavon affair and that of the ministerial committee. Ben-Gurion and his supporters now took up their positions for the last battle at the party conference. Conference alone had the authority to reverse decisions taken by executive organs of the party.

The main strength of the young guard was concentrated in the two most important urban branches, Haifa and Tel Aviv. The veterans had control of the agricultural wing of the party and the smaller branches, and had the great advantage of dominance in government and at all levels of party-key officialdom. Last-minute attempts to bring about a re-conciliation between Ben-Gurion and Eshkol were to no avail. The conference gave vent to intense emotion which came to a peak when Sharett, painfully ill and approaching the end of his life, made one of the best speeches of his career denouncing Ben-Gurion's adventurism. By about sixty per cent to forty the conference voted to refuse Ben-Gurion's claims in the matter of the ministerial committee, and by a slightly larger margin endorsed the alignment with Ahdut Ha'avodah.

The minority refused to accept defeat. Now with Ben-Gurion's blessing they organized a campaign for his return as the party's candidate for head of government in the general election due in November 1965. The majority of the party executive voted in the summer in favour of going into the election under Eshkol's banner. Ben-Gurion decided to enter the election as head of an opposition list. Even some of his closest supporters balked at splitting the party outright. Dayan himself did not wish to run in an election campaign tied up with Ben-Gurion's personal obsession. Ben-Gurion nevertheless proceeded undeterred to announce the formation of the Israel Workers' List (Rafi), open to all who wished to join him. Thereupon the disciplinary organs of Mapai had no choice but to expel Ben-Gurion and his followers from the party. The split was formally complete.

Dayan agreed to join the new list when its platform relegated the Lavon affair issues to the background and pushed to the fore a general critique of the Histadrut and the ideology of the alignment. Rafi failed to preclude the alignment from winning a majority, albeit slender, in the Histadrut elections.[7] Similarly, the elections to the Knesset[8] gave Ben-Gurion a clear no for an answer. The era of his leadership had come to a close.

Mapai remained in power under its veteran leaders. They now ruled in their own right rather than as appendages of the old man. Ben-Gurion had been mistaken in supposing that his colleagues of a lifetime were expendable. The party which he had created survived by re-asserting its traditional social-democratic ideology, by refusing to accept Ben-Gurion in his new guise as moral and ideological mentor. The classical Histadrut rhetoric prevailed for the time being over the new political vocabulary that had evolved under the sign of independence, industrialization and military prowess.

From war to war

The unrelenting Arab hostility to Israel from 1948 to 1956 engendered Israeli attitudes and policies which fertilized and fortified that hostility. Whether or not a conciliatory approach by Israel might have succeeded in breaking the vicious circle, Sharett's defeat by Ben-Gurion effectively sealed that option. After the Sinai war both sides were trapped in the unyielding logic of sworn enmity. On the Israeli side the Sinai victory strengthened the plausibility of the 'activist' theory while the relatively tranquil borders after the war confirmed for the public the validity of the policy of intimidation. Few now questioned that Israel's security must be based on coercive power. As for the Arabs, Israel's collusion with the western powers in the Suez engagement confirmed the widespread suspicion that Israel's role in the region was that of a western imperial wedge undermining the independence of the Arab world.

Although among the Arabs and in some other quarters

its reputation was in this way tarnished by the war, on the whole Israel's international position was strengthened by its new western connection. Israel was now able to overcome its diplomatic isolation. In the decade after the war strong relations with the newly independent states throughout Africa were developed on the basis of 'functional' diplomacy. France continued to co-operate closely with Israel even after the settlement in Algeria swept away the initial rationale of the policy. Under de Gaulle France fostered a virtual alliance between the two countries. Relations with Britain became warm for the first time. Labour's repudiation of the Suez engagement introduced a temporary chill so far as the opposition party was concerned, but for the first time the ruling Conservatives approached Israel with enthusiasm and a sense of shared interests. Under Ben-Gurion's constant prodding the Israeli leadership and public began to welcome ties with Germany, and military bargains were now added to the economic bonds.[9] Harmony between Israel and America was quickly restored to supersede the tension of the Suez summer. The major penetration of Soviet power in the middle east now drove America to seek in Israel a military counterweight. American policy was no longer merely a reflection of strategic Jewish voting power, and favour to Israel was no longer limited to the democratic party which benefited most from Jewish electoral support. In the early 'sixties for the first time the United States directly sold arms to Israel, including missiles and tanks.

At the same time Nasser, in spite of his defeat on the battlefield, was borne on a high tide of popularity throughout the Arab world. This led him to press Egypt's claims to pan-Arab hegemony, thereby exacerbating inter-Arab tensions and weakening the Arab world in relation to Israel. Nasser posed a direct threat to the Saudi Arabian monarchy and to American interests in the peninsula by committing heavy forces to the civil war in Yemen. Egypt's army was tied down for years and its military capacity drained by the war, while its policies spurred America to promote further its growing military links with Israel. By the mid-'sixties military supplies from America to Israel included Skyhawk fighter bombers and heavy tanks.

The Sinai war gave Israel a long respite from terrorist attack and border incursions. The policy of retaliation could now be replaced by the strategic doctrine of deterrence. The military brilliance of the Sinai campaign was strenuously exaggerated as a psychological deterrent, to become the prevailing myth of the region. This was nourished and sustained by the intensive modernization of the army on the basis of a procurement programme of unprecedented scale, made possible by the new western appraisal of Israel's potentiality as a brake at least on the military component of Soviet imperial penetration.

Upon the completion of Israel's national water carrier in the summer of 1964, tension again spread throughout the region. In engineering the plan to bring water from the Jordan in the north to the Negev desert, Israel meticulously followed the prospectus of the Johnston plan for regional irrigation, thereby avoiding impingement on the interests of the riparian Arab states. Syria nevertheless tried to foil the plan by initiating a major diversion of the Jordan at the sources within its territory. Immediate Israeli air attacks put a stop to the attempt. Now Syria responded by bombarding Israeli settlements from the Golan heights. In the summer of 1965 the Palestinian national movement, despairing of the Arab governments that had hitherto represented their cause, launched a campaign of terror and sabotage deep inside Israel. Syria sponsored the Palestinians but ensured that their attacks were launched from Jordanian territory, thus widening the area of tension. The relative calm of nearly a decade was shattered and the region again came under the cloud of war.

Israel's economy had taken a steep plunge with the reduction of immigration to a trickle, while emigration and unemployment rose sharply. The economic malaise and the renewed violence diminished public confidence in the Eshkol government, thereby undermining its poise.

Deterrence had run its course and Israel reverted to retaliation and intimidation. A heavy Israeli raid on Samu inside Jordan in November 1966 almost brought down the weak regime of King Hussein. The Israeli attack appeared to be a displacement of anger at Syria. Although it was reluctant to engage Syria directly in view of the pervasive Soviet presence there, Israel made it plain that it would not permit Syria to continue its harassment unchecked.

While Egypt had been second to none in the stridency of its anti-Israel rhetoric its practical policies in relation to Israel had been essentially passive. With his forces bogged down in the interminable Yemen adventure Nasser knew that he was in no position to seek an early military showdown with Israel. Syrian militancy clumsily manipulated by the Soviet Union now succeeded in drawing Nasser against his better judgement into the direct military confrontation with Israel that he had so studiously avoided. Prodded by Syria and the Soviet Union and misled by the apparent hesitancy of the Israeli government and its incapacity to resolve its deepening economic crisis, Nasser lost his balance and faced Israel with the crisis of May 1967 which culminated in the June war.

CHAPTER 17

FOUNDATIONS OF NATIONAL
IDENTITY (1948-67)

Israel is a new nation. Like many of the political communities of Asia it is a new nation rooted in an ancient cultural heritage, religious in form. Like many other new nations today, Israel was delivered by a caesarian operation: by European surgery on the abdomen of Asia. The national identity of the new society has been largely determined by these two connections, by the relation of Israel to Jewry and by its relation to the Arabs.

The establishment of the Jewish state in the territory of Palestine was the achievement of the movement inspired by the Zionist critique of Jewish life in the conditions of its territorial dispersion. The adherents of Zionism were but a small minority of Jews throughout the world. The Jews, alleged by Zionism to comprise a nation, have not typically regarded themselves as such nor have they shown any desire to settle in the land claimed by Zionism for their national redemption. Before the establishment of the state the majority of immigrants were refugees from the carnage which accompanied the breakdown of European civilization beginning in 1914 and culminating in the Nazi holocaust. After 1948, in addition to the remnant of European Jewry that survived the second great war, the immigrants were Jews from the Arab world where they had come under pressure as a result of the circumstances in which Israel was established. Just as the Zionists had been a minority among the Jews abroad, so too were they a minority among the Jewish settlers in Palestine. Only a minority of the adult immigrants of the present and previous generations came to the country by choice, out of devotion to the idea of national rebirth. It was this creative minority which shaped institutions capable of providing a viable refuge for the uprooted Jews of other lands, and capable also of forging a sufficiently coherent basis of national life as to lend credibility to the claim to Jewish statehood when the time was ripe.

The forces which conjured the state into being were not in themselves sufficient to create a new nation, neither as to its identity nor its rationale. At its foundation Israel comprised a population of immigrants brought together under the auspices of a national movement which provided a rationale for their migration and an ideological structure for their integration within the settler community. Israel's accession to statehood brought about a significant change in the bearing of the national ideology. Zionism had elaborated the myth of a Jewish nation in order to create a Jewish state. Immediately upon its establishment the state then became the foremost instrument for the creation of a new nation, the Israelis.

The ideological and political constitution of the new state and its embryonic national offspring were intrinsically bound up with Jewish immigration. The new national identity at its core was moulded in the substance and the myth of Jewish immigration, in both its aspects as the major source of Israel's population and as a national claim exerted on Jews everywhere. The state came into being as a result of the need of the Jews for a place of free immigration. When the state was established the roles were reversed, and it was the state itself which needed the immigration for its own survival. The Zionist movement, having failed to transform the Jews into a nation, bequeathed to the Zionist state the mission of creating a nation of Jews. This was the new myth which, through its component doctrine of Jewish immigration, afforded continuity with the earlier Zionist aspiration and also a continuing link with world Jewry. Thus, while undertaking to forge a nation of Israelis from its heterogeneous elements, the state purported to create a nation of Jews. In this way the state could bridge the chasm that separated the state-making doctrine derived from nineteenth-century European conditions from the reality of nation-making under conditions of sovereign power in the twentieth-century middle east.

Mass immigration from a hundred sources, overwhelmingly non-Zionist in composition, challenged the relevance of the nineteenth-century ideological foundations of the state. In this context Ben-Gurion strove to place the ancient Jewish heritage at the centre of the public myth, not merely as a source of inspiration but as a vital instrument of national unification. Given the great diversity of cultural origins of the population and given that the great majority did not practice orthodox Judaism, it was only by a backward leap of the imagination across two thousand years that a common national consciousness could be quickly synthesized. Only by reference to a remote past through the medium of the Hebrew language could the diverse geographic experience of the population be reconciled with national history. Only Zionism conflated with millennial history could press into a common frame of reference the heterogeneous cultural freight introduced by the immigrants. The ideology of the new nation sought to transcend the faulty articulation of the geography and history of the people. The complexities and ambiguities of the recent Jewish past were thus submerged by the millennial imprint of the national identity card.

The land itself with its vivid ancient relics supplied a material foundation for the nourishment of a national consciousness in which the biblical prophets and the Macabees came alive. But, while assisting the non-orthodox majority to establish common roots, this atavistic mythology differentiated the Israelis more sharply from the non-orthodox majority of Jews abroad, whose contemporary adaptation left little scope or disposition to entertain ancient ghosts. It was simultaneously necessary, while reverting to the psychological anchorage of the ancient past and its glories, to develop national doctrines relating Israelis to the Jews abroad and especially to those of the west who were regarded as the country's most loyal political ally and as its main potential source of future immigration. This was not rendered easier by the vehement Zionist repudiation of the traditional culture of the east-European Pale of Settlement in which most of modern

Jewry outside Israel had its roots, nor by the associated habit of criticism by which Zionism in the period before the state had related itself to the unresponsive Jewish majorities. Nor did the need to provide Israel with a psychic orientation towards the major Jewries of the west correspond with the background or indeed the cultural integrity and dignity of the oriental Jews who were to become the majority of the people.

The emotion-laden memory of the European holocaust afforded the strongest immediate bond with the Jewish communities of the west. The European trauma has been a pervasive motif in the political consciousness of Israel, accounting in large part for the characteristically apocalyptic responses of the people to the issues of security posed by Arab enmity. When the Sinai war extended the privilege of military pride and confidence from the generation of 1948 to the population at large, as though redeeming the apparent passivity of European Jewry in the hands of its butchers, the people felt better able to consult its dark sorrow in the light of day.

Ben-Gurion seized the opportunity of Eichmann's capture by Israeli secret agents in May 1960 to elicit an emotional affirmation of Israel's national being. Through exposure to Eichmann's trial under the law of the Jewish state the older generation could subdue its nightmare by catharsis while the youth of Israel would directly experience the validation of the Zionist passport mediating its national identity. The Kastner trial as an investigation of the troubled Jewish conscience had vented an adolescent brooding of the national spirit. The trial of the chief Nazi executioner would be a more fertile catalyst of mature national canon. At the same time as in this manner educating the national sensibility of the young Israeli generation, the very proceeding would impart the fixity of legal engrossment to the Zionist tenet by which Israel strove to harness the identity of world Jewry to the service of its own national myth.[1]

Following a year of meticulous investigation the trial of Eichmann was staged in Jerusalem, continuing for about four months. The court then spent another four months preparing its judgement which it delivered in December 1961. Upon the failure of his appeal to the supreme court and the refusal of clemency by the president of state, Eichmann was executed on

31 May 1962. For a full two years from the moment he was apprehended in Argentina to the disposal of his ashes beyond Israel territorial waters, Eichmann exercised and dominated the mind of the Israeli public.

Eichmann's role in the liquidation of European Jewry was so central that the trial compelled the Israeli public (and indeed Germany and the rest of the world with eyes glued to Jerusalem) to witness as through a microscope the scatological investigation of the insane Nazi empire. The overwhelming grief of the survivors was discharged from the pent-up silence of the years. The young were challenged to the limits of their endurance to comprehend the meaning of their relation to the people asphyxiated in the intestines of European civilization.

The youth of Israel in exploring the anguished external sources of its national being experienced an excruciating sense of the solitariness of Europe's Jews as they met their terminal fate. With the shock of recognition they likened this to their own feeling of isolation surrounded by a sea of Arab hatred. Israel's youth reacted with bitter cynicism to the rhetorical solicitude of the gentile world for its tortured Jews. Self-assuredness to the point of claustrophilia characterized the response of the young generation. If the Jews in dispersion had lived as the 'tremble of history', Israel's history would be that of the wind. National independence, if it had failed to dispel collective enmity to the Jews as Zionism had promised, would at least afford the means of effective resistance. If it was as Jews that they incurred the hatred of the Arabs, then as Israelis they would know how to fight back. The Eichmann trial toughened this typical Israeli posture by evoking for the first time an acute sense of identification by the young with their doomed European relatives. There was now a greater interest in Jewry beyond Israeli's shores. But the common mourning, the linkage through death, was an insufficient vehicle for affinity among the living. Jewry abroad remained as foreign as ever to the Israelis. While promoting appreciation of the indivisibility of Jewish fate the Eichmann trial at the same time enhanced the plausibility of the Zionist doctrine asserting the inevitability of persecution of the Jews in diaspora. To the Israeli majority the Jewish minorities abroad appeared as the pitiful victims of a fatal illusion.

While in its national consciousness Israel searched the implications of its ideological connection with Jewry it also had to formulate the legal boundaries of Jewish identity in order to administer and regulate the status of its citizens. For the great majority of Jews outside Israel the secularization processes of some two centuries have all but eliminated the religious foundations of Jewish identity, but the nominal source of the identity in Judaism persists. This requires individual Jews to relate themselves in some fashion, even if negatively, to the religious heritage. The same necessity arises for the Israelis. But in this case the 'Jewish' state as the author and embodiment of the official theory of its citizens' identity must formulate the relation on a general plane.

Given the dual sources of Jewish identity in the religious and secular social order the general doctrine comprehending the identity of all Jewish individuals could only be adumbrated by formalizing the relation between religion and state. Abundant paradoxes and contradictions, amenable to practical mitigation through political compromises but hardly capable of resolution in principle, therefore characterized the relation between the secular and religious spheres in the constitution of Israel. Although it was undoubtedly a secular political order the state officially claimed to be a Jewish state. Yet Judaism was not ranked as the 'established' religion. Citizens were ascribed a religious identity to determine their location in the administration of personal status by the religious courts. But Judaism, Islam and Christianity as collective religious communions were subject to regulation by secular statute on a basis of equality: any differential applications of law arose not from favour towards Judaism but from the diversity of religious canon, and bore on citizens as individuals.

The secularist majority of Jews did not for the most part wish to relegate religious life entirely to the private realm. Unless the secularists maintained some public institutional expressions of Judaic provenance the link with world Jewry on which the rationale of Jewish statehood depended for its sustenance would be sapped of vitality. On the other hand, the orthodox population did not wish to implement theocratic rule (if one be permitted to discount its official avowals to the contrary) and thereby undertake responsibility for the whole range of public administration. The religious law and the rabbinical jurisprudence had evolved through centuries on the assumption that secular power was under alien control. It therefore did not develop adaptations, aptitudes and doctrines adequate to comprehend the challenges of extensive public administration in a society based on modern technology. Religious sources viewed in this context were archaic, yielding little guidance on the drawing up of military budgets or the perfection of sanitation. The obligation to rule by theocratic norms would in fact necessarily transform the substance of classical and rabbinical Judaism. Although avowedly theocrats, the orthodox leaders were in fact more concerned to preserve historical Judaism than to adapt it to the requirements of secular power.[2] Hence, rather than a *kulturkampf* between secularist and theocratic theories of government, the public realm manifested clerical politics. The secularist majority willingly undertook to honour a large body of Jewish tradition in public life while the orthodox were glad to accept the 'alien' rule of the secularists as a guarantor of traditional Judaism.

If Judaism was not installed as the established religion of the state, neither was the relation between religion and state determined by 'separation'. In yielding its theocratic aspiration the orthodox community had no choice but to submit to the secularization of religious law. The divergent legal sources governing the two orders were mutually exclusive: there could be no intermediate realm between theocracy and democracy. The constitutional source of secular law in Israel is the will of the people as expressed through representative institutions. Its highest norm is in the politically defined and perceived optimum of human interests. Religious law, by contrast, rests on the authority of divine revelation as interpreted by its believers in the custody of its qualified sages. Human interests are held subordinate to divine worship. The divergence meant that the state could be either theocratic or secular. The state could and did assign authority to the religious judiciary, and also incorporated a host of symbolic and substantive religious contrivances into public life, on political grounds. In thus giving coercive effect to religious norms within certain limits, secular government played host to religious claims much as had all the alien rulers the Jews had known.

417

In this ideological context the definition of 'a Jew' became a political problem of reconciling and adjusting the practice of secularist bureaucracies to that of the rabbinical judiciary as politically represented by the orthodox parties. The Law of Return, the Law of Registration, the Law of Nationality and the Rabbinical Courts Jurisdiction Law, among others, imposed on citizens in their capacity as Jews. But the political bargain between Mapai and the orthodox parties did not unequivocally resolve the issue: who is a Jew? None of these laws defined 'Jew'. This was deliberately left to administrative determination in the respective jurisdictions, to avoid burdening the text of the laws with definitions offensive to the orthodox. (Definition based on religious authority, apart from its incongruity with its secular auspices, would not encompass the sociological reality of the immigration.)

The issue most directly involved the ministry of the interior, responsible for registration of the population at ports of entry. The minister was required by law to maintain a register, and citizens to hold identity cards, recording personal attributes including nationality and religion. Registrars were empowered, at their discretion, to demand and peruse documents for verification before recording particulars. For the most part secular agents, not being concerned with the religious implications of their acts nor claiming any religious jurisdiction, were disposed to accept and record the statements of registrands, subject to consistency. A person claiming to be Jewish would be so regarded for the record. The loose secular criteria of Jewish nationality and religion did not correspond with the religious connotations of these terms. In religious law a Jew is defined as anyone born of a Jewish mother or converted to Judaism by authoritative procedures. Religious authorities, in determining eligibility for marriage or other personal transactions within their jurisdiction, had their own devices for ascertaining the validity of claims to being Jewish. Since the registration was a matter of indifference to the religious authorities in applying their own criteria there was little friction with the ministry of interior during the first years of immigration. However, the somewhat informal understanding between the religious parties and their secular partners in the coalition government came under strain in

1958 when Ahdut Ha'avodah, one of the most militant secularist groups, held the interior portfolio.

Given the vagueness of the law and the incompatability of secularist and orthodox canon, civil servants tended to meet hard cases, such as those presented by 'mixed' marriages and their children, by improvisation. Precision was avoided in order to deter a political showdown. It was possible to leave the issues indeterminate at the cost of occasional injustice to individuals rather than to risk unsettling the collective equilibrium since in principle no general rule was available which could obviate individual hardship. In March 1958 the minister of interior took a different view. He issued explicit instructions to registrars in an attempt to surmount inconsistencies of practice.

The minister stipulated that registrars must record without verification the information supplied in good faith by registrands, and also that in the case of a couple declaring their child to be Jewish the child must be registered as such, even if the mother was non-Jewish and the child accordingly was non-Jewish in religious law. In the minister's view the secular definition of nationality carried no religious implication whatever and was the province of his ministry. Nor did his instruction change existing practice except to clarify it explicitly, since it was well known that the rabbinical authorities did not accept registration as evidence of Jewish identity for their purposes.

In the secular vocabulary of Israel, 'nationality' (unlike Israeli citizenship) differentiated Jew and Arab. The concept of nationality is derived from the Zionist theory of Jewish peoplehood rather than from Judaism. Secular nationality is therefore devoid of religious purport. In the religious view Jewish nationality and religion are indivisible. The orthodox leaders apprehended the minister's act as a challenge since it created a situation in which a specific registration offensive to religious sensibility would now be mandatory.[3] When a cabinet committee of inquiry reported in a sense upholding the minister's view Ben-Gurion failed to persuade the religious leaders of its validity. In June 1958 the religious ministers resigned from the coalition, bringing down the government on the grounds that the minister's instructions changed the *status quo*.

The importance of the issue to the orthodox community derived from the fear that a gradual validation of secularist criteria of Jewish identity would create a schism in Jewry as a whole. The link with Jewry abroad as well as social cohesion within Israel would be damaged beyond repair if marriage in Israel and between Israelis and Jews abroad became increasingly difficult due to the impairment of the credentials of identity (paramount in the religious administration of status) of large numbers. Even the avowedly atheistic Jew born of a Jewish mother could be rescued for orthodoxy by marriage, while the devout Jew whose origins or conversion were dubious was lost to the orthodox community. From the secularist Zionist standpoint the issue was no less important, since it involved the power to constitute the Jewish nationality giving substance to the concept of the state as Jewish. To yield this power would be to abdicate the secularist Zionist hegemony in favour of theocratic rule.

Ben-Gurion resolved to dramatize the issue as link with foreign Jewry. In October 1958 he consulted forty-five eminent rabbinical authorities, secular jurists and scholars in Israel and abroad, seeking their views on the appropriate procedure for registration of the children of mixed marriages both of whose parents wished them to be registered as Jews.[4] Meanwhile the government withdrew the minister of interior's instructions. When the replies of those consulted were complete several months later, it was clear that they overwhelmingly recommended the application of religious criteria alone. Ben-Gurion's somewhat bizarre correspondence had pointed up the divergence between Jewry abroad and in Israel. The issue was put to rest by a decision to leave the register and identity cards of children of mixed marriages blank under the headings of nationality and religion.

Friction inevitably recurred from time to time between the ministries, and between the judiciary and the government. Where the vagueness of the law inflicted hardship on an individual litigation would often occur, placing on civil judges the onus of formulating the boundaries of Jewish identity. A *cause célèbre* was that of Oswald Rufeisen (Brother Daniel), a Polish Jew who had heroically saved hundreds of Jews from the Nazis. While in hiding in a convent he had converted to Catholicism and became a Carmelite monk. In 1958 he immigrated to Israel and claimed citizenship under the Law of Return. He considered himself a Jewish national of the Catholic religion. Following the refusal of the ministry of interior to grant automatic citizenship, the case came before the supreme court. According to religious law a person does not cease to be a Jew on account of conversion to another religion. In the secular view, on the other hand, a professing Christian could not be considered a Jew. The supreme court upheld the ministry's contention, formulating the paradox of Jewish identity in Israel in its sharpest form. On *secular* grounds the court ruled that a person professing a non-Jewish *religion* could not be a Jewish *national*, while the religious view as expressed in a dissenting opinion on the court held that regardless of his religion a born Jew remained a Jewish national.

The elaboration of Jewish identity in its Israeli context was further complicated by the social cleavage between Ashkenazi and Sephardi Jews on the one hand, and between Jews and Arabs on the other. The cleavage within the Jewish population (arising from its diversity of origin as between the western and eastern regions of Jewish settlement in the dispersion) was regarded as an ethnic division. Use of the term *eda* to distinguish Jews of Ashkenazi and Sephardi origin implied that the Jewish population was religiously homogeneous but ethnically divided. As applied to the Arabs, however, the terms connoted religious differentiation (mainly between Muslims and Christians), implying common ethnicity. Zionist doctrine in this context thus affirmed the religious basis of Jewish identity and the national basis of Arab identity.

In the case of oriental Jews in Israel the paradox of identity is convoluted, given that they are for the most part simultaneously Arab *and* Jewish in their geographic and cultural origins. In the Arab world the Jews have historically been seen as Jewish Arabs, that is Arabs of a minority religion. Transplanted to Israel the Jews of the middle east were redefined as Arab Jews, that is Jews of a minority national culture. Just as in the Arab world where, at least since the modern national revolution, religious diversity is more easily assimilable than national diversity, so in Israel there is difficulty in assimilating the Arabs as a national group, although the confessional diversity is incorporated with relative ease. The 'Jewish' state, although its definition is derived from religious sources, in fact discriminates against Arab nationals rather than non-Jewish religions. The existence of a sizeable Arab minority, seen as nationally foreign, thus presses on the identity of oriental Jews in Israel. While all the other Jewish immigrants carry an ethnic label from their countries of origin, only those from the middle east, even though they have become a majority, bear a label identifying them with a foreign minority within the country. As Arab Jews they thus present a challenge to the validity of the Zionist national theory which governs the terms of their assimilation.

The European Zionist movement originated and evolved in the conditions of eastern Europe at the turn of the century when the spreading national movement of the host countries pressed on the separate identity of the Jews. Transplanted to the middle east, Zionism now presses in the same fashion on the identity of the oriental Jews. The moment Israel was established as a nation-state the status of the Jews in the middle east was transformed and they became inassimilable within Arab society. This was most clearly exemplified in Iraq, where age-old religious co-existence was terminated the moment Jews came to be seen as a national entity. Expelled from Arab society as Jewish nationals, they came to Israel where they found themselves virtual Jewish religionists of Arab nationality. The price of their assimilation in Israel is therefore the shedding of their Arab culture. The oriental Jews can be assimilated only on European terms, by denying and submerging their own heritage. Otherwise the new nation would become necessarily bi-national and predominantly Arab, reversing the victory of Zionism which provided the rationale of the Jewish state tied to the Jewries of the west.

The new Israeli nation which was established in the nineteen years between the declaration of its independence and the crisis of May 1967 had borrowed heavily on both Jewry abroad and on the Arabs of Palestine to secure its own identity. The elimination of the Palestinian identity was a corollary of the Zionist rationale by which the relation of the state to western Jewry was sustained. To the Jews abroad Israel said, in effect, 'abandon the material fleshpots which offer only hollow satisfaction, and come here to live an inspiring national life,' while to the Arabs of Palestine it said, 'give up this national folly and enjoy the material benefits to be derived from our dynamism.' Palestinians were fated to be either refugees abroad or second-class citizens within Israel. The promotion of a bi-national theory of independence would have swept away the basis of foreign Jewish support. The Zionist underpinning of the Jewish state thus required Israel to dictate to the surrounding Arabs the structure of their own national life.

By adding more than a million Arabs to the population under Israeli control, the occupation of the Gaza Strip and the western bank of Jordan after the 1967 war sharpened the issue of the place of the Palestinians in relation to the Jewish state. The regular financial support of Jewry abroad had enabled Israel to implement the coercive approach to the Arabs on which security policy was based. After 1967 the policy was reinforced by the efficacy of vicarious military pride as an emotional source of foreign Jewish support. In this way Israel drew foreign Jewries into conflict with the Arab world. The process reached its culmination after 1967 in the outpouring of Jewish financial help on an unprecedented scale to maintain the occupation of Egyptian, Jordanian and Syrian territories.

The disastrous policy of the occupation, which squandered the fruits of the military victory of 1967 and made Israel less secure than at any time in its history, was not only uncritically accepted by foreign Jewries but had become the very source of their enthusiasm. The occupation itself had in fact *become* the security problem of Israel. And yet the Israeli government could never have counted on comparable Jewish support for a policy, say, of integrating the Arab minority fully within the national life of the country. It was Israel as conqueror that evoked the most generous support, launching the country after 1967 on its most buoyant economic expansion yet.

The Meir government, politically out of its depth, built its fortunes on the furtherance of the most dangerous tendency inherent in the Ben-Gurion legacy, failing to appreciate that the old man himself would never have done so. The government came to believe in the myth of its own military infallibility while assiduously squandering its greatest military asset, the flexible offensive capacity of its forces, in favour of an army of occupation geared to the rigid defence of remote foreign territories. After 1967 Israel developed its imperial personality to correspond with the Arab stereotype of it. The democratic institutions and political ethos that had been painstakingly built up for nearly a century have been subjected to a process of degeneration from which it is doubtful whether they can recover. The occupation cannot endure, for the Arabs will not endure it. Then there will be a reckoning in Israel in which it will be hard pressed to restore its classical identity against the pressures towards permanent military rule.

EPILOGUE

Experts are all experts in things that have already happened; there are no experts in things that have never happened.

David Ben-Gurion

I am disturbed less than most of my countrymen, by the fact that some appraisals of Israeli policy are critical, because I don't believe that criticism of a policy is inherently an unfriendly act.

Abba Eban

EPILOGUE (1967-73)

The manuscript of this work was completed in June 1973, three months before the outbreak of the fourth Israel-Arab war of the quarter century. Throughout the years of writing it had been clear to the author that the war of June 1967 and the Israeli occupation of Arab territories in its aftermath were an incomplete episode which would culminate in a new war of greater magnitude, rendering Israel's policies obsolete. It therefore seemed prudent to conclude the narrative at the spring of 1967. The war of October 1973 brought the six-year period to a peremptory close. Some discussion of the period and the new prospect yielded by its termination, in the light of the preceding history, is therefore called for.

The detailed coverage accorded to recent events in the middle east by the news media will undoubtedly have enabled the reader to approach this history from a vivid topical perspective. If the work has any merit it should now enable the reader to approach the current scene from a vivid historical perspective. Of course the historian can claim no authority for prognostications about the future. Any discussion of the fluid contemporary scene risks being overtaken by events by the time it appears in print. With all due caution, nevertheless, the reader of history may legitimately hope that close study of the past can help to distinguish the more authentic from the more spurious alternative prospects latent in circumstances.

While topical interest centres on the changed prospect in Israel-Arab relations, the student of Israeli history will be interested also in other changes which have taken place over the past six years, many of which will be no less significant for the future. In the delineation of Israeli-Jewish identity, for example, new legislation and judicial decisions have further elaborated the theory of nationality and the place of religion

427

in the life of the state. The economy as a whole and industry in particular were transformed by an unprecedented influx of foreign investment capital, and by the induction of a sizeable Arab labour force commuting from the occupied territories. The labour parties managed to extend and maintain a semblance of unity by postponing the resolution of the succession issue, while its inclusion for three years in a national-unity coalition lent new political weight to the right-wing opposition. Persistent Israeli pressure on the Soviet Union, carried out with the help of Zionists in the west, was rewarded by a steady influx of Jewish immigrants from Russia. This, in conjunction with a tide of private American investment in luxury housing, bedevilled the integration of earlier immigrants and exacerbated tensions between the oriental majority and those of European extraction. Eventually these and other changes will require detailed study on a scale symmetrical with the treatment of earlier periods. But whatever the consequences of such changes, they will in large part be determined by the context of Israel-Arab relations and the pattern of peace or war.

The six-day war

Until the middle of May 1967, when the whole region was suddenly gripped in crisis, there were few in the middle east or elsewhere who expected an early war between Israel and Egypt. Of course the chronic conflict remained unresolved, as manifested in increased violence following the emergence of a militant Palestinian nationalism in 1965. It was an avowed aim of this movement to draw the Arab states into war with Israel. Encouraged by the Syrian government which now claimed the leadership of the Arab struggle against Israel, Palestinian saboteurs stepped up their actions inside Israel at the beginning of 1967. Tension mounted when Israel's cultivation of the disputed lands in the demilitarized zone on the Syrian border led to an air battle on 7 April in which six Syrian MIGs were shot down. Torn between its desire to punish the Syrian regime which it held responsible for Palestinian acts of terror and its reluctance to anger the regime's Soviet backers, Israel deferred physical retaliation while issuing strident verbal warnings for a longer period than had been its past practice. These warnings led Syria to invoke its joint defence pact with Egypt on the grounds that a full-scale Israeli attack was imminent. But Nasser had for a decade repeatedly enunciated his view, at the risk of his personal prestige, that the Arab states must avoid any major battle with Israel until they were sufficiently prepared to enable them to inflict a decisive defeat. With fifty thousand Egyptian troops bogged down in the Yemen war, earning little credit for Egyptian arms or political acumen, the spring of 1967 did not appear an auspicious time for Nasser to engage the lithe Israeli war machine in battle. Yet within two weeks from the middle of May to the end of the month Nasser had reversed his policy and had created a situation in which war became inevitable.

There is some uncertainty and a good bit of controversy surrounding the explanation of Nasser's somersault. The most probable account is that, in danger of losing his leadership of pan-Arabism to the more militant rhetoricians, he sought to regain initiative by seizing the issue of Israel more firmly. Not at first wishing for war, he thought he could bluff his way to a diplomatic victory over Israel. Then, dazzled by the array of Egyptian force which he hastily assembled in the Sinai peninsula, he became intoxicated to the point of greatly over-estimating the Egyptian military capability. At the same time, the apparent hesitancy of the Israeli government in responding to his challenge led him to a new appraisal in which he grossly underestimated Israel's military strength. Step by step he thus allowed himself against his better judgement to be drawn into a confrontation, until it was too late to revert to his original goal of a technical affront to Israel. As diplomatic cover for provoking war he used the allegation sponsored by Syria and the Soviet Union that Israel was concentrating forces for an immediate attack on Syria. There is good reason to believe that Nasser knew that no such Israeli assault was in fact in preparation. (It is rather more difficult to fathom the Soviet role. Whatever Russia's aim in fomenting the crisis it is clear that it acted with great clumsiness, unless it actually wanted a full-scale war in the region.)

The crisis broke on 14 May when Nasser placed Egyptian forces on maximum alert and began deploying his army in the Sinai peninsula. Egypt then requested the UNEF commander to withdraw from the Gaza strip. Nasser may have intended to secure only a partial withdrawal of UNEF to facilitate the deployment of his forces, but when the Secretary-General of UNO intimated that only a complete withdrawal would be consistent with UNEF's role, Nasser confirmed that this was his wish. By 21 May Egyptian troops had occupied the positions vacated by UNEF, including Sharm el-Sheikh on the Tiran Straits commanding the entrance to the Gulf of Akaba. It had now become impossible for Egypt, without intolerable loss of prestige, to allow the passage of Israeli shipping through the straits. Nasser announced a blockade on 22 May, well knowing that Israel was unequivocally committed to construing this as an act of war requiring a military response. The hasty inclusion of Jordan within the Egyptian military command and the entry of Iraqi troops into Jordan completed the irreversible Arab commitment to war.

Premier Eshkol's fumbling style created an atmosphere of uncertainty and weakness in Israel which belied the actual vigour and determination of the political and military elites. But there was a real malaise that went deeper than the style of leadership. The economic recession which began in 1965 had assumed crisis proportions by the end of 1966. There were few signs of improvement in the spring of 1967. Emigration increased and morale was low. As in the early fifties, the economic crisis coincided with increased sabotage and terror inside Israel. The al-Fatah movement, under Syrian tutelage since the Damascus coup of February 1966, did not so much threaten the security of Israel as its sense of security. The public had begun to lack confidence in the government. A political crisis thus compounded the economic and military stress, and a general gloom descended to displace the verve that had come to typify public life.

In this context Nasser was the more prone to mis-read the hesitancy of Eshkol's response to his initial challenge, failing to appreciate Israel's latent strength and resilience. In fact the Israeli leadership was completely confident that it could trounce the Egyptian forces and any other Arab armies it might be compelled to engage. Its initial hesitancy reflected its assessment of the military balance, on the basis of which it assumed that Nasser could not intentionally risk war. But when the UNEF force was dislodged Israel acted decisively enough, mobilising its forces on 19 May. That Israel then chose to explore the possiblity of a diplomatic solution, in view of the western commitment to freedom of passage in the Tiran Straits, was due not to any doubts about the capacities of its military forces but to its reluctance to go to war, and its need for time to absorb the shock of Nasser's unexpected provocation. Eshkol's despondent and inarticulate broadcast to the Israeli public on 28 May, in which he relayed the government's decision to attempt to counter Nasser by diplomatic means, aggravated the public's lack of confidence in his leadership. Eshkol now reluctantly agreed to relinquish the defence ministry to Moshe Dayan in order to restore the waning confidence of the general staff in the government, and to boost public morale. When it became clear at the beginning of June that the United States could not muster the support of other western powers for physical action to secure freedom of navigation, and that it was unwilling to attempt this alone, the Israeli government resolved on military action.

The fear that gripped Israel's friends around the world, Jewish and non-Jewish, followed from the consistency of Nasser's avowals that he would not go to war until the Arabs were ready to destroy Israel. While Israel saw the value of this widespread sympathy in diminishing the political dangers of a pre-emptive strike, and so did nothing to dispel exaggerated fears for its survival, it did not itself create the atmosphere of impending doom. In this instance apocalyptic propaganda did not emanate from Israel, but from Nasser and other Arab leaders. The propaganda backfired on the Arabs by evoking the greatest diplomatic and financial support for Israel that it had ever received.

Israel's pre-emptive strike on the morning of 5 June, in which at a stroke it destroyed Arab air power, determined the outcome of battle. The Egyptian forces were quickly routed throughout the Sinai peninsula. King Hussein of Jordan (though in the context of inter-Arab politics he probably had little choice but to participate in battle), was deceived by Nasser into mounting a full-fledged attack on Jerusalem in the belief that Egyptian air power was intact. A few days sufficed for Israel to conquer the whole of the West Bank of Jordan and to take over the Syrian Golan Heights from which Israeli settlements had been subjected to regular bombardment.

The six-year war*

Israel's military prowess was not matched by the political skill of its leaders. The policy of remaining in occupation of the Arab territories taken in battle† resulted from a lack of preparation for the contingency of conquest on such a scale. This was the only redeeming feature of the policy. Only a total withdrawal from the conquered territories, immediately the cease-fire was implemented, could have rewarded Israel with the political fruits of its military victory. Peace might not have been possible, but at the very least the irredentist will of the Arab states and even the Palestinians might have faltered. After all, the debacle of the Sinai campaign of 1956 gave the Arabs pause for a decade, although on that occasion Israel had not defeated Egypt single-handed.

In maintaining the occupation Israel transformed the structure of its insecurity greatly to its own military disadvantage. To retain its hold on remote foreign territory Israel had to sustain casualties as numerous as those that had previously been hallowed in defence of its own borders. The advantage of shortened borders was illusory, being far outweighed by the atrophy of the military posture and its associated skills that had been so successfully adapted for deterrence and offensive defence. But even the deterioration of its strategic imagination was a minor flaw in Israel's new status, compared to the political costs of the occupation policy.

Israel at first had no policy to deal with the conquered territories. The disastrous policy of occupation evolved by

* Lest he be accused of abusing hindsight, the author should point out that the observations in this section are based on articles and talks he delivered in student forums between 1967–71.

† The Egyptian Sinai peninsula and Gaza strip with a population of about 400,000; old Jerusalem with some 66,000 and the West Bank (Judea and Samaria) of Jordan with some 600,000; and the Syrian Golan Heights with a Druze population of about 6,000.

a process of drift, until within a few months it was so deeply invested with the imagery of deterrence and security that it became irreversible, creating the conditions of its own justification. The government of Eshkol and his successor Golda Meir lacked the sense of direction which distinguishes statesmanship from petty politics. Quite out of their depth in the arena of grand politics, they allowed desire for the territories to grow to an irresistible intensity until it dictated the policy, which they then rationalised in terms of a misguided doctrine of security.

The initial fatal step in the evolution of the policy was the annexation on 27 June of the old city of Jerusalem, which Jordan had appropriated in 1949. (Jordan's negligent custody of the holy places had certainly earned no superior legitimacy for its proprietorship.) Defying the wishes of the seventy thousand Arab residents of the old city and its environs, the emotional act of annexation extinguished the political imagination of the Israeli government and public in relation to the Palestinian people of the West Bank. The corollary of the appropriation of the potential capital of the Palestinian nation was the repression of political activity throughout the West Bank in order to prevent the emergence of a Palestinian national personality capable of effectively claiming self-determination. The war had re-created the Palestine of 1947, for the first time in twenty years bringing the Palestinian issue back into the centre of the Israel-Arab conflict, in circumstances in which a constructive solution might for a brief period have been possible. The Israeli government, rather than build on the possibility of accommodation with the masses of people who had been dispossessed at Israel's birth, chose to pursue the elegant diplomacy of rapprochement with King Hussein.

Before the Arab 'summit' conference at Khartoum at the end of August 1967 the Israeli government hoped that by bargaining with the occupied territories it could reach a peace settlement with the Arab states. The government reasoned that the withdrawal from the Tiran Straits and the Gaza strip in the spring of 1957 had made possible the war of 1967. That they interpreted the situation in this way, rather than concluding that the military victory in 1956 followed by the withdrawal had made possible a decade of relative quiescence, reflected an absolutism that had come to pervade their concept of peace in proportion to its elusiveness. In the early fifties Sharett had advocated the acceptance of short-term sacrifices of security in the interest of nurturing the conditions for long-term peace, while Ben-Gurion assigned priority to short-term security in the belief that peace would be unattainable for a generation. Ben-Gurion's heirs now elevated absolute peace to top priority on the assumption that the occupation of the conquered territories guaranteed short-term security. The false security of remote shortened borders had superseded Ben-Gurion's authentic security of the centres of population, while the mirage of peace at a stroke of the pen had superseded Sharett's pursuit of the conditions of peace. Israel's demand for total peace based on assumed invincibility now became the main obstacle to peace and security alike.

At a press conference in mid-August 1967 the Israeli foreign minister presented the official view that the war had shattered the armistic agreements, conveying the inference (later substantiated) that Israel's boundaries of 1949 no longer held, and that definitive borders could only be determined by negotiation. Following the Khartoum conference at the end of August at which the Arab leaders enunciated their guiding principles of no peace, no recognition and no negotiation with Israel, the peace demands of Israel became more absolute, and more hollow. The initial post-war expectation of withdrawal by negotiation gave way to the hardened formula of maintaining the cease-fire lines of 1967 pending direct negotiations with the Arabs to re-draw the map. The taste of possession of old Jerusalem began to whet the appetite for control of the West Bank, which in its own way also fired the religious imagination. At the end of October a prominent rabbinical authority in an official position of state stipulated that the religious law denied Israel the right to yield a single inch of occupied territory on the West Bank. There was less talk of withdrawal and more of secure, recognised boundaries. This was increasingly accompanied by discussion of various plans for Jewish settlement in occupied lands.

After the war the Israeli government was unable to achieve any consensus on the disposal of the occupied territories. Unable to see the risks and costs of the policy of staying put, the public came to enjoy the enlarged living space. Before long the occupation produced the conditions that lent plausibility to the security rationale that was attached to it. Enjoyment of the prize was thus enhanced by the belief that holding on to it was the safest way to handle it. Within a few months of the war Israel settled into a Maginot mentality, losing the initiative with which its military strength had endowed it, and in effect relinquishing to the Arabs the responsibility of determining its fate.

The assertion that its boundaries of 1949 were nugatory crystallized the enormity of Israel's political error. For nearly twenty years Israel had sought Arab recognition of its boundaries, and indeed their rectification by negotiation. Now, when its victory might for the first time have made such recognition attainable, it renounced those boundaries and officially rendered indeterminate its own configuration on the map. It has often been pointed out that at each successive stage in the advance of Zionism the Arabs showed a willingness to accept the previous *status quo* which they had sought to alter by force. In the earlier period of its advance Zionism was unwilling to revert to any previous status which fell short of its aspiration for independence. After the war of independence it was unwilling to contemplate reverting to the boundaries of the partition proposed by UNO, understandably in view of the Jordanian and Egyptian annexations of parts of the land and the absence of a willing Palestinian society capable of implementing the other half of the partition. The Zionists therefore rested their case on the borders of the 1949 armistice agreements and succeeded in obtaining world-wide recognition of these borders as an approximation of Israel's legitimate territorial status, subject to minor rectifications if and when conditions allowed. In 1967, instead of seizing (or at least exploring or seeking to create) the political opportunity to obtain Arab recognition of these borders and so demonstrating that it was not bent on expansion as the Arabs believed, Israel squandered its historical legitimacy and opened up the question of the extent of its claims. Well might the Arabs ask which Israel they were supposed to deal with! Instead of clinging at all costs with great force and persistence to the boundaries that the international system had institutionalized, legalized and recognized, and which had held good and proved to be defensible for two decades, Israel by its own choice became an indeterminate quantity, its territorial identity a question mark. In this sort of context the selection of 1947 or for that matter 1917 as benchmarks for definition does not sound so unreasonable as it does in the context of official Israeli rhetoric. The spokesmen of Israeli expansionism assert that 'whoever gives up our right to Nablus questions our right to Tel Aviv'. Actually, it is the other way about: whoever in Israel claims the right to Nablus calls in question the right to Tel Aviv.

In effect, the Israeli leaders after Khartoum realized that they would be unable to dictate the terms of peace, but at the same time they continued to believe that the occupation would afford security because the Arabs would remain incapable of mounting an effective military campaign. Israel failed to distinguish the political effects of its military victory from the contrary effects of its continued occupation of the Arab territories. The possible deterrent effect of its military triumph was dissipated in proportion to the intensification of Arab resistance due to the occupation.

Like any other people under military occupation, the Arabs could not regard the return of portions of their own territory as representing 'concessions' for peace. The Israeli formula of secure and recognized (but putative) boundaries had a hollow ring for the three states in the region whose *actual* boundaries had been consigned to oblivion by Israeli power. To the Arabs at least it was clear that they could win back their lands only by war.

The occupation exerted a dramatic impact throughout the Arab world. With Israeli soldiers encamped on the Suez canal and Egyptian life in the canal-zone brought to a standstill by the perennial shooting match of attrition, the Egyptian people for the first time experienced Israel as a palpable reality. So far as the Egyptian public was concerned, the Israeli presence on Egyptian soil translated the issue of Palestine from the realm of poetic abstraction to that of physical pain. Nor was the Palestinian population of the West Bank and Gaza strip any more disposed to acquiesce in Israeli rule than would Israel have been willing to accept the rule of an Arab majority. Above all, the occupation transformed the Palestine liberation movement from being a mere appendage of the Syrian and Egyptian regimes to becoming a political force in its own right, capable of dictating the terms on which its hosts gave it cover. Unable to dent the Israeli armour, the Palestinian radicals launched a campaign of unrelenting terror aimed at random targets throughout the world. Although the movement lacked popular support and hence also the potential to pose any serious military threat to Israel, and although the cruelty and frequent ineptitude of its terrorist practice earned it little sympathy in the world, it nevertheless succeeded in establishing the image of its cause as the quest of a victimized people for national self-determination, rather than a neglected refugee problem as it had hitherto been widely regarded.* Hussein's ruthless butchery of the radicals in September 1970, when they went too far in defying the authority of his throne, eliminated the military nucleus of the movement and thereby drove the rump based in Syria and Lebanon to new excesses. While the militants failed to mobilize the refugees and the people of the West Bank, the majority of whom would probably wish for an honourable modus vivendi with Israel if that were but forthcoming, they nevertheless gathered increased tacit support. Israel's repressive administration of the West Bank created a political vacuum. Thus the voice of terror remained the only audible voice of Palestine, with the result that the political status of the movement greatly surpassed its social coherence at the grassroots.

As Israel's imperial persona matured the Palestinian people emerged as a political entity in the struggle for its homeland, while the Arab states focused on the recovery of their own lost territories. The Arab cause had now become very much more respectable than when it had been a mere plaything of pan-Arab politics framed in the rhetoric of annihilation, while the corresponding Israeli rhetoric of survival rang less true with every passing day. The occupation imparted a new legitimacy to Arab belligerency as resistance. In the degree

* There is no escaping the analogy with Zionism in the late forties.

that the illusions of pan-Arabism receded the actuality of Arab unity grew, nurtured by the determination to recover the occupied territories.

The October war and aftermath

Early in October 1967, after the Arab conference at Khartoum, the Israeli minister of defence pointed out that Israeli withdrawal from the occupied territories was not a viable method for obtaining peace, because no Arabs were promising peace if she withdrew. That he did not at the same time note that all Arabs were promising war if she did not withdraw, reflected the already prevalent Israeli confidence that its military supremacy held a permanent lease on the map of the region.

The re-armament of Egypt under Soviet patronage began in 1968, and within a few years had elevated its military technology to a level on which it could counter Israeli air power. The presence of the United States and the Soviet Union behind their respective clients ensured the continuance of the familiar arms race. Sadat, if less flamboyant, was proving to be a steadier hand than Nasser. Arab war plans were carefully prepared and co-ordinated on two fronts on the basis of close unity of purpose, rather than ramshackle alliance as in 1967. When he chose his moment in October 1973 Sadat took Israel by surprise by means of brilliantly executed 'indirection'.

The Israeli army was rusty with the tedium of the administration of its conquests. This time its men were fighting far from home, defensively, rather than against an enemy on the run. The Arabs had the initiative, and were fighting for their own land. Israel was isolated in the world except for its American patron. The loyalty of the United States held firm not because of any American commitment to the thesis that the defence of Tel Aviv required an Israeli army on the Suez canal, so much as on account of the American reluctance to allow a victory of Russian arms over American arms. Other countries, if well enough disposed towards Israel, were not disposed to accept the view that the battle for Egyptian and Syrian territories was a battle for Israeli survival. For most of Israel's friends, even a resumption of Syrian control of the

Golan Heights overlooking Israeli settlements that had good reason to fear it would not credibly call in question the existence of Haifa. Nor were any but the more ignorant of Israel's friends abroad inclined to interpret the Arab attempt to recover their own territory as a war of aggression.

Although they achieved no decisive victory in the October war, the Arabs did succeed in altering the military balance, with maximum political effect. At the very least they checked the arrogance by which Israel, acting like a great power, had come to assume its right to dictate to its neighbours the terms of national existence in the middle east. By itself renouncing the territorial arrangements which had imparted some fixity to its national claims, Israel lost the rare opportunity that arose in 1967 to convince its neighbours that neither could they hope to dictate to Israel the terms of its existence. As a result, Israel is now in a much weaker position if any effort towards mutual accommodation should occur. For in the long run, if military factors were indeed to be the sole basis of determination, at the cost of national annihilation of one of the parties to the conflict, then Israel would be doomed.

During and after the war the Arabs took their first steps towards realizing their vast potential power. As a result of the October war a concrete unity may be expected to evolve at the core of the Arab world, accelerated by the momentum of success instead of being limited as in the past to the desperate rhetoric of failure. In these circumstances Israel will be obliged to seize any gestures for partial peace the Arabs may offer. Their partial victory may give the Arabs a desire for partial peace, the benefits of which in turn may produce a desire for its extension. If Israel were to continue to insist on absolute peace as a starting point, it might find before many years that the Arabs were sufficiently strong to do without partial peace.

Israel was deeply shocked by the cost of the war. Many people began immediately to question the false assumptions and illusions on which the public had fed for six years. The general election campaign of December 1973 showed some of the sobering effects of the war, but at the same time gave grounds for the prognosis that the damage done by six years of intoxication may require more than another six to repair.

It is true that the October war generated a discussion in Israel in which the 'doves' appeared to carry more weight than they had immediately after the war of 1967. But the discussion that will be necessary if peace is to become possible did not take place, and it is doubtful whether it can take place. Discussion which goes to the heart of the relationship between Israel and the Arabs in general, and the Palestinians in particular, will have to be taken outside the salons of the intellectuals and into the centre of the political arena. This is where there are grounds for pessimism, for the political institutions of the country may be unable to withstand such a *kulturkampf*.

Egypt's statement at the end of November 1973, announcing its readiness to enter into negotiations for the disengagement of forces, called for a complete Israeli withdrawal and for the restoration of Palestinian national rights. The revised election manifesto issued by the labour alliance a few days later discarded its pre-October nonsense about absolute peace on Israel's terms, and substituted the formula 'defensible' borders. But it reiterated both the Israeli repudiation of the boundaries of 4 June 1967 and the denial of freedom to the Palestinian people to arrange their national existence on the West Bank in any way they might wish, with or without King Hussein.

The election campaign showed that the country was deeply divided, along the same lines as it had been after the war of June 1967. The October war strengthened the belief of the 'hawks' that the occupation had conduced to security since the territories had bought time, while it reinforced the view of the 'doves' that the price of occupation was exorbitant. But the terms of the debate as laid down after the war of 1967 had become somewhat irrelevant to the situation as it stood after October 1973. The debate between 'hawks' and 'doves' was as out of date after October 1973 as previously it had been illusory. The pattern of policy after June 1967 and the controversy that arose within that framework were premised on the assumption of Israeli military preponderance sufficient to deter an Arab assault. Owing to the dialectic of resistance set in motion by the occupation, that assumption had been false, and after October 1973 it could be seen to have been false.

Israel's political institutions have for a quarter of a century been locked in a stable equilibrium sustained by the assumption of military invincibility. This assumption, rather than merely the challenge of Arab enmity, had been a condition of political cohesion. Bereft of this assumption the political equilibrium may become a political deadlock. This is the crux of Israel's internal dilemma in the aftermath of the October war.

Before 1967 the national identity of Israel had become relatively firm and finite. After 1967 a new battle for the delineation of the national identity divided the country on a false issue: whether that identity should have an imperial hawkish profile or an imperial dovish profile. The war of October 1973 has revealed the bankruptcy of that debate, while the continuation of the debate in the aftermath of the war revealed the possible incapacity of the country to face the Arab issue outside its framework. Now that the Arabs have seized the military and political initiative Israel may be compelled to re-assess its relationships with the Arab world on a basis of equality. Yet it may well lack the psychological and institutional resources to do so.

Just as the Arabs have become more united by their unaccustomed success, so Israel has become more deeply divided by the unaccustomed failure of its policies. The October war may be expected to place the 'doves' in the ascendant, for chauvinism in Israel tends to thrive on success. (If election statistics suggest the contrary, that is a superficial indication. The important clue is the state of opinion within the Mapai alliance.) However, even if the 'doves' should achieve preponderance their influence may fall short of generating a radical re-assessment of the Arab issue in its multiple facets. Throughout three-quarters of a century the Zionist movement was unable to tackle these issues squarely, while Israel in its quarter-century has never found it necessary to do so, as long as its arms triumphed and the Arabs remained a weak enemy. The very attempt to bring these problems into the centre of political life might threaten to subvert the centripetal authority of the ideological components of the national personality. The older generation of immigrants whose leaders have retained power for half a century cannot be expected to accomplish the necessary feat of imagination, since every detail of the apocalyptic Jewish trauma and the bitter historical struggle with the Arabs in Palestine is imprinted on their political consciousness. Only the younger generation, whose Israeli identity is a firm and naturalistic existential reality, free of the complexities that adhere to that of its revolutionary makers, are likely to be able to reconstruct its contours in tune with the changing realities of existence in the middle east. However, even given an exercise of imagination adequate to the challenge, it might be politically impossible to escape from the inertia of the past and effect a reconstruction of the terms of national life.

The maintenance of civilian democratic rule in Israel has been assisted by the civilian acceptance of the military point of view, and it has been resilient so long as that point of view, *vis-à-vis* the Arab world, was efficacious. The most profound danger to Israel, apart from the resumption of war if it fails to do so, is that if it attempts to face the Arab issue on a basis other than the military calculus, its institutions locked in the equilibrium of victory may be so deadlocked and disrupted as to make way for the installation of permanent military rule. This would not require a *coup d'état*, nor would such a development necessarily have any bearing on the direction of policy. Israel has a citizen army. Its generals in their civilian clothes now occupy all the key positions in government and throughout the economy. The Arabs would presumably know how to take advantage of political paralysis in Israel, by increasing the pressure. In such circumstances the army would comprise the only pervasive organizational network capable of maintaining order and production.

It would undoubtedly be more difficult today for Israel to implement a full withdrawal to the armistice boundaries, as a basis for the negotiation of rectifications and demilitarization, than it would have been before the occupation generated, incrementally from year to year, the conditions for its own validation. The political error of the occupation has become much harder to undo, as a result of its own impact on the structure of the conflict. If the Arabs continue, as may be expected, to consider that any vestige of occupation of their

territories constitutes a cause for war, then the disengagement
of forces in the Sinai peninsula and the possible negotiation of
further withdrawals will merely register the Egyptian gains
of 1973. Partial withdrawals by negotiation may be a mere
charade, postponing the next round rather than progressing
towards peace. This is how the Israeli 'hawks' see it, and
they are probably correct, although their conclusion that
Israel should therefore stay put is probably wrong; but not
even the 'doves' would now be likely to go the whole way,
to conclude that Israel should withdraw by its own volition,
unilaterally, without the illusory compension of a *quid pro quo*
for every kilometre.

The danger of renewed war is greater than ever. Every
successful stage of negotiation may be expected to excite
Palestinian radicals to new extremes of violence inside Israel
and abroad. So far as the Golan Heights is concerned, perennial bloodshed is certain, with or without withdrawal. No
detente with the volatile Syrian regime can be expected for
many years, until at least a stable accommodation can be
reached with Egypt. This is more difficult than ever to achieve,
because in 1967 Egypt learned the cost of allowing Israel the
first strike, as Nasser chose to do, while in 1973 Israel learned
the cost of allowing Egypt to strike the first blow, as Meir
chose to do. Slender as the hope may therefore be, the Egyptian
decision to advance by diplomacy offers the only immediate
prospect for a reduction of tension.

Israel's resistance, or at least that of the immigrant generation of leaders, to the fact of Palestinian national consciousness, helped to obscure the profoundly different nature of the
conflict between Israel and the Palestinians and that between
Israel and the Arab states. The war of October 1973 helped
to clarify this difference. Initial disengagement of forces by
Egypt and Israel and even eventual disengagement on the
Golan Heights might be followed by further negotiations and
further withdrawals, or not. In either event the recurrence of
war may be considered inevitable unless and until definitive
boundaries are drawn up by mutual agreement. If there is a
recurrence of battle, regardless of its outcome, or if there is
agreement, regardless of its terms, the issue will remain untouched at heart until the relationship between Israel and the

Palestinians is placed on a new footing. If Israel's mental and institutional resources should fail to transcend this necessity, then only civil war within Jordan, reverberating throughout the region in a new conflagration, will remain in prospect.

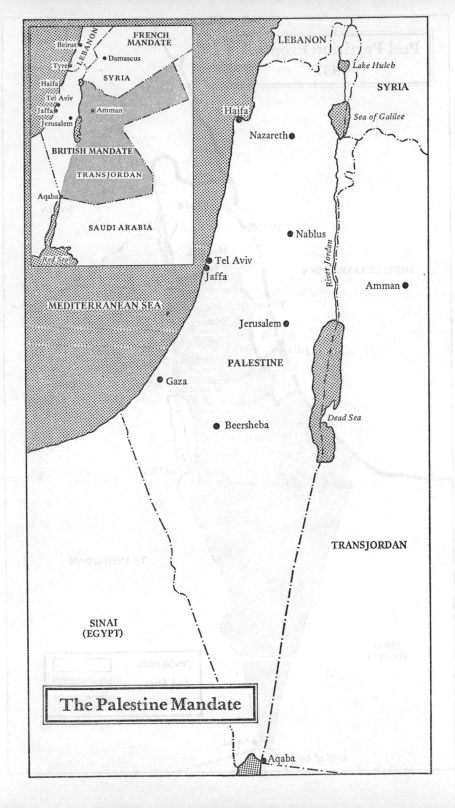

The Palestine Mandate

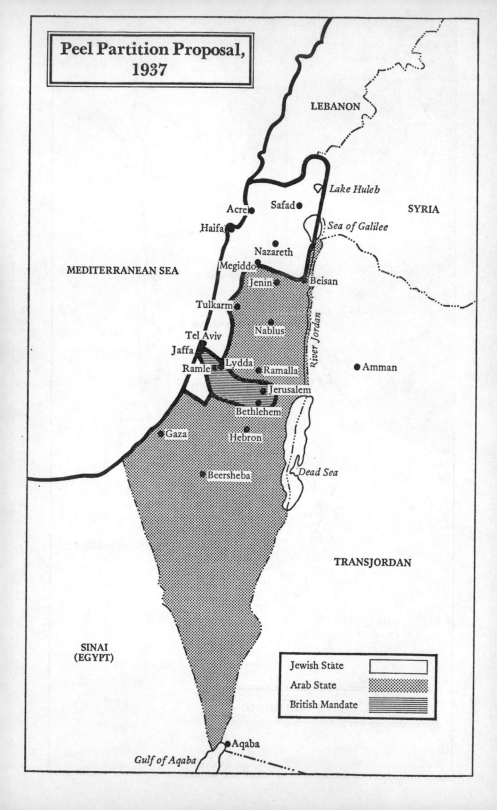

Peel Partition Proposal, 1937

LEBANON

Lake Huleb

SYRIA

Acre● Safad●

Haifa● *Sea of Galilee*

Nazareth●

MEDITERRANEAN SEA

Megiddo●

Jenin● ●Beisan

Tulkarm●

Nablus●

River Jordan

Tel Aviv●

Jaffa●

Ramle● Lydda●

●Ramalla ●Amman

●Jerusalem

Bethlehem●

Gaza● Hebron●

Beersheba● *Dead Sea*

TRANSJORDAN

SINAI
(EGYPT)

Jewish State

Arab State

British Mandate

●Aqaba

Gulf of Aqaba

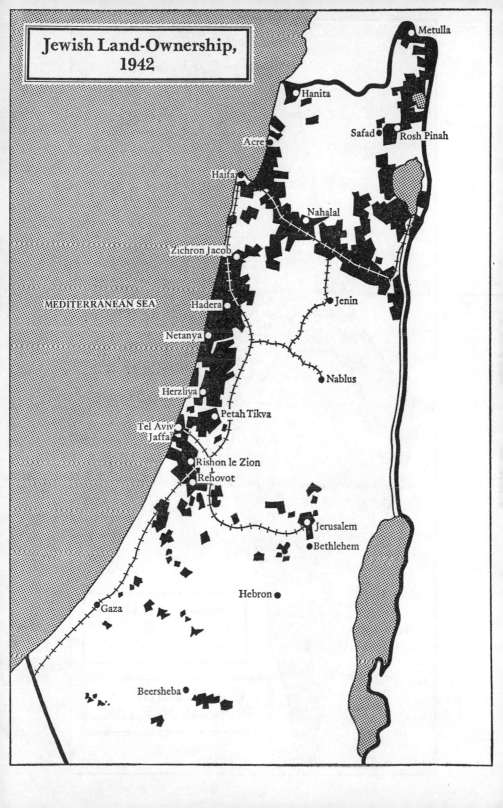

Jewish Land-Ownership, 1942

Metulla

Hanita

Safad

Rosh Pinah

Acre

Haifa

Nahalal

Zichron Jacob

MEDITERRANEAN SEA

Jenin

Hadera

Netanya

Nablus

Herzliya

Petah Tikva

Tel Aviv
Jaffa

Rishon le Zion

Rehovot

Jerusalem

Bethlehem

Hebron

Gaza

Beersheba

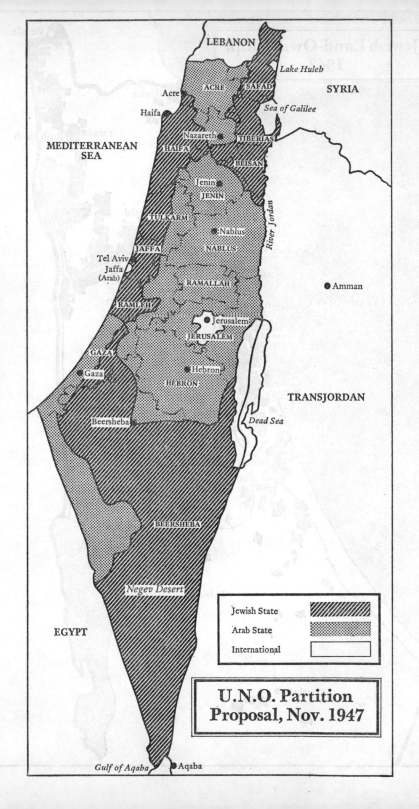

LEBANON

Lake Huleb

SYRIA

ACRE

SAFAD

Acre

Sea of Galilee

Haifa

MEDITERRANEAN
SEA

Nazareth

TIBERIAS

HAIFA

BEISAN

Jenin

River Jordan

JENIN

TULKARM

Nablus

JAFFA

NABLUS

Tel Aviv

Jaffa
(Arab)

RAMALLAH

Amman

RAMLEH

Jerusalem

JERUSALEM

GAZA

Hebron

Gaza

HEBRON

TRANSJORDAN

Beersheba

Dead Sea

Negev Desert

BEERSHEBA

Jewish State	
Arab State	
International	

EGYPT

**U.N.O. Partition
Proposal, Nov. 1947**

Gulf of Aqaba

Aqaba

ISRAEL
(Armistice
Boundaries, 1949)

LEBANON

Lake Huleh

SYRIA

Galilee

Sea of Galilee

Haifa

MEDITERRANEAN SEA

River Jordan

Tel
Aviv

JORDAN

Jerusalem

Gaza

Gaza Strip

Dead Sea

Beersheba

Negev Desert

SINAI PENINSULA
(EGYPT)

Demilitarized Zone

Eilat

Aqaba

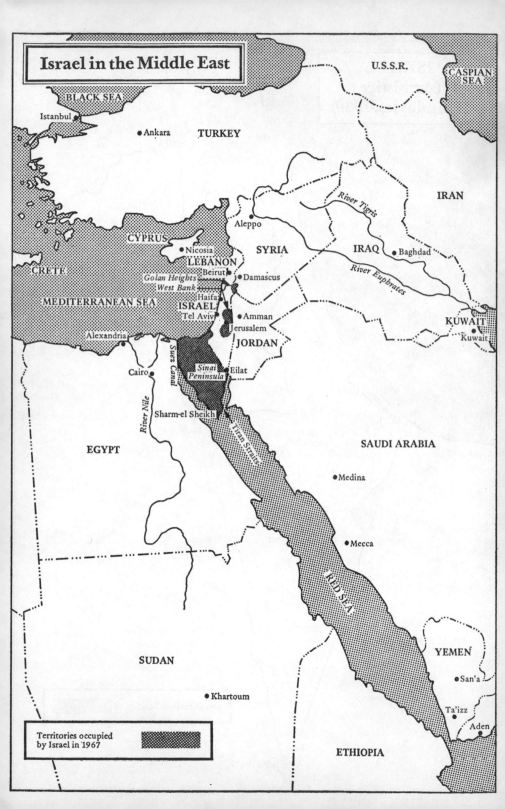

Israel in the Middle East

Territories occupied
by Israel in 1967

NOTES

To avoid proliferation of footnotes they are reserved as far as possible for reference to Hebrew sources and materials otherwise relatively inaccessible to the general reader. The author's indebtedness to works in the English language is recorded below in the bibliography. Except where attributed to English-language sources, all quotations from Hebrew given in the text are translated by the author. While in the text transliterations are based on simple usage, those in the footnotes are more pedantically formulated.

CHAPTER 1 THE JEWS OF EUROPE IN THE NINETEENTH CENTURY

1. For an elaboration of this view see J. B. Agus, *The Meaning of Jewish History* (New York, 2 vols., 1963), I, chapters 2 and 3.
2. S. W. Baron, *Modern Nationalism and Religion* (New York, 1960), p. 241. It should be emphasized that the foregoing generalizations apply to the nineteenth century. It is necessary to recast the analysis to account for Jewish responses in the twentieth century. Major events such as the growth of American Jewry, the Nazi massacre of European Jewry, the emergence of the Zionist movement and the establishment of the state of Israel posed new challenges to the maintenance of Jewish identity no less demanding than emancipation.

CHAPTER 2 ZIONIST DOCTRINES AND NINETEENTH-CENTURY PALESTINE

1. Cf. I. Yeshayahu and A. Zadok (eds), *Shevut Teman* (Tel Aviv, 1945).
2. M. Braslavsky, *Tenu'at ha-Po'alim ha-Erez-Yisraelit* (Tel Aviv, 4 vols, 1955, 1956, 1959, 1962), I, p. 19; Z. Even-Shoshan (Rozenstein), *Toledot Tenu'at ha-Po'alim be-Erez-Yisrael* (Tel Aviv, 3 vols, 1955, 1966), I, pp. 17–31; S. N. Eisenstadt, *Perakim be-Toledot Tenu'at ha-Po'alim ha-Yehudit ad 1905* (Merhavia, 1944), I.
3. The total investment by the Baron in Palestine is estimated at over £5 million.
4. As a result of misinformation at the time this has become known in Zionist historiography as the 'Uganda' proposal. Actually, the territory offered corresponds to a portion of Kenya.

CHAPTER 3 FOUNDING FATHERS: THE SECOND IMMIGRATION (1904–14)

1. L. Greenberg, *The Jews in Russia* (New Haven, 2 vols, 1944, 1951), II, p. 74.
2. Even-Shoshan, *Toledot Tenu'at ha-Po'alim*, I, pp. 266–7.
3. Braslavsky, *Tenu'at ha-Po'alim*, I, p. 81; Y. Ben-Zvi, *Po'alei Zion be-Aliyah ha-Sheniyya* (Tel Aviv, 1950); J. C. Brenner, *Perake Keriya mi-Ketavav* (Tel Aviv, no date, ?1946); B. Habbas, *Sefer ha-Aliyah ha-Sheniyya* (Tel Aviv, 1947); D. Kalai, *Ha-Aliyah ha-Sheniyya* (Tel Aviv, 1954).
4. Berl Katznelson, as quoted in Even-Shoshan, *Toledot Tenu'at ha-Po'alim*, I, pp. 62–3, and in M. Shmueli, *Perakim bi-Toledot ha-Zionut ve-Tenu'at ha-Avodah*, 4th ed. (Tel Aviv, 1953), II, pp. 101–2; see also B. Katznelson, *Perakim le-Toledot Tenu'at ha-Po'alim (Ketavim*, XI), 2nd ed. (Tel Aviv, 1949); Y. Erez, *Berl Katznelson: Ha-Ish u-Pe'alo* (Tel Aviv, no date); D. Tidhar, *Enzeklopedia le-Haluzei ha-Yishuv u-Bonav* (Tel Aviv, 10 vols, 1947–59).
5. A. Hertzberg, *The Zionist Idea* (New York, 1960), p. 369; M. Kushnir (ed.), *A. D. Gordon: Zikhronot ve-Divrei Ha'arakha* (Tel Aviv, 1947).
6. S. Avineri, in a suggestive article, 'Israel in the Post-Ben-Gurion Era', *Midstream* (September, 1965), pp. 16–32, argues forcibly that the democratic political culture of Israel is derived from the traditions of the *kehillah*. Of course, this is not a researchable issue. But it appears to the present author that a better hypothesis might attribute to the religious and communal tradition of east-European Jewry the dynastic, oligarchical and autocratic tendencies manifest in Israeli politics, while reserving to the pioneering 'frontier' conditions and socialist ideology the paternity of democratic values.
7. S. Zemach, *An Introduction to the History of Labour Settlement in Palestine*, 2nd ed., trans. S. Satten (Tel Aviv, 1946), p. 40.
8. Even-Shoshan, *Toledot Tenu'at ha-Po-alim*, I, p. 183 and p. 204.
9. J. S. Bentwich, *Education in Israel* (London, 1965), p. 14.

CHAPTER 4 FOUNDING FATHERS: THE THIRD IMMIGRATION (1914–24)

1. Trumpeldor had served with distinction in the Tsarist army in the Russo-Japanese war.
2. A facsimile of the letter is reproduced in L. Stein, *The Balfour Declaration* (London, 1961), frontispiece.
3. J. Klausner, *Mannihei ha-Yesod shel Medinat Yisrael* (Jerusalem, 1955), pp. 196–251, gives the best summary of Jabotinsky's views in this context.
4. As quoted in M. Bar-Zohar, *The Armed Prophet* (London, 1967), p. 32. The source of the quotation is not given, but comparable remarks by Ben-Gurion in 1915 are found in D. Ben-Gurion, *Anakhu u-Shekheineinu* (Tel Aviv, 1931), pp. 1–12.

5. D. Ben-Gurion, *Zikhronot* (Tel Aviv, 1971), p. 97.
6. Quoted in B. Litvinoff, *Ben-Gurion of Israel* (New York, 1954), p. 84; see also Ben-Gurion, *Zikhronot*, p. 166.
7. See especially, *Kuntras* (published by Ahdut ha-Avodah) and *Ha-Po'el ha-Zair* (published by the party of that name).
8. Literally, 'organization' or 'federation', the colloquial abbreviation of *Ha-Histadrut ha-Kelalit shel ha-Ovdim ha-Ivrim be-Erez-Yisrael* (The General Federation of Hebrew Workers in Palestine). Following the admission of Arab workers to full membership the name was modified in 1959 to become The General Federation of Labour in Israel.
9. For details of the founding convention see D. Kalai, *Eikh Noseda ha-Histadrut?*, 4th ed. (Tel Aviv, 1952); Even Shoshan, *Toledot Tenu'at ha-Po'alim*, I, pp. 431–47; Braslavsky, *Tenu'at ha-Po'alim*, I, pp. 198–204; Katznelson, *Ketavim*, XI, pp. 212–17.
10. Together with two colleagues who later found their place in the second echelon of national leadership. Ben-Gurion was effectively the executive officer of the movement in its first years.
11. D. Ben-Gurion, *Mi-Ma'amad le'Am* (Tel Aviv, 1955), pp. 210–15, gives the complete text of his proposal, and pp. 182–209 reproduce his report to the convention of 1923; the constitution as adopted is in Histadrut Executive Committee, *Hukot ha-Histadrut*, 2nd ed. (Tel Aviv, 1952), pp. 21–9.

CHAPTER 5 THE ARABS, THE JEWS AND THE BRITISH (1917–39)

1. The first census was conducted by the British administration in October 1922, giving a total population of approximately 757,000, including 591,000 Muslims, 75,000 Christians, 7,000 Druzes, and 84,000 Jews. The accuracy of the census findings was called in question by both Arab and Zionist spokesmen.
2. However painful to those displaced, the proportions of the problem caused by Jewish purchases were probably exaggerated by propaganda. Dispossession of the fellahin during the mandate was on a relatively small scale because most of the land acquired by the Zionists was uninhabited wilderness or swamp. Much displacement was due to transactions within the Arab economy, reflecting a process of concentration of ownership by Arab landowners and usurers. The steady increase of the Arab population unaccompanied by improved cultivation was also a factor pressing on the land. The Palestine government reported that at the end of 1935 there were 664 Arab families made landless by Zionist purchases: Esco Foundation For Palestine, *Palestine: A Study of Jewish, Arab, and British Policies* (New Haven, 1947), II, pp. 704–22.
3. This estimate is given by A. Cohen, *Israel and the Arab World* (London 1970), p. 225. A large portion of Zionist funds reaching the Arab sector of the economy came into the hands of the landowners and was therefore of dubious benefit to the fellahin.

4. Although Samuel, Bentwich and Hyamson were Jews they may properly be described as 'British-Zionists' since they had little affinity for the east-European and Palestinian Zionism. In matters of policy they displayed some affinity for 'cultural Zionism', the movement which provided perhaps the only link between non-Jewish and Jewish Zionists outside the socialist movement. Only Bentwich fully under stood Palestinian Zionism, but this was due to the extraordinary breadth of his sympathies rather than to common ideological or political ground. As for Storrs, no Zionist then and few today would concede his description as 'British' or any other sort of Zionist. But the reader of his memoirs could hardly mistake the profoundly romantic Zionism suffusing them.

5. The British High Commissioners were Sir Herbert Samuel (1920–5), Field Marshall Lord Plumer (1925–8), Sir John Chancellor (1928–31), General Sir A. Wauchope (1931–8), Sir Harold MacMichael (1938–44), Field Marshall Lord Gort (1944–5), and General Sir A. Cunningham (1945–8).

CHAPTER 6 FOUNDATIONS OF JEWISH SELF-GOVERNMENT (1917–39)

1. M. Michaeli, *Sehar ha-Huz u-Yevu ha-Hon be-Yisrael* (Tel Aviv, 1963), p. 2, and R. Shershevsky, *Mivneh ha-Meshek ha-Yehudi be-Erez-Yisrael u-be-Yisrael* (Jerusalem, 1968).

2. Histadrut Executive Committee, *Bi-Shenat ha-Sheloshim* (Tel Aviv, no date, ?1952), Table A, pp. 3–4 and Table 2, p. 32. The lack of an authoritative census of the labour force made it difficult for the Histadrut accurately to estimate its degree of organization among those eligible for membership.

3. Cf. Histadrut Executive Committee, *Pirkei Din ve-Heshbon le-Ve'ida ha-Shiv'it* (Tel Aviv, 1949), pp. 391–3.

4. Contributions by American trade unions to the Histadrut budget ranged from two-thirds to three-quarters of its revenue: Histadrut Executive Committee, *Ha-Bikkoret ba-Histadrut* (Tel Aviv, 1949), pp. 46–7.

5. Even-Shoshan, *Toledot Tenu'at ha-Po'alim*, III, pp. 225–40. A third of the *kevuzah* groups were organized for hired labour in the rural towns, and had not yet settled on their own lands.

6. A compendium of speeches and unity proposals put forward in the mid-thirties is B. Katznelson (ed.), *Ha-Kibbutz ve-ha-Kevuzah: Yalkut li-Birur She'elat ha-Ihud* (Tel Aviv, 1940); cf. also Katznelson's address to a labour convention: '*Hevelei Ihud u-Shelavei Ihud*', *Ha-Po'el ha-Za'ir* (Tel Aviv, 1938).

7. Even-Shoshan, *Toledot Tenu'at ha-Po'alim*, III, pp. 257–66.

8. Moshe Smilansky, in 1938, as quoted by D. Gildai, 'Yuzema Peratit, Hon Le'ummi ve-Gibbush Politi shel ha-Yemmin', in *Ha-Mivneh ha-Hevrati shel Yisrael*, ed. S. N. Eisenstadt *et al.* (Jerusalem, 1966), pp. 85–97. This section is indebted to Giladi's analysis.

9. The following table (adapted from Braslavsky, *Tenu'at ha-Po'alim*, I,

p. 267 and II, p. 37), shows the results of the Histadrut elections in 1923 and 1927:

Party	Convention delegates, 1923	1927
Ahdut ha-Avodah	69	108
Ha-Po'el ha-Zair	36	54
Ha-Shomer ha-Za'ir and left-wing opposition groups	17	34
Others	8	5
Total mandates	130	201

10. Abraham Stavsky, a young revisionist just arrived in the country, was charged with the murder, convicted in the trial court, and acquitted on appeal for lack of evidence. Tension between the Histadrut and the revisionist movement was greatly exacerbated by the murder and the trial, and bad feeling persisted for many years. Insiders in the labour movement were sure that the murder was a revisionist conspiracy, while the revisionists were equally sure that the trial was rigged by collusion between Mapai and the British police. The records of the trial betray a hasty and ill-conceived prosecution case, which, if it did not prove Stavsky's innocence, certainly did not prove him guilty in the light of accepted judicial norms: Hassolel Partnership, *The Arlosoroff Murder Trial, Speeches and Documents* (Jerusalem, 1934), and H. B. Samuel, 'Who Killed Arlosoroff?' (unpublished typescript by Stavsky's defence attorney, no date, available at the Wiener Library in London). One of the men who had been involved in a senior capacity in the police investigation of the murder revealed (or alleged) in 1955 that two Arabs had confessed to the murder but had been pressed by British officials to withdraw their confession so as to rescue the police from having to admit that they had mistakenly charged Stavsky. (The police were at the time pursuing the revisionist youth movement which had begun to resort to arms in the underground). See Jewish Telegraphic Agency, *Daily News Bulletin*, 208, 16 June 1955.

11. The following table, adapted from Braslavsky, *Tenu'at ha-Po'alim*, II, p. 263 and III, p. 145, shows the results of elections to the fourth and fifth Histadrut conventions:

Party	Delegates		Delegates	
	1933	% votes	1942	% votes
Mapai	165	81·5	278	69·3
Ha-Shomer ha-Zair	16	8·1	77	19·2
Left Po'alei Zion	16	8·1	17	4·3
Others	4	2·3	20	5·0
Totals	201	100·0	*392	*97·8

(* Nine mandates representing 2·2 per cent of the vote were unfilled, following the expulsion from the convention of an anti-Zionist communist group.)

12. For the early evolution of the party see E. Margalit, *Ha-Shomer ha-Ẓa'ir: mi-Eidat Ne'urim li-Marksizm Mahapkhani* (Tel Aviv, 1971).

13. The rise of the labour movement to ascendancy within the international Zionist movement is shown in the following table of election results for congresses held between 1921 and 1939, adapted from Braslavsky, *Tenu'at ha-Po'alim*, II, p. 245 and III, p. 509; I. Cohen, *The Zionist Movement* (New York, 1946), p. 365.

Congress	Year	% Labour delegates
12th	1921	8
13th	1923	21
14th	1925	18
15th	1927	22
16th	1929	26
17th	1931	29
18th	1933	44
19th	1935	45
20th	1937	42
21st	1939	41

14. M. Atias (ed.), *Sefer ha-Te'udot shel ha-Va'ad ha-Le'ummi li-Keneset Yisrael bi-Ereẓ Yisrael, 1918–1948* (Jerusalem, 1963); S. Sager, 'Pre-State Influences on Israel's Parliamentary System', *Parliamentary Affairs*, XXV, 1 (London, Winter 1971/2), pp. 29–49.

CHAPTER 7 THE TRIANGULAR CONFLICT (1920–39)

1. In a speech at a Zionist meeting, published in 1907, as quoted by Cohen, *Israel and Arabs*, p. 67 (emphasis in original).

2. In 1932, in a mood of apparent despondency, Haim Arlosoroff wrote to Weizman on the problem of Zionist-Arab relations. In his letter he contemplated a forcible seizure of power by the Zionists as a necessary means to contain Arab opposition: H. Arlosoroff, *Mivhar Katavim u-Pirkei Ḥayyim* (Tel Aviv, 1958), pp. 326–36.

3. The failure of their movement to influence events has tended to eliminate these men from the pages of history. Since they correctly foresaw the consequences of Zionist policy it may be not inappropriate to accord them the space of a footnote. In addition to those mentioned in the text, the advocates of bi-nationalism included Jacob Thon (1880–1950), director of the Palestine Land Development Corporation; Ḥayyim Margalit Kalvarisky (1868–1947), the director of PICA (Baron Rothschild's land trust); Moshe Smilansky (1874–1953), the distinguished head of the Farmers' Federation. It is interesting that Ruppin and the others, who were those most directly involved in land transactions with the Arabs, were unanimously impressed by the necessity for bi-national co-operation. The magazine of the movement, *Ner*, was published by 'Reb Binyamin' (Joshua Redler-Feldman, 1880–1957). Among the prominent academic expo-

nents of bi-nationalism were Professors Scholem, Bergmann, and Simon of the Hebrew University. W. Senator, a 'non-Zionist' member of the Jewish Agency executive, and Edwin (later Viscount) Samuel, the son of the first High Commissioner, were also associated with the movement.

4. A memorandum on these lines was submitted to the Jewish Agency in 1930 by Ernst Simon (b. 1899), quoted at length in S. L. Hattis, *The Bi-National Idea in Palestine During Mandatory Times* (Haifa, 1970), pp. 53–4.

5. Ben-Gurion, *Zikhronot*, p. 299.

6. D. Ben-Gurion, *Medinat Yisrael ha-Mehudeshet*, I, p. 57, and Ben-Gurion, *Mi-Ma'amad le'Am*, pp. 474–7.

7. A. Ruppin, *Be-Vinyan ha-Arez ve-ha-Am, 1920–1942 (Perake Hayyim, III)* (Tel Aviv, 1968), p. 203 and pp. 255–8.

8. D. Ben-Gurion, *Pegishot im Manhigim Aravim* (Tel Aviv, 1967), p. 84, and M. Sharett, *Yoman Medini* (Tel Aviv, 1968), p. 159.

9. In July 1932, in a speech to a Mapai conference, quoted in D. Ben-Gurion, *Rebirth and Destiny of Israel* (New York, 1954), p. 75; cf. Ben-Gurion, *Zikhronot*, pp 511–19

10 Ben-Gurion, *Rebirth*, p 81.

11. B. Katznelson, *Revolutionary Constructivism* (New York, 1937), p. 31.

12. The Haycraft Commission.

CHAPTER 8 FOUNDATIONS OF JEWISH SELF-DEFENCE (1920–39)

1. E. Golomb, 'Rashei Perakim be-Toledot ha-Haganah', in M. Bogdan (ed.), *Ma'asim u-Megamot* (Tel Aviv, 1942), pp. 233–90. Also, Ben-Zion Dinur (general editor), *Sefer Toledot ha-Haganah*, I; H. H. Ben-Sasson and S. Avigur, *Mi-Hitgonnenut le-Haganah*, 2nd ed. (Tel Aviv, 1964), Part 2, pp. 659–65, and II; Y. Slutsky, *Mi-Haganah le-Ma'avak*, 3rd ed. (Tel Aviv, 1971), Part 1, pp. 95–109.

2. Dinur (ed.), *Haganah*, I, Ben-Sasson and Avigur, *Mi-Hitgonnenut*, Part 2, p. 658.

3. Golomb (1893–1945), although still a teenager, was from that time the leading political spokesman of the labour movement on defence matters.

4. Dinur (ed.), *Haganah*, II; Slutsky, *Mi-Haganah*, Part 1, pp. 426–32 and pp. 574–85.

5. Haganah 'B' was also known as Irgun 'B', for *Irgun Zevai Le'ummi* (National Military Organization); this title was officially adopted by the revisionist group seceding from Haganah 'B': Dinur (ed.), *Haganah*, II; Slutsky, *Mi-Haganah*, Part 2, p. 1053. The name was commonly abbreviated 'Ezel' or 'Irgun'.

6. The first phase of the Arab revolt, which reached a peak in August 1936, took the lives of eighty Jews, while in the second phase 415 Jews were killed: Dinur (ed.), *Haganah*, II; Slutsky, *Mi-Haganah*, part 2, p. 650 and p. 801.

7. Financed in the main by the Jewish community organs with some assistance from the British authorities.

8. Wingate (1903–44) later achieved great fame as a major-general in command of the 'Chindits' in the Burmese theatre during the second world war.

9. In mid-1938 the National Council, representing all parties but the revisionists, imposed a defence levy on the community. This was a voluntary tax assessed by local committees and collected by volunteers, backed by effective social sanctions and occasional intimidation by Haganah members. In its first year of operation the community defence treasury raised over P£150,000, covering seventy per cent of Haganah's expenditure: cf. Y. Avidar, *Ba-Derekh le-Ẓahal: Zikhronot* (Tel Aviv, 1970), p. 114.

10. A scientist at the Haifa Technion who had acquired military experience in Russia during the first world war.

CHAPTER 9 THE STRUGGLE FOR THE SUCCESSION:
PALESTINE AND THE EUROPEAN HOLOCAUST (1937–45)

1. The following table summarizes the results of the election to the sixth convention in 1944, adapted from Histadrut Executive Committee, *Sekira al Pe'ulot ha-Va'ad ha-Po'el bi-Shanim 1956–1959* (Tel Aviv, 1960), p. 157.

Party	Votes	%	Delegates
Mapai	57,135	53·8	216
Ha-Shomer ha-Ẓa'ir	21,959	20·7	83
Le-Aḥdut ha-Avodah	18,840	17·8	71
Others	8,368	7·7	31
Totals	106,302	100·0	401

2. In July 1938, on the initiative of President Roosevelt, the representatives of thirty-one countries held a conference at Evian in France to discuss the rescue of refugees from Nazism. Apart from the Dominican Republic, which offered asylum for a hundred thousand Jews from Germany and Austria, none of the participating countries showed willingness to receive refugee immigration on a large scale. The Zionists were not displeased by the failure of the Evian conference, since the opening up of barriers to immigration elsewhere would have eased the pressure on Palestine. On the other hand, the reluctance of the western countries to accept large numbers of refugees strengthened the Zionist claim that the Jews had nowhere else to go but Palestine.

CHAPTER 10 THE STRUGGLE FOR THE SUCCESSION:
THE STATE OF ISRAEL ESTABLISHED (1939–48)

1. Israel Rokaḥ (1896–1959), mayor of Tel Aviv, was the leading spokesman of the non-labour wing of the Haganah. As head of the largest municipality in the country he exerted the strongest influence on the revenue arm of the Haganah.

2. Dori (b. 1899) was Haganah commander of the Haifa district since 1931. An engineer by training, he later became president of the Haifa Technion.
3. Galili (b. 1910) was a member of the left wing of Mapai, later a leader of Le'Ahdut ha-Avodah and a minister in the government of Israel.
4. Sneh (1909–72) was a man of acute intellect and great ability, a doctor by training. Immediately upon his arrival in the country in 1940 from Poland he came into the higher councils of Palestine Jewry. Later he moved gradually leftwards in politics, eventually becoming leader of the Communist Party.
5. Allon (b. 1918) was born in Palestine. Along with his rival Dayan, he learned military practice with Yizhak Sade. He later became a leader of *Le'Ahdut ha'Avodah* and a minister in the government of Israel.
6. David Razi'el (1910–41) was regarded by the Irgunists as a military genius and magnetic leader.
7. Quotation from S. Katz, *Days of Fire* (London, 1968), pp. 83–4.
8. Sneh immediately committed to writing his account of the conversation. It is reproduced in full in Dinur (ed.), *Haganah*, III; Y. Slutsky, *Mi-Ma'avak le-Milhama* (Tel Aviv, 1972), Part 3, pp. 1887–93. Begin gave his account several years later in M. Begin, *Ha-Mered* (Jerusalem, 1950), published in English as *The Revolt* (Tel Aviv, no date, ?1951), pp. 137–41. The two recollections are not identical, but neither are they incompatible.
9. The committee of twelve was made up of six Britons and six Americans, and was to report its findings to both governments. Three of its members have published detailed accounts of the inquiry: see bibliography.
10. Critics of British rule, from a variety of ideological standpoints, have contended that Britain had consciously followed a policy of 'divide and rule' throughout the mandatory period. This is perhaps somewhat exaggerated. For most of the mandatory period the evidence does not justify this generalization.
11. He was under surveillance rather than detention, but was not legally permitted to leave France pending possible requests for his extradition as a war criminal. In Palestine it was suspected by many Zionists that Britain had assisted the Mufti's flight in order to counter Zionist activism. Another view held that France had assisted the escape in order to impede British policies in the middle east.
12. The King David Hotel outrage was the occasion of much dispute and recrimination between the Haganah and the Irgun. The two bodies had jointly planned the operation, but Sadeh, the acting Haganah chief of staff, claimed that the Irgun had ignored a Haganah order to delay the attack, and also that the Irgun had executed the plan at a different hour from that which had been agreed, without informing the Haganah. The Irgun, on the other hand, felt that the Haganah evaded its responsibility in order to bring odium on the

Irgun when it became likely that the heavy casualties would evoke British reprisals on the population. The Irgun gave ample warning by telephone of the impending explosion. It was rumoured at the time that a high British official had contemptuously chosen to ignore warnings to evacuate the building. Dinur (ed.), *Haganah*, III; Slutsky, *Mi-Ma'avak*, Part 2, pp. 898–901; Begin, *Revolt*, pp. 212–30.

13. UNSCOP was composed of the representatives of eleven countries: Australia, Canada, Czechoslovakia, Guatemala, India, Iran, Netherlands, Peru, Sweden, Uruguay and Yugoslavia.

14. Australia abstained out of deference to Britain.

15. Kaplan (1891–1952), had for long been treasurer of the Jewish Agency, and was the chief economic spokesman of Mapai.

16. Remez (1886–1951), succeeded Ben-Gurion as head of the Histadrut when the latter moved to the centre of the national stage. He also served as chairman of the National Council.

17. The instrument is officially designated the 'Scroll of the establishment of the State of Israel'.

CHAPTER 11 WAR, ARMISTICE AND IMMIGRATION (1947–51)

1. D. Ben-Gurion, 'Mi-Ḥazon ha-Medina ad Milḥemet ha-Kommemiut', in Ẓahal, *Toledot Milḥemet ha-Kommemiut* (Tel Aviv, 1959), p. 43.

2. It is not possible to assess the armoury of the Haganah with exactitude. But even sources that wish to show that the Haganah's own accounts are gross underestimates concede in effect that the available arms were insufficient to provide for the available manpower: see Khalidi (ed.), *From Haven To Conquest* (Beirut, 1971), pp. 861–6.

3. Irgun spokesmen persistently deny that the Dir Yassin operation was a massacre, describing this as a blood libel. Although the Israeli foreign ministry (naturally enough) in its propaganda abroad seeks to mitigate the atrocity, if not to exonerate its perpetrators, the semi-official history of the Haganah, for Israeli readers, is quite unequivocal in the severity of its judgement: Dinur (ed.), *Haganah*, III; Slutsky, *Mi-Ma'avak*, Part 3, pp. 1546–8.

4. Over a third of these were from areas outside Israel's borders as designated by the UNO partition plan.

5. Israel has since that time maintained that the Arab flight was due to instructions by Arab leaders to their people to leave their homes, to make way for the incoming Arab armies. This is not, however, a very plausible account, and it has never been substantiated by valid evidence. An article by Erskine Childers, 'The Other Exodus', in *The Spectator* (London, 12 May 1961), and the correspondence to which it gave rise, provide a summary of the range of disputed explanations of the flight. Although it is inconclusive on the score whether any broadcasts by Arab radio ordering evacuation actually took place, the BBC monitoring of broadcasts in the region certainly disclosed no such radio orders, while it did catch several broadcasts

in a contrary sense. The flight of Arabs within Palestine was first considered noteworthy by monitors at the end of January 1948: Monitoring Service of the British Broadcasting Corporation, *Summary of World Broadcasts* (Reading, 1947–9), Nos. 1–99, 36, p. 52. That the Haganah in the early phase of the war was concerned to restrain the flight may be inferred from a Haganah broadcast in Arabic on 18 February, relaying an article from the Egyptian press which branded Arabs who left Palestine as cowards: 39, p. 67. A Damascus Radio broadcast picked up by American monitors on 4 April 1948 relayed a communique of the Arab Higher Committee calling on all Arab employees in Palestine to continue at their posts (the reference appears to be to government employees), 45, p. 64. On 24 April American monitors recorded a Lebanese broadcast reporting that there were 23,000 old men, women and children in the country, refugees from Palestine, and that 'young men who were able to fight have been returned to Palestine in compliance with the request of the Arab authorities,' 48, p. 60.

6. The number of refugees is, of course, another of the many issues of fact disputed by the parties to the conflict. The best estimate, based on thorough investigation not too distant from the events, would appear to be that of the Clapp Mission (Economic Survey Mission for the Middle East) set up by UNO in 1949, which placed the refugee total at 726,000 as at 30 September 1949. These were distributed as follows: the Arab portion of Palestine which came under Jordanian control, 280,000; Egypt, 7,000; Gaza (held by Egypt), 190,000; Iraq, 4,000; Jordan, 70,000; Lebanon, 100,000; Syria, 75,000: D. Peretz, *Israel and the Palestine Arabs* (Washington, 1958), p. 30.

7. In the summer of 1947 Ben-Gurion had appointed Galili head of command and asked Dori to continue as chief of staff. At the outbreak of the war Dori was unable to work regularly owing to illness, and Galili acted as military chief of staff in addition to his other responsibilities. Yigal Sukenik (Yadin) was chief of operations in the general staff and Yigal Allon headed the Palmach. These were among Ben-Gurion's closest advisers in the early part of the war.

8. On the day the state was declared the Haganah was able to field some 30,000 troops of whom 40 per cent bore rifles (in addition to the static settlement defences of about the same number): Dinur (ed.), *Haganah*, III; Slutsky, *Mi-Ma'avak*, Part 2, pp. 1457–62. Estimates of the invasion forces (in addition to the 5–7,000 of the Arab Liberation Army already engaged) range from 21,500 (J. and D. Kimche, *A Clash of Destinies*, New York, 1960, p. 162) to less than 14,000 (Khalidi, ed., *Conquest*, p. 867). The main discrepancy between conflicting estimates is in reference to the size of the invading Egyptian force.

9. The truce was not immediately implemented on all fronts. At Sejera in the north Kaukji's forces continued an attack begun on the previous day, and bombarded the settlement until 13 June. During

this action, on 11 June 1948, Captain Isaiah Morris, M.C., a volunteer doctor from Britain, was killed while tending the wounded on the frontline: Dinur (ed.), *Haganah*, III; Slutsky, *Mi-Ma'avak*, Part 2, p. 1470.

10. The conflicting versions of the incident are given in Begin, *Revolt*, pp. 154–76, and Katz, *Days of Fire*, pp. 233–50 on the one hand, and Ben-Gurion, *Medinat Yisrael*, I, pp. 179–96, on the other. Whether Ben-Gurion and Galili trapped the Irgun into a staged showdown with the government or whether they had acted in good faith in the belief that the Irgun was preparing a coup, it was clear that the persisting partisan habits of the Irgun were a threat to government authority and national security. From the accounts of Begin and Katz it is clear that the Irgun saw the arrival of the *Altalena* with its weapons as the crowning triumph of the 'revolt', the climax of the organization's heroic struggle. They seemed to believe that these weapons would save the country from military disaster. What they failed to appreciate was that the government was the better judge of the need for arms, and that the Irgun campaign for funds to finance its own procurement, *after* the state was established, was a disruptive and possibly dangerous activity. Ben-Gurion's diary records on 15 June the arrival or despatch of over thirty thousand rifles and three thousand machine guns, with millions of rounds of ammunition, in addition to heavy equipment including thirty-one aircraft. The Irgun's belief that its own efforts would determine the country's security had become a pathetic illusion.

CHAPTER 12 CONSTITUTIONAL TRANSITION (1948–53)

1. See especially, Mazkirut Va'adat ha-Mazav, 'Minhal ha-Memshala be-Medina ha-Ivrit: Haza'a le-Mivne ha-Mahlekot, Mangenonan, ve-Takziveihen' (Jerusalem/Tel Aviv, April 1948), mimeo; and 'Gilyon Minhelet ha'Am, Zavim ve-Hoda'ot' (Tel Aviv, May 1948).

2. To remove doubt about the territorial application of Israeli law the government on 16 September 1948 enacted the Area of Jurisdiction and Powers Ordinance, Government Printer, *Laws of The State of Israel, Authorised Translation* (Jerusalem, 1948), I, *Ordinances 5708–1948*, 29, p. 64. The ordinance stipulated that any law applying to the whole state would be deemed applicable to any part of Palestine which the minister of defence designated as occupied by the army.

3. The Law and Administration Ordinance, *L.S.I.*, I (*Ordinances, 1948*), pp. 7–12, in effect conferred on the government and its several ministers the emergency powers that the British High Commissioner had assumed under the Palestine (Defence) Order-In-Council of 18 March 1937 (Great Britain, *Parliamentary Papers: Statutes, Rules and Orders*, 225), to deal with the Arab revolt. The High Commissioner in 1945 extended and codified his powers (to deal now with Zionist terrorism) by issuing the Defence (Emergency) Regulations, 1945, *The Palestine Gazette, 1442, Regulations and Orders, Supplement 2*, pp.

1055–98. In 1951 the Knesset almost unanimously ruled that the regulations were incompatible with democratic government, and resolved to annul and replace them. This has not so far been done.

4. Results of the elections to the seventh convention of the Histadrut are summarized in the following table, adapted from Ha-Va'ad ha-Po'el shel ha-Histadrut, *Ha-Ve'ida ha-Shiv'it shel ha-Histadrut* (Tel Aviv, 1949), pp. 410–11.

Party	Votes	%
Mapai	79,286	57·06
Mapam	47,888	34·43
Ha'Oved ha-Zioni	5,227	3·76
Communist	3,658	2·63
Ha'Oved ha-Dati	2,948	2·12

5. *Divrei ha-Knesset*, 5, p. 1743.

6. In 1969 the Supreme Court (in Bergman v The Minister of Finance) asserted judicial review in a ruling in which it attributed supremacy to 'entrenched' portions of fundamental law.

7. Cf. Professor M. Silberg (Justice of the Supreme Court), *Ha-Ma'amad ha-Ishi be-Yisrael* (Jerusalem, 1965), pp. 62–76 and pp. 347–97.

CHAPTER 13 IDEOLOGICAL AND POLITICAL TRANSITION (1948–56)

1. Adapted from tables in Central Bureau of Statistics, *Statistical Abstract of Israel, 17* (Jerusalem, 1966), pp. 644–5 and 650.

2. However, since the period of anti-British terrorism in the 'forties, the religious parties had displayed an affinity with the nationalist right on issues involving the boundaries of Jewish sovereignty. Upon the re-emergence of such issues with the occupation of the west bank of Jordan after the 1967 war, religious nationalism has brought the orthodox factions into closer collusion with the right wing, a process which could well become the occasion for termination of the 'stable coalition'.

3. This small faction was composed of orthodox workers who tended to support Mapai, disapproving of party organization along religious lines.

4. Various accounts of the fiasco have been published, although Israel has maintained an understandable official silence about it. It appears that the spy-ring was instructed to sabotage western installations in Egypt on the theory that the resulting tension and instability would lead Britain to reconsider evacuating the Suez base. The spy-ring was apprehended and its members brought to trial; two were executed and one committed suicide in prison, while others were imprisoned and later released in an exchange of captives with Israel.

5. This became known when the 'Lavon Affair' broke in 1960, see chapter 16. While there did not appear to be any doubt that the forgery and perjury were contrived to implicate Lavon, this in itself did not prove that Lavon bore no responsibility for the fiasco.

CHAPTER 14 ECONOMIC AND SOCIAL DEVELOPMENT
(1952–64)

1. *Laws of the State of Israel*, IV, 20, pp. 68–82.
2. The complicated legal procedures of confiscation shrouded the process in obscurity. Estimates of the land of *Israeli* Arabs taken under the wing of the Development Authority range from forty to sixty per cent of their total holdings. In effect this was nationalized in the interests of immigrant absorption and extension of the areas farmed by the kibbuẓim adjoining Arab villages. See especially Peretz, *Palestine Arabs,* chapter 9, and Sabri Jirysis, *The Arabs in Israel, 1948–1966* (Beirut, 1968), chapter 2; also Walter Schwarz, *The Arabs in Israel* (London, 1959). Discussion in the Knesset and in the press in the spring of 1953 vented strong opposition to the government's confiscation policy. However, the general public was not well informed of the details of the land policy and knew little of the depredations suffered by the Arabs who had remained in the country. Official compensation for their lands was spurned by most of the Arabs and the episode embittered the Arab minority perhaps more than any other of their sufferings.
3. Business leaders frequently complained that private enterprise was excluded from heavy long-term investment by governmental favouritism to the Histadrut, and not on account of any unwillingness to undertake the risks.
4. This consisted not only in exposure to the egalitarian mores associated with the co-operative ideology. The settlement agencies regulated financial assistance to new moshavim in such a way as to compensate for poor land, so that the potential income of settlers was equalized, regardless of conditions.
5. A summary of the issue of wage differentials is given in English by M. Derber, 'Israel's Wage Differential: A Persisting Problem', in *University of Illinois Bulletin* (Institute of Labor and Industrial Relations), LX, 67, March 1963, Reprint Series 125; and 'National Wage Policy in Israel, 1948–1962', LX, 97, June 1963, Reprint Series 128.
6. This finding is presented by G. Hanoch, 'Income Differentials in Israel', in The Falk Project for Economic Research in Israel, Fifth Report: 1959 and 1960 (Jerusalem, 1961), pp. 37–130. According to a study based on data compiled for 1963–5, 25–30 per cent of Jewish children in Israel grew up in 'socially deprived' families, nearly ninety per cent of which were of African or Asian birth. Nearly two-thirds of these immigrated in the years immediately following the establishment of the state, and about a sixth of all those who immigrated from the orient remained in the class of the 'most deprived', nearly half of them living in new towns. Most of these had indeed been materially worse off in the countries from which they emigrated, but in Israel their expectations were higher and their position was worse relative to the rest of the population: J. M. Rosenfeld and E. Morris, 'Socially Deprived Jewish Families in Israel' in A. Jarus *et al.* (eds), *Children and Families in Israel: Some Mental Health Perspectives* (New York, 1970), pp. 427–64.

CHAPTER 15 THE ROAD TO WAR (1948–57)

1. According to Walter Eytan, who as director-general of the foreign ministry represented Israel at the talks, three separate groups of Palestinian refugees at their own expense sent representatives to the conference, only to be shunned by the delegates of the Arab states. They succeeded in making good contact only with the Israeli delegation: W. Eytan, *The First Ten Years* (New York, 1958), p. 54.
2. It has been alleged that Allen Dulles, head of the CIA, knew the outlines of the impending war but did not inform the President.
3. Bound by secrecy (not honoured by other participants), Ben-Gurion has never admitted taking part in this meeting.

CHAPTER 16 IDEOLOGICAL AND POLITICAL DEVELOPMENT (1955–66)

1. The following table summarizes the results of elections to the fourth Knesset, held in 1959:

Party	% vote	Seats
Mapai	38·2	47
Herut	13·5	17
General-Zionist	6·2	8
Mizrahi-ha-Po'el ha-Mizrahi	9·9	12
Agudah-Po'ale Agudah	4·7	6
Ahdut ha-Avodah	6·0	7
Mapam	7·2	9
Communist	2·8	3
Progressive	4·6	6
Arab parties (Mapai)	4·7	5
Others	2·2	—
Totals	100·0	120

For comparison with the 1955 results see p. 312 above, and note 1, chapter 13.

The following table summarizes results of the elections to the eighth and ninth Histadrut conventions, showing the relative positions of the parties in 1955 and 1959:

Party	1955 votes	%	1959 votes	%
Mapai	236,956	57·8	266,386	55·4
Ahdut ha-Avodah	59,968	14·6	81,860	17·0
Mapam	51,506	12·5	66,902	13·9
Liberal	21,543	5·2	27,754	5·8
General-Zionist	15,618	3·8	16,735	3·5
Communist	16,806	4·1	13,442	2·8
Ha-Oved ha-Dati	8,034	2·0	7,544	1·6

Adapted from the table in Histadrut Executive Committee, *Ha-Histadrut bein Ve'ida le-Ve'ida: Pirkei Din ve-Heshbon, 1959–1965* (Tel Aviv, no date, ?1965), p. 394.

2. For details of the Lavon affair and the range of disputed versions, see especially: E. Hasin and D. Horowitz, *Ha-Parasha* (Tel Aviv, 1961); Y. Arieli, *Ha-Kenunya* (Tel Aviv, 1965), a withering critique from a 'Lavonist' point of view; N. Yanai, *Kera be-Zameret* (Tel Aviv, 1969), a brilliant analysis (biassed in support of Ben-Gurion); D. Ben-Gurion, *Medinat Yisrael*, I, pp. 448–53 and II, pp. 597–647, 730–47; D. Ben-Gurion, *Devarim Kehavayatam* (Tel Aviv, 1965); A. Ziv (ed.), *Ha-Arez 1948–1958: Eser ha-Shanim ha-Rishonot* (Tel Aviv, 1958), and S. Shihor (ed.), *Ha-Arez 1958–1961: Yoman Iru'ei Shalosh ha-Shanim* (Tel Aviv, 1961).

3. The following table summarizes the results of the 1961 election:

Party	% vote	Seats
Mapai	34·7	42
Herut	13·8	17
Liberals (General-Zionist and Progressive)	13·6	17
Mizrahi-ha-Po'el ha-Mizrahi	9·8	12
Agudah-Po'alei Agudah	5·6	6
Ahdut ha-Avodah	6·6	8
Mapam	7·5	9
Communist	4·2	5
Arab parties (Mapai)	3·9	4
Others	0·3	—
Totals	100·0	120

Adapted from CBS, *Statistical Abstract 17*, pp. 644–5, 650.

4. His return to active electoral politics in 1965 led his enemies to infer that he had not intended irrevocably to withdraw from government. But the balance of evidence favours the view that he did so intend; his 1965 return was based on an *opposition* platform, and there is little likelihood that he expected to resume office as a result of the 1965 election.

5. To this end he assumed a conciliatory posture on matters on which Ben-Gurion had nursed old grievances: e.g., he permitted Jabotinsky's remains to be brought to Israel for burial; he became the first prime minister to visit the Arab community of Nazareth, and took initiative to relax military rule in border areas; he also sought to counteract the hostility to the Soviet Union which had long characterized the Israeli press, and arranged for his brother who lived in Russia to come on a visit to Israel.

6. In this they were assisted by Reuven Barkatt, the party secretary (later Speaker of the Knesset), who had become an antagonist of Lavon when the latter removed him from the top leadership of the Histadrut.

7. The following table summarizes the results of the election to the tenth convention of the Histadrut:

Party	Votes	%
Ma'arakh (Alignment of Mapai, Aḥdut ha-Avodah and Ha-Oved ha-Dati	333,068	50·88
Mapam	95,028	14·51
Rafi	79,428	12·13
Liberal	28,934	4·42
Ḥerut-General-Zionist	99,559	15·20
Israeli Communist	10,335	1·58
New Communist	8,369	1·28

Adapted from Histadrut Executive, *Pirkei Din ve-Ḥeshbon 1959–1965*, p. 394.

8. The following table summarizes the results of elections to the sixth Knesset:

Party	% vote	Seats
Alignment (Mapai and Aḥdut ha-Avodah)	36·7	45
Rafi	7·9	10
Mizraḥi-ha-Po'el ha-Mizraḥi	8·9	11
Agudah	3·3	4
Po'ale Agudah	1·8	2
Gaḥal (Ḥerut and General-Zionist)	21·3	26
Independent Liberal (Progressive)	3·8	5
Mapam	6·6	8
Communist	1·1	1
New Communist	2·3	3
Ha-Olam ha-Ze	1·2	1
Arab parties (Mapai)	3·8	4
Others	1·3	—
Totals	100·0	120

Adapted from CBS, *Statistical Abstract 17*, pp. 644–5, 650.

9. See M. Bar-Zohar, *Ha-Memuneh* (Jerusalem, 1971), p. 240, for an account of secret military ties with Germany.

CHAPTER 17 FOUNDATIONS OF NATIONAL IDENTITY

1. By asserting in international law its right to represent world Jewry, Israel in effect unilaterally defined the identity of Jews abroad in terms of its own national ideology, and imposed this on them in a context in which their resistance could be expected to be minimal.

2. This analysis is argued by Prof. Y. Leibowitz in an article published in 1953 in *Be-Terem*, and reproduced as 'The Crisis of Religion and the State of Israel' in Z. Zinger and A. Avi-Hai (eds), *Trends in Religion, Culture and Political Thought in Eretz Yisrael in the 20th Century* (Jerusalem, 1971), pp. 25–30. A useful discussion of Leibowitz' article is H. Weiner, 'Church and State in Israel', *Midstream* (New York, Winter 1962), pp. 3–14; a contrary view is presented in E.

Simon, 'Are We Israelis Still Jews?', in *Commentary* (New York, 1953), pp. 357–64. See also Y. Leibowitz, *Torah u-Mizvot ba-Zeman ha-Ze* (Tel Aviv, 1954), and 'Din Torah ke-Mishpat Medinat Yisrael?' in M. Smith (ed.), *Ha-Dat ve-ha-Medina* (Jerusalem, 1971), pp. 25–39.

3. Z. Bernstein, *Be-Ma'arakha li-Sheleimut ha-Umma* (Tel Aviv, 1959), summarizes the religious view of the issue.

4. The responsa and opinions have been collected and published by B. Litvin in S. B. Hoenig (ed.), *Jewish Identity* (Jerusalem-New York, 1970).

SELECT BIBLIOGRAPHY
OF WORKS IN ENGLISH

In addition to the Hebrew sources on which I have relied, many of which are referred to in the footnotes, I have also tried to acquaint myself with the relevant materials in the English language. In this note my aim is to give a sparse selection indicating those works which I most closely consulted, and at the same time to offer guidance for further reading to the student who may not read Hebrew, but who may wish to pursue particular aspects of the subject in greater detail. It will therefore be clear that this is not a bibliography. I have had to discard many familiar titles to prevent the list from becoming unwieldy. (Sometimes I have done this with reluctance, sometimes with relief that I can thereby avoid criticizing the work of others.) While keeping the selection as lean as possible I have tried to represent the whole range of issues and views pertaining to the century of history which is the subject of the text. To avoid undue expansion of the annotation I have marked with an asterisk those titles which in my judgement are of outstanding merit or usefulness. With a few exceptions I have excluded official documents and academic articles, but have starred those works with a good bibliography of primary sources and periodicals. Taken together the starred titles comprise my personal short-list of recommended reading. Although many titles have relevance to more than one part of the text, I have mentioned each title only once.

Part 1

The serious student of Israel will undoubtedly require some familiarity with the background of Jewish history, both ancient and modern, and also with Jewish religious traditions and beliefs. A useful first step for orientation would be to consult Shlomo Shunami, *Bibliography of Jewish Bibliographies* (2nd enlarged edition, Magnes Press, Jerusalem, 1965), which lists works in several languages. Also helpful is Issacher Joel (comp.), *Index of Articles on Jewish Studies*, an annual series published in Jerusalem by the Magnes Press since 1969.

A brief but adequate introduction to the Jewish religion is provided by I. Epstein, *Judaism* (Penguin Books, 1959). The divergence between western and oriental Jewry in its religious aspects is treated by Rabbi Dr. H. J. Zimmels, *Ashkenazim and Sephardim: Their Relations, Differences* *and Problems as Reflected in the Rabbinical Responsa* (OUP, London, 1958). Gershom G. Scholem, *Major Trends in Jewish Mysticism* (Schocken, New York, 1954), is supplemented by another great work by the same author, *The Messianic Idea in Judaism and Other Essays on Jewish Spirituality** (Allen and Unwin, London, 1971), which explores the connections between mysticism and messianism and clarifies the distinctions between Jewish and Christian messianic concepts.

An encyclopaedic introduction to the sociology of contemporary Jewry is provided by Louis Finkelstein (ed.), *The Jews, Their History, Culture and Religion* (2 vols, 2nd ed., Harper, New York, 1955). Particularly useful are the essays on statistics of Jewish population and migration. The best brief outline of contemporary world Jewry is Barnet Litvinoff, *A Peculiar People: Inside the Jewish World Today** (Weidenfeld and Nicolson, London, 1969). For the student who is unfamiliar with Judaism and Jewry a very lucid summary of the historical background is the second chapter of Louvish, *The Challenge of Israel* (Jerusalem, 1968).

The classics of nineteenth-century Jewish historiography have been superseded by the prolific work of the greatest contemporary Jewish historian, Salo W. Baron. A bibliography of his work is given in Joseph L. Blau *et al.*, *Essays on Jewish Life and Thought Presented in Honor of Salo Wittmayer Baron* (Columbia UP, New York, 1959). For the period up to the mid-seventeenth century the student will wish to sample Baron's *A Social and Religious History of the Jews* (2nd ed., 14 vols, JPSA and Columbia UP, 1952–1969). The most rewarding selection from Baron's monumental output would include *The Jewish Community: Its History and Structure to the American Revolution* (3 vols, JPSA, 1942); *History and Jewish Historians: Essays and Addresses* (compiled by Arthur Hertzberg and Leon A. Feldman (JPSA, 1964); and *Modern Nationalism and Religion** (Meridian Books, New York, 1960). A brilliant original interpretation of Jewish history since ancient times is Jacob Bernard Agus, *The Meaning of Jewish History** (2 vols, Abelard-Schuman, New York, 1963). A popular introduction of poetic intensity, for the coffee table rather than the study, is Abba Eban, *My People: The Story of The Jews* (Weidenfeld and Nicolson, London, 1969). A useful aid to study is Martin Gilbert, *Jewish History Atlas* (Weidenfeld and Nicolson, London, 1969).

An introduction to anti-semitism, stressing its religious origins, is James Parkes, *The Conflict of the Church and The Synagogue* (Soncino Press, London, 1934). The same author, in *Antisemitism* (Vallentine Mitchell, London, 1963), gives a good account including the modern period, though it is marred by a misleading concluding chapter on Israeli-Arab relations. A thorough and distinguished monograph on the modern period is Norman Cohn, *Warrant for Genocide: The Myth of the Jewish World-Conspiracy and The Protocols of the Elders of Zion* (Penguin Books, 1970). Perceptive and stimulating, if controversial, essays in the social psychology of anti-semitism are Part 1 of Hannah Arendt, *The Origins of Totalitarianism* (Meridian Books, New York, 1959), and Jean-Paul Sartre, *Anti-Semite and Jew* (Schocken, New York, 1965). A neglected but rewarding work emphasizing the religious motives of anti-semitism, but enhanced by a most perceptive concluding essay on the modern period by the author's son, is Count Heinrich Coudenhove-Kalergi (ed. Richard Coudenhove-Kalergi), *Anti-Semitism Throughout the Ages* (Hutchinson, London, 1935).

The multitude of fine monographs on particular aspects of early-modern and modern Jewish history threatens to overwhelm the student. Even the most economical selection must make room for S. D. Goitein, *Jews and Arabs* (Schocken, New York, 1955), which traces the contacts of the two people in their most fertile aspects. A masterly account of Jewish communal organization and traditions in eastern Europe is Jacob Katz, *Tradition and Crisis: Jewish Society at the End of the Middle Ages** (Free Press, Glencoe, Illinois, 1961). The same author has carried forward his study of these themes into the modern period in *Exclusiveness and Tolerance: Studies in Jewish-Gentile Relations in Medieval and Modern Times* (OUP, London, 1961), and *Emancipation and Assimilation: Studies in Modern Jewish History* (Gregg International, 1972). A more critical analysis of the Jewish social structure stressing its inherent antagonisms is Raphael Mahler, *A History of Modern Jewry 1780–1815* (London, 1971) (which also includes a good chapter on Palestine in that period, pp. 602–77). The efforts of Marx and Kautsky on this topic appear as pertinent but unconsummated efforts alongside the brilliant essay by Abram Leon, *The Jewish Question: A Marxist Interpretation** (with an equally challenging introduction by Nathan Weinstock), now made more widely available by Pathfinder Press, New York, 1970. One of Baron's best works is *The Russian Jews Under Tsars and Soviets* (Macmillan, New York, 1964), and some useful essays are also to be found in J. Frumkin *et al.* (eds), *Russian Jewry (1860–1917)* (Yoseloff, 1966). A drier work, but thorough and reliable is Louis Greenberg, *The Jews in Russia* (2 vols, Yale UP, 1944, 1951). Simon Dubnow's history of Russian and Polish Jewry is still useful, but perhaps not so enlightening as his *Nationalism and History: Essays on Old and New Judaism* (Meridian Books, New York, 1961). A sympathetic anthropological account of east-European Jewish culture is M. Zborowski and E. Herzog, *Life is With People: The Jewish Little-Town of Eastern Europe* (New York, 1952) reproduced with an introduction by Margaret Mead in 1962. A provocative account of east-European Jewish life is M. Selzer, *The Wineskin and the Wizard* (London, 1970). Moving westward, Michael A. Meyer offers a detailed analysis of *The Origins of the Modern Jew: Jewish Identity and European Culture in Germany, 1749–1824* (Wayne State UP, 1967). A comparable work on France is M. R. Marrus, *The Politics of Assimilation: A Study of the French Jewish Community at the Time of the Dreyfus Affair* (Clarendon Press, Oxford, 1971). A more comprehensive analysis of exceptional quality is A. Hertzberg, *The French Enlightenment and the Jews** (New York, 1968). A good statistical account of the migrations which accompanied the process of Jewry's entry into the modern world is Mark Wischnitzer, *To Dwell in Safety: The Study of Jewish Migration since 1800* (JPSA, 1948).

For an introduction to the ideological ferment within Jewry in the context of rampant nationalism and socialism at the end of the nineteenth century see F. Gross and B. J. Vlavianos, *Struggle For Tomorrow* (New York, 1954). A brilliant lecture placing Zionism in the perspective of European nationalism is Professor Trevor Roper's *Jewish and Other Nationalisms* (Weidenfeld and Nicolson, London, 1962). For an understanding of the connections between Jewish nationalism and the socialist movement see the unpublished doctoral dissertation by Jonathan Frankel, 'Socialism and Jewish Nationalism in Russia, 1892–1907' (Cambridge, 1961). More accessible are A. L. Patkin, *The Origins of the Russian-Jewish Labour Movement* (F. W. Cheshire Pty., Melbourne, 1947); Ezra Mendelsohn, *Class Struggle in the Pale: The Formative Years of the Jewish Workers' Movement in Tsarist Russia* (Cambridge UP, 1970); and H. J. Tobias, *The Jewish Bund in Russia From Its Origins in 1905* (Stanford UP, 1972). This latter work has an exhaustive bibliography and provides a good map of the Pale of Settlement. A most perceptive and revealing analysis of Israel's social image as derived from east-European culture is given by Sir Isaiah Berlin in a lecture delivered in 1953 and reproduced as 'The Origins of Israel', in W. Z. Laqueur (ed.), *The Middle East in Transition* (London, New York, 1958).

A superb introduction to Zionist thought is the collection edited by Arthur Hertzberg, *The Zionist Idea: A Historical Analysis and Reader** (Meridian Books, New York, 1960). For the extended writings of Zionist thinkers one may begin with Moses Hess, *Rome and Jerusalem*, an edition of which was published in New York in 1943. Leo Pinsker's *Auto-Emancipation* was published in 1935. Ahad Ha'am is best represented by *Ten Essays on Zionism and Judaism* which appeared in London in 1922; and by Leon Simon (trans. and ed.), *Ahad Ha-Am: Essays, Letters, Memoirs** (Phaidon Press, Oxford, 1946). Sylvia d'Avigdor has translated Theodor Herzl, *The Jewish State: An Attempt at a Solution of the Jewish Question* (London, 1936), while his novel *Old-New Land* appeared in New York in 1941, and was issued again by the Herzl Press in New York in 1959. Raphael Patai (ed.), *The Complete Diaries of Theodor Herzl* (trans. Harry Zohn) (Herzl Press and Thomas Yoseloff, 1960) offers more detail than most readers would require. The less devout will find Marvin Lowenthal (ed. and trans.), *The Diaries of Theodor Herzl* (Dial Press, New York, 1956), an adequate introduction and abridgement. A standard biography is Alexander Bein, *Theodor Herzl* (Philadelphia, 1940). An interesting essay showing the links and divergencies between its three subjects is Josef Fraenkel, *Dubnow, Herzl and Ahad Ha-Am* (Ararat Pub., London, 1963). An edition of Nachman Syrkin, *Essays on Socialist Zionism*, was published in New York in 1935 while Marie Syrkin gives her father's biography in *Nachman Syrkin* (New York, 1961). The best edition of Borochov in English is introduced with a superb essay by A. G. Duker, *Nationalism and the Class Struggle: A Marxian Approach to the Jewish Problem** (New York, 1937). Solomon Schiller, *Principles of Labor Zionism* (trans. Arlosoroff, 1928), is a lucid account, while labour-Zionism is placed in a broader frame of reference by Hayim Greenberg, *The Inner Eye: Selected Essays** (New York, 1958). For a detailed account of 'territorialism' see Joseph Leftwich, *Israel Zangwill* (James Clarke, London,

1957), and Maurice Simon (ed.), *Speeches, Articles and Letters of Israel Zangwill* (Soncino Press, London, 1937). A fine monograph on the 'Uganda' episode is Robert G. Weisbrod, *African Zion: The Attempt to Establish a Jewish Colony in the East Africa Protectorate 1903–1905* (JPSA, 1968). Under the general editorship of Meyer W. Weisgal three volumes of Weizman's papers have so far been issued, *The Letters and Papers of Chaim Weizmann* (OUP, 1968, 1971 and 1972), covering the period from 1885–1904.

For the history of Palestine itself, a general cultural history since ancient times is given by M. Avi-Yonah, *The Holy Land* (Thames and Hudson, London, 1972), and the same author has edited *A History of the Holy Land* (Weidenfeld and Nicolson, London, 1969). James Parkes, *Whose Land: A History of the Peoples of Palestine*, first published by Gollancz and re-issued by Penguin Books in 1970, and Berl Locker, *A Stiff-Necked People: Palestine in Jewish History* (Gollancz, London, 1946), trace the vicissitudes of the land from a Zionist standpoint.

Part 2

A selection of the work of A. D. Gordon is conveniently presented in *Selected Essays* (trans. F. Burnce) (New York, 1938). The early activities of the socialist Zionists is not adequately told in English, but a start may be made with B. Katznelson, *Revolutionary Constructivism* (New York, 1937); Arthur Ruppin, *The Agricultural Colonization of the Zionist Organization in Palestine* (London, 1926); and S. Zemach, *An Introduction to the History of Labour Settlement in Palestine* (2nd cd., Tel Aviv, 1946). Most useful also are R. Katznelson-Rubashov (ed.), *The Plough Woman* (New York, 1932); Joseph Baratz, *A Village By The Jordan* (London, 1954); S. Dayan, *The Promised Land* (Routledge, London, 1961); and Alex Bein, *Return to the Soil* (Jerusalem, 1952). Arthur Ruppin, *Building Israel: Selected Essays 1907–1935* (Schocken, New York, 1949), is also enlightening. S. Spiegel, *Hebrew Reborn* (London, 1930), gives a somewhat scanty introduction to the Hebrew revival, which may be supplemented by the biography of Eliezer Ben Yehuda, Robert St John, *Tongue of the Prophets* (New York, 1958).

The Royal Institute of International Affairs publishes a companion to its surveys in the form of an annual collection of documents. Other useful documentary anthologies are Walter Laqueur (ed.), *The Israel-Arab Reader* (Weidenfeld and Nicolson, London, 1969), and a more detailed collection in two volumes edited by J. C. Hurewitz, *Diplomacy in the Near and Middle East* (Van Nostrand, London, 1956).

The intricate middle-east dealings of the powers during the first world war continue to engage the industry of historians and exacerbate their disagreements. The leanest list would have to include Neville Mandel, 'Turks, Arabs and Jewish Immigration into Palestine, 1882–1914', reproduced in St Antony's Papers 17 (OUP, 1965); the first issue of Middle Eastern Studies in 1964 offers 'Attempts at an Arab-Zionist Entente: 1913–14', by the same author; J. Nevakivi, *Britain, France and the Arab*

Middle East, 1914–1920 (Athlone Press, London, 1969), restores to life issues traversed with masterly insight and authority by E. Kedourie, *England and the Middle East** (Bowes and Bowes, London, 1956); some of the choicest products of the professional historian's art are offered in E. Kedourie, *The Chatham House Version and Other Middle Eastern Studies** (Weidenfeld and Nicolson, London, 1970); Leonard Stein, *The Balfour Declaration* (Vallentine Mitchell, London, 1961), for long was regarded as the definitive study of this topic but has now been capped by I. Friedman, *The Question of Palestine, 1914–1918: British-Jewish-Arab Relations* (Routledge and Kegan Paul, London, 1973). A masterly survey (giving excellent references) of the complex British and Zionist diplomacy during and after the war by Elizabeth Monroe is 'The Origins of the Palestine Problem' in Peter Mansfield (ed.), *The Middle East: A Political and Economic Survey* (4th ed., OUP, 1973), while a short provocative essay by Jon Kimche, *The Unromantics: The Great Powers and the Balfour Declaration* (London, 1968), provides a good introduction.

A. Engle, *The Nili Spies* (Hogarth Press, London, 1959), traces the details of a little-known episode of Palestinian involvement in the allied cause during the first world war, while the story of *The Jewish Legion* is told by its prime mover, V. Jabotinsky. H. N. Howard, *The King-Crane Commission* (Beirut, 1963), gives a scholarly account of the abortive American attempt to counter European imperial dealings in the aftermath of the war. The forces which created the Palestinian mandate and its territorial shape are carefully traced by H. F. Frischwasser-Ra'anan, *The Frontiers of a Nation* (Batchworth Press, London, 1955).

The history of Zionism itself is a surprisingly neglected subject. A major study of great complexity, subtle and rewarding, is B. Halpern, *The Idea of the Jewish State* (2nd ed., Harvard UP, 1969). Walter Laqueur, *A History of Zionism** (Weidenfeld and Nicolson, London, 1972), which appeared too late to be of use to the author in the preparation of the present work, will be most useful to students, though they should perhaps be warned that it is a series of erudite extended essays on various aspects of Zionism, rather than a history. A masterly, perceptive and scholarly account which is at the same time a literary gem is Barnet Litvinoff, *Road to Jerusalem: Zionism's Imprint on History** (Weidenfeld and Nicolson, London, 1965). A good elementary introduction is Israel Cohen, *The Zionist Movement* (New York, 1946). Older works, still useful for their wealth of detail, are N. Sokolow, *History of Zionism 1600–1918*, 2 vols (London, 1919), and R. J. Gottheil, *Zionism* (Philadelphia, 1914). O. K. Rabinowicz, *Vladimir Jabotinsky's Conception of a Nation* (New York, 1946), is an admirer's tribute to Jabotinsky's thought, which succeeds only in showing that the philosophical prowess of Jabotinsky in no way matched his platform appeal. The historian and Zionist leader L. B. Namier wrote many pieces on Zionism, which may be sampled in *Conflicts* (London, 1942). After several decades in which Arab propaganda displayed a shallow understanding of Zionism, the Institute for Palestine Studies at Beirut has now built up a formidable list of analytical works. Perhaps the most outstanding of these to date, which should be required reading, is Walid Khalidi (ed.), *From Haven to Conquest: Readings in Zionism and the Palestine Problem Until 1948** (Beirut, 1971). The evolution of Zionism was closely affected by conditions in Poland between the wars, which may be studied through H. M. Rabinowicz, *The Legacy of Polish Jewry* (Yoseloff, 1965); B. K. Johnpoll, *The Politics of Futility: The General Jewish Workers' Bund of Poland 1917–43* (Cornell UP, 1967); and V. Jabotinsky, *The Jewish War Front* (London, 1940).

For the history of Palestine in the period between the two world wars an indispensable detailed work is Esco Foundation For Palestine, *Palestine: A Study of Jewish, Arab, and British Policies** (Yale UP, New Haven, 1947), in two volumes. A sensitive account is that by J. C. Hurewitz, *The Struggle for Palestine** (W. W. Norton, 1950, reprinted by Greenwood Press, 1968). A fine early study with much useful detail and a superb bibliography is F. F. Andrews, *The Holy Land Under Mandate* (2 vols, Cambridge, Mass., 1931). Two judicious and well-informed accounts by British Jews who held high positions in the Palestine administration are Norman Bentwich, *Fulfilment in the Promised Land 1917–1939* (London, 1937), and A. M. Hyamson, *Palestine Under The Mandate, 1920–1948* (London, 1950). Christopher Sykes, *Cross Roads to Israel* (Collins, London, 1965), is the best available comprehensive introduction from the standpoint of British interests and sensibilities. P. L. Hanna, *British Policy in Palestine* (Washington, 1942), is an acute analysis, while J. M. N. Jeffries, *Palestine: The Reality* (London, 1939), although passionately hostile to Zionism, is formidable and perceptive. Alan R. Taylor, *Prelude to Israel: An Analysis of Zionist Diplomacy, 1897–1947* (New York, 1959), is a sharp critique of Zionism, while Jon Kimche, *Seven Fallen Pillars* (London, 1950), and Arthur Koestler, *Promise and Fulfilment* (London, 1949), are searing indictments of British policies. Koestler's book is unsurpassed in the genre of historical journalism, vivid, provocative and illuminating. Also, the serious student will not miss the report of the Peel Commission (Command Papers 5479) and the accompanying minutes of evidence heard in public, published by HMSO in 1937.

A sampling of personal memoirs and biography should include the two-volume study by Blanche Dugdale, *Arthur James Balfour* (London, 1936); Viscount Samuel, *Memoirs* (Cresset Press, London, 1945); Sir Ronald Storrs, *Orientations* (London, 1937), suffused with erudite romantic conceit, offers the most economical education in the mind and habit of the British imperial elite; Chaim Weizmann, *Trial and Error** (London, 1949), is mandatory reading, but should be taken in conjunction with Oscar K. Rabinowicz, *Fifty Years of Zionism: A Historical Analysis of Dr. Weizman's Trial and Error* (2nd ed., Anscombe, London, 1952); a superb analytical biography is (eds.) M. Weisgal and J. Carmichael, *Chaim Weizman: A Biography by Several Hands** (Weidenfeld and Nicolson, London, 1962); Richard Crossman, perhaps the most gifted of Israel's friends who wield the pen, gives an acute assessment in *A Nation Reborn: A Personal Account of the Roles Played by Weizmann, Bevin and Ben-Gurion in the Story of Israel** (Atheneum, New York, 1960); the major biography of Jabotinsky is the two-volume study by J. B. Schechtman, *The Jabotinsky*

Story (New York, 1956, 1961); Nahum Goldmann, *Memories* (Weidenfeld and Nicolson, London, 1970), is an indispensable critical account of Zionist history told from the inside; Arthur Ruppin, *Memories, Diaries, Letters* (Weidenfeld, Jerusalem, 1971), is a translation of this key figure's papers. Ben-Gurion has so far eluded adequate representation in English. For the pre-state period the best works are *Ben-Gurion Looks Back in Talks with Moshe Pearlman** (Weidenfeld and Nicolson, London, 1965), and *Rebirth and Destiny of Israel* (New York, 1954), while the best biography is Barnet Litvinoff, *Ben-Gurion of Israel* (New York, 1954); *Orde Wingate* is the subject of a superb biography by Christopher Sykes (Collins, London, 1959); R. Meinertzhagen, *Middle East Diary 1917–1956* (London, 1959), combines personal eccentricity and acute perceptiveness; Edwin Samuel (the second Viscount Samuel), *A Lifetime in Jerusalem* (Jerusalem, 1970), is a benevolent memoir, while Horace B. Samuel, *Unholy Memories of the Holy Land* (Hogarth Press, London, 1930), is a candid and revealing essay in disillusionment. A brilliant reporter, Vincent Sheean, gives his personal response to the riots of 1929 in *Personal History* (London, 1969) (first published in 1935 as *In Search of History*).

For the social, economic and political development of the national home, the best comprehensive introduction is Nathan, Gass and Creamer, *Palestine: Problem and Promise** (Washington, 1946). An excellent monograph on the early evolution of Jewish political institutions is M. Burstein, *Self-Government of the Jews in Palestine Since 1900* (Tel Aviv, 1934). Norman Bentwich, *England in Palestine* (London, 1932), is a model account of the administrative practice of the British authorities. A. Revusky, *Jews in Palestine* (3rd ed., New York, 1945), and the same author's *Histadrut* (New York, 1938), are fine detailed outlines of the Jewish society, giving proper weight to the activities of the labour movement; for further study of the theory and practice of Jewish colonization, see A. Granott, *The Land System in Palestine* (London, 1952). Rambling, discursive and at times irritating for lack of editing, but nevertheless a valuable documentary account of the evolution of the economic institutions of the labour movement, in seven volumes, is Harry Viteles, *A History of the Cooperative Movement in Israel*; the first four volumes (London, 1966, 1967, 1968) are particularly useful. Less ambitious, but reliable, is G. Muenzner, *Jewish Labour Economy in Palestine* (London, 1945). For the early growth of the agricultural co-operatives, a good introduction is Weintraub *et al.*, *Moshava, Kibbutz and Moshav* (Cornell UP, 1969), and also H. Darin-Drabkin, *The Other Society* (London, 1962); the journal *Social Problems* published by Brandeis University, in autumn 1957 devoted a special issue to the kibbutz, including a particularly interesting discussion by S. Diamond, the editor. Martin Buber, the philosopher, in *Paths in Utopia* (London, 1949), helpfully locates the kibbutz movement within the wider context of socialism.

For the early encounters between Zionism and the Arabs, a start may be made with the classic George Antonius, *The Arab Awakening* (London, 1938). A very uneven anthology containing some useful material, is I. Abu-Lughod (ed.), *The Transformation of Palestine* (Northwestern UP,

1971). G. Mansur, *The Arab Worker Under The Palestine Mandate* (Jerusalem, 1936 (?1939)), introduces the impact of the Histadrut on the labour market from an Arab point of view, while the labour-Zionist approaches are best treated in E. Sereni and R. E. Asheri, *Jews and Arabs in Palestine: Studies in a National and Colonial Problem** (New York, 1936); and Histadrut Executive Committee, *Documents and Essays on Jewish Labour Policy in Palestine* (Tel Aviv, 1930). An excellent historical monograph on the Jewish movement for a bi-national Palestine is S. L. Hattis, *The Bi-National Idea in Palestine During Mandatory Times** (Haifa, 1970). J. Magnes and M. Buber, *Arab-Jewish Unity* (London, 1947), is a good statement of the thinking of this wing of Zionism, as presented in evidence before the 1946 Anglo-American inquiry. Also useful here are Norman Bentwich's biography, *Judah L. Magnes* (London, 1955), and Hashomer Hatzair Executive, *The Case For a Bi-National Palestine* (Tel Aviv, 1946).

The student of the European holocaust should consult the series of several volumes, begun in 1957, published by the Yad Washem Remembrance Authority in Jerusalem, *Yad Washem Studies in the European Jewish Catastrophe and Resistance*. These Studies include strong criticisms of the more widely available works, such as Gerald Reitlinger, *The Final Solution* (London and New York, 1953); Leon Poliakov, *Harvest of Hate* (Syracuse UP, 1954); and Raoul Hilberg, *The Destruction of European Jews* (Chicago, 1961). A careful monograph is Schleunes, *The Twisted Road to Auschwitz* (University of Illinois Press, 1970). Arthur D. Morse, *While Six Million Died* (Random House, New York, 1967), is a popular account highlighting American apathy, while H. L. Feingold, *The Politics of Rescue* (New Jersey, 1970), is a more substantial analysis of the political responses and pressures within the Roosevelt administration in relation to the plight of European Jewry. Y. Bauer, *Flight and Rescue: Brichah** (Random House, New York, 1970), is a pioneer work tracing the intricate post-war migration of European Jews under the auspices of Zionist and other rescue agencies. Jon and David Kimche, *The Secret Roads* (London, 1954), is a more popular narrative treatment of the illegal migrations and the obstacles they overcame in gaining entry to Palestine; on the same lines is M. Mardor, *Strictly Illegal* (London, 1964), told by one of the top directors of the rescue movement. A. Weissberg and Joel Brand, *Desperate Mission* (New York, 1958), recounts the disaster of Hungarian Jewry as told by one of the principals of the 'Kastner trial'. Herbert Agar, *The Saving Remnant* (London, 1960), is a standard history of the rescue activities of the Joint Distribution Committee.

For the struggle for the establishment of the Jewish state, the best treatment of the wartime period is Yehuda Bauer, *From Diplomacy to Resistance: A History of Jewish Palestine 1939–1945** (Philadelphia, 1970). Martin W. Wilmington, *The Middle East Supply Centre* (London, 1972), is a good account in which Palestine may be seen in the regional context of the war. George Kirk, *The Middle East 1945–50* (OUP, 1954), which supplements the Royal Institute of International Affairs wartime survey, is an object lesson in the uses of scepticism in historical reconstruction and at the same time in the dangers of supplanting partisan bias by generalized misanthropy. This may be too waspish a comment on the work of a brilliant historian. Harry Sacher, *Israel: The Establishment of a State* (London, 1952), is a good account from a Zionist standpoint. Menahem Begin, *The Revolt** (Tel Aviv, ?1951), is an indispensable source for insight into the Jewish terrorist movement, and may be supplemented by a comparable account, S. Katz, *Days of Fire* (London, 1968). Three members of the Anglo-American inquiry of 1946 have given their personal accounts: Richard Crossman, *Palestine Mission* (London, 1947); Bartley Crum, *Behind the Silken Curtain* (London, 1947); and James MacDonald, *My Mission in Israel* (London, 1951); the Palestine government itself prepared for the commission a detailed *Survey of Palestine**, in two volumes, December 1945 and January 1946, which is the best official account of the political conflict. On the role of America in the creation of Israel, Frank E. Manuel, *The Realities of American-Palestine Relations* (Washington, 1949), is a judicious account sympathetic to Zionism, while a contrary bias is manifested in R. P. Stevens, *American Zionism and U.S. Foreign Policy 1942–1947* (New York, 1950). Samuel Halperin, *The Political World of American Zionism* (Wayne UP, 1961), is a lucid analysis of the evolution of American Zionism as a political force. For the diplomacy in the United Nations arena, J. B. Schechtman, *The United States and the Jewish State Movement* (New York, 1966), should be consulted; and also J. Garcia-Granados, *The Birth of Israel* (New York, 1948), and E. B. Glick, *Latin America and the Palestine Problem* (New York, 1958). Eliahu Elath, *Israel and Elath: The Political Struggle For The Inclusion of Elath in the Jewish State* (London, 1966), is a revealing account of a special issue within the wider diplomatic context.

Part 3

The best starting point for the study of Israel is Ben-Gurion's personal account, now available in a good English translation: David Ben-Gurion, *Israel: A Personal History** (New English Library, London, 1972). The late premier modestly sacrificed his initial resolve to write a general history, and the result is an indispensable personal memoir told with candour, which greatly illuminates the centre of the political stage. Of the many general discussions of Israel one of the most acute and readable is Amos Elon, *The Israelis: Founders and Sons** (Weidenfeld and Nicolson, London, 1971). Ferdynand Zweig, *Israel: The Sword and the Harp* (Heineman, 1969), offers some good sociological insights. Georges Friedmann, *The End of the Jewish People?* (London, 1967), is an intelligent discussion despite its shallow foundations. Uri Avnery, *Israel Without Zionists** (New York, 1968), is a radical critique by a maverick politician, challenging and irresistible. Nadav Safran, *The United States and Israel* (Harvard UP, 1963), is a reliable guided tour. For scathing American criticism of Zionism Alfred M. Lilienthal, *What Price Israel* (Chicago, 1953), or *The Other Side of The Coin* (New York, 1965), are most provocative and possibly salutary. Maxim Rodinson, *Israel and the Arabs* (Penguin, 1968), although superficial and frequently in error, shows some Marxian acumen. Abdullah Schleifer, *The Fall of Jerusalem** (Monthly Review Press, 1972), is much more substantial in the same genre, and although it is concerned with the situation after 1967, its analysis has sufficient historical depth to afford a challenging introduction to the subject as a whole. M. Selzer, *The Aryanization of the Jewish State* (New York, 1967), is a withering critique. H. M. Sachar, *Aliyah: The Peoples of Israel* (Cleveland, 1961), is very rewarding for the reader willing to bear with irrelevant personal anecdote. G. Nikitina, *The History of Israel* (Progress Publishers, Moscow, 1973), although slapdash and full of error is useful for an understanding of the Soviet view of Israel. G. H. Jansen, *Zionism, Israel and Asian Nationalism** (Beirut, 1971), is a sharp critique which, while failing to understand Zionism, nevertheless places it within a useful framework for comparison with other movements. A trifle sycophantic, but authoritative, is Michael Bar-Zohar, *The Armed Prophet: A Biography of Ben-Gurion* (London, 1967). Terence Prittie, *Eshkol of Israel: The Man and the Nation* (London, 1967), has captured much significant detail which will whet the appetite of the student restricted to English.

A standard semi-official account of Israel's war of independence is Netanel Lorch, *The Edge of the Sword* (New York, 1961). More original and bold, while yet remaining authoritative within the Israeli perspective, is Jon and David Kimche, *A Clash of Destinies* (New York, 1960). Harry Levin, *Jerusalem Embattled: A Diary of the City Under Siege* (London, 1950), is candid, while Dov Joseph, *The Faithful City* (London, 1950), is a trifle apologetic. Count Bernadotte, *To Jerusalem* (London, 1951), is most useful for its detachment. An indispensable account of the implementation of sovereignty in May 1948 is Z. Sharef, *Three Days** (London, 1962). For those who like their wars reported with the smell of smoke and blood there are two extraordinarily well researched accounts in great detail: D. Kurzman, *Genesis 1948* (New American Library, 1970), and L. Collins and D. Lapierre, *O Jerusalem!* (London, 1972). For a statistical account of the initial mass immigration M. Sicron, *Immigration to Israel 1948-1953* (Jerusalem, 1957), provides a good survey which will be of use to the student who might not wish to risk getting lost among the excellent annual statistical abstracts issued by the Israeli government in English and Hebrew.

For an introduction to the military evolution of Israel, a substantial beginning is S. Peres, *David's Sling: The Arming of Israel* (London, 1970), and Yigal Allon, *The Making of Israel's Army* (London, 1971). Samuel Rolbant, *The Israeli Soldier* (London, 1970), is a good general description of the army. Badly written and not edited at all, but nevertheless well-informed and useful, if opinionated, is Amos Perlmutter, *Military and Politics in Israel* (Frank Cass, 1969). J. C. Hurewitz, *Middle East Politics: The Military Dimension* (London, 1969), is thorough and painstaking, with a useful account of Israel's military capacities in the wider regional context. Fuad Jabber, *Israel and Nuclear Weapons* (London, 1971), is speculative rather than reliable, but gives food for thought.

For the government and politics of Israel the student is assisted by excellent official publications, such as the annual yearbooks, the authorized annual translation of the *Laws of the State of Israel*, and *Selected Judgements of the Supreme Court of Israel*, so far in three volumes covering the period from 1948–60. A superb formal account of the governmental system from a legalistic standpoint is Y. Freudenheim, *Government in Israel** (Oceana, New York, 1967). Some searching articles are included in G. Tedeschi and U. Yadin (eds), *Studies in Israel Legislative Problems* (Magnes Press, Jerusalem, 1966) (Scripta Hierosolymitana XVI, distributed by OUP). M. D. Gouldmann, *Israel Nationality Law* (Jerusalem, 1970), is a sure guide through the maze of technicalities surrounding this topic. Peter Y. Medding, *Mapai in Israel** (Cambridge UP, 1972) is the best analysis of Israeli politics for those to whom the language of academic political science is not prohibitive. An excellent account of the early constitutional debates of the new state is E. Rackman, *Israel's Emerging Constitution* (New York, 1955). M. H. Bernstein, *The Politics of Israel* (Princeton UP, 1957), is recommended for its elucidation of economic and administrative issues. E. S. Likhovski, *Israel's Parliament* (Oxford, 1971), is an interesting discussion, more analytical than A. Zidon, *Knesset: The Parliament of Israel* (New York, 1967), which is, however, a good text for reference. H. E. Baker, *The Legal System of Israel* (Jerusalem, 1968), is a clear introductory text. A lively journalistic discussion in scholarly garb is Leonard J. Fein, *Israel: Politics and People* (Boston, 1968). A helpful introduction to the party system is B. Akzin, 'The Role of Parties in Israeli Democracy', which appeared in the Journal of Politics, XVII, 1955. E. Birnbaum, *The Politics of Compromise: State and Religion in Israel* (Fairleigh Dickinson UP, 1970), is a fair, if somewhat shallow, introduction to this topic. A useful discussion of Israeli administrative practice is B. Akzin and Y. Dror, *Israel: High Pressure Planning* (Syracuse UP, 1966). Michael Brecher, *The Foreign Policy System of Israel: Setting, Images, Procedures* (OUP, London, 1972), is perhaps over-elaborate and detailed, but useful for reference.

For the economic problems and development of Israel there is a wealth of sophisticated material in English. The professional economist will look elsewhere for guidance, but the lay student of Israeli society might find the following titles sufficient for a general introduction. The Economic Planning Authority of the Prime Minister's Office, *Israel: Economic Development: Past Progress and Plan for the Future**, Final Draft (Jerusalem, 1968), is an indispensable comprehensive survey. Also a most lucid survey, reliable and analytical without being too technical, is N. Halevi and R. Klinov-Malul, *The Economic Development of Israel** (New York, 1968). Eliyahu Kanovsky, *The Economic Impact of the Six-Day War* (New York, 1970), contains a fine introduction to the Israeli economy in the period since independence. Also useful for the early period is Emanuel Levy, *Israel Economic Survey 1953–54* (Jerusalem, 1955). Don Patinkin, *The Israeli Economy: The First Decade* (Jerusalem, 1959), is a masterly critical account by the leading authority, that will be rewarding for the economically literate, while Alex Rubner, *The Economy of Israel* (London, 1960), is perhaps less challenging for the lay reader. (The student who requires more detailed economic analyses would do well to consult Praeger's list of special studies, especially works by Heth, Gaathon, Finger and Ofer. Also the annual reports of the Bank Leumi.)

The best introduction to the general problems of immigrant absorption is Raphael Patai, *Israel Between East and West** (Philadelphia, 1953), a sensitive work by an anthropologist. A sociological approach is S. N. Eisenstadt, *The Absorption of Immigrants* (London, 1954), while more recent works of the same genre are J. Matras, *Social Change in Israel* (Chicago, 1965); Judith T. Shuval, *Immigrants on the Threshold* (New York, 1963); Don Weintraub and Associates, *Immigration and Social Change* (Manchester, 1971); E. Baldwin, *Differentiation and Cooperation in an Israeli Veteran Moshav* (Manchester, 1972); M. Shokeid, *The Dual Heritage* (Manchester, 1971); D. Willner, *Nation-Building and Community in Israel* (Princeton, 1969). For the specific study of the kibbutz and moshav forms of settlement, one should begin with the general context of agricultural policy, as described by A. Granott, *Agrarian Reform and the Record of Israel* (London, 1956). Raanan Weitz, *From Peasant to Farmer* (Columbia UP, 1971), contains a helpful survey of planning methods in Israeli rural development. On this topic see also H. Darin-Drabkin, *Pattern of Cooperative Agriculture in Israel* (Tel Aviv, 1962); H. Halperin, *Changing Patterns in Israeli Agriculture* (London, 1957); and the same author's *Agrindus* (London, 1963).

The kibbutz is itself the subject of a considerable literature, to which a good introduction is Rabin, *Kibbutz Studies: Digest of Books and Articles* (Michigan State UP, 1971). Two pioneering studies by Melford E. Spiro, *Venture in Utopia* (Harvard, 1956), and *Children of The Kibbutz* (Harvard, 1958), give an anthropological insight, while an excellent monograph from another standpoint is E. Kanovsky, *The Economy of the Israeli Kibbutz* (Harvard, 1966). A brilliant controversial discussion is Bruno Bettleheim, *The Children of the Dream** (New York, 1970).

Sabri Jiryis, *The Arabs in Israel, 1948–1966** (Beirut, 1968), is the best introduction to the situation of the Arab minority as seen by one of its members. Abner Cohen, *Arab Border-Villages in Israel* (Manchester, 1965), is a careful study of the impact of Israeli society on Arab social organization, while Jacob M. Landau, *The Arabs in Israel: A Political Study* (OUP, 1969), although it fails to live up to its sub-title since it ignores the basic conflicts underlying the Arab position in Israeli society, is useful for much of its detail. A good journalistic sketch of the Arab minority is Walter Schwarz, *The Arabs in Israel* (London, 1959).

For the issues of foreign policy and in particular the Israel-Arab conflicts a convenient work of reference is the fourth volume of J. H. Wiener (ed.), *Great Britain: Foreign Policy and the Span of Empire 1689–1971: A Documentary History* (New York, 1972), which includes a good collection of official documents pertaining to the middle east in the period from 1936–67. J. C. Hurewitz (ed.), *Soviet-American Rivalry in the Middle East* (New York, 1969), is a fine collection of articles including an acute short survey by Professor Elie Kedourie. W. Z. Laqueur, *Communism and Nationalism in the Middle East* (New York, 1956), and *The*

Struggle for the Middle East (London, 1969), gives useful information on the growth of Soviet influence in the region. Malcolm Kerr, *The Arab Cold War 1958–1964* (OUP, 1965), is the best general outline of inter-Arab political developments. Abba Eban, *Voice of Israel* (New York, 1957), and Walter Eytan, *The First Ten Years* (New York, 1958), offer the rhetoric and history of Israeli foreign policy in its early evolution. I. Deutschkron, *Bonn and Jerusalem* (Philadelphia, 1970), and N. Balabkins, *West German Reparations to Israel* (Rutgers UP, 1971), are enlightening on the course of German-Israel relations, while A. Dagan, *Moscow and Jerusalem* (New York, 1970), gives a less satisfactory account of Soviet-Israeli relations, which is nevertheless useful for reference.

Aharon Cohen, *Israel and the Arab World** (London, 1970), is an excellent work, though at fault in placing too much emphasis on the British administration as a factor exacerbating Zionist-Arab conflict. Don Peretz, *Israel and the Palestine Arabs** (Washington, 1958), is a strenuous and excellent effort to determine the facts of the Palestine refugee problem and the situation of the Arabs within Israel. Much less careful but with some significant detail is R. E. Gabbay, *A Political Study of the Arab-Jewish Conflict* (Libraire E. Droz, Geneva, 1959). E. Eliachar, *Israeli Jews and Palestinian Arabs* (Jerusalem, 1970), is a criticism of Israeli policy by a leader of the oriental Jews in Israel, while Sami Hadawi, *Palestine: Loss of a Heritage* (Texas, 1965), and *Bitter Harvest: Palestine Between 1914–1967* (New York, 1967), vigorously present the Arab experience of Zionism in Palestine, giving detail on the little-known history of land transactions. F. J. Khouri, *The Arab-Israeli Dilemma* (Syracuse UP, 1968), and Henry Cattan, *Palestine, The Arabs and Israel: The Search for Justice* (London, 1969), more coolly provide an Arab perspective on the conflict. Kodsy and Lobel, *The Arab World and Israel: Two Essays* (Monthly Review Press, 1970), are perhaps doctrinaire rather than radical as intended, but the second essay (by Lobel) sheds some light. Y. Harkabi, *Arab Attitudes to Israel* (Jerusalem, 1971) is a controversial but influential analysis of Arab political psychology by a distinguished and well-informed Israeli scholar.

On more specific aspects of the conflict, S. Rosenne, *Israel's Armistice Agreements with The Arab States: A Juridical Interpretation* (Tel Aviv, 1951), gives an official Israeli view. N. Bar-Yaacov, *The Israel-Syrian Armistice: Problems of Implementation, 1949–1966* (Magnes Press, Jerusalem, 1967), and S. N. Saliba, *The Jordan River Dispute* (The Hague, 1968), are careful detailed accounts. Legal polemics in support of Israeli doctrines are N. Feinberg, *The Arab-Israeli Conflict in International Law* (Jerusalem, 1970), and Y. Z. Blum, *Secure Boundaries and Middle East Peace* (Jerusalem, 1971). Earl Berger, *The Covenant and the Sword: Arab-Israeli Relations 1948–1956* (London and Toronto, 1965), is an excellent clear account of the events leading up to the war of 1956, which may be supplemented by E. L. M. Burns, *Between Arab and Israeli* (London, 1962). Of the very many books on this subject perhaps the most valuable single volume is Nadav Safran, *From War to War: The Arab-Israeli Confrontation, 1948–1967** (New York, 1969). For the war of 1956 an economical selection would include Hugh Thomas, *The Suez Affair* (Penguin Books, 1970); M. and S. Bromberger, *Secrets of Suez* (transl.) (Pan Books, London, 1957); and Major-General Moshe Dayan, *Diary of the Sinai Campaign 1956* (London, 1966). Of the many works on the role of UNO the best is Rosalyn Higgins, *United Nations Peacekeeping 1946–1967* (London, 1969).

Many works which focus on the period after 1967, although their subject-matter is beyond the scope of the present work, offer a good perspective on less recent events and are therefore of use to the student of the earlier period. These include Michael Curtis (ed.), *People and Politics in the Middle East* (New Jersey, 1971); I. Howe and Carl Gershman, *Israel, The Arabs and The Middle East* (Bantam Books, London, 1972); Y. Alexander and N. Kittrie, *Crescent and Star** (New York, 1973); S. Avineri (ed.), *Israel and the Palestinians* (New York, 1971). On the 1967 war Walter Laqueur has written his best work, *The Road to War 1967: The Origins of the Arab-Israeli Conflict** (London, 1969). Extraordinarily good accounts of the war and of the Israeli occupation respectively are S. Teveth, *The Tanks of Tammuz* (London, 1969), and *The Cursed Blessing* (London, 1970). Other rapidly produced but more than passable accounts are D. Kimche and D. Bawly, *The Sandstorm* (London, 1968); I. Abu-Lughod (ed.), *The Arab-Israeli Confrontation of June 1967: An Arab Perspective* (Northwestern UP, 1970); and Theodore Draper, *Israel and World Politics: Roots of the Third Arab-Israeli War* (New York, 1968). An indispensable work of reference for the year 1967 is D. Dishon (ed.), *Middle East Record, Volume Three, 1967** (Jerusalem, 1971).

The chief prosecutor gives a detailed account of the Eichmann trial in G. Hausner, *Justice in Jerusalem* (Nelson, London, 1967), while Hannah Arendt, *Eichmann in Jerusalem: A Report on the Banality of Evil* (New York, 1963), displayed all her gifts of critical observation to incur the wrath of the Israeli public. P. Papadatos, *The Eichmann Trial* (London, 1964), is a good elementary introduction to the legal aspects of the trial.

A searching essay on the meaning and future of Zionism in the context of the Jewish state is Mordecai M. Kaplan, *A New Zionism* (New York, 1959), while Michael Selzer (ed.), *Zionism Reconsidered: The Rejection of Jewish Normalcy* (sic) (Macmillan, New York, 1970), is a collection drawn from several decades. Two withering critiques of Zionism from its origins to its modifications under Israeli auspices are by W. T. Mallison Jr: 'The Zionist-Israel Juridical Claims to Constitute "The Jewish People" Nationality Entity and to Confer Membership in it', The George Washington Law Review, XXXII, 1964, pp. 963–1075; and 'The Legal Problems Concerning The Juridical Status and Political Activities of the Zionist Organisation/Jewish Agency', William and Mary Law Review, IX, Spring 1963, pp. 556–629, reproduced as a pamphlet, Beirut, 1968. A quite superb erudite analysis of the relation between religion and state in Israel is Emile Marmorstein, *Heaven at Bay: The Jewish* Kulturkampf *in the Holy Land** (OUP, 1969). Also excellent on this topic are I. Domb, *The Transformation* (London, 1958), written from an orthodox-religious anti-Zionist standpoint, and K. Kahana, *The Case for Jewish Civil Law in the Jewish State* (Soncino Press, London, 1960). Herbert Weiner, *The Wild*

Goats of Ein Gedi: A Journal of Religious Encounters in the Holy Land* (Philadelphia and Cleveland, 1963), is a brilliant and delightful account in the readable medium of a personal quest. S. P. Colbi, *Christianity in The Holy Land Past and Present* (Tel Aviv, 1969), is a superb monograph with historical depth. W. Zander, *Israel and the Holy Places of Christendom* (London, 1971), is a fascinating study.

Isaac Deutscher, *The Non-Jewish Jew and Other Essays* (OUP, 1968), is an articulate expression of the dilemmas of Jewish identity unanchored in religious commitment. B. Litvin (comp.) and S. B. Hoenig (ed.), *Jewish Identity: Modern Responsa and Opinions on the Registration of Children of Mixed Marriages – David Ben-Gurion's Query to Leaders of World Jewry** (Jerusalem, 1970), is an indispensable guide to the student of this problem. Haim H. Cohen (ed.), *Jewish Law in Ancient and Modern Israel* (New York, 1971), includes some most significant essays. Simon N. Herman, *Israelis and Jews: The Continuity of an Identity* (New York, 1970), explores attitudes in Israel and skilfully analyses the results.

Finally, the erudition of J. L. Talmon elucidates with great economy the broadest range of themes encompassed by the Jewish and Israeli experiences, in three essays gathered under the title *Israel Among the Nations* (London, 1970).

AUTHOR INDEX

(Where an author is directly quoted in the text, the page-reference of the quotation is given in bold type, followed by the footnote reference in parenthesis.)

GENERAL INDEX

mentions, 42, 70, 140, 145, 173, 177, 202, 216, 217, 227, 234, 316, 320, 321, 413, 414, 420, 424, 425, 434 *see also* author index
Bentwich, Norman, 114, 145, 454n *see also* author index
Ben-Yehuda, Eliezer, 63, 64
Ben-Zvi, Yitzhak, becomes President, 318; other mentions, 42, 50, 69 *see also* author index
Bergmann, Professor Hugo, 457n
Bergmann v Minister of Finance, 463n
Bermuda conference on war refugees, 201
Bernadotte, Count Folke, 259, 261, 264–5 *see also* author index
Betar youth movement, 175
Bevin, Ernest, 224, 225, 231
Biltmore programme, 190, 192, 193
Biluim, 25–6
bi-nationalism, 144–51, 193, 456–7n *see also* Ihud Association
Blaudan conference, 226
Borochov, Ber, 34, 35, 36–8, 49, 84, 154 *see also* author index
Brit Shalom, 146–7, 150 *see also* bi-nationalism
Britain (London government), diplomacy in first world war, 71–2; occupies Palestine, 67, 94; issues Balfour Declaration, 71; post-war diplomacy, 94–7; installs civil government in Palestine, 96; Zionist sentiments, 96–7, 113–14, 454n; despatches Zionist Commission, 96, 104; transfers Palestine affairs from Colonial Office to Foreign Office, 96; Haycraft Commission, 457n; Churchill White Paper, 116; Shaw-Hope Simpson reports, 160; Passfield White Paper, 161; Peel Commission, 162, 164–5; Woodhead Commission, 165; Macdonald White Paper, 108, 109, 194, 198–9, 220, 221, 222; concern for regional security, 165–6, 195–6; holds St

James' Conference (1939), 165; in second world war, 195–6; and Palestine war effort, 199–202, 209; and Jewish Brigade, 200–1, 216; talks with US on refugees, 201–2; and Jewish refugees in Europe, 221–6, 231; labour government continues policies, 222; appoints Anglo-American inquiry, 224–5; establishes Arab League, 222; considers military base in Palestine, 226; recognizes Transjordan independence, 226; relinquishes mandate to UNO, 231; assists Arabs in 1947–8, 235, 249; Morrison-Grady Plan, 229; presses Israel to withdraw from Egypt (1948), 266; excludes Israel from Sterling Area and freezes balances, 270; releases blocked sterling, 275; joins in Tripartite Declaration guaranteeing boundaries, 366; evacuates Suez base, 367, 463n; courts Nasser, 380; after canal nationalization seeks Nasser's overthrow, 381; plans Suez war, 382–3; co-ordinates Suez plan with Sinai war, 383–5; hesitant conduct of Suez attack, 385–8; improved Israel-British relations, 408
British Administration (Palestine), military administration, 94–6; concept of national home, 114–15; relations with Arabs, 115–16; relations with Zionists, 96–7, 113–18, 213ff; regulates immigration, 107–9; assists Arab agriculture, 111; recognizes Jewish Agency, 105; provides for religious autonomy, 115; fails to obtain Arab-Jewish co-operation, 135; changes over three decades, 118; develops hostility to Zionism, 114, 216–21; suppresses Arab revolt, 162–3, 178; co-operation with Haganah, 178–80, 211, 220; intercepts illegal craft, 195; suppresses illegal immi-

491